Third Workshop on NLP for Similar Languages, Varieties and Dialects 2016 (VarDial 3)

Osaka, Japan
12 December 2016

ISBN: 978-1-5108-3328-9

Preface

VarDial is a well-established series of workshops, attracting researchers working on a range of topics related to the study of linguistic variation, e.g., on building language resources for language varieties and dialects or in creating language technology and applications that make use of language closeness and exploit existing resources in a related language or a language variant.

The research presented in the two previous editions, namely VarDial'2014, which was co-located with COLING'2014, and LT4VarDial'2015, which was held together with RANLP'2015, focused on topics such as machine translation between closely related languages, adaptation of POS taggers and parsers for similar languages and language varieties, compilation of corpora for language varieties, spelling normalization, and finally discrimination between and identification of similar languages. The latter was also the topic of the DSL shared task, held in conjunction with the workshop.

We believe that this is a very timely series of workshops, as research in language variation is much needed in today's multi-lingual world, where several closely-related languages, language varieties, and dialects are in daily use, not only as spoken colloquial language but also in written media, e.g., in SMS, chats, and social networks. Language resources for these varieties and dialects are sparse and extending them could be very labor-intensive. Yet, these efforts can often be reduced by making use of pre-existing resources and tools for related, resource-richer languages.

Examples of closely-related language varieties include the different variants of Spanish in Latin America, the Arabic dialects in North Africa and the Middle East, German in Germany, Austria and Switzerland, French in France and in Belgium, etc. Examples of pairs of related languages include Swedish-Norwegian, Bulgarian-Macedonian, Serbian-Bosnian, Spanish-Catalan, Russian-Ukrainian, Irish-Gaelic Scottish, Malay-Indonesian, Turkish–Azerbaijani, Mandarin-Cantonese, Hindi–Urdu, etc.

This great interest of the community has made possible the third edition of the Workshop on NLP for Similar Languages, Varieties and Dialects (VarDial'2016), co-located with COLING'2016.

As part of the workshop, we organized the third edition of the Discriminating between Similar Languages (DSL) shared task, which offered an opportunity for researchers and developers to investigate the performance of computational methods to distinguishing between closely-related languages and language varieties, thus bridging an important gap for language identification. For the first time, the DSL task was divided into two sub-tasks: Sub-task 1 focusing on similar languages and language varieties, and Sub-task 2 on Arabic dialect identification.

The third edition of the DSL shared task received a very positive response from the community and a record number of participants. A total of 37 teams subscribed to participate in the DSL shared task, 24 of them submitted official runs, and 20 of the latter also wrote system description papers, which appear in this volume along with a shared task report by the task organizers. These numbers represent a substantial increase in participation compared to the 2014 and 2015 editions of the DSL task.

We further received 13 regular VarDial workshop papers, and we selected nine of them to be presented at the workshop and to appear in this volume.

Given the aforementioned numbers, we consider the workshop a success, and thus we are organizing a fourth edition in 2017, which will be co-located with EACL'2017.

We take the opportunity to thank the VarDial program committee and the additional reviewers for their thorough reviews, and the DSL Shared Task participants, as well as the participants with regular research papers, for the valuable feedback and discussions. We further thank our invited speakers, Mona Diab and Robert Östling, for presenting their interesting work at the workshop.

The organizers: Preslav Nakov, Marcos Zampieri, Liling Tan, Nikola Ljubešić, Jörg Tiedemann, and Shervin Malmasi

Organisers

Preslav Nakov (Qatar Computing Research Institute, HBKU, Qatar)
Marcos Zampieri (University of Cologne, Germany)
Liling Tan (Singapore University of Technology and Design, and Saarland University, Germany)
Nikola Ljubešić (Jožef Stefan Institute, Slovenia, and University of Zagreb, Croatia)
Jörg Tiedemann (University of Helsinki, Finland)
Shervin Malmasi (Harvard Medical School, USA)

DSL Shared Task Organisers

Marcos Zampieri (University of Cologne, Germany)
Preslav Nakov (Qatar Computing Research Institute, HBKU, Qatar)
Shervin Malmasi (Harvard Medical School, USA)
Liling Tan (Singapore University of Technology and Design, and Saarland University, Germany)
Nikola Ljubešić (Jožef Stefan Institute, Slovenia, and University of Zagreb, Croatia)
Jörg Tiedemann (University of Helsinki, Finland)
Ahmed Ali (Qatar Computing Research Institute, HBKU, Qatar)

Programme Committee

Željko Agić (IT University of Copenhagen, Denmark)
Cesar Aguilar (Pontifical Catholic University of Chile, Chile)
Laura Alonso y Alemany (University of Cordoba, Argentina)
Tim Baldwin (The University of Melbourne, Australia)
Jorge Baptista (University of Algarve and INESC-ID, Portugal)
Eckhard Bick (University of Southern Denmark, Denmark)
Francis Bond (Nanyang Technological University, Singapore)
Aoife Cahill (Educational Testing Service, USA)
David Chiang (University of Notre Dame, USA)
Paul Cook (University of New Brunswick, Canada)
Marta Costa-Jussà (Institute for Infocomm Research, Singapore)
Jon Dehdari (Saarland University and DFKI, Germany)
Liviu Dinu (University of Bucharest, Romania)
Stefanie Dipper (Ruhr University Bochum, Germany)
Sascha Diwersy (University of Montpellier, France)
Mark Dras (Macquire University, Australia)
Tomaž Erjavec (Jožef Stefan Institute, Slovenia)
Mikel L. Forcada (Universitat d'Alacant, Spain)
Binyam Gebrekidan Gebre (Phillips Research, Holland)
Cyril Goutte (National Research Council, Canada)
Nizar Habash (New York University Abu Dhabi, UAE)
Chu-Ren Huang (Hong Kong Polytechnic University, Hong Kong)
Jeremy Jancsary (Nuance Communications, Austria)
Lung-Hao Lee (National Taiwan Normal University, Taiwan)
Marco Lui (Rome2Rio Ltd., Australia)
Teresa Lynn (Dublin City University, Ireland)

John Nerbonne (University of Groningen, Netherlands and University of Freiburg, Germany)
Graham Neubig (Nara Institute of Science and Technology, Japan)
Kemal Oflazer (Carnegie-Mellon University in Qatar, Qatar)
Maciej Ogrodniczuk (Institute of Computer Science, Polish Academy of Sciences, Poland)
Petya Osenova (Bulgarian Academy of Sciences, Bulgaria)
Santanu Pal (Saarland University, Germany)
Reinhard Rapp (University of Mainz, Germany and University of Aix-Marsaille, France)
Paolo Rosso (Polytechnic University of Valencia, Spain)
Tanja Samardžić (University of Zürich, Switzerland)
Felipe Sánchez Martínez (Universitat d'Alacant, Spain)
Kevin Scannell (Saint Louis University, USA)
Yves Scherrer (University of Geneva, Switzerland)
Serge Sharoff (University of Leeds, UK)
Kiril Simov (Bulgarian Academy of Sciences, Bulgaria)
Milena Slavcheva (Bulgarian Academy of Sciences, Bulgaria)
Marko Tadić (University of Zagreb, Croatia)
Elke Teich (Saarland University, Germany)
Joel Tetreault (Grammarly, USA)
Francis Tyers (UiT Norgga árktalaš universitehta, Norway)
Duško Vitas (University of Belgrade, Serbia)
Taro Watanabe (Google Inc., Japan)
Pidong Wang (Machine Zone Inc., USA)

Additional Reviewers

Johannes Bjerva (University of Groningen, Netherlands)
Marc Franco Salvador (Polytechnic University of Valencia, Spain)
Aleksander Wawer (Institute of Computer Science, Polish Academy of Sciences, Poland)

Invited Speakers

Mona Diab (George Washington University, USA)
Robert Östling (University of Helsinki, Finland)

Table of Contents

Conference Program

Monday, December 12, 2016

9:00–9:10   *Opening*

9.10–9.30   *Discriminating between Similar Languages and Arabic Dialect Identification: A Report on the Third DSL Shared Task*
Shervin Malmasi, Marcos Zampieri, Nikola Ljubešić, Preslav Nakov, Ahmed Ali and Jörg Tiedemann

9.30–10.00   *Discriminating Similar Languages with Linear SVMs and Neural Networks*
Çağrı Çöltekin and Taraka Rama

10.00–10.30   *LSTM Autoencoders for Dialect Analysis*
Taraka Rama and Çağrı Çöltekin

10.30–11.00   *The GW/LT3 VarDial 2016 Shared Task System for Dialects and Similar Languages Detection*
Ayah Zirikly, Bart Desmet and Mona Diab

11.00–12.00   Invited talk 1

Processing Dialectal Arabic: Exploiting Variability and Similarity to Overcome Challenges and Discover Opportunities
Mona Diab

12.00–14.00   *Lunch*

14.00–14.30   *Language Related Issues for Machine Translation between Closely Related South Slavic Languages*
Maja Popović, Mihael Arcan and Filip Klubička

14.30–15.00   *Romanized Berber and Romanized Arabic Automatic Language Identification Using Machine Learning*
Wafia Adouane, Nasredine Semmar and Richard Johansson

Monday, December 12, 2016 (continued)

15.00–16.00   **Invited talk 2**

How Many Languages Can a Language Model Model?
Robert Östling

16.00–16.30   ***Coffee break***

16.30–18.00   **Poster Session**

Automatic Detection of Arabicized Berber and Arabic Varieties
Wafia Adouane, Nasredine Semmar, Richard Johansson and Victoria Bobicev

Automatic Verification and Augmentation of Multilingual Lexicons
Maryam Aminian, Mohamed Al-Badrashiny and Mona Diab

Faster Decoding for Subword Level Phrase-based SMT between Related Languages
Anoop Kunchukuttan and Pushpak Bhattacharyya

Subdialectal Differences in Sorani Kurdish
Shervin Malmasi

Enlarging Scarce In-domain English-Croatian Corpus for SMT of MOOCs Using Serbian
Maja Popović, Kostadin Cholakov, Valia Kordoni and Nikola Ljubešić

Arabic Dialect Identification in Speech Transcripts
Shervin Malmasi and Marcos Zampieri

DSL Shared Task 2016: Perfect Is The Enemy of Good Language Discrimination Through Expectation–Maximization and Chunk-based Language Model
Ondřej Herman, Vit Suchomel, Vít Baisa and Pavel Rychlý

Byte-based Language Identification with Deep Convolutional Networks
Johannes Bjerva

Classifying ASR Transcriptions According to Arabic Dialect
Abualsoud Hanani, Aziz Qaroush and Stephen Taylor

N-gram and Neural Language Models for Discriminating Similar Languages
Andre Cianflone and Leila Kosseim

Discriminating Between Similar Languages and Arabic Dialect Identification: A Report on the Third DSL Shared Task

Shervin Malmasi[1,2], Marcos Zampieri[3], Nikola Ljubešić[4,5]
Preslav Nakov[7], Ahmed Ali[7], Jörg Tiedemann[6]

[1]Harvard Medical School, USA, [2]Macquarie University, Australia
[3]University of Cologne, Germany, [4]University of Zagreb, Croatia
[5]Jožef Stefan Institute, Slovenia, [6]University of Helsinki, Finland
[7]Qatar Computing Research Institute, HBKU, Qatar

Abstract

We present the results of the third edition of the Discriminating between Similar Languages (DSL) shared task, which was organized as part of the VarDial'2016 workshop at COLING'2016. The challenge offered two subtasks: subtask 1 focused on the identification of very similar languages and language varieties in newswire texts, whereas subtask 2 dealt with Arabic dialect identification in speech transcripts. A total of 37 teams registered to participate in the task, 24 teams submitted test results, and 20 teams also wrote system description papers. High-order character n-grams were the most successful feature, and the best classification approaches included traditional supervised learning methods such as SVM, logistic regression, and language models, while deep learning approaches did not perform very well.

1 Introduction

The Discriminating between Similar Languages (DSL) shared task on language identification was first organized in 2014. It provides an opportunity for researchers and developers to test language identification approaches for discriminating between similar languages, language varieties, and dialects. The task was organized by the workshop series on NLP for Similar Languages, Varieties and Dialects (VarDial), which was collocated in 2014 with COLING, in 2015 with RANLP, and in 2016 again with COLING.

In its third edition, the DSL shared task grew in size and scope featuring two subtasks and attracting a record number of participants. Below we present the task setup, the evaluation results, and a brief discussion about the features and learning methods that worked best. More detail about each particular system can be found in the corresponding system description paper, as cited in this report.

2 Related Work

Language and dialect identification have attracted a lot of research attention in recent years, covering a number of similar languages and language varieties such as South-Slavic languages (Ljubešić et al., 2007), English varieties (Lui and Cook, 2013), varieties of Mandarin in China, Taiwan and Singapore (Huang and Lee, 2008), Malay vs. Indonesian (Ranaivo-Malançon, 2006), Brazilian vs. European Portuguese (Zampieri and Gebre, 2012), and Persian vs. Dari (Malmasi and Dras, 2015a), to mention just a few. The interest in this aspect of language identification has motivated the organization of shared tasks such as the DSL challenge, which allowed researchers to compare various approaches using the same dataset.

Along with the interest in similar languages and language variety identification, we observed substantial interest in applying natural language processing (NLP) methods for the processing of dialectal Arabic with special interest in methods to discriminate between Arabic dialects. Shoufan and Al-Ameri (2015) presented a comprehensive survey on these methods including recent studies on Arabic dialect identification such as (Elfardy and Diab, 2014; Darwish et al., 2014; Zaidan and Callison-Burch, 2014;

Proceedings of the Third Workshop on NLP for Similar Languages, Varieties and Dialects,
pages 1–14, Osaka, Japan, December 12 2016.

Tillmann et al., 2014; Malmasi and Dras, 2015a). Methods for Arabic dialect detection present significant overlap with methods proposed for similar language identification. For this reason, in the 2016 edition of the DSL challenge we offered a subtask on Arabic dialect identification.

Below, we discuss some related shared tasks including the first two editions of the DSL challenge.

2.1 Related Shared Tasks

Several shared tasks related to the DSL task have been organized in recent years. Two examples are the ALTW language identification shared task (Baldwin and Lui, 2010) on general-purpose language identification, and the DEFT 2010 shared task (Grouin et al., 2010), which focused on language variety identification of French texts with a temporal dimension. In the DEFT 2010 shared task, systems were asked to predict *when* and *where* texts were published. The DEFT 2010 shared task is most similar to our DSL task, but is limited to French language varieties, while our task is multilingual and includes several groups of similar languages and language varieties.

Language identification on Twitter and other platforms of user-generated content is a popular research direction (Ljubešić and Kranjčić, 2015). This interest has motivated the shared task on Language Identification in Code-Switched Data (Solorio et al., 2014), which focused on tweets containing a mix of two or more languages, and the TweetLID shared task (Zubiaga et al., 2014; Zubiaga et al., 2015), which targeted language identification of tweets focusing on English and on languages spoken on the Iberian peninsula, namely Basque, Catalan, Spanish, and Portuguese.

The most recent related shared task is the task on geolocation prediction in Twitter (Han et al., 2016).[1] The organizers of this task provided a large training set collected from one million users, and asked to predict the location of each user (user-level prediction) and of each tweet (*tweet*-level prediction).

2.2 Previous Editions of the DSL Task

For the first edition of the DSL task (Zampieri et al., 2014), we compiled v1.0 of the DSL corpus collection (DSLCC), which contained excerpts of newspaper texts written in thirteen languages divided into the following groups: Group A (Bosnian, Croatian, Serbian), Group B (Indonesian, Malay), Group C (Czech, Slovak), Group D (Brazilian Portuguese, European Portuguese), Group E (Peninsular Spanish, Argentinian Spanish), and Group F (American English, British English).[2]

Team	Closed	Open	System Description Paper
NRC-CNRC	**0.957**	-	(Goutte et al., 2014)
RAE	0.947	-	(Porta and Sancho, 2014)
UMich	0.932	0.859	(King et al., 2014)
UniMelb-NLP	0.918	**0.880**	(Lui et al., 2014)
QMUL	0.906	-	(Purver, 2014)
LIRA	0.766	-	-
UDE	0.681	-	-
CLCG	0.453	-	-
Total	**8**	**2**	**5**

Table 1: Results for the DSL 2014 shared task: accuracy.

Eight teams developed systems and submitted results for this first edition of the task. All eight teams participated in the closed track, which was limited to training on the DSL corpus only, and two teams took part in the open track, which also allowed using external resources; five teams submitted system description papers. The results are summarized in Table 1, where the best-performing submissions, in terms of accuracy, are shown in bold.[3]

The best score in the closed submission track was achieved by the *NRC-CNRC* team (Goutte et al., 2014), which used a two-step classification approach: they first predicted the language group, and then

---

[1]https://noisy-text.github.io/2016/geo-shared-task.html

[2]Group F was excluded from the official evaluation results due to a number of republications present in the dataset.

[3]For a comprehensive discussion of the first two editions of the DSL shared task, see (Goutte et al., 2016).

discriminated between the languages from this predicted language group. Members of this team also participated in 2015 under the name *NRC*. *UMich* (King et al., 2014) and *UniMelb-NLP* (Lui et al., 2014) were the only teams that compiled and used additional training resources and the only teams to make open submissions. However, their open submissions performed worse than their closed submissions: accuracy dropped from 93.2% to 85.9% for *UMich*, and from 91.8% to 88.0% for *UniMelb-NLP*.

For the 2015 edition of the task (Zampieri et al., 2015b), we created v2.0 of the DSLCC, which included the following languages and language varieties grouped by similarity: Bulgarian vs. Macedonian, Bosnian vs. Croatian vs. Serbian, Czech vs. Slovak, Malay vs. Indonesian, Brazilian vs. European Portuguese, Argentinian vs. Peninsular Spanish, and a group of various other languages,[4] which were included to emulate a more realistic language identification scenario. We had two test datasets. Test set A contained the original unmodified text excerpts, while in test set B we replaced the capitalized named entities by placeholders. The results for the participating systems in the 2015 edition of the DSL task are presented in Table 2; again, the best submissions are shown in bold. We can see that the 2015 edition of the task attracted more submissions compared to 2014.

Team	Closed A	Closed B	Open A	Open B	System Description Paper
BOBICEV	0.941	0.922	-	-	(Bobicev, 2015)
BRUNIBP	0.937	-	-	-	(Ács et al., 2015)
INRIA	0.839	-	-	-	-
MAC	**0.955**	**0.940**	-	-	(Malmasi and Dras, 2015b)
MMS*	0.952	0.928	-	-	(Zampieri et al., 2015a)
NLEL	0.640	0.628	0.918	0.896	(Fabra-Boluda et al., 2015)
NRC	0.952	0.930	**0.957**	**0.934**	(Goutte and Léger, 2015)
OSEVAL	-	-	0.762	0.753	-
PRHLT	0.927	0.908	-	-	(Franco-Salvador et al., 2015)
SUKI	0.947	0.930	-	-	(Jauhiainen et al., 2015)
Total	**9**	**7**	**3**	**3**	**8**

Table 2: Results for the DSL 2015 shared task: accuracy.

The best-performing system in the open submission track, that of *MAC*, used an ensemble of SVM classifiers and achieved 95.5% accuracy on test set A and 94.0% accuracy on test set B. Unlike in the 2014 edition, in which open submissions performed substantially worse than closed ones, this time this was not the case, e.g., for the *NRC* team. However, the additional resource they used was external only technically; in fact, it was the previous version of the DSL corpus.[5]

Moreover, the use of two test sets allowed us to evaluate the impact of named entities. In the 2014 edition of the task, we had noticed that names of people, places, and organizations could be quite helpful for discriminating texts from different geographical locations, e.g., Argentinian vs. Peninsular Spanish, and we were worried that this is what systems critically relied on, i.e., that they were focusing on country of origin rather than language variety prediction. However, the results for test set A vs. B in 2015 show that the influence of named entities was not as great as we feared, and that the participating systems were able to capture lexical and, in some cases syntactic, variation using n-gram models even when the original named entities were not present.

3   Task Setup

Here, we describe the setup of the 2016 DSL shared task: the subtasks, the tracks, and the data.

3.1   General Setup

This year, the DSL challenge included two subtasks:

---

[4]This group of languages included Catalan, Russian, Slovene, and Tagalog.

[5]The *NLEL* team reported a bug in their closed submission, which might explain their low performance in this track.

- **Subtask 1:** *Discriminating between Similar Languages and Language Varieties*
  For this subtask, we compiled a new version of the DSL corpus, which included for the first time French language varieties, namely Hexagonal French vs. Canadian French, and further excluded pairs of similar languages that proved to be very easy to discriminate between in previous editions (e.g., Czech vs. Slovak and Bulgarian vs. Macedonian).

- **Subtask 2:** *Arabic Dialect Identification*
  This subtask focused on discriminating Arabic dialects in speech transcripts. We used the dataset compiled by Ali et al. (2016), which contained Modern Standard Arabic (MSA) and four Arabic dialects: Egyptian (EGY), Gulf (GLF), Levantine (LAV), and North African (NOR).

As in previous editions of the DSL task, we allowed teams to use external data. We therefore divided each subtask in two tracks:

- **Closed:** using only the corpora provided by the organizers;

- **Open:** using any additional data.[6]

Participation this year increased substantially compared to previous years, as the statistics in Table 3 show. We believe that this is due to the addition of an Arabic subtask as well as to the out-of-domain tweet test sets for the English subtask.

Year	Venue	(Sub-)tasks	Subscriptions	Submissions	Papers
2014	VarDial at COLING	1	22	8	5
2015	LT4VarDial at RANLP	1	24	10	8
2016	VarDial at COLING	2	37	24	20

Table 3: The evolution of the DSL task from 2014 to 2016.

3.2 Data

In this section, we present the datasets we used this year. For subtask 1, we compiled v3.0 of DSLCC with a new language variety (French) as well as out-of-domain test sets with tweets, and for subtask 2, we use a corpus of Arabic transcribed speeches presented in (Ali et al., 2016).

3.2.1 Subtask 1 Data

We compiled a new version 3.0 of DSLCC, following the methodology we used in previous years (Tan et al., 2014).[7] The resulting corpus contains short newspaper texts written in twelve languages and language varieties. Table 4 shows the languages included in the DSL v3.0 grouped by similarity.

We provided participants with 20,000 instances per language variety divided into 18,000 instances for training and 2,000 for development. Most language groups included in v3.0 were also present in v1.0 and v2.0. We further added French from Canada and from France, as well as Mexican Spanish.[8]

We used three test sets for subtask 1: one in-domain (A), and two out-of-domain (B1 and B2). Test set A contained journalistic data including 1,000 instances per language sampled from the same distribution as for the DSLCC v3.0. It is also comparable to the test sets released in DSLCC v1.0 and v2.0.

We further created test sets B1 and B2 in order to evaluate the performance of the participating systems on out-of-domain data. Each of the two datasets included 100 Twitter users per language/variant, and a varying number of tweets per user. Note that these test sets cover only two groups of closely-related languages: South-Slavic (Bosnian, Croatian, Serbian) and Portuguese (Brazilian and European).

We used the TweetGeo (Ljubešić et al., 2016) and TweetCat (Ljubešić et al., 2014) tools for data collection. TweetGeo allows us to collect geo-encoded tweets over a specified perimeter via the Twitter

---

[6]For subtask 1, using previous versions of the DSL corpus also made a submission open.

[7]The dataset is available at `http://ttg.uni-saarland.de/resources/DSLCC`

[8]Mexican Spanish was already present for the unshared task in 2015, but now it is part of the main DSL shared task.

Language/Variety	Class	Train and Dev.		Testing					
		Instances	**Tokens**	**A**	**Tokens**	**B1**	**Tokens**	**B2**	**Tokens**
Bosnian	bs	20,000	743,732	1,000	37,630	100	209,884	100	170,481
Croatian	hr	20,000	874,555	1,000	42,703	100	179,354	100	119,837
Serbian	sr	20,000	813,076	1,000	41,153	100	181,185	100	124,469
Indonesian	id	20,000	831,647	1,000	42,192	—	—	—	—
Malay	my	20,000	618,532	1,000	31,162	—	—	—	—
Brazilian Portuguese	pt-BR	20,000	988,004	1,000	49288	100	151,749	100	19,567
European Portuguese	pt-PT	20,000	908,605	1,000	45173	100	134,139	100	13,145
Argentine Spanish	es-AR	20,000	999,425	1,000	50,135	—	—	—	—
Castilian Spanish	es-ES	20,000	1,080,523	1,000	53,731	—	—	—	—
Mexican Spanish	es-MX	20,000	751,718	1,000	47,176	—	—	—	—
Canadian French	fr-CA	20,000	772,467	1,000	38,602	—	—	—	—
Hexagonal French	fr-FR	20,000	963,867	1,000	48,129	—	—	—	—
Total		240,000	10,346,151	12,000	527,074	500	856,331	500	323,030

Table 4: DSLCC v3.0: the languages included in the corpus grouped by similarity. Note that a test example in test set A is an excerpt of text, whereas in test sets B1 and B2 it is a collection of multiple tweets by the same user (with 98.88 and 50.47 tweets per user on average for B1 and B2, respectively).

Stream API. We set up one perimeter over the South-Slavic speaking countries, another one over Portugal, and a final one over Brazil. We then collected data over a period of one month. Once ready, we filtered the users by number of tweets collected per user and by language the user predominantly used. Finally, we used the TweetCat tool to collect whole timelines for users matching the following criteria: the user has posted at least five tweets (otherwise language identification would be hard), and the language(s) given langid.py's prediction are (hr, sr, bs) for the first variant and (pt) for the second one.

We then proceeded to manual annotation. We had a single human annotator for each language/variety group. The annotation procedure was the following: the annotator read one tweet after the other, starting with the most recent tweet, and marking the tweet at which he made the decision about the language/variety used by the Twitter user. In the South-Slavic group, the average number of analyzed tweets per user was 70.5 for Bosnian, 51.5 for Croatian, and 49 for Serbian. In the Portuguese group, these were 6 for European Portuguese, and 8 for Brazilian Portuguese. While part of the difference between the two groups may be due to different criteria the two annotators used, the differences inside groups show important trends, e.g., that identifying Bosnian users requires on average 40% more tweets compared to identifying Serbian or Croatian ones.

Having the information about the number of tweets that were needed for a human decision enabled us to prepare the harder B2 test set in which only that minimum number of tweets was included. On the other hand, the B1 test set, being a proper superset of B2, contained much more tweets per user, and we had to cap the overall number of tweets in the dataset at 50,000 due to restrictions of the Twitter Developer Agreement.

It is important to stress that no filtering over the user timeline (such as removing tweets written in different languages or with no linguistic information) was performed, offering thereby a realistic setting.

3.2.2 Subtask 2 Data

For the Arabic subtask, we used transcribed speech in MSA and in four dialects (Ali et al., 2016): Egyptian (EGY), Gulf (GLF), Levantine (LAV), and North African (NOR). The data comes from a multi-dialectal speech corpus created from high-quality broadcast, debate and discussion programs from Al Jazeera, and as such contains a combination of spontaneous and scripted speech (Wray and Ali, 2015). We released 7,619 sentences for training and development, without a train/dev split;[9] a breakdown for each dialect is shown in Table 5. We further used 1,540 sentences for evaluation. We extracted text from ten hours of speech per dialect for training, and from two hours per dialect for testing.

---

[9]http://alt.qcri.org/resources/ArabicDialectIDCorpus/varDial_DSL_shared_task_2016_subtask2

Note that even though the origin of our data is speech, in our corpus we only used written transcripts. This makes the task hard as it may be difficult, or even impossible in certain contexts, to determine unambiguously the dialect of a written sentence if it contains graphemic cognates common across multiple dialects of colloquial and of Standard Arabic. This ambiguity is less pronounced in the presence of speech signal. Thus, we plan to make available acoustic features in future challenges.

Dialect	Dialect	Training		Testing	
		Examples	Words	Examples	Words
Egyptian	EGY	1,578	85K	315	13K
Gulf	GLF	1,672	65K	256	14K
Levantine	LAV	1,758	66K	344	14K
Modern Standard	MSA	999	49K	274	14K
North African	NOR	1,612	52K	351	12K
Total		7,619	317K	1,540	67K

Table 5: The Arabic training and testing data.

3.3 Evaluation

Regarding evaluation, in the previous editions of the DSL task, we used average accuracy as the main evaluation metric. This was because the DSL datasets were balanced with the same number of examples for each language variety. However, this is not true for this year's Arabic dataset, and thus we added macro-averaged F1-score, which is the official score this year.

Moreover, following common practice in other shared tasks, e.g., at WMT (Bojar et al., 2016), this year we carried out statistical significance tests using McNemar's test in order to investigate the variation of performance between the participating systems. Therefore, in all tables with results, we rank teams in groups taking statistical significance into account,[10] rather than using absolute performance only.

4 Results for Subtask 1: DSL Dataset

A total of 17 teams participated in the shared task. Table 6 shows statistics about the participating teams.

Team	A (Closed)	A (Open)	B (Closed)	B (Open)	System Description Paper
andre	✓				(Cianflone and Kosseim, 2016)
ASIREM	✓				(Adouane et al., 2016)
Citius_Ixa_Imaxin	✓	✓	✓	✓	(Gamallo et al., 2016)
eire	✓		✓		(Franco-Penya and Sanchez, 2016)
GW_LT3	✓		✓		(Zirikly et al., 2016)
HDSL	✓		✓		—
hltcoe	✓		✓		(McNamee, 2016)
mitsls	✓				(Belinkov and Glass, 2016)
nrc	✓	✓	✓	✓	(Goutte and Léger, 2016)
PITEOG	✓		✓	✓	(Herman et al., 2016)
ResIdent	✓		✓		(Bjerva, 2016)
SUKI	✓	✓	✓	✓	(Jauhiainen et al., 2016)
tubasfs	✓		✓		(Çöltekin and Rama, 2016)
UniBucNLP	✓		✓		(Ciobanu et al., 2016)
Uppsala	✓		✓		—
UPV_UA	✓		✓		—
XAC	✓		✓		(Barbaresi, 2016)
Total	17	3	14	4	14

Table 6: Teams participating in subtask 1 (here, we group test sets B1 and B2 under B).

---

[10]This means that systems not significantly different to the top system are also assigned rank 1, and so on.

4.1 Results on Test Set A

We received submissions by 17 teams for the closed training training condition. The results and a brief description of the algorithm and of the features used by each team are shown in Table 7. Note that the teams were allowed to submit up to three runs, and here we only show the results for the best run from each participating team. The best results in the closed condition were achieved by the *tubasfs* team with F1-score of 89.38% and by the *SUKI* team with F1-score of 88.77% (both ranked first, as they are not statistically different). A group of five teams scored between 88.14% and 88.70%, and they were all ranked second (as they were not statistically different).

Rank	Team	Run	Accuracy	F1	Approach
1	tubasfs	run1	**0.894**	**0.894**	SVM, char n-grams (1-7)
	SUKI	run1	0.888	0.888	Lang. models, word uni-, char n-grams (1-6)
2	GW_LT3	run3	0.887	0.887	Hierarchical log. regression, char/word n-grams
	nrc	run1	0.886	0.886	Two-stage probabilistic and SVM, char 6-grams
	UPV_UA	run1	0.883	0.884	String kernels and kernel discriminant analysis
	PITEOG	run3	0.883	0.883	Chunk-based language model
	andre	run1	0.885	0.881	Language models, char n-grams
3	XAC	run3	0.879	0.879	Unsupervised morphological model
	ASIREM	run1	0.878	0.878	SVM, char 4-grams
	hltcoe	run1	0.877	0.877	Prediction by partial matching, char 5-grams
4	UniBucNLP	run2	0.865	0.864	Hierarchical log. reg. w/ word 1/2-grams
5	HDSL	run1	0.853	0.852	SVM, word and char n-grams
	Citius_Ixa_Imaxin	run2	0.853	0.850	Naive Bayes, word unigrams
	ResIdent	run3	0.849	0.846	Deep neural net with byte embeddings
6	eire	run1	0.838	0.832	Naive Bayes, char bigrams
	mitsls	run3	0.830	0.830	Character-level convolutional neural network
7	Uppsala	run2	0.825	0.824	Word-level convolutional neural network

Table 7: Results for subtask 1, test set A, *closed* training condition.

Rank	Team	Run	Accuracy	F1	Approach
1	nrc	run1	**0.890**	**0.889**	Two-stage probabilistic and SVM, char 6-grams
	SUKI	run1	0.884	0.884	Lang. models, word uni-, char n-grams (1-7)
2	Citius_Ixa_Imaxin	run2	0.871	0.869	Naive Bayes, word unigrams

Table 8: Results for subtask 1, test set A, *open* training condition.

The open training track for test set A attracted only three teams as shown in Table 8. For the first two teams, the difference compared to their closed submission is marginal: *nrc* gained less than half a point absolute in terms of accuracy and F1, while *SUKI* lost about the same. However, the third team, *Citius_Ixa_Imaxin*, managed to gain about two points absolute in both measures.

Overall, we observe that the teams used a wide variety of algorithms and features, which are summarized in the results tables. They are also described in more detail in the corresponding system description papers. Note that some teams, such as *ResIdent* and *Uppsala*, used neural network-based approaches, but their results were not competitive to those that used simpler, standard classifiers such as SVM and logistic regression.

4.2 Results on Test Sets B1 and B2

The results of the participating teams on test set B1 (out-of-domain, tweets) for the closed training condition are shown in Table 9. Once again, we group the submissions based on statistical significance. Three teams shared the first place, namely *GW_LT3*, *nrc*, and *UniBucNLP*, with an F1-score ranging from 89.69% to 91.94%.

Rank	Team	Run	Accuracy	F1	Approach
1	GW_LT3	run1	**0.920**	**0.919**	Log. reg. with char/word n-grams
	nrc	run1	0.914	0.913	Two-stage probabilistic and SVM, char 6-grams
	UniBucNLP	run1	0.898	0.897	Log. reg. w/ word 1/2-grams
2	UPV_UA	run2	0.888	0.886	String kernels and kernel discriminant analysis
	tubasfs	run1	0.862	0.860	SVM, char n-grams (1-7)
3	eire	run1	0.806	0.793	Naive Bayes, char bigrams
	PITEOG	run1	0.800	0.793	Expectation maximization, word unigrams
4	Citius_Ixa_Imaxin	run1	0.708	0.713	Dictionary-based ranking method
	ResIdent	run3	0.688	0.687	Deep neural net with byte embeddings
	HDSL	run1	0.698	0.686	SVM, word and char n-grams
	Uppsala	run2	0.682	0.685	Word-level convolutional neural network
	SUKI	run3	0.688	0.672	Lang. models, word uni-, char n-grams (1-8)
5	XAC	run2	0.618	0.594	Unsupervised morphological model
6	hltcoe	run1	0.530	0.510	Prediction by partial matching, char 5-grams

Table 9: Results for subtask 1, test set B1, *closed* training condition.

Rank	Team	Run	Accuracy	F1	Approach
1	nrc	run1	**0.948**	**0.948**	Two-stage probabilistic and SVM, char 6-grams
2	SUKI	run3	0.822	0.815	Lang. models, word uni-, char n-grams (1-8)
	PITEOG	run1	0.800	0.815	Expectation maximization, word unigrams
4	Citius_Ixa_Imaxin	run1	0.664	0.634	Dictionary-based ranking method

Table 10: Results for subtask 1, test set B1, *open* training condition.

Rank	Team	Run	Accuracy	F1	Approach
1	GW_LT3	run1	**0.878**	**0.877**	Log. reg. with char/word n-grams
	nrc	run1	**0.878**	**0.877**	Two-stage probabilistic and SVM, char 6-grams
	UPV_UA	run2	0.858	0.857	String kernels and kernel discriminant analysis
2	UniBucNLP	run2	0.838	0.838	Hierarchical log. reg. w/ word 1/2-grams
	tubasfs	run1	0.822	0.818	SVM, char n-grams (1-7)
3	PITEOG	run1	0.760	0.757	Expectation maximization, word unigrams
	eire	run1	0.740	0.727	Naive Bayes, char bigrams
4	Citius_Ixa_Imaxin	run1	0.686	0.698	Dictionary-based ranking method
	ResIdent	run2	0.698	0.694	Deep neural net with byte embeddings
	Uppsala	run2	0.672	0.675	Word-level convolutional neural network
	HDSL	run1	0.640	0.626	SVM, word and char n-grams
	SUKI	run1	0.642	0.623	Lang. models, word uni-, char n-grams (1-6)
5	XAC	run2	0.576	0.552	Unsupervised morphological model
	hltcoe	run2	0.554	0.513	Prediction by partial matching, char 5-grams

Table 11: Results for subtask 1, test set B2, *closed* training condition.

Rank	Team	Run	Accuracy	F1	Approach
1	nrc	run1	**0.900**	**0.900**	Two-stage probabilistic and SVM, char 6-grams
2	SUKI	run2	0.796	0.791	Lang. models, word uni-, char n-grams (1-8)
3	PITEOG	run1	0.728	0.759	Expectation maximization, word unigrams
	Citius_Ixa_Imaxin	run1	0.692	0.695	Dictionary-based ranking method

Table 12: Results for subtask 1, test set B2, *open* training condition.

Note that the higher results obtained on test set B1 compared to test set A are somewhat misleading: test set B1 is out-of-domain and is thus generally harder, but it also involves less languages (five for test set B1 as opposed to twelve for test set A), which makes it ultimately much easier.

In Table 10 we present the results for the four teams that participated under the open training condition for test set B1, i.e., using external data. We can see that the *nrc* team performed best with an F1 score of 94.80%. This result is a few percentage points better than the 91.34% F1-score obtained by *nrc* in the closed training condition, which indicates that the use of additional training data was indeed helpful. This is an expected outcome as no suitable training data has been provided for test sets B1 and B2, which contain tweets, and are out of domain compared to the training data (newspaper texts).

Table 11 shows the results on test set B2 under the closed training condition. As expected, this test set turned out to be more challenging than test set B1, and this was the case for almost all teams. Moreover, we can see that there was some minor variation in the ranks of teams on B1 and on B2 (closed training condition), e.g., the *UniBucNLP* team was ranked among the first on B1, but for B2 it switched places with the *UPV UA* team.

Finally, Table 12 presents the results on test set B2 in the open training condition. Once again, the results of *nrc* were higher here than in the closed training condition.

4.3   Open Training Data Sources

Collecting additional training data is a time-consuming process. Therefore, in line with our expectations given our past experience in the previous editions of the DSL task, we received far fewer entries in the open training condition for both subtasks.

For subtask 1, a total of four teams used additional training data across the three test sets. According to the system description papers, the data was compiled from the following sources:

- *Citius_Ixa_Imaxin* augmented the training data with the corpus released in the second edition of the DSL task in 2015.

- *nrc* augmented the provided training data with the corpora from the two previous DSL shared tasks (DSLCC v1.0 and DSLCC v2.1), plus additional text crawled from the web site of the newspaper *La Presse* from Quebec.

- *PITEOG* used their own custom web-based corpus, with no further details provided.

- *SUKI* created an additional dataset using web pages in the Common Crawl corpus.

5   Results for Subtask 2: Arabic Dialect Identification

The eighteen teams that participated in subtask 2 along with the reference to their system description papers are shown in Table 13.[11]

5.1   Results on Subtask C

The results obtained by the teams that participated in the closed training condition are shown in Table 14. The best results were obtained by *MAZA*, *UnibucKernel*, *QCRI*, and *ASIREM*, which achieved an F1-score ranging between 49.46% and 51.32%, and thus shared the first place. The *MAZA* team proposed an approach based on SVM ensembles, which was also ranked first in the 2015 edition of the DSL task (Malmasi and Dras, 2015b), which confirms that SVM ensembles are a suitable method for this task. The *UnibucKernel* team approached the task using string kernels, which were previously proposed for native language identification (Ionescu et al., 2016).

Table 15 shows the results obtained by the three teams that participated in subtask 2 under the open training condition. They showed very different performance (statistically different), and saw very different outcomes when using external training data.

---

[11] We acknowledge that team *MAZA* included two DSL shared task organizers. Yet, the team had no unfair advantage, and competed under the exactly same conditions as the other participants.

Team	C (Closed)	C (Open)	System Description Paper
AHAQST	✓		(Hanani et al., 2016)
ALL	✓		(Alshutayri et al., 2016)
ASIREM	✓	✓	(Adouane et al., 2016)
cgli	✓		(Guggilla, 2016)
Citius_Ixa_Imaxin	✓		(Gamallo et al., 2016)
eire	✓		(Franco-Penya and Sanchez, 2016)
GW_LT3	✓	✓	(Zirikly et al., 2016)
HDSL	✓		—
hltcoe	✓		(McNamee, 2016)
MAZA	✓		(Malmasi and Zampieri, 2016)
mitsls	✓		(Belinkov and Glass, 2016)
PITEOG	✓		(Herman et al., 2016)
QCRI	✓	✓	(Eldesouki et al., 2016)
SUKI	✓		(Jauhiainen et al., 2016)
tubasfs	✓		(Çöltekin and Rama, 2016)
UCREL	✓		—
UnibucKernel	✓		(Ionescu and Popescu, 2016)
UniBucNLP	✓		(Ciobanu et al., 2016)
Total	**18**	**3**	**15**

Table 13: The teams that participated in subtask 2 (Arabic).

Rank	Team	Run	Accuracy	F1	Approach
1	MAZA	run3	0.512	**0.513**	Ensemble, word/char n-grams
	UnibucKernel	run3	0.509	0.513	Multiple string kernels
	QCRI	run1	**0.514**	0.511	SVM, word/char n-grams
	ASIREM	run1	0.497	0.495	SVM, char 5/6-grams
2	GW_LT3	run3	0.490	0.492	Ensemble, word/char n-grams
	mitsls	run3	0.485	0.483	Character-level convolutional neural network
	SUKI	run1	0.488	0.482	Language models, char n-grams (1-8)
	UniBucNLP	run3	0.475	0.474	SVM w/ string kernels (char 2-7 grams)
	tubasfs	run1	0.475	0.473	SVM, char n-grams (1-7)
3	HDSL	run1	0.458	0.459	SVM, word and char n-grams
	PITEOG	run2	0.461	0.452	Expectation maximization, word unigrams
4	ALL	run1	0.429	0.435	SVM, char trigrams
	cgli	run3	0.438	0.433	Convolutional neural network (CNN)
	AHAQST	run1	0.428	0.426	SVM, char trigrams
	hltcoe	run1	0.412	0.413	Prediction by partial matching, char 4-grams
5	Citius_Ixa_Imaxin	run1	0.387	0.382	Dictionary-based ranking method
5	eire	run1	0.358	0.346	Naive Bayes, char bigrams
6	UCREL	run2	0.261	0.244	Decision tree (J48), word frequencies

Table 14: Results for subtask 2 (Arabic), *closed* training condition.

Rank	Team	Run	Accuracy	F1	Approach
1	ASIREM	run3	**0.532**	**0.527**	SVM, char 5/6-grams
2	GW_LT3	run3	0.491	0.493	Ensemble, word/char n-grams
3	QCRI	run1	0.379	0.352	SVM, word/char n-grams

Table 15: Results for subtask 2 (Arabic), *open* training condition.

The best-performing system proposed by the *ASIREM* team achieved higher results in the open vs. the closed training condition (52.74% vs. 49.46% F1-score); the second-best system by the *GW_LT3* team performed very similarly in the two conditions (an F1-score of 49.29% for open and 49.22% for closed training); and the third team, *QCRI*, actually performed much better in the closed training condition than in the open one (51.12% vs. 35.20% F1-score). This variation can be explained by looking at the additional training data these teams used, which we will do in the next subsection.

5.2   Open Training Data Sources

The three teams who participated in the open training condition used the following sources:

- *ASIREM* used 18,000 documents (609,316 words) collected manually by native speakers from social media. This yielded results that outperformed the best system in the closed training track, thus demonstrating that out-of-domain training data can be quite useful for this task.

- The *GW_LT3* team made use of dialectal dictionaries and data they collected from Twitter, which also worked quite well.

- The *QCRI* team used a multi-dialect, multi-genre corpus of informal written Arabic (Zaidan and Callison-Burch, 2011).

6   Approaches and Trends

6.1   Features

Almost all teams relied on standard word and character n-grams. Key trends here were that character n-grams outperformed their word-based counterparts, and that higher-order n-grams (5-, 6- and 7-grams) did very well. In fact, the top teams in all categories made use of high-order n-grams. The two teams that were ranked first in test set A used only character n-grams of order 1–7, which demonstrates that combining the n-grams of different orders can be useful.

6.2   Machine Learning Approaches: Traditional vs. Deep Learning Methods

When analyzing the results, we observed several trends about how machine learning approaches were used. For example, we found that traditional supervised learning approaches, particularly SVM and logistic regression, performed very well. In fact, the winner of each category used one of these approaches. This is not surprising given that these methods are suitable for tasks with large numbers of features. Complex learning approaches, such as ensemble methods or hierarchical classifiers, also performed well. Many of the winning runs or those in the top-3 for each category used such an approach.

In contrast, numerous teams attempted to use new deep learning-based approaches, with most of them performing poorly compared to traditional classifiers. One exception is the character-level CNN used by the *mitsls* team, which ranked in sixth place for test set C. Several teams submitted runs using both simple classifiers and deep learning methods, with most noting that the simple methods proved difficult to beat even when comparing against very sophisticated neural network architectures. Others noted the memory requirements and long training times, which made the use of deep learning methods difficult. For example, one team mentioned that their model needed ten days to train.

7   Conclusion

The 2016 DSL shared task was once again a very fruitful experience for both the organizers and the participants. The record number of 37 subscriptions and 24 submissions confirms the interest of the community in discriminating between dialects and similar languages.

This year, we split the task into two subtasks: one on similar languages and varieties and one on Arabic dialect identification. For subtask 1, we provided an in-domain test set (A) compiled from news corpora and an out-of-domain test sets (B1 and B2) collected from social media; the latter case was more challenging. The new subtask on Arabic dialects and the new datasets we released brought even more attention to the DSL task, which ultimately resulted in a record number of submissions.

We are delighted to see many teams developing systems and testing approaches in both subtasks. We observed that more teams used deep learning in comparison to previous editions of the DSL task. Yet, the best results were obtained by simpler machine learning methods such as SVM and logistic regression.

Acknowledgments

We would like to thank all participants in the DSL shared task for their valuable suggestions and comments. We further thank the VarDial Program Committee for thoroughly reviewing the system papers and for their feedback on this report.

References

Judit Ács, László Grad-Gyenge, and Thiago Bruno Rodrigues de Rezende Oliveira. 2015. A Two-level Classifier for Discriminating Similar Languages. In *Proceedings of the LT4VarDial Workshop*.

Wafia Adouane, Nasredine Semmar, Richard Johansson, and Victoria Bobicev. 2016. ASIREM Participation at the Discriminating Similar Languages Shared Task 2016. In *Proceedings of the VarDial Workshop*.

Ahmed Ali, Najim Dehak, Patrick Cardinal, Sameer Khurana, Sree Harsha Yella, James Glass, Peter Bell, and Steve Renals. 2016. Automatic Dialect Detection in Arabic Broadcast Speech. In *Proceedings of Interspeech*.

Areej Alshutayri, Eric Atwell, Abdulrahman Alosaimy, James Dickins, Michale Ingleby, and Janet Watson. 2016. Arabic Language WEKA-Based Dialect Classifier for Arabic Automatic Speech Recognition Transcripts. In *Proceedings of the VarDial Workshop*.

Timothy Baldwin and Marco Lui. 2010. Multilingual Language Identification: ALTW 2010 Shared Task Data. In *Proceedings of ALTA*.

Adrien Barbaresi. 2016. An Unsupervised Morphological Criterion for Discriminating Similar Languages. In *Proceedings of the VarDial Workshop*.

Yonatan Belinkov and James Glass. 2016. A Character-level Convolutional Neural Network for Distinguishing Similar Languages and Dialects. In *Proceedings of the VarDial Workshop*.

Johannes Bjerva. 2016. Byte-based Language Identification with Deep Convolutional Networks. In *Proceedings of the VarDial Workshop*.

Victoria Bobicev. 2015. Discriminating between Similar Languages Using PPM. In *Proceedings of the LT4VarDial Workshop*.

Ondrej Bojar, Rajen Chatterjee, Christian Federmann, Yvette Graham, Barry Haddow, Matthias Huck, Antonio Jimeno Yepes, Philipp Koehn, Varvara Logacheva, Christof Monz, et al. 2016. Findings of the 2016 Conference on Machine Translation. In *Proceedings of WMT*.

Çağrı Çöltekin and Taraka Rama. 2016. Discriminating Similar Languages with Linear SVMs and Neural Networks. In *Proceedings of the VarDial Workshop*.

Andre Cianflone and Leila Kosseim. 2016. N-gram and Neural Language Models for Discriminating Similar Languages. In *Proceedings of the VarDial Workshop*.

Alina Maria Ciobanu, Sergiu Nisioi, and Liviu P. Dinu. 2016. Vanilla Classifiers for Distinguishing between Similar Languages. In *Proceedings of the VarDial Workshop*.

Kareem Darwish, Hassan Sajjad, and Hamdy Mubarak. 2014. Verifiably Effective Arabic Dialect Identification. In *Proceedings of EMNLP*.

Mohamed Eldesouki, Fahim Dalvi, Hassan Sajjad, and Kareem Darwish. 2016. QCRI @ DSL 2016: Spoken Arabic Dialect Identification Using Textual Features. In *Proceedings of the VarDial Workshop*.

Heba Elfardy and Mona Diab. 2014. Sentence Level Dialect Identification in Arabic. In *Proceedings of ACL*.

Raül Fabra-Boluda, Francisco Rangel, and Paolo Rosso. 2015. NLEL UPV Autoritas participation at Discrimination between Similar Languages (DSL) 2015 shared task. In *Proceedings of the LT4VarDial Workshop*.

Hector-Hugo Franco-Penya and Liliana Mamani Sanchez. 2016. Tuning Bayes Baseline for Dialect Detection. In *Proceedings of the VarDial Workshop*.

Marc Franco-Salvador, Paolo Rosso, and Francisco Rangel. 2015. Distributed Representations of Words and Documents for Discriminating Similar Languages. In *Proceedings of the LT4VarDial Workshop*.

Pablo Gamallo, Iñaki Alegria, and José Ramom Pichel. 2016. Comparing two Basic Methods for Discriminating Between Similar Languages and Varieties. In *Proceedings of the VarDial Workshop*.

Cyril Goutte and Serge Léger. 2015. Experiments in Discriminating Similar Languages. In *Proceedings of the LT4VarDial Workshop*.

Cyril Goutte and Serge Léger. 2016. Advances in Ngram-based Discrimination of Similar Languages. In *Proceedings of the VarDial Workshop*.

Cyril Goutte, Serge Léger, and Marine Carpuat. 2014. The NRC System for Discriminating Similar Languages. In *Proceedings of the VarDial Workshop*.

Cyril Goutte, Serge Léger, Shervin Malmasi, and Marcos Zampieri. 2016. Discriminating Similar Languages: Evaluations and Explorations. In *Proceedings of LREC*.

Cyril Grouin, Dominic Forest, Lyne Da Sylva, Patrick Paroubek, and Pierre Zweigenbaum. 2010. Présentation et Résultats du Défi Fouille de Texte DEFT2010 Où et Quand un Article de Presse a-t-il Été Écrit? In *Proceedings of DEFT*.

Chinnappa Guggilla. 2016. Discrimination between Similar Languages, Varieties and Dialects using CNN and LSTM-based Deep Neural Networks. In *Proceedings of the VarDial Workshop*.

Bo Han, Afshin Rahimi, Leon Derczynski, and Timothy Baldwin. 2016. Twitter Geolocation Prediction Shared Task of the 2016 Workshop on Noisy User-generated Text. In *Proceedings of the W-NUT Workshop*.

Abualsoud Hanani, Aziz Qaroush, and Stephen Taylor. 2016. Classifying ASR Transcriptions According to Arabic Dialect. In *Proceedings of the VarDial Workshop*.

Ondřej Herman, Vit Suchomel, Vít Baisa, and Pavel Pavel Rychlý. 2016. DSL Shared task 2016: Perfect Is The Enemy of Good Language Discrimination Through Expectation–Maximization and Chunk-based Language Model. In *Proceedings of the VarDial Workshop*.

Chu-ren Huang and Lung-hao Lee. 2008. Contrastive Approach towards Text Source Classification based on Top-Bag-of-Word Similarity. In *Proceedings of PACLIC*.

Radu Tudor Ionescu and Marius Popescu. 2016. UnibucKernel: An Approach for Arabic Dialect Identification based on Multiple String Kernels. In *Proceedings of the VarDial Workshop*.

Radu Tudor Ionescu, Marius Popescu, and Aoife Cahill. 2016. String Kernels for Native Language Identification: Insights from Behind the Curtains. *Computational Linguistics*, 43(3):491–525.

Tommi Jauhiainen, Heidi Jauhiainen, and Krister Lindén. 2015. Discriminating Similar Languages with Token-based Backoff. In *Proceedings of the LT4VarDial Workshop*.

Tommi Jauhiainen, Krister Lindén, and Heidi Jauhiainen. 2016. HeLI, a Word-Based Backoff Method for Language Identification. In *Proceedings of the VarDial Workshop*.

Ben King, Dragomir Radev, and Steven Abney. 2014. Experiments in Sentence Language Identification with Groups of Similar Languages. In *Proceedings of the VarDial Workshop*.

Nikola Ljubešić and Denis Kranjčić. 2015. Discriminating Between Closely Related Languages on Twitter. *Informatica*, 39(1).

Nikola Ljubešić, Nives Mikelic, and Damir Boras. 2007. Language identification: How to distinguish similar languages? In *Proceedings of ITI*.

Nikola Ljubešić, Darja Fišer, and Tomaž Erjavec. 2014. TweetCaT: a Tool for Building Twitter Corpora of Smaller Languages. In *Proceedings of LREC*.

Nikola Ljubešić, Tanja Samardžić, and Curdin Derungs. 2016. TweetGeo – A Tool for Collecting, Processing and Analysing Geo-encoded Data. In *Proceedings of COLING*.

Marco Lui and Paul Cook. 2013. Classifying English Documents by National Dialect. In *Proceedings of ALTA*.

Marco Lui, Ned Letcher, Oliver Adams, Long Duong, Paul Cook, and Timothy Baldwin. 2014. Exploring Methods and Resources for Discriminating Similar Languages. In *Proceedings of VarDial*.

Shervin Malmasi and Mark Dras. 2015a. Automatic Language Identification for Persian and Dari Texts. In *Proceedings of PACLING*.

Shervin Malmasi and Mark Dras. 2015b. Language Identification using Classifier Ensembles. In *Proceedings of the VarDial Workshop*.

Shervin Malmasi and Marcos Zampieri. 2016. Arabic Dialect Identification in Speech Transcripts. In *Proceedings of the VarDial Workshop*.

Paul McNamee. 2016. Language and Dialect Discrimination Using Compression-Inspired Language Models. In *Proceedings of the VarDial Workshop*.

Jordi Porta and José-Luis Sancho. 2014. Using Maximum Entropy Models to Discriminate between Similar Languages and Varieties. In *Proceedings of the VarDial Workshop*.

Matthew Purver. 2014. A Simple Baseline for Discriminating Similar Language. In *Proceedings of VarDial Workshop*.

Bali Ranaivo-Malançon. 2006. Automatic identification of close languages - case study: Malay and Indonesian. *ECTI Transactions on Computer and Information Technology*, 2:126–134.

Abdulhadi Shoufan and Sumaya Al-Ameri. 2015. Natural Language Processing for Dialectical Arabic: A Survey. In *Proceedings of the Arabic NLP Workshop*.

Thamar Solorio, Elizabeth Blair, Suraj Maharjan, Steven Bethard, Mona Diab, Mahmoud Ghoneim, Abdelati Hawwari, Fahad AlGhamdi, Julia Hirschberg, Alison Chang, and Pascale Fung. 2014. Overview for the First Shared Task on Language Identification in Code-Switched Data. In *Proceedings of the CodeSwitch Workshop*.

Liling Tan, Marcos Zampieri, Nikola Ljubešić, and Jörg Tiedemann. 2014. Merging Comparable Data Sources for the Discrimination of Similar Languages: The DSL Corpus Collection. In *Proceedings of the BUCC Workshop*.

Christoph Tillmann, Saab Mansour, and Yaser Al-Onaizan. 2014. Improved Sentence-Level Arabic Dialect Classification. In *Proceedings of the VarDial Workshop*.

Samantha Wray and Ahmed Ali. 2015. Crowdsource a little to label a lot: labeling a speech corpus of dialectal Arabic. In *Proceedings of Interspeech*.

Omar F. Zaidan and Chris Callison-Burch. 2011. Crowdsourcing translation: Professional quality from non-professionals. In *Proceedings of ACL-HLT*.

Omar F Zaidan and Chris Callison-Burch. 2014. Arabic Dialect Identification. *Computational Linguistics*, 40(1):171–202.

Marcos Zampieri and Binyam Gebrekidan Gebre. 2012. Automatic Identification of Language Varieties: The Case of Portuguese. In *Proceedings of KONVENS*.

Marcos Zampieri, Liling Tan, Nikola Ljubešić, and Jörg Tiedemann. 2014. A Report on the DSL Shared Task 2014. In *Proceedings of the VarDial Workshop*.

Marcos Zampieri, Binyam Gebrekidan Gebre, Hernani Costa, and Josef van Genabith. 2015a. Comparing Approaches to the Identification of Similar Languages. In *Proceedings of the VarDial Workshop*.

Marcos Zampieri, Liling Tan, Nikola Ljubešić, Jörg Tiedemann, and Preslav Nakov. 2015b. Overview of the DSL Shared Task 2015. In *Proceedings of the LT4VarDial Workshop*.

Ayah Zirikly, Bart Desmet, and Mona Diab. 2016. The GW/LT3 VarDial 2016 Shared Task System for Dialects and Similar Languages Detection. In *Proceedings of the VarDial Workshop*.

Arkaitz Zubiaga, Inaki San Vicente, Pablo Gamallo, José Ramom Pichel, Inaki Alegria, Nora Aranberri, Aitzol Ezeiza, and Víctor Fresno. 2014. Overview of TweetLID: Tweet Language Identification at SEPLN 2014. In *Proceedings of the TweetLID Workshop*.

Arkaitz Zubiaga, Iñaki San Vicente, Pablo Gamallo, José Ramom Pichel, Iñaki Alegria, Nora Aranberri, Aitzol Ezeiza, and Víctor Fresno. 2015. TweetLID: A Benchmark for Tweet Language Identification. *Language Resources and Evaluation*, pages 1–38.

Discriminating similar languages: experiments with linear SVMs and neural networks

Çağrı Çöltekin
Department of Linguistics
University of Tübingen, Germany
ccoltekin
@sfs.uni-tuebingen.de

Taraka Rama
Department of Linguistics
University of Tübingen, Germany
taraka-rama.kasicheyanula
@uni-tuebingen.de

Abstract

This paper describes the systems we experimented with for participating in the discriminating between similar languages (DSL) shared task 2016. We submitted results of a single system based on support vector machines (SVM) with linear kernel and using character ngram features, which obtained the first rank at the closed training track for test set A. Besides the linear SVM, we also report additional experiments with a number of deep learning architectures. Despite our intuition that non-linear deep learning methods should be advantageous, linear models seem to fare better in this task, at least with the amount of data and the amount of effort we spent on tuning these models.

1 Introduction

Automatic language identification if often considered a solved task. Very high levels of accuracies in automatic identification of languages from text had been reported in studies over two decades ago (Beesley, 1988; Cavnar and Trenkle, 1994; Dunning, 1994). For example, Dunning (1994) reports over 99 % accuracy for test strings of 100 characters, the reported accuracy goes up to 99.90 % for 500-character strings. Even short strings of 20 characters were enough for over 90 % accuracy. The results above were obtained when a training set of 50k characters were considered 'large' training data, and many of the machine learning methods were in their infancy. Considering the amount of data, computation power and the methods we have at hand today, the automatic language identification task is, indeed, an almost solved problem. However, there are at least two cases where we are not close to the solution yet. The first is when the languages to be discriminated are closely related (Tiedemann and Ljubešić, 2012; Zampieri et al., 2014; Zampieri et al., 2015), and the second is when the documents of interest contain multiple languages, including code mixing or code switching (Nguyen and Dogruöz, 2013; Lui et al., 2014). Discriminating between Similar Languages (DSL) shared task (Malmasi et al., 2016) aims to address the first issue.

This paper describes the models we experimented with for participating in the DSL shared task. In this work, we describe and report results from two families of models. The first family is the linear models with character-ngram features, including the linear support vector machine (SVM) model which obtained the first rank at the closed training track for test set A, and obtained fair results in other test sets despite the fact that it was not particularly optimized for them. In our experiments, the (simple) linear models with character ngram features were proven difficult to beat.

The second family of models we experimented with are a number of deep neural network architectures. These models has been our initial motivation for participating in the shared task. Besides their recent success in many natural language processing methods, these models are interesting for discriminating between similar languages because of (at least) two reasons. First, it seems success in discriminating between distant/different languages and discriminating between similar languages require different types of models and/or features. This observation is supported by the fact that one of the most popular and successful approaches in earlier DSL shared tasks has been hierarchical systems that use different models

---

15

Proceedings of the Third Workshop on NLP for Similar Languages, Varieties and Dialects,
pages 15–24, Osaka, Japan, December 12 2016.

for discriminating language groups and individual languages within each group (Goutte et al., 2014; Goutte and Léger, 2015; Fabra Boluda et al., 2015; Ács et al., 2015). The potential benefit of a deep learning model here is the possibility of building a single (hierarchical) model that addresses both issues jointly.

The second potential benefit of deep learning architectures comes from the fact that, unlike linear models, they can capture non-additive non-linear interactions between input features. For example, although none of the features marked with boldface in (1) below are conclusive for 3-way discrimination between Bosnian (1a), Croatian (1b) and Serbian (1c), a non-linear combination of these features are definitely useful.[1]

(1)   a. *Član 3. **Svako** ima pravo na život, slobodu i **ličnu sigurnost**.*

      b. *Članak 3. **Svatko** ima pravo na život, slobodu i **osobnu sigurnost**.*

      c. *Član 3. **Svako** ima pravo na život, slobodu i **ličnu bezb(j)ednost**.*

        Article 3. Everyone has the right to life, liberty and security of person.

As a result, given enough training data and appropriate model architecture, we expect deep networks to perform well in discriminating both languages across the language groups and languages within the language groups. Below, we describe both family of models in detail (Section 2), report results of both on the shared task training data (Section 3), and discuss the results obtained (Section 4).

2   Approach

We originally intended to participate in the shared task using deep neural network models, with the motivations that are discussed in Section 1. However, our efforts did not yield better results than the 'baseline' models that we initially implemented just for the sake of comparison. As a result, we participated in the shared task with our best baseline, which also obtained good results among the other participated systems. In this section, we first briefly described the 'baseline' models that constitute our official participation to the DSL shared task. We also describe some of the deep learning architectures we have experimented with in this section, and report results obtained by both models – linear and deep learning – and compare them in Section 3. The implementations of all models described below are available at `https://doi.org/10.5281/zenodo.163812`.

2.1 Linear models

The results we submitted to the shared task use a multi-class (one-vs-one) support vector machine (SVM) model with linear kernel. Although we experimented with various features, our final model included character ngrams of length one to seven. The features are weighted using sub-linear tf-idf scaling (Jurafsky and Martin, 2009, p.805). The models we describe here are almost identical to the model of Zampieri et al. (2015) in the DSL 2015 shared task. Similar to them, we also experimented with logistic regression as well, using both one-vs-rest and one-vs-one multi-class strategies. In our experiments, different linear models performed comparably. However, the SVM models always performed slightly better than logistic regression models. In this paper, we only describe the SVM models and discuss the results obtained using them.

We did not apply any filtering (e.g., case normalization, tokenization) except truncating the input documents to 70 white-space-separated tokens. In all experiments reported in this paper, we fixed the single model parameter (SVM margin or regularization parameter, C) at 1.00. Unlike results reported by Purver (2014), in our experiments, the model accuracy was not affected drastically with the changes in the regularization parameter within a reasonable range (not reported here). Although stronger regularization was useful for models employing larger number of features, the effect was not noteworthy.

All linear models were implemented with scikit-learn (Pedregosa et al., 2011) and trained and tested using Liblinear back end (Fan et al., 2008).

---

[1] The example (article 3 of the Universal Declaration of Human Rights) is taken from `https://en.wikipedia.org/wiki/Comparison_of_standard_Bosnian,_Croatian,_Montenegrin_and_Serbian`.

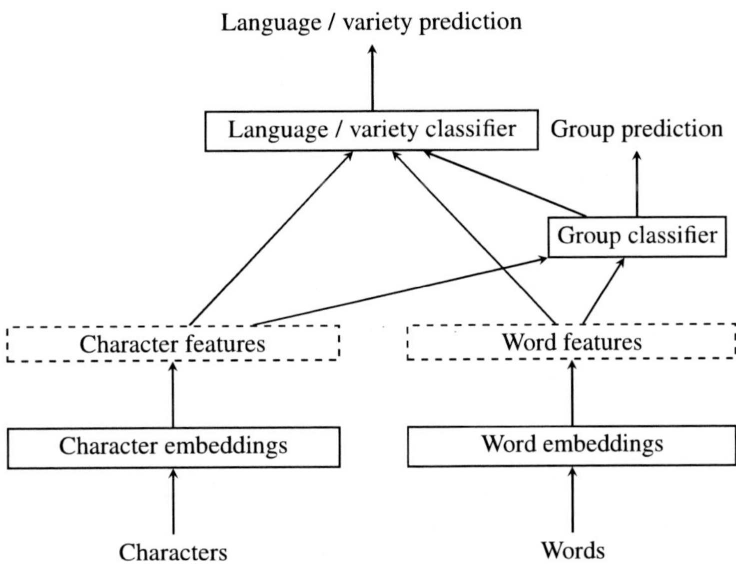

Figure 1: The schematic representation of general neural network architecture.

2.2 Deep learning models

FastText. The FastText model is a recent model proposed by Joulin et al. (2016). The main idea behind this model is to represent a sentence as a sequence of word embeddings (dense vectors) and then employ average the vectors across the sentence to yield a single dense representation of a sentence. Formally, given a sentence of length N, each word w_n is represented as a vector $e_n \in \mathbb{R}^K$ where K is the dimension of the dense representation. At this step, the sentence is now represented as matrix $E \in \mathbb{R}^{k \times n}$. The average pooling step transforms the matrix into a single vector $X \in \mathbb{R}^k$ and $X_k = \frac{\sum E_k}{n}$ where, X_k is the kth element in X. We tested with both character embeddings and word embeddings in our experiments.

This model is similar to the system of Franco-Salvador et al. (2015) in the DSL 2015 shared task, since it represents the documents as an average vectors of their components (characters or words). However, crucially, the embeddings used in this model are learned specifically for the discrimination task rather than being general word vectors capturing syntactic/semantic properties.

Hierarchical character + word models. The general architecture used for our hierarchical network model is presented in Figure 1. In this model, we use both character and word embeddings to train our model. Similar to FastText model discussed above, the embeddings are task-specific. They are trained during learning to discriminate the languages varieties. As a result, the expectation is that the input features (characters words) that are indicative of a particular label (rather than words that are semantically similar) cluster in the same region of the space defined by the embeddings.

The model is an example of multi-label classification. During training, model parameters are optimized to guess both the group, and the specific language variety correctly. Furthermore, we feed the model's prediction of the group to the classifier predicting the specific language variety. For instance, we would use the information that *es-ar* and *es-mx* labels belong to the Spanish group. The intuition behind this model is that, it will use the highly accurate group prediction during test time to tune into features that are useful within a particular language group for predicting individual varieties. In principle, the boxes 'Group classifier' and 'Language / variety classifier' in Figure 1 may include multiple layers for allowing the classifier to generalize based on non-linear combinations in its input features. However, in the experiments reported in this paper, we did not use multiple layers in both classifiers, since it did not improve the results.

The dashed boxes in Figure 1 turn the sequence of word and character embeddings into fixed-size feature vectors. In principle, any model that extracts useful features from a sequence of embeddings are useful here. The convolutional and recurrent neural networks are typical choices for this step. We have experimented with both methods. However, simple averaging of the embedding as in the FastText model described above performed better. As a result we only report results from a simple feature extraction step where the features are averaged embedding vectors.

The model we use for the results reported in Section 3.3 below has the following components.

1. A character embeddings model and a word embeddings model similar to FastText.

2. A group label classifier is trained on the concatenation of the representation from character and word embeddings.

3. The softmax score of the group classifier is concatenated again with the character and word representations' concatenation to train a final language variety classifier based on softmax classifier.

In the experiments reported below, the documents are padded or truncated to 512 characters for the character embedding input, and they are padded or truncated to 70 tokens for the word embeddings input. We used character embeddings of size 20 and word embeddings of size 32. For both embedding layers, we used dropout with rate 0.20 to prevent overfitting. As noted above, the feature extraction step is only averaging over all embedding vectors. Both classifiers in the figure were single layer networks (with softmax activation function), predicting one-hot representations of groups and varieties. The network was trained using categorical cross entropy loss function for both outputs using Adam optimization algorithm. To prevent overfitting, the training was stopped when validation set accuracy stopped improving. All neural network experiments are realized using Keras (Chollet, 2015) with Tensorflow backend (Abadi et al., 2015).

3   Experiments and results

This section presents the results obtained with the approaches described in Section 2. We first introduce the data sets used briefly. Then we present the result we received from the shared task organizers, followed by the results from the models that we did not submit to the shared task.

3.1   Data

The DSL shared shared task (Malmasi et al., 2016) included two tasks. The data for the first task (*task 1*) comes from Tan et al. (2014), and contains a set of 12 language varieties belonging to 5 groups. The data for the second task (*task 2*) comes from Ali et al. (2016), and contains five varieties of Arabic. The first task included two test sets. Test set A contains in-domain documents including all languages or language varieties listed in Table 1. Test set B contains out-of-domain documents (tweets) in Bosnian, Croatian, Serbian, Brazilian Portuguese and European Portuguese. The test set B comes in two varieties, B1 and B2, differing in the way documents were sampled (Malmasi et al., 2016).

The languages/varieties included in task 1 are presented in Table 1, and the Arabic dialect data for task 2 is presented in Table 2. Besides the codes and short descriptions of the varieties, Table 1 also presents the average document length in number of words and characters for each variety in the training set. Although training set for task 1 is balanced in number of documents, there is a slight amount of imbalance with respect to token and character features available in the training data. The overall average length of the documents in task 1 training data was 34.80 words (sd=14.42) and 185.48 characters (sd=76.52). Besides average number of characters and words, Table 1 also presents the number of documents belonging to each variety in the training set for task 2. The data for task 2 contains ASR transcripts. The lengths of the documents in the task 2 training set vary more. The average length of the documents in task 2 training set is 183.79 (sd=271.81) characters and 41.45 (sd=60.68) tokens. In particular, the task 2 training data consists mainly of short documents (27 % of the documents are less than 50 characters, cf. 1.50 % for task 1 training set). However, there are also occasional very long documents (longest document contains 18 017 characters).

Code	Language / variety	Characters	Tokens
bs	Bosnian	168.36	31.13
hr	Croatian	203.56	37.02
sr	Serbian	180.04	34.27
es-ar	Argentinian Spanish	213.11	41.47
es-es	European Spanish	224.49	44.77
es-mx	Mexican Spanish	151.92	30.85
fr-ca	Canadian French	147.22	28.34
fr-fr	European French	181.98	35.06
id	Indonesian	207.62	33.51
my	Malay	157.94	25.51
pt-br	Brazilian Portuguese	202.82	39.53
pt-br	European Portuguese	186.66	36.18

Table 1: The DSL 2016 data set for the task 1. The number of documents in both training (18 000) and development (2 000) sets were balanced. The columns labeled 'characters' and 'tokens' present the average number of non-space characters and white-space-separated tokens for the documents belonging to each language variety in the training set.

Code	Language / variety	Documents	Characters	Tokens
egy	Egyptian	1578	236.63	53.83
glf	Gulf	1672	168.53	38.33
lav	Levantine	1758	163.16	37.67
msa	Modern Standard Arabic	999	231.62	49.04
nor	North-African	1612	140.77	32.01

Table 2: The DSL 2016 data set for the task 2. The column 'documents' number of documents that belong to each language variety in the training set. The columns labeled 'characters' and 'tokens' present the average number of non-space characters and white-space-separated tokens for documents belonging to each language variety.

Test Set	Run	Accuracy	F1 (micro)	F1 (macro)	F1 (weighted)	Rank
A	run1	0.8938	0.8938	0.8938	0.8938	1
A	run2	0.8905	0.8905	0.8904	0.8904	1
B1	run1	0.862	0.862	0.6144	0.8602	5
B1	run2	0.86	0.86	0.6126	0.8576	5
B2	run1	0.822	0.822	0.5839	0.8175	5
B2	run2	0.81	0.81	0.5745	0.8044	5
C	run2	0.4747	0.4747	0.4703	0.4725	9

Table 3: The results submitted to the closed track of DSL shared task 2016. All results are obtained using the same model parameters (an SVM using character ngram features of length one to seven). In *run1*, the model is trained on combined training and development corpus, the model is trained only on the training corpus in *run2*. Since task 2 (test set C) did not have a development set, we only list the results of *run2*.

3.2 Main results

We submitted two sets of results (runs) to the DSL shared task. Both runs were obtained with identical models, the linear SVM described in Section 2.1. The differences between the runs were the data used for the training. For *run1*, we used the all the data available to the closed track participants (training and development sets), while we used only the training set for *run2*. Since test-set C did not have any development set, both runs were identical. We optimized the hyperparameters (the regularization parameter of the SVM model and the range of character n-grams) on the development set of task 1 which is most similar to test set A, and used the same parameters for all sub-tasks of task 1 (test sets A, B1 and B2) and task 2 (test set C). We did not perform any cleanup or filtering on test sets B1 and B2. We only participated in the closed track. The results, as calculated by the shared task organizers, are presented in Table 3.

All results are substantially higher than the trivial (random or majority) baselines, which are 0.08, 0.20 and 0.23 for test sets A, B and C, respectively. The baseline scores are random baselines for test sets A and B, and the majority baseline, which is slightly higher than the random baseline (0.20) for test set C, due to class imbalance.

The differences between *run1* and *run2* are small enough that it does not affect the system's rank in the shared task. However, small but consistent increase in scores of *run1* in comparison to *run2* suggests that more data is useful for this task.

In task 1, our results are better for test set A. Besides the fact that this test set contained in-domain documents, our results are also better here probably because the hyperparameters (regularization constant, and range of character ngrams used) are tuned for this particular task. The performance scores obtained on the gold standard test data is also very close to the scores we have obtained on the development set. We also note that test set A results are, in general, lower than last year's shared task (Zampieri et al., 2015). Despite the fact that there is no 'other' label in this year's data, it seems to be more challenging in some other reasons.

Our results in task 2 are the worse among the results reported in Table 3. The rank we obtained in this task is also relatively low, 9th among 18 participants. However, the scores on this task are rather close to each other, with best accuracy of 0.51. It is also noteworthy that the scores obtained on the gold standard data is substantially lower than the scores we obtained using cross validation on the training data (0.65 accuracy, 0.65 weighted F_1 score). This may be due to differences between the domain (or some other characteristics) of the test set and the gold standard data. Another reason for relatively low score obtained on test set C is due the fact that we truncated the documents to 70 tokens. Since the test set C contains a large number of rather long documents, the truncation choice seems to hurt the performance up to 1 % in cross validation scores, which may have affected the rank of the system a few steps if the difference was reflected to the testing on the gold standard data.

We also present the confusion tables for each test set in Table 4, Table 5 and Table 6, for test sets A,

B and C, respectively. As expected, most confusion occurs within the language groups. There are very few instances of out-of-group confusions. Among the groups the most confusions occur within *bs-hr-sr* group and the Spanish varieties. This may be due to genuine difficulties of discriminating between these languages, but there may also be some effect of amount of data available for each class. The varieties with least recall often corresponds with the varieties with shorter documents on average, for example, *bs* and *es-mx* which have the smallest number of characters and words within their group (see Table 1).

		bs	hr	sr	es-ar	es-es	es-mx	fr-ca	fr-fr	id	my	pt-br	pt-pt
							Predicted label						
True Label	bs	774	125	98	0	1	0	0	2	0	0	0	0
	hr	138	846	15	0	0	0	0	0	0	0	1	0
	sr	65	12	920	0	0	0	0	2	0	0	1	0
	es-ar	0	0	0	846	43	108	0	2	0	0	1	0
	es-es	0	0	0	43	779	172	0	4	0	0	1	1
	es-mx	0	0	0	90	112	798	0	0	0	0	0	0
	fr-ca	0	0	0	0	0	0	958	42	0	0	0	0
	fr-fr	0	0	0	0	1	0	58	940	0	0	1	0
	id	1	0	0	0	0	0	0	2	977	20	0	0
	my	0	0	0	0	0	0	0	0	14	986	0	0
	pt-br	0	0	0	0	0	0	0	0	0	0	959	41
	pt-pt	0	0	0	0	0	0	0	0	0	0	57	943

Table 4: Confusion table for task 1, test set A. The language labels are explained in Table 1.

The confusion matrices presented in Table 5 also show the same trend. Almost no confusions across the language groups, and the *bs-hr-sr* group also seems to be harder to discriminate here as well. The confusion table between the Arabic dialects, presented in Table 5, shows more confusions overall, as expected from low scores presented in Table 3. Gulf variety seems to be difficult to identify for the system, without a clear pattern. We also observe a relatively poor recall for the North African variety which is mostly confused with, probably not surprisingly, Egyptian Arabic.

							Predicted label						
		Test set B1						Test set B2					
		bs	hr	sr	pt-br	pt-pt	other	bs	hr	sr	pt-br	pt-pt	other
True Label	bs	62	31	5	0	0	2	59	31	8	0	0	2
	hr	2	97	1	0	0	0	0	99	1	0	0	0
	sr	2	1	97	0	0	0	2	1	97	0	0	0
	pt-br	0	0	0	98	2	0	0	0	0	94	6	0
	pt-pt	0	0	0	22	77	1	0	0	0	36	62	2

Table 5: Confusion table for task 1, test sets B1 and B2. The predicted label other refers to all labels that did not occur in the gold standard. This amounts to, *bs–id* and *bs–es-ar* confusion for both tests sets, a single *pt-pt–id* confusion in test set B1, and *bs–id* and *bs–es-ar* confusions in test set B2.

3.3 Results with deep learning architectures

We present the performance scores of FastText and the hierarchical neural network model described in Section 2.2 in Table 7. The models are evaluated on the gold standard test data released after the shared

		Predicted label			
	egy	glf	lav	msa	nor
egy	171	33	54	27	30
glf	52	86	44	57	17
lav	54	65	157	33	35
msa	27	26	25	179	17
nor	73	59	45	36	138

(The rows egy–nor are labelled "True Label".)

Table 6: Confusion table for test set C. The language labels are explained in Table 2.

Model	Features	Variety accuarcy			Group accuracy		
		A	B1	B2	A	B1	B2
FastText	char	55.69					
	word	76.75					
Hierarchical	char+word	86.42	60.20	70.20	99.66	86.40	92.00

Table 7: The accuracy values obtained on *task 1* by the neural network models. The models are tested on the gold standard testing data.

task results were announced. We evaluate the models only on task 1. The hierarchical model clearly performs better than the FastText baseline, both using character or word features. Although the accuracy on the test set A is not as good as the SVM model discussed above, if we had submitted the results with this model it would have obtained a mid-range rank in the shared task. The group accuracy on test set A is almost perfect. The results on test set B1 and B2 are lower than ones obtained by the SVM model. The performance on B is also noticeably bad for the group prediction. Furthermore, the drop of performance on test sets B in comparison to test set A also seem to be more steep in comparison to the linear models, despite the fact that we prevented overfitting using multiple measures (see Section 2.2). This may be an indication that even though the system may not be overfitting in the usual sense, it may be 'overfitting' to the domain.

4 Discussion and conclusions

In this paper we reported on our contribution to the DSL 2016 shared task. We described and reported results from two (families of) models. The linear SVMs, that we originally intended to use as a baseline, and deep learning methods that we expected to perform well in this task. In our experiments the 'baseline' SVM model outperformed a number of neural network architectures we have experimented with, and it also obtained the first rank in the test set A of on closed track of the shared task. Our neural network models, on the other hand, did not perform as well in this task, although they have some attractive features discussed in Section 1. Within alternative neural network architectures, simple ones seem to perform better, despite some apparent shortcomings. Furthermore the neural network models seem to be more sensitive to domain differences during the training and testing time.

Our findings show that linear models, in general simpler models, are quite useful and hard to beat in this particular setup. Our experiments with the neural network architectures are rather preliminary, and can probably be improved, for example, through better architectures, better hyper-parameters and more training data.

Acknowledgements

The second author has been supported by the ERC Advanced Grant 324246 EVOLAEMP, which is gratefully acknowledged.

References

Martín Abadi, Ashish Agarwal, Paul Barham, Eugene Brevdo, Zhifeng Chen, Craig Citro, Greg S. Corrado, Andy Davis, Jeffrey Dean, Matthieu Devin, Sanjay Ghemawat, Ian Goodfellow, Andrew Harp, Geoffrey Irving, Michael Isard, Yangqing Jia, Rafal Jozefowicz, Lukasz Kaiser, Manjunath Kudlur, Josh Levenberg, Dan Mané, Rajat Monga, Sherry Moore, Derek Murray, Chris Olah, Mike Schuster, Jonathon Shlens, Benoit Steiner, Ilya Sutskever, Kunal Talwar, Paul Tucker, Vincent Vanhoucke, Vijay Vasudevan, Fernanda Viégas, Oriol Vinyals, Pete Warden, Martin Wattenberg, Martin Wicke, Yuan Yu, and Xiaoqiang Zheng. 2015. TensorFlow: Large-scale machine learning on heterogeneous systems. Software available from tensorflow.org.

Judit Ács, László Grad-Gyenge, and Thiago Bruno Rodrigues de Rezende Oliveira. 2015. A two-level classifier for discriminating similar languages. In *Proceedings of the Joint Workshop on Language Technology for Closely Related Languages, Varieties and Dialects (LT4VarDial)*, pages 73–77.

Ahmed Ali, Najim Dehak, Patrick Cardinal, Sameer Khurana, Sree Harsha Yella, James Glass, Peter Bell, and Steve Renals. 2016. Automatic dialect detection in arabic broadcast speech. In *Interspeech 2016*, pages 2934–2938.

Kenneth R Beesley. 1988. Language identifier: A computer program for automatic natural-language identification of on-line text. In *Proceedings of the 29th Annual Conference of the American Translators Association*, volume 47, page 54. Citeseer.

William B. Cavnar and John M. Trenkle. 1994. N-gram-based text categorization. In *Proceedings of the Third Symposium on Document Analysis and Information Retrieval*, pages 161–175.

François Chollet. 2015. Keras. `https://github.com/fchollet/keras`.

Ted Dunning. 1994. Statistical identification of language. Technical report, Computing Research Laboratory, New Mexico State University.

Raül Fabra Boluda, Francisco Rangel, and Paolo Rosso. 2015. Nlel upv autoritas participation at discrimination between similar languages (dsl) 2015 shared task. In *Proceedings of the Joint Workshop on Language Technology for Closely Related Languages, Varieties and Dialects (LT4VarDial)*, pages 52–58, Hissar, Bulgaria.

Rong-En Fan, Kai-Wei Chang, Cho-Jui Hsieh, Xiang-Rui Wang, and Chih-Jen Lin. 2008. LIBLINEAR: A library for large linear classification. *Journal of Machine Learning Research*, 9:1871–1874.

Marc Franco-Salvador, Paolo Rosso, and Francisco Rangel. 2015. Distributed representations of words and documents for discriminating similar languages. In *Proceedings of the Joint Workshop on Language Technology for Closely Related Languages, Varieties and Dialects (LT4VarDial)*, pages 11–16.

Cyril Goutte and Serge Léger. 2015. Experiments in discriminating similar languages. In *Joint Workshop on Language Technology for Closely Related Languages, Varieties and Dialects*, page 78.

Cyril Goutte, Serge Léger, and Marine Carpuat. 2014. The nrc system for discriminating similar languages. In *Proceedings of the First Workshop on Applying NLP Tools to Similar Languages, Varieties and Dialects*, pages 139–145.

Armand Joulin, Edouard Grave, Piotr Bojanowski, and Tomas Mikolov. 2016. Bag of tricks for efficient text classification. *arXiv preprint arXiv:1607.01759*.

Daniel Jurafsky and James H. Martin. 2009. *Speech and Language Processing: An Introduction to Natural Language Processing, Computational Linguistics, and Speech Recognition*. Pearson Prentice Hall, second edition.

Marco Lui, Jey Han Lau, and Timothy Baldwin. 2014. Automatic detection and language identification of multilingual documents. *Transactions of the Association for Computational Linguistics*, 2:27–40.

Shervin Malmasi, Marcos Zampieri, Nikola Ljubešić, Preslav Nakov, Ahmed Ali, and Jörg Tiedemann. 2016. Discriminating between similar languages and arabic dialect identification: A report on the third DSL shared task. In *Proceedings of the 3rd Workshop on Language Technology for Closely Related Languages, Varieties and Dialects (VarDial)*, Osaka, Japan.

Dong Nguyen and A. Seza Dogruöz. 2013. Word level language identification in online multilingual communication. In *Conference on Empirical Methods in Natural Language Processing*, pages 857–862. Association for Computational Linguistics.

F. Pedregosa, G. Varoquaux, A. Gramfort, V. Michel, B. Thirion, O. Grisel, M. Blondel, P. Prettenhofer, R. Weiss, V. Dubourg, J. Vanderplas, A. Passos, D. Cournapeau, M. Brucher, M. Perrot, and E. Duchesnay. 2011. Scikit-learn: Machine learning in Python. *Journal of Machine Learning Research*, 12:2825–2830.

Matthew Purver. 2014. A simple baseline for discriminating similar languages. In *Proceedings of the First Workshop on Applying NLP Tools to Similar Languages, Varieties and Dialects (VarDial)*, pages 155–160.

Liling Tan, Marcos Zampieri, Nikola Ljubešic, and Jörg Tiedemann. 2014. Merging comparable data sources for the discrimination of similar languages: The dsl corpus collection. In *Proceedings of the 7th Workshop on Building and Using Comparable Corpora (BUCC)*, pages 11–15, Reykjavik, Iceland.

Jörg Tiedemann and Nikola Ljubešić, Ljubešić. 2012. Efficient discrimination between closely related languages. In *Proceedings of COLING 2012*, pages 2619–2634.

Marcos Zampieri, Liling Tan, Nikola Ljubešić, and Jörg Tiedemann. 2014. A report on the dsl shared task 2014. In *Proceedings of the First Workshop on Applying NLP Tools to Similar Languages, Varieties and Dialects*, pages 58–67.

Marcos Zampieri, Liling Tan, Nikola Ljubešic, Jörg Tiedemann, and Preslav Nakov. 2015. Overview of the dsl shared task 2015. In *Joint Workshop on Language Technology for Closely Related Languages, Varieties and Dialects*, pages 1–9.

LSTM autoencoders for dialect analysis

Taraka Rama
Department of Linguistics
University of Tübingen, Germany
`taraka-rama.kasicheyanula`
`@uni-tuebingen.de`

Çağrı Çöltekin
Department of Linguistics
University of Tübingen, Germany
`ccoltekin`
`@sfs.uni-tuebingen.de`

Abstract

Computational approaches for dialectometry employed Levenshtein distance to compute an aggregate similarity between two dialects belonging to a single language group. In this paper, we apply a sequence-to-sequence autoencoder to learn a deep representation for words that can be used for meaningful comparison across dialects. In contrast to the alignment-based methods, our method does not require explicit alignments. We apply our architectures to three different datasets and show that the learned representations indicate highly similar results with the analyses based on Levenshtein distance and capture the traditional dialectal differences shown by dialectologists.

1 Introduction

This paper proposes a new technique based on state-of-the-art machine learning methods for analyzing dialectal variation. The computational/quantitative study of dialects, *dialectometry*, has been a fruitful approach for studying linguistic variation based on geographical or social factors (Goebl, 1993; Nerbonne, 2009). A typical dialectometric analysis of a group of dialects involve calculating differences between pronunciations of a number of items (words or phrases) as spoken in a number of sites (geographical location, or another unit of variation of interest). Once a difference metric is defined for individual items, item-by-item differences are aggregated to obtain site-by-site differences which form the basis of further analysis and visualizations of the linguistic variation based on popular computational methods such as clustering or dimensionality reduction. One of the key mechanisms for this type of analysis is the way item-by-item differences are calculated. These distances are often based on Levenshtein distance between two phonetically transcribed variants of the same item (Heeringa, 2004). Levenshtein distance is often improved by weighting the distances based on pointwise mutual information (PMI) of the aligned phonemes (Wieling et al., 2009; Prokic, 2010).

In this paper we propose an alternative way for calculating the distances between two phoneme sequences using unsupervised (or self supervised) deep learning methods, namely Long Short Term Memory (LSTM) autoencoders (see Section 2 for details). The model is trained for predicting every pronunciation in the data using the pronunciation itself as the sole predictor. Since the internal representation of the autoencoder is limited, it is forced to learn compact representations of words that are useful for reconstruction of the input. The resulting internal representations, *embeddings*, are (dense) multi-dimensional vectors in a space where similar pronunciations are expected to lie in proximity of each other. Then, we use the distances between these embedding vectors as the differences between the alternative pronunciations. Since the distanced calculated in this manner are proper distances in an Euclidean space, the usual methods of clustering or multi-dimensional scaling can be applied without further transformations or normalizations.

There are a number of advantages of the proposed model in comparison to methods based on Levenshtein distance. First of all, proposed method does not need explicit alignments. While learning to reconstruct the pronunciations, the model discovers a representation that places phonetically similar

Proceedings of the Third Workshop on NLP for Similar Languages, Varieties and Dialects,
pages 25–32, Osaka, Japan, December 12 2016.

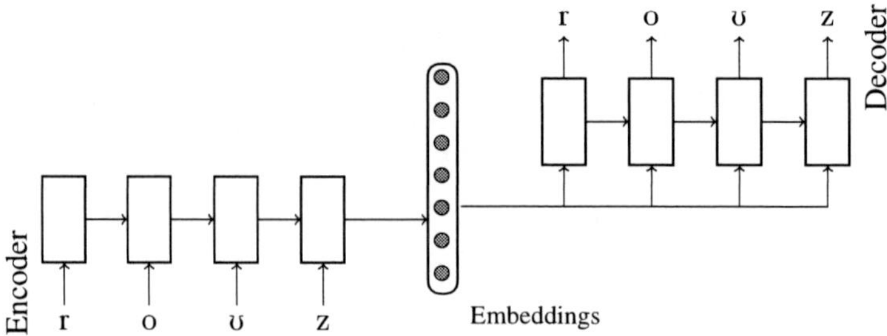

Figure 1: The demonstration of LSTM autoencoder using an example pronunciation [roʊz] (rose). The encoder part represents the whole sequence as a fixed-size embedding vector, which is converted to the same sequence by the decoder.

variants together. However, unlike other alternatives, the present method does not need pairs of pronunciations of the same item. Another advantage of the model is its ability to discover potential non-linear and long-distance dependencies within words. The use of (deep) neural networks allow non-linear combinations of the input features, where LSTMs are particularly designed for learning relationships at a distance within a sequence. The model can learn properties of input that depend on non-contiguous long-distance context features (e.g., as in vowel harmony) and it can also learn to combine features in a non-linear non-additive way, (e.g., when the effect of vowel harmony is canceled in presence of other contextual features).

The rest of the paper is organized as follows. In section 2, we describe our model and the reasons for the development and employment of such a model. In section 3, we discuss our experimental settings and the results of our experiments. We discuss our results in section 4. We conclude the paper in section 5.

2   Model

As mentioned in the previous section, the computational approaches in dialectometry compare words using Levenshtein distance and aggregate the Levenshtein distance across concepts to project the distance matrix on a map. In this paper, we propose the use of autoencoders (Hinton and Salakhutdinov, 2006) based on Long Short Term Memory neural networks (LSTMs) (Hochreiter and Schmidhuber, 1997) for capturing long distance relationships between phonemes in a word. Originally, autoencoders were used to reduce the dimensionality of images and documents (Hinton and Salakhutdinov, 2006). Hinton and Salakhutdinov (2006) show that the deep fully connected autoencoders, when applied to documents, learn a dense representation that separates documents into their respective groups in two dimensional space.

Unlike standard deep learning techniques which learn the neural network weights for the purpose of classification, autoencoders do not require any output label and learn to reconstruct the input. Typical autoencoders feature a hour-glass architecture where the lower half of the hour glass architecture is used for learning a hidden representation whereas, the upper half of the architecture (a mirror of the lower half) learns to reconstruct the input through back-propagation. The learned intermediate representation of each word is a concise representation its pronunciation. The network is forced to use information-dense representations (by removing or reducing redundant features in the input) to be able to construct the original pronunciation. These representations, which are similar to well-known word embeddings (Mikolov et al., 2013; Pennington et al., 2014) in spirit, can then be used for many tasks. In our case, we use the similarities between these internal vector representations for quantifying the similarities of alternative pronunciations. Although the lengths of the pronunciations vary, the embedding representations are fixed. Hence each pronunciation is mapped to a low dimensional space, $\mathbb{R}^k$, such that similar pronunciations are mapped to close proximity of each other.

In this paper, we employ a LSTM based autoencoder (cf. figure 1) to learn an internal representation of a word. The LSTM autoencoder has two parts: encoder and decoder. The encoder part transforms the input sequence $(x_1, \ldots x_T)$ to a hidden representation $h \in \mathbb{R}^k$ where, k is a predetermined dimensionality of h. The decoder is another LSTM layer of length T. The $h_t = h$ representation at each time step t is fed to a softmax function ($\frac{e^{h_{tj}}}{\sum_k e^{h_{tk}}}$) that outputs a $\hat{x}_t \in \mathbb{R}^{|P|}$ length probability vector where P is the set of phonemes in the language or the language group under investigation.

In this paper, we represent a word as a sequence of 1-hot-$|P|$ vectors and use the categorical cross-entropy function ($-\sum_t x_t log(\hat{x}_t) + (1 - x_t)log(1 - \hat{x}_t)$) where x_t is a 1-hot vector and $\hat{x}_t$ is the output of the softmax function at timestep t) to learn both the encoder and decoder LSTM's parameters.

We tested with both unidirectional ($\overrightarrow{h}$) and bidirectional encoder representations in our experiments. The bidirectional encoder consists of a bidirectional LSTM where the input word is scanned in both directions to compute a concatenated $\overrightarrow{h} \bigoplus \overleftarrow{h}$ which is then fed to a decoder LSTM layer for reconstructing the input word.

The model we use is different from the *seq2seq* model of Sutskever et al. (2014) in that the *seq2seq* model supplies the hidden representation of the input sequence to predict the first symbol in a target sequence and then uses the predicted target symbol as an input to the LSTM layer to predict the current symbol. Our architecture, is simpler than the *seq2seq* model due to the following reasons:

1. Unlike *seq2seq*, we work with dialects of a single language which do not require explicit language modeling that features in cross-language sequence learning models.

2. Our model is essentially a sequence labeling model that learns a dense intermediate representation which is then used to predict the input sequence. Moreover, unlike neural machine translation, the source and target sequences are identical, hence, have the same length in our case.

The motivation behind the use of autoencoders is that a single autoencoder network for all the site data would learn to represent similar words with similar vectors. Unlike Levenshtein distance, the LSTM autoencoders can learn to remember and forget the long distance dependencies in a word. The general idea is that similar words tend to have similar representations and a higher cosine similarity. By training a single autoencoder for the whole language group, we intend to derive a generalized across-concept representation for the whole language group.

Once the network is trained, we use the similarities or differences between internal representations of different pronunciations to determine similarities or differences between alternative pronunciations. Since embeddings are vectors in an Euclidean space, similarity can easily be computed using cosine of the angle between these vectors. Then, we use Gabmap (Nerbonne et al., 2011; Leinonen et al., 2016) for analyzing the distances and visualizing the geographic variation on maps. Since Gabmap requires a site-site distance matrix to visualize the linguistic differences between sites, we convert the cosine similarity to a distance score by shifting a similarity score by 1.0 followed by a division by 2.0. The shifted similarity score is then subtracted from 1.0 to yield a distance score. The distance for a site pair is obtained by averaging the word distances across concepts. In case of synonyms, we pick the first word for each concept.

3 Experiments and Results

3.1 Data

We test the system with data from three different languages, English, Dutch and German. The English data comes from Linguistic Atlas of the Middle and South Atlantic States (LAMSAS; Kretzschmar (1993)) The data includes 154 items from 67 sites in Pennsylvania. The data is obtained from Gabmap site,[1] and described in Nerbonne et al. (2011).

The Dutch dialect data is form the Goeman-Taeldeman-Van Reenen Project (Goeman and Taeldeman, 1996) which comprises 1876 items collected from more than 600 locations in the Netherlands and

---

[1] http://www.gabmap.nl

Flanders between 1979–1996. It consists of inflected and uninflected words, word groups and short sentences. The data used in this paper is a subset of the GTRP data set and consist of the pronunciations of 562 words collected at 613 locations. It includes only single word items that show phonetic variation.

German dialect data comes from the project 'Kleiner Deutscher Lautatlas – Phonetik' at the 'Forschungszentrum Deutscher Sprachatlas' in Marburg. The data was recorded and transcribed in the late 1970s and early 1990s (Göschel, 1992). In this study, we the data from Prokić et al. (2012) which is a subset of the data that consists of the transcriptions of 40 words that are present at all or almost all 186 locations evenly distributed over Germany.

3.2 Experimental setup

In our experiments, we limit T, the length of the sequence processed by the LSTM, to 10 for Dutch and German dialect datasets and 20 for Pennsylvanian dataset. We trained our autoencoder network for 20 epochs on each dataset and then used the encoder to predict a hidden representation of length 8 for each dataset. We used the continuous vector representation to compute the similarities between words. We used a batch size of 32 and the *Adadelta* optimizer (Zeiler, 2012) to train our neural networks. All our experiments were performed using Keras (Chollet, 2015) and Tensorflow (Abadi et al., 2016).

3.3 Results

In this section we first present an example visualization of the learned word representations in the hidden dimensions of LSTM autoencoders. To present the model's success in capturing geographical variation, we present visualizations from three different linguistic areas. The maps and the MDS plots in this section were obtained using Gabmap.

3.4 Similarities in the embedding space

Figure 2 presents first two dimensions of the PCA projection of the embedding vectors for alternative pronunciations of German word *acht* 'eight'. As the figure shows, similar pronunciations are closer to the each other in this projection.

Although the representation in Figure 2 show that similar pronunciations are close to each other in this projection, we note that the vector representation are already dense. As a result, unlike many data sets with lots of redundancy, the first two PCA components does not contain most of the information present in all 8 dimensions used in this experiment. The first two PCA component above only explains 50% of the total variation. Hence, half of the variation is not visible in this graph, and some of the similarities or differences shown in the figure may be not be representative of their actual similarities or differences. However, as the analyses we present next confirm, the distances between these representations in the unreduced 8 dimensional space captures the geographical variation well.

3.4.1 Pennsylvanian dialects

An interesting dialect region often analyzed in the literature is the Pennsylvanian dialects. We visualize the distances between sites by reducing the distances using MDS and projecting it on a map for both unidirectional and bidirectional LSTM autoencoders and for a typical Levenshtein distance analysis (using Gabmap with default settings). Figure 3 presents a shaded map where shades represent the first MDS dimension. The reduction to a single dimension preserves 88%, 90% and 96% of the original distances for unidirectional LSTM, Levenshtein distance and bidirectional LSTM, respectively. The results are again similar to the earlier analyses (Nerbonne et al., 2011). Here all analyses indicate a sharp distinction between the 'Pennsylvanian Dutch' area and the rest of Pennsylvania. This distinction is even sharper in the maps produced by the LSTM autoencoders. However, within each group distances indicated by the LSTM autoencoders are smaller, hence, transitions are smoother. The famous 'Route 40' boundary is also visible in all analyses, however, it is sharper in the classical Levenshtein distances in comparison to the LSTM autoencoders.

To visualize the groups of sites with more than two dimensions we also present first two MDS dimensions plotted in Figure 4. In all figures, the group of the dots at the bottom parts of the graphs represent sites in the 'Pennsylvanian Dutch' area. As also indicated by Figure 3, the grouping is clearer between

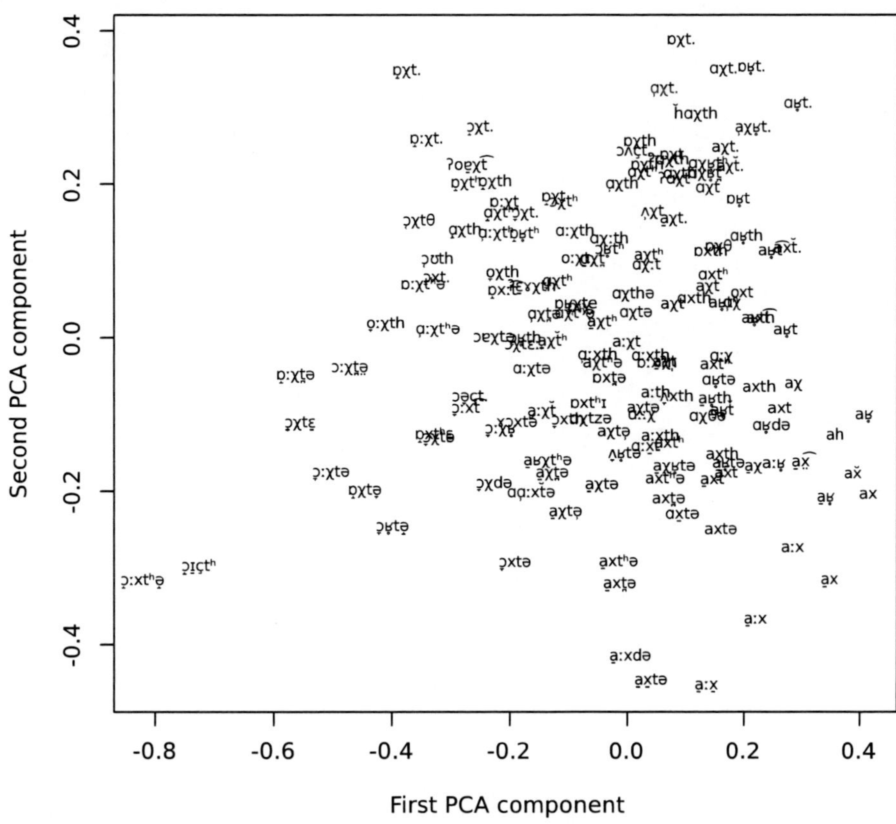

Figure 2: PCA analysis of the dense representation of the German word *acht* 'eight'.

this area and the rest in the LSTM autoencoder output but not as strong in the results with Levenshtein differences.

3.4.2 Dutch dialects

Figure 5 presents the multi-dimensional scaling (MDS) applied to distances based on both unidirectional and bidirectional LSTM autoencoder in comparison to classical Levenshtein distance. The distances in the first three dimensions of MDS are mapped to RGB color space. The correlation between the distances in the first three dimensions and the distances in the unreduced space are 89% for Levenshtein and unidirectional LSTM autoencoder, and 94% for the bidirectional LSTM autoencoder. All methods yield similar results which are also in-line with previous research (Wieling et al., 2007). The colors indicate different groups for Frisian (north west), Low Saxon (Groningen and Overijsel, north east), Dutch Franconian varieties (middle, which seem to show gradual changes from North Holland to Limburg), and Belgian Brabant (south east) and West Flanders (south west).

Although the overall results seem similar, the visualization in Figure 5 indicate that the distances based on both LSTM autoencoders indicate a smoother change compared to the Levenshtein distance.

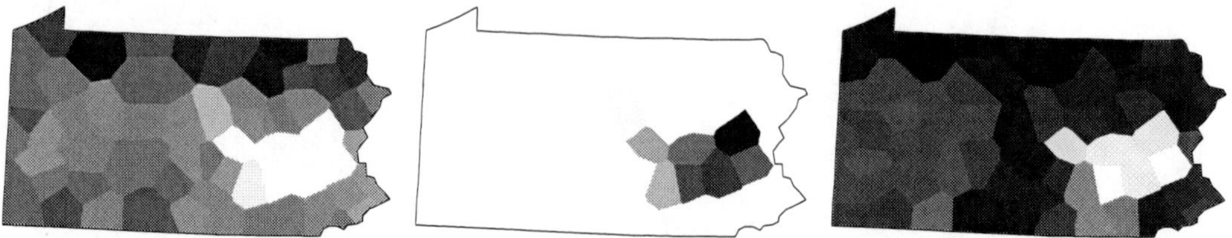

Figure 3: MDS analysis of Pennsylvanian dialects. The shades represent only the first MDS dimension. The distances are based on distances of bidirectional recurrent autoencoder representations (left), unidirectional (middle) and aggregate Levenshtein distance (right). Note that the colors are arbitrary, only the differences (not the values) are meaningful.

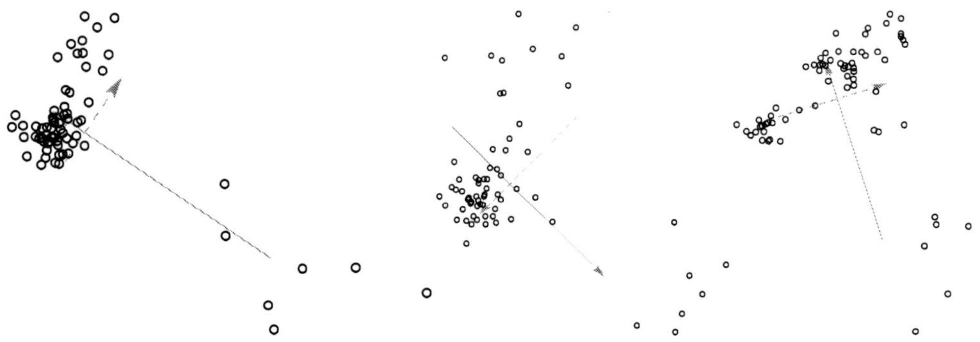

Figure 4: First two MDS dimensions plotted against each other for the Pennsylvania data. Distances are based on concatenated bidirectional LSTM autoencoder representation (left), unidirectional LSTM encoder (middle) and classical aggregate Levenshtein difference (right).

Figure 5: MDS analysis of Dutch dialects. First three MDS dimensions are mapped to RGB color space. The distances are based on distances of bidirectional recurrent autoencoder representations (left), unidirectional (middle) and aggregate Levenshtein distance (right). As in figure 3 the colors are arbitrary, only the differences (not the values) are meaningful.

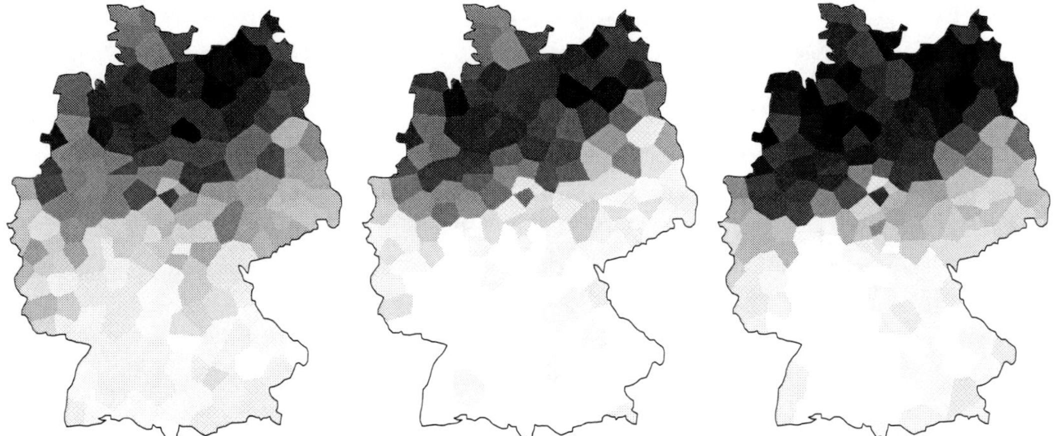

Figure 6: MDS analysis of the German dialects. The shades represent only the first MDS dimension. The distances are based on distances of bidirectional recurrent autoencoder representations (left), unidirectional (middle) and aggregate Levenshtein distance (right).

3.4.3 Dialects of Germany

Figure 6 presents similar analyses for dialects of Germany. Similar to Pennsylvania data, we only visualize the first MDS dimension, with correlations with the original distances 62%, 68% and 70% for unidirectional LSTM, bidirectional LSTM and Levenshtein distances, respectively. The MDS maps of the German dialects show the traditional two-way classification along the North-South dimension. The unidirectional autoencoder shows a higher transition boundary as compared to the bidirectional autoencoder. This seems to be in line with the observation that autoencoders represent a smoother transition in comparison to Levenshtein distance.

4 Discussion

The results of the above visualization show that sequence-to-sequence autoencoders capture similar information to that of pair-wise Levenshtein distance. The autoencoders only require list of words in a uniformly transcribed IPA format for learning the dense representation as compared to the pair-wise approach adopted in Levenshtein distance. We hypothesize that the dense representation of a word causes the smooth transition effect that is absent from the maps of Levenshtein distance. Our experiments suggest that the autoencoders require few thousands of words to train and the visualizations of the site distances correlate well with the traditional dialectological knowledge. An advantage of autoencoders is that they do not require explicit alignment and can train to reconstruct the input.

5 Conclusions

In this paper, we introduced the use of LSTM autoencoders for the purpose of visualizing the shifts in dialects for three language groups. Our results suggest that LSTM autoencoders can be used for visualizing the transitions across dialect boundaries. The visualizations from autoencoders correlate highly with the visualization produced with the standard Levenshtein distance (used widely in dialectometry). LSTM autoencoders do not require explicit alignment or a concept based weighting for learning realistic distances between dialect groups. In the future, we aim to apply the LSTM autoencoders to speech recordings of dialects for the purpose of identifying dialect boundaries.

Acknowledgements

The first author has been supported by the ERC Advanded Grant 324246 EVOLAEMP, which is gratefully acknowledged.

References

Martín Abadi, Ashish Agarwal, Paul Barham, Eugene Brevdo, Zhifeng Chen, Craig Citro, Greg S Corrado, Andy Davis, Jeffrey Dean, Matthieu Devin, et al. 2016. Tensorflow: Large-scale machine learning on heterogeneous distributed systems. *arXiv preprint arXiv:1603.04467*.

François Chollet. 2015. Keras: Deep learning library for theano and tensorflow.

Hans Goebl, 1993. *Dialectometry: a short overview of the principles and practice of quantitative classification of linguistic atlas data*, pages 277–315. Springer Science & Business Media.

Antonie Goeman and Johan Taeldeman. 1996. Fonologie en morfologie van de nederlandse dialecten. een nieuwe materiaalverzameling en twee nieuwe atlasprojecten. *Taal en Tongval*, 48:38–59.

Joachim Göschel. 1992. Das Forschungsinstitut für Deutsche Sprache "Deutscher Sprachatlas". Wissenschaftlicher Bericht, Das Forschungsinstitut für Deutsche Sprache, Marburg.

Wilbert Jan Heeringa. 2004. *Measuring dialect pronunciation differences using Levenshtein distance*. Ph.D. thesis, University of Groningen.

Geoffrey E Hinton and Ruslan R Salakhutdinov. 2006. Reducing the dimensionality of data with neural networks. *Science*, 313(5786):504–507.

Sepp Hochreiter and Jürgen Schmidhuber. 1997. Long short-term memory. *Neural computation*, 9(8):1735–1780.

William A Kretzschmar. 1993. *Handbook of the linguistic atlas of the Middle and South Atlantic States*. University of Chicago Press.

Therese Leinonen, Çağrı Çöltekin, and John Nerbonne. 2016. Using Gabmap. *Lingua*, 178:71–83.

Tomas Mikolov, Ilya Sutskever, Kai Chen, Greg S Corrado, and Jeff Dean. 2013. Distributed representations of words and phrases and their compositionality. In *Advances in neural information processing systems*, pages 3111–3119.

John Nerbonne, Rinke Colen, Charlotte Gooskens, Peter Kleiweg, and Therese Leinonen. 2011. Gabmap – a web application for dialectology. *Dialectologia*, Special Issue II:65–89.

John Nerbonne. 2009. Data-driven dialectology. *Language and Linguistics Compass*, 3(1):175–198.

Jeffrey Pennington, Richard Socher, and Christopher D Manning. 2014. Glove: Global vectors for word representation. In *EMNLP*, volume 14, pages 1532–1543.

Jelena Prokić, Çağrı Çöltekin, and John Nerbonne. 2012. Detecting shibboleths. In *Proceedings of the EACL 2012 Joint Workshop of LINGVIS & UNCLH*, pages 72–80. Association for Computational Linguistics.

Jelena Prokic. 2010. Families and resemblances.

Ilya Sutskever, Oriol Vinyals, and Quoc V Le. 2014. Sequence to sequence learning with neural networks. In *Advances in neural information processing systems*, pages 3104–3112.

Martijn Wieling, Wilbert Heeringa, and John Nerbonne. 2007. An aggregate analysis of pronunciation in the goeman-taeldeman-van reenen-project data. *Taal en Tongval*, 59(1):84–116.

Martijn Wieling, Jelena Prokić, and John Nerbonne. 2009. Evaluating the pairwise string alignment of pronunciations. In *Proceedings of the EACL 2009 workshop on language technology and resources for cultural heritage, social sciences, humanities, and education*, pages 26–34.

Matthew D Zeiler. 2012. Adadelta: an adaptive learning rate method. *arXiv preprint arXiv:1212.5701*.

The GW/LT3 VarDial 2016 Shared Task System for Dialects and Similar Languages Detection

Ayah Zirikly
George Washington University
Washington, DC
`ayaz@gwu.edu`

Bart Desmet
LT3, Ghent University
Ghent, Belgium
`bart.desmet@ugent.be`

Mona Diab
George Washington University
Washington, DC
`mtdiab@gwu.edu`

Abstract

This paper describes the GW/LT3 contribution to the 2016 VarDial shared task on the identification of similar languages (task 1) and Arabic dialects (task 2). For both tasks, we experimented with Logistic Regression and Neural Network classifiers in isolation. Additionally, we implemented a cascaded classifier that consists of coarse and fine-grained classifiers (task 1) and a classifier ensemble with majority voting for task 2. The submitted systems obtained state-of-the-art performance and ranked first for the evaluation on social media data (test sets B1 and B2 for task 1), with a maximum weighted F1 score of 91.94%.

1 Introduction

The 2016 DSL shared task objective was to correctly identify the different variations of similar languages (Malmasi et al., 2016). DSL2016 covered two main subtasks:

- Task 1: discriminating between similar languages from the same language family and between national language varieties. Covered languages and varieties are:

  I Bosnian (`bs`), Croatian (`hr`) and Serbian (`sr`) from the South Slavic language family

  II Malay (`my`) and Indonesian (`id`) from the Austronesian language family

  III Portuguese from Brazil (`pt-BR`) and Portugal (`pt-PT`)

  IV Spanish from Argentina (`es-AR`), Mexico (`es-MX`) and Spain (`es-ES`)

  V French from France (`fr-FR`) and Canada (`fr-CA`)

- Task 2: Arabic dialect identification. The task includes Modern Standard Arabic (`MSA`) and the Egyptian (`EGY`), Gulf (`GLF`), Levantine (`LAV`) and North African (`NOR`) dialects.

Both tasks were evaluated in two tracks: closed (no external resources or additional training data are allowed) and open. The shared task involves predicting different languages for groups I and II from Task 1, identifying different variants of the same language in groups III, IV, V from Task 1, and predicting dialects in Task 2. Furthermore, Task 1 was evaluated on in-domain and out-of-domain test sets.

The experimental approaches described in this paper include preprocessing methods to prepare the data, feature engineering, various machine learning methods (Logistic Regression, Support Vector Machines and Neural Networks) and system architectures (one-stage, two-stage and ensemble classifiers). Additionally, we collected Twitter training data for Task 2 and studied its impact on prediction performance. GW/LT3 participated in Task 1 *(closed)* and Task 2 *(closed and open)*.

The rest of the paper is organized as follows: Section 2 presents a brief overview of work in similar languages identification and previous DSL tasks. Section 3 describes the overall methodology, whereas Section 4 and 5 discuss the datasets, preprocessing, experimental results and analysis in detail for each task. Section 6 concludes this paper.

Proceedings of the Third Workshop on NLP for Similar Languages, Varieties and Dialects,
pages 33–41, Osaka, Japan, December 12 2016.

2   Related Research

Language identification is an active field of research, where in recent years increased attention has been given to the identification of closely related languages, language variants and dialects, which are harder to distinguish. The three editions of the DSL shared task on detecting similar languages have provided a forum for benchmarking various approaches. For a detailed overview of the previous editions and their related work, we refer to the overview papers of Zampieri et al. (2014) and Zampieri et al. (2015).

State-of-the-art approaches to related language identification rely heavily on word and character n-gram representations. Other features include the use of blacklists and whitelists, language models, POS tag distributions and language-specific orthographical conventions (Bali, 2006; Zampieri and Gebre, 2012). For systems, a wide range of machine learning algorithms have been applied (Naive Bayes and SVM classifiers in particular), with work on optimization and dimensionality reduction (Goutte et al., 2014), and on ensembling and cascading, which yielded the best-performing systems in the 2015 edition (Goutte and Léger, 2015; Malmasi and Dras, 2015).

Previous approaches for Arabic dialect detection, a new task introduced in this shared task edition, use similar approaches. Sadat et al. (2014) argue that character n-gram models are well suited for dialect identification tasks because most of the variation is based on affixation, which can be easily modeled at the character level.

Also new to this edition of the shared task is the evaluation on social media data. In 2014, the Tweet-LID shared task specifically addressed the problem of language identification in very short texts (Zubiaga et al., 2014). This brought to light some of the challenges inherent to the genre: a need for a better external resources to train systems, low accuracy on underrepresented languages and the inability to identify multilingual tweets.

3   System Description

We experiment with a number of machine learning methods that range from conventional methods such as Logistic Regression to Deep Learning.

Feature Set   We experimented with a simple feature set similar to those that proved effective in previous DSL tasks (Goutte and Léger, 2015). We employ word and character n-gram representations as features in the closed submission for Task 1. Additionally, we incorporate lexical features based on Arabic dialect dictionaries. We generated `GLF`, `EGY`, `LAV`, and `NOR` noisy dictionaries that are collected from Twitter where a filter based on the geolocation field from Twitter API is applied to reflect the targeted dialects (e.g. `KW` → `GLF`). The `MSA` dictionary is based on the unique vocabulary set in Arabic Gigaword. The dictionary features are a set of 5 features (one per dialect) where each feature value represents the in-dictionary occurrence frequencies (e.g. *kdh mA ySH$* [EN: *This is not right*]: `GLF_dic:1, EGY_dic:3, MSA_dic:1, LAV_dic:1, NOR_dic:1`).

Classifiers
Support Vector Machines (SVM): we experimented with SVMs and found that it produces worse results in comparison to other classifiers. As a result, we did not submit a run that implements SVM.
Logistic Regression (LR) classifier: the intuition behind using LR as opposed to Support Vector Machines (SVM) is that LR works better in scenarios where the classes are close to each other and when the predictors can near-certainly determine the output label. We use LR for both Task 1 and Task 2 as one of the submitted runs, where LR produces state-of-the-art results for Task 1 on out-of-domain data. All LRs are trained with L2 regularization and a cost C of 1.
Neural Network (NN) classifier: we also experiment with NNs, because they have proven effective in modelling a wide range of complex NLP tasks. All NNs are trained with a single hidden layer of 500 neurons, using softmax activation and Adaptive Moment Estimation (Adam) to optimize the stochastic gradient descent.
Two-stage classifier: for Task 1, we implemented a two-stage classifier where we first train a system to predict the coarse-grained language group class. Then, for every language group we built a model

that predicts the fine-grained variant class. A detailed description of this classifier is depicted in Figure 1. **Ensemble with majority voting:** for Task 2, we implemented an ensemble classifier that takes

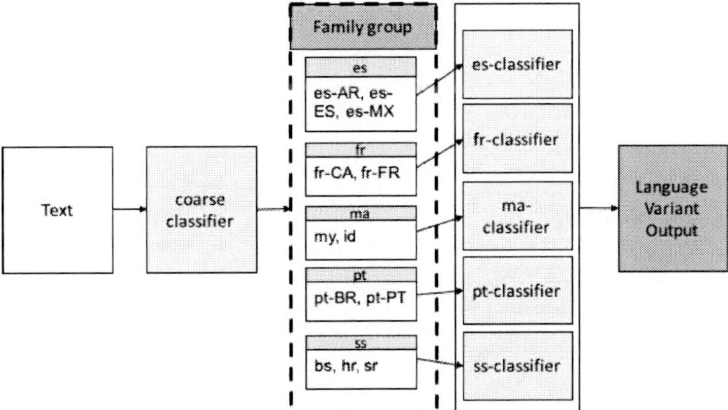

Figure 1: Two-stage coarse-fine classifier

the majority vote of 1 LR and 2 NN classifiers' output and produces the majority label. Ties are broken by taking the output of the best-performing individual classifier. The number and selection of classifiers participating in the ensemble was determined experimentally on the development data.

4   Task 1

Task 1 focuses on predicting the correct label of language variant among classes of similar languages and variants.

4.1   Datasets

The dataset provided contains:

- Training and development data: a balanced train and dev set containing fragments from newswire text (18000 training and 2000 dev instances per class)

- Test data: class-balanced in-domain (test set A: 12000 instances) and out-of-domain data collected from social media (test sets B1 and B2 with 500 instances each, pertaining to the South Slavic and pt families)

4.2   Preprocessing

In order to reduce data dimensionality and improve lexical recall, preprocessing was applied to the datasets. This was especially relevant for the out-of-domain datasets B1 and B2, which were noisy in nature since they had been collected from Twitter. We performed the following normalization operations:

- number masking (e.g. 1990 $\Rightarrow$ 8888)

- URL replacement (e.g. *ttg.uni-saarland.de/vardial2016* $\Rightarrow$ *URL*)

- in words elongated with character flooding, repetitions are limited to two occurrences (e.g. *goooood* $\rightarrow$ *good*)

- removal of at-mentions, retweets and HTML tags

- lowercasing of all text

Additionally, we applied language filtering on the tweets in datasets B1 and B2. The task was to determine the primary language variant of a Twitter user, given a collection of his or her tweets. However, Twitter users do not consistently tweet in the same language: some tweets may be in a different language entirely, and some may have internal code switching. Because such tweets can confuse a classifier, we removed all tweets that could not be confidently assigned to one of the language groups under study. We used the probability outputs of a NN coarse-grained classifier to remove all tweets that had less than 95% of the probability mass concentrated in one category.

Ana Skledar Matijević, prodekanica za nastavu na Veleučilištu Baltazar Adam Krčelić #portrait https://t.co/9WeYAOC4Dq Vinko Morović, dekan i osnovač Veleučilišta Baltazar Adam Krčelić | Dean and co-founder of BAK University #portrait https://t.co/qkmzgompWZ Željko Turk, gradonačelnik Grada Zaprešića | The Mayor of Zaprešić #portrait https://t.co/xiwg1euit8 Robert Vrdoljak, direktor tvrtke Specijalni Projekti d.o.o. | Director of Specijalni Projekti d.o.o. #portrait https://t.co/twZVgyL9m6 Ivica Vugrinec, direktor tvrtki Vugrinec d.o.o. i Golubovečki kamenolomi d.o.o. #portrait https://t.co/KppT6TrgJa   @brankocovic Tajna je ;) Beauty dish ispred, sofbox lijevo i jedan na pozadini. @brankocovic Hvala tebi. Drago mi je da ti se sviđa :) @brankocovic Polako... ja sam isto počela s dva kišobrana :) Ante Žaja, ravnatelj Muzeja Matija Skurjeni u Zaprešiću | Director of the Marija Skurjeni Museum #portrait https://**t.co/tEgnfLJeXx**   **I would rather be kind than right. Palm trees of Doha** @ Doha, Qatar https://t.co/0mZkzB33nh

Figure 2: Example of out-of-domain dataset entry

4.3 Postprocessing

For the B1 and B2 test sets, which only contain 2 of the 5 language groups, we normalize predictions pertaining to an incorrect language group by backing off to the highest-probability available class. In the case of the cascaded classifier, this is done in the first stage.

4.4 Results

The GW/LT3 team submitted to the closed track for Task 1, where no external training data or resources could be used. For each dataset, three systems were submitted (as explained in Section 3), with the following settings:

- LR: character (2-6) and word n-grams (1-3) with term-frequency weighting

- NN: binary character n-gram features (2-6), 35 epochs of training

- Cascade: both the coarse (language group) and fine-grained classifier use LR, with the same feature set as described above for LR

GW/LT3 ranked **first** in the out-of-domain evaluation (test sets B1&B2) and **third** for in-domain test set A. As shown in Table 1, the LR classifier yields the best performance on the B1 and B2 test sets, with an accuracy of 92.0% and 87.8%, respectively. It is narrowly beaten by the cascaded approach on test set A (88.7%).

The state-of-the-art performance on the B1 and B2 test sets may indicate that adequate preprocessing is a prerequisite when dealing with noisy social media data. Both the normalization steps and the aggressive filtering of code-switched tweets based on language family detection may have been effective for improving performance over competing systems.

Data Metric	A			B1			B2		
	LR	NN	2-stage[3]	**LR**[1]	NN	2-stage	**LR**[1]	NN	2-stage
Accuracy	88.59	85.02	**88.70**	**92.00**	89.60	91.20	**87.80**	86.00	87.20
F1-weighted	88.60	84.93	**88.70**	**91.94**	89.45	91.12	**87.73**	85.81	87.13

Table 1: Task 1 results. System ranks are indicated in superscript.

Based on the confusion matrices for the in-domain dataset, we note a very similar behavior among the three different approaches, especially LR & two-stage. We note that NN consistently performs worse than the other two approaches with a marked accuracy degradation in the more closely language variants,

Method \ Variant	hr	bs	sr	es-ar	es-es	es-mx	fr-ca	fr-fr	id	my	pt-br	pt-pt
	A											
LR	85	77	90	85	80	77	94	93	98	98	93	93
NN	82	75	88	79	73	63	92	91	96	96	91	91
2-stage	85	77	90	85	80	78	94	93	98	98	94	93
	B1											
LR	93	86	92	-	-	-	-	-	-	-	94	94
NN	88	82	95	-	-	-	-	-	-	-	92	91
2-stage	93	86	92	-	-	-	-	-	-	-	93	92
	B2											
LR	92	85	91	-	-	-	-	-	-	-	86	84
NN	90	80	92	-	-	-	-	-	-	-	85	82
2-stage	92	84	91	-	-	-	-	-	-	-	85	83

Table 2: Task 1 per-variant F1-score

such as the Portuguese and Spanish language groups. The NN approach performs notably poorly for the detection of Mexican Spanish with a recall of 58% in comparison to 81% for LR. However, it is worth noting that performance for Mexican Spanish is poor across classifiers (Table 2). Together with Bosnian (across datasets), it appears to be harder to predict than other language variants.

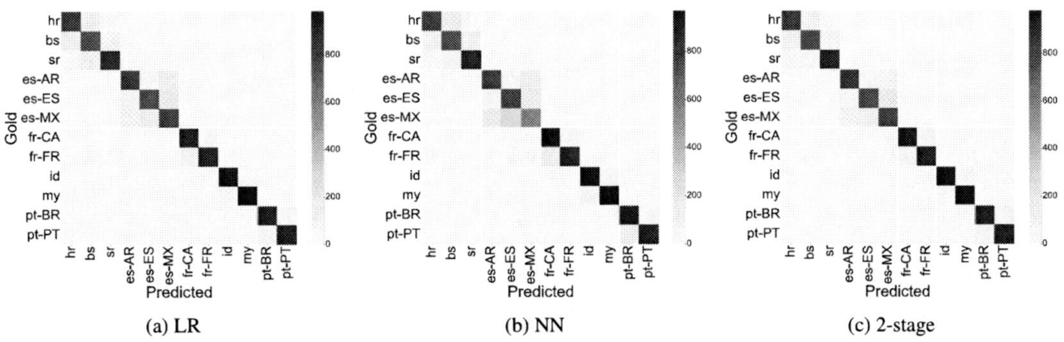

(a) LR   (b) NN   (c) 2-stage

Figure 3: A Confusion Matrices

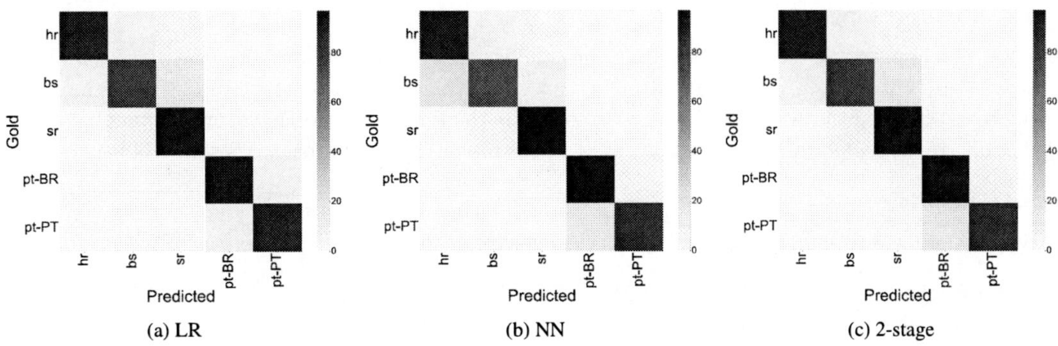

(a) LR   (b) NN   (c) 2-stage

Figure 4: B1 Confusion Matrices

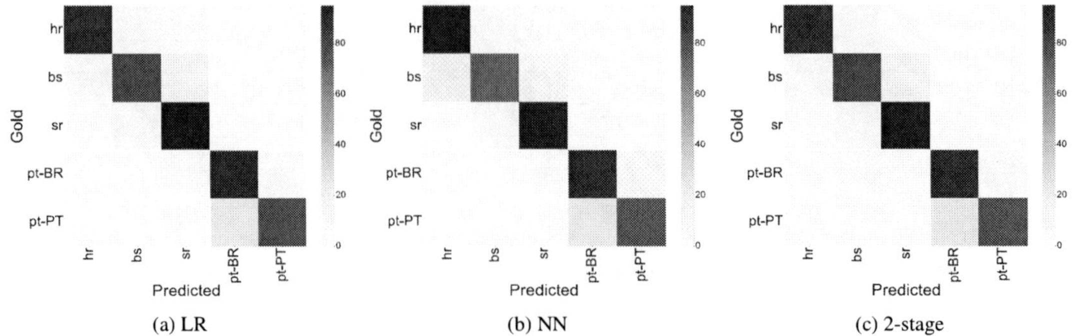

Figure 5: B2 Confusion Matrices

5   Task 2

Task 2 aims to predict the correct Arabic dialect from a set of 5 different dialects. GW/LT3 submitted systems to both the open and closed for the Arabic subtracks.

5.1   Datasets

The dataset (Ali et al., 2016) provided contains Automatic Speech Recognition (ASR) transcripts in Buckwalter encoding[1] and is divided into:

- Training data: unlike Task 1, the training data is unbalanced and contains 1578 EGY, 1672 GLF, 1758 LAV, 999 MSA, and 1612 NOR instances (total of 7619)

- Test data: ASR transcripts containing 315 EGY, 256 GLF, 344 LAV, 274 MSA, and 351 NOR instances (total of 1540)

External datasets   For the open submission, we used dialect dictionaries to make in-vocabulary frequency count features (as explained in 3). For MSA, we used the Arabic Gigaword vocabulary, whereas for other dialects we built dictionaries based on data collected from Twitter. We are aware that using social media data invariably introduces noise, both in terms of misspelled vocabulary entries and with relation to incorrect geographical information. However, as argued by Mubarak and Darwish (2014), such information still provides acceptable dialectal corpora. We filtered the collected tweets based on the countries of interest that map to the targeted dialects of the shared task (e.g. $Syria \rightarrow LAV$). Before creating the dictionaries, we apply normalization (hamza normalization, emoji and URL removal, ...). The resulting dictionary sizes were 76,721 for GLF, 22,003 for EGY, 10,000 for LAV, 286,559 for MSA and 6,343 for NOR.

5.2   Preprocessing

We tested applying letter normalization during the train/dev phase, where we normalized the different shapes of hamza $(', |, >, \&, <, ,)$ to Alif (A). However, we noted that this type of normalization did not improve performance, which is why it was omitted in the final systems. However, preprocessing on the dictionaries collected from Twitter was applied in a similar fashion as the one described in 4.2.

5.3   Results

Settings of the 3 submitted runs for both tracks (as explained in Section 3), were as follows:

- LR: character (2-6) and word n-grams (1-3) without term-frequency weighting, additional dictionary features for the open track

- NN: binary character n-gram features (2-6), 35 epochs of training

---

[1] http://www.qamus.org/transliteration.htm

- Ensemble: 1 NN classifier with character (3-5) and word (1) n-grams, 1 NN classifier with character n-grams (2-6) and 1 LR classifier with character n-grams (1-6) with MSA dictionary features for the open track

GW/LT3 ranks 2nd and 5th in the open and closed settings respectively, using the ensemble approach (EMV) described in Section 3. Table 3 shows the three submitted runs' performance under the closed and open settings. We note that adding extra features using the external resources, or even adding them as extra training data during the train/dev phase, did not improve the performance of the systems. This can likely be explained by limited overlap in genre between the training and test data and the Twitter data. In Table 4, we note that EMV produces the best performance per dialect, with MSA being the easiest dialect to identify. This may be explained by the fact that MSA is highly distinguishable from other dialects, as opposed to the high overlap between dialects' vocabularies.

Data / Metric	Closed			Open		
	LR	NN	EMV[5]	LR	NN	EMV[2]
Accuracy	44.42	49.03	**49.03**	44.35	49.03	**49.09**
F1-weighted	44.79	49.17	**49.22**	44.74	49.17	**49.29**

Table 3: Task 2 results. System ranks are indicated in superscript.

Method / Dialect	EGY	GLF	LAV	MSA	NOR
	CLOSED				
LR	45	33	43	54	48
NN	52	**35**	48	61	49
EMV	**52**	34	**48**	**61**	**50**
	OPEN				
LR	44	33	43	55	48
NN	52	35	48	61	49
EMV	**52**	**35**	**48**	**61**	**50**

Table 4: Task 2 dialects F1-score

Based on Figure 6 and 7, we note that our systems perform in a very similar behavior under the open and closed settings, which is due to the small number of added features under the open settings as opposed to the closed. GLF dialect represents the highest challenge for our systems with F1-score of 35% (as shown in Table 4). Based on the confusion matrix, we note that GLF is often mispredicted as LAV or MSA. Additionally, we note that MSA yields the best performance among the various dialects, a result aligning with the findings of Zaidan and Callison-Burch (2014). EMV produces the best overall accuracy and F-score results with a performance that is very close to the NN system, as two of the three votes belong to NN systems with different parameters.

6 Conclusion & Future Work

In this paper, we discussed the collaborative work between George Washington University (GW) and Ghent University (LT3), where GW/LT3 submitted systems to both 2016 DSL Task 1 (closely related languages and variants) and Task 2 (Arabic dialect identification). The performance of our best run on out-of-domain data for Task 1 ranked first, using a Logistic Regression classifier. We hypothesize that adequate preprocessing of noisy social media data may be a prerequisite for good performance. Complex system architectures such as cascaded classification or ensembling did not yield significant improvements over the one-stage classifiers. Given the promising results of the single-layer Neural Networks for the Arabic dialect detection task, we intend to investigate alternative Deep Learning methodologies in future work.

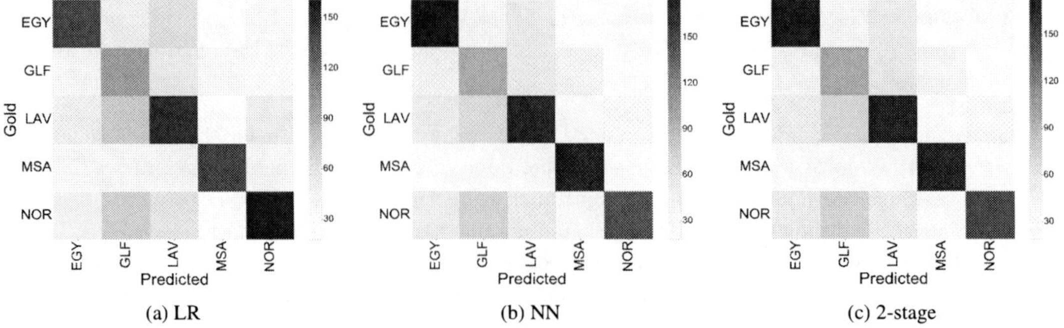

(a) LR   (b) NN   (c) 2-stage

Figure 6: C Closed Confusion Matrices

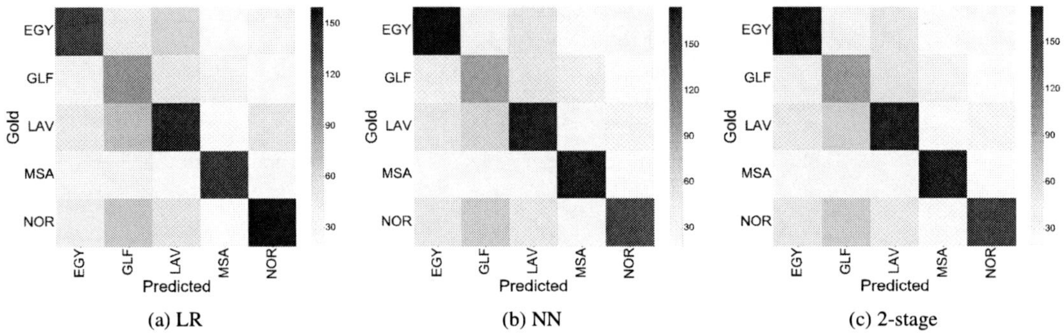

(a) LR   (b) NN   (c) 2-stage

Figure 7: C Open Confusion Matrices

Acknowledgements

We would like to thank the organizers for an interesting shared task. The first and third author were partially funded by DARPA DEFT subcontract from Columbia University. The second author was funded by the Flemish government agency for Innovation by Science and Technology, through the AMiCA project (IWT SBO 120007).

References

Ahmed Ali, Najim Dehak, Patrick Cardinal, Sameer Khurana, Sree Harsha Yella, James Glass, Peter Bell, and Steve Renals. 2016. Automatic dialect detection in Arabic broadcast speech. In *Interspeech 2016*, pages 2934–2938.

Ranaivo-Malançon Bali. 2006. Automatic identification of close languages–case study: Malay and Indonesian. *ECTI Transaction on Computer and Information Technology*, 2(2):126–133.

Cyril Goutte and Serge Léger. 2015. Experiments in discriminating similar languages. In *Joint Workshop on Language Technology for Closely Related Languages, Varieties and Dialects*, page 78.

Cyril Goutte, Serge Léger, and Marine Carpuat. 2014. The NRC system for discriminating similar languages. In *Proceedings of the First Workshop on Applying NLP Tools to Similar Languages, Varieties and Dialects*, pages 139–145.

Shervin Malmasi and Mark Dras. 2015. Language identification using classifier ensembles. In *Joint Workshop on Language Technology for Closely Related Languages, Varieties and Dialects*, page 35.

Shervin Malmasi, Marcos Zampieri, Nikola Ljubešic, Preslav Nakov, Ahmed Ali, and Jörg Tiedemann. 2016. Discriminating between similar languages and Arabic dialect identification: A report on the third DSL shared task. In *Proceedings of the 3rd Workshop on Language Technology for Closely Related Languages, Varieties and Dialects (VarDial), Osaka, Japan*.

Hamdy Mubarak and Kareem Darwish. 2014. Using Twitter to collect a multi-dialectal corpus of Arabic. *ANLP 2014*, page 1.

Fatiha Sadat, Farnazeh Kazemi, and Atefeh Farzindar. 2014. Automatic identification of Arabic language varieties and dialects in social media. *Proceedings of SocialNLP*.

Omar F Zaidan and Chris Callison-Burch. 2014. Arabic dialect identification. *Computational Linguistics*, 40(1):171–202.

Marcos Zampieri and Binyam Gebrekidan Gebre. 2012. Automatic identification of language varieties: The case of Portuguese. In *KONVENS2012-The 11th Conference on Natural Language Processing*, pages 233–237. Österreichischen Gesellschaft für Artificial Intelligende (ÖGAI).

Marcos Zampieri, Liling Tan, Nikola Ljubešic, and Jörg Tiedemann. 2014. A report on the DSL shared task 2014. In *Proceedings of the First Workshop on Applying NLP Tools to Similar Languages, Varieties and Dialects*, pages 58–67.

Marcos Zampieri, Liling Tan, Nikola Ljubešic, Jörg Tiedemann, and Preslav Nakov. 2015. Overview of the DSL shared task 2015. In *Joint Workshop on Language Technology for Closely Related Languages, Varieties and Dialects*, page 1.

Arkaitz Zubiaga, Inaki San Vicente, Pablo Gamallo, José Ramom Pichel Campos, Iñaki Alegría Loinaz, Nora Aranberri, Aitzol Ezeiza, and Víctor Fresno-Fernández. 2014. Overview of TweetLID: Tweet language identification at SEPLN 2014. In *TweetLID@ SEPLN*, pages 1–11.

Processing Dialectal Arabic: Exploiting Variability and Similarity to Overcome Challenges and Discover Opportunities (invited talk)

Mona Diab
Department of Computer Science
George Washington University
`mtdiab@email.gwu.edu`

Abstract

We recently witnessed an exponential growth in dialectal Arabic usage in both textual data and speech recordings especially in social media. Processing such media is of great utility for all kinds of applications ranging from information extraction to social media analytics for political and commercial purposes to building decision support systems. Compared to other languages, Arabic, especially the informal variety, poses a significant challenge to natural language processing algorithms since it comprises multiple dialects, linguistic code switching, and a lack of standardized orthographies, to top its relatively complex morphology. Inherently, the problem of processing Arabic in the context of social media is the problem of how to handle resource poor languages. In this talk I will go over some of our insights to some of these problems and show how there is a silver lining where we can generalize some of our solutions to other low resource language contexts.

Biography

Mona Diab is an Associate Professor in the Department of Computer Science, George Washington University (GW). She is the founder and Director of the GW NLP lab CARE4Lang. Before joining GW, She was Research Scientist (Principal Investigator) at the Center for Computational Learning Systems (CCLS), Columbia University in New York. She is also co-founder of the CADIM group with Nizar Habash and Owen Rambow, which is one of the leading reference points on computational processing of Arabic and its dialects. Her research interests span several areas in computational linguistics/natural language processing: cross linguistic modeling and multilingual processing, computational lexical semantics, social media processing, information extraction & text analytics, machine translation, resource building, and computational socio-pragmatics. She has a special interest in low resource language processing with a focus on Arabic dialects.

Proceedings of the Third Workshop on NLP for Similar Languages, Varieties and Dialects,
page 42, Osaka, Japan, December 12 2016.

Language related issues for machine translation between closely related South Slavic languages

Maja Popović[1] **Mihael Arčan**[2] **Filip Klubička**[3]

[1] Humboldt University of Berlin, Germany
`maja.popovic@hu-berlin.de`

[2] Insight Centre for Data Analytics, National University of Ireland, Galway
`mihael.arcan@insight-centre.org`

[3] Department of Information and Communication Sciences, University of Zagreb, Croatia
`fklubick@ffzg.hr`

Abstract

Machine translation between closely related languages is less challenging and exhibits a smaller number of translation errors than translation between distant languages, but there are still obstacles which should be addressed in order to improve such systems. This work explores the obstacles for machine translation systems between closely related South Slavic languages, namely Croatian, Serbian and Slovenian. Statistical systems for all language pairs and translation directions are trained using parallel texts from different domains, however mainly on spoken language i.e. subtitles. For translation between Serbian and Croatian, a rule-based system is also explored. It is shown that for all language pairs and for both translation systems, the main obstacles are the differences between syntactic properties.

1 Introduction

Machine translation (MT) between (closely) related languages is a specific field in the domain of MT which has attracted the attention of several research teams. Nevertheless, it has not attracted as much attention as MT between distant languages. This is, on the one side, due to the fact that speakers of these languages often easily understand each other without switching to the foreign language. Furthermore, many documents are distributed in their original language, even in the neighbouring countries. Another fact is that MT between related languages is less problematic than between distant languages (Kolovratník et al., 2009).

Still, there is a need for translation even between very closely related language pairs such as Serbian and Croatian, for example, for the sake of producing standard official documents which exixst in one language but not the other. Another application of such systems is the two-stage (also called "pivot") MT (Babych et al., 2007): for example, if an adequate English-Croatian system is available whereas an English-Serbian system is not, or is of poor quality, English source sentences can first be translated into Croatian, and then the obtained output is further translated into Serbian by a Croatian-Serbian MT system. A similar application can also include enriching parallel training corpora by producing "synthetic" data in the less resourced related language (Bertoldi and Federico, 2009).

This work examines MT systems between three closely related South Slavic languages, namely Croatian, Serbian and Slovenian. Therefore we used the *Asistent*[1] phrase-based translation system (Arčan et al., 2016), which was developed to translate text between English and the morphological complex south Slavic languages: Slovene, Serbian and Croatian. Additionally, an RBMT system[2] (Klubička et al., 2016) is analysed for translation between Croatian and Serbian in both directions in order to explore advantages and disadvantages of both approaches for very close language pairs.

[1] `http://server1.nlp.insight-centre.org/asistent/`
[2] `http://translator.abumatran.eu`

Proceedings of the Third Workshop on NLP for Similar Languages, Varieties and Dialects,
pages 43–52, Osaka, Japan, December 12 2016.

Research questions

Taking into account the language differences among Croatian, Serbian and Slovenian, our main questions are:

- What are the main obstacles for machine translation between these languages?

- Considering the closeness between Serbian and Croatian, which approach exhibits fewer errors, SMT or RBMT? What are the most important differences between the two approaches?

1.1 Related work

Although all South Slavic languages are still rather under-resourced and under-investigated, in the last decade several MT systems have been built between these languages and English. Nevertheless, the translation between them has been investigated to a much lesser extent.

A rule-based translation system between Slovenian and Serbian has been described in Vičič (2008) and automatic scores (BLEU, METEOR and edit-distance) as well as adequacy and fluency are reported. Another work on RBMT between Serbian, Croatian and Slovenian is presented in Peradin et al. (2014). The SUMAT project[3] included a statistical approach for Serbian and Slovenian subtitles (Etchegoyhen et al., 2014). Nevertheless, a deeper analysis of translation errors or problems has not been performed in any of these articles.

Evaluation of several scenarios with different models and data-sets involving Croatian are explored in Toral et al. (2016) in the framework of the Abu-MaTran project[4], but only for translation from and to English. Three MT systems between Croatian and Serbian for the news domain are described in Popović and Ljubešić (2014), one very basic rule-based system and two SMT systems trained on small and on large parallel texts. Their performance was not examined in detail however, as they are only used as a bridge for translation from and into English.

Analysis of problems for MT between closely related languages together with a comparison between an RBMT and an SMT system is presented in Kubon and Vičič (2014) for the Czech-Slovak language pair. Similar analysis for South Slavic languages has been performed in Popović and Arčan (2015), though not for translation between these languages but from and into English and German.

To the best of our knowledge, no systematic investigation of actual difficulties for MT systems translating between South Slavic languages has been carried out yet.

2 Language properties – similarities and differences

2.1 Common properties

All three languages, Croatian, Serbian and Slovenian, belong to the South-Western Slavic branch. As Slavic languages, they have a very rich inflectional morphology for all word classes. There are six distinct cases affecting not only common nouns, but also proper nouns as well as pronouns, adjectives and some numbers. Some nouns and adjectives have two distinct plural forms depending on the number (less than five or not). There are also three genders for the nouns, pronouns, adjectives and some numbers leading to differences between the cases and also between the verb participles for past tense and passive voice. When it comes to verbs, person and many tenses are expressed by the suffix, and, similarly to Spanish and Italian, the subject pronoun (e.g. *I, we, it*) is often omitted. In addition, negation of three quite important verbs, *biti* (all languages) (*to be*), *imati* (Croatian, Serbian) / *imeti* (Slovenian) (*to have*) and *ht(j)eti* (Croatian, Serbian) / *hoteti* (Slovenian) (*to want*), is formed by adding the negative particle to the verb as a prefix. There are also two verb aspects, and so many verbs have perfective and imperfective form(s) depending on the duration of the described action. The different forms are lexicalized, and are often either different but very similar (e.g. *skakati-skočiti*), or are distinguished only by prefix (e.g. *gledati-pogledati*). It should be noted that this phenomenon is less prominent in Slovenian.

As for syntax, all three languages have quite a free word order, and neither language uses articles, either definite or indefinite. In addition to this, multiple negation is always used.

---

[3]http://www.sumat-project.eu
[4]http://www.abumatran.eu/

It should be also noted that while the Latin alphabet is common for all three languages, Serbian also uses the Cyrillic script. However, this poses no problem regarding MT because a Cyrillic Serbian text can be easily transliterated into Latin, as there is one-to-one correspondence between the characters.

2.2 Differences between Croatian and Serbian

Croatian and Serbian exhibit a large overlap in vocabulary and a strong morpho-syntactic similarity so that the speakers can understand each other without difficulties. Nevertheless, there is a number of small but notable and also frequently differences occurring differences between them.

The largest differences between the two languages are in vocabulary: some words are completely different, some however differ only by one or two letters. In addition, Serbian language usually phonetically transcribes foreign names and words although both transcription and transliteration are allowed, whereas the Croatian standard only transliterates.

Apart from lexical differences, there are also structural differences mainly concerning verbs: modal verb constructions, future tense, conditional, as well as constructions involving the verb *trebati* (to need, should). When it means *should*, in Croatian it takes the tense according to the subject and it is transitive as in English (*trebam raditi* equals *I should work*). In Serbian however, it is impersonal followed by the conjunction da and the present of the main verb (*treba da radim* equals *I should work*). When it means *to need*, the Croatian structure is the same (*trebam posao* equals *I need a job*, *Petar treba knjige* equals *Petar needs books*), whereas in Serbian, the verb is conjugated according to the needed object, and the subject which needs something is an indirect grammatical object in dative case (*meni treba posao = I need a job*, *Petru trebaju knjige = Petar needs books*). The Serbian structure is also possible in Croatian, although the other one is preferred. Impersonal constructions (*treba uraditi = it should be done*) are same in both languages, namely the verb *trebati* in third person singular is followed by infinitive of the main verb.

Regarding other modal verbs, the infinitive is prescribed in Croatian (*moram raditi = I have to work*), whereas the construction with conjunction *da* (en. *that/to*) and present tense is preferred in Serbian (*moram da radim*). The mentioned difference partly extends to the future tense which is formed in a similar manner to English, i.e. using present of the verb *ht(j)eti* as the auxiliary verb. The infinitive is formally required in both variants, however, when *da*+present is used instead, it can additionally express the subject's will or intention to perform the action. This form is frequent in Serbian (*ja ću da radim = I will work*), whereas in Croatian only the infinitive form is used (*ja ću raditi*). Another difference regarding future tense exists when the auxiliary and main verb are reversed: in Croatian, the final *i* of the infinitive is removed (*radit ću*), whereas in Serbian the main and the auxiliary verb merge into a single word (*radiću*).

2.3 Differences from Slovenian

Even though Slovenian is very closely related to Croatian and Serbian, and the languages share a large degree of mutual intelligibility, a number of Croatian/Serbian speakers may have difficulties with Slovenian and the other way round.

The nature of the lexical differences is similar to the one between Croatian and Serbian, namely a number of words is completely different and a number only differs by one or two letters. However, the amount of different words is much larger. In addition to that, the set of overlapping words includes a number of false friends (e.g. *brati* means *to pluck* in Croatian and Serbian but *to read* in Slovenian).

The amount of grammatical differences is also larger and includes local word order, verb mood and/or tense formation, question structure, dual in Slovenian, usage of some cases, structural properties for certain conjunctions as well as some other structural differences. Local word order differences include, for example, the order of auxiliary and main verbs: Slovenian allows the auxiliary verb to be at the beginning of the clause, whereas Croatian and Serbian do not (*sem videl/videl sem = video sam = I've seen*). Also, the place of reflexive pronoun is different (*se vidi = vidi se = it can be seen*, *se mi zdi = čini mi se = it seems to me*).

Constructions involving the Croatian/Serbian verb *trebati* differ significantly: in Slovenian, the meaning *should* is expressed by the adverb *treba* (*bi bilo treba = trebalo bi = it should*). For the meaning *to need*, the verb *potrebovati* is used in the same form as the verb *trebati* in Croatian, i.e. it requires the needed object in accusative case (*potrebujem knjigo = trebam knjigu = I need a book*).

The main difference regarding tense formation is the future tense. In Slovenian, it is formed using the auxiliary verb *biti* and the past participle of the main verb – in Croatian and Serbian, another auxiliary verb is used, *ht(j)eti* with the infinitive or *da* + present tense of the main verb (*jaz bom videl = ja ću da vidim = ja ću vid(j)eti = I will see*). Another important difference is Slovenian conditional formed using the adverb *lahko* and present tense of the main verb: in Croatian and Serbian it is formed by the modal verb *moći* (*can* and infinitive or *da* + present tense (*lahko vidim = mogao bih da vidim = mogao bih videti = I could see*).

Some conjunctions and/or require completely different structuring. For example, Slovenian *tudi* (en. *also, too*) has a direct equivalent in Croatian and Serbian (*takodje(r)*), but it is often translated by *i*. For negation form *neither* in Slovenian the construction *tudi ne* is used, whereas in Croatian and Serbian a negation conjunction *ni* is used. Slovenian conjunction *pa* also has different usage and structural requirements, and it can also be considered as a false friend.

Another important difference is the Slovenian dual grammatical number which refers to two entities (apart from singular for one and plural for more than two). It requires additional sets for noun, adjective and verb inflexion rules not existing either in Croatian or in Serbian.

3   Experimental set-up

3.1   Machine translation systems

The statistical phrase-based systems (Koehn, 2004) were trained using the Moses toolkit (Koehn et al., 2007) with MERT tuning. The word alignments were built with GIZA++ (Och and Ney, 2003) and a 5-gram language model was built with kenLM (Heafield, 2011). The parallel texts used to train the SMT systems were mostly obtained from the OPUS[5] web site (Tiedemann, 2009), which contains various corpora of different sizes and domains. Although corpora in distinct domains, e.g., legal, medical, financial, IT, exist for many language pairs including some of the South Slavic languages and English, parallel data between South Slavic languages pairs consist mostly of the OpenSubtitles[6] corpus and a little portion of the technical domain. For Serbian-Croatian language pair, the SEtimes corpus from the news domain (Tyers and Alperen, 2010) is also available. In total, about 15 million of sentence/segment pairs containing about 100 million of running words was used for training (Table 1). For tuning, 2000 sentence pairs were used for each language pair.

The Croatian-Serbian RBMT system is a bidirectional rule-based system which is based on the open-source Apertium platform (Forcada et al., 2011) and has been built collaboratively between several institutions as part of the aforementioned Abu-MaTran project. The process involved several workshops that employed the work of experts and non-experts to gather the necessary data to build a bilingual dictionary and to verify correct transfer rules automatically inferred using a tool developed by Sánchez-Cartagena et al. (2015). Work on the translator has continued since, and at the time of writing this paper the bilingual dictionary has quite a high coverage, containing a total of 88521 bilingual lemma entries, while the number of defined transfer rules in the Serbian-Croatian direction is 99, and 86 in the Croatian-Serbian direction. At the time of publication, the system was automatically evaluated on 351 Serbian sentences gathered from newspaper texts that were manually translated into Croatian, and when compared to *Google Translate*, the only other available system at the time, the RBMT system yielded higher scores. For more details on the construction and evaluation of the system, refer to Klubička et al. (2016).

3.2   Test sets

The in-domain data set used for evaluating SMT performance consists of about 2000 sentences for each language pair isolated from the training data set. Therefore, the test data consist mostly out of the Open-Subtitles corpus, since this corpus builds the largest part (95%) of the data used to train the translation models.

---

[5]http://opus.lingfil.uu.se/
[6]http://www.opensubtitles.org

Corpus Name	Slovene-Croatian	Slovene-Serbian	Croatian-Serbian
Gnome	4K	600K	300K
KDE	85K	49k	33.2k
OpenSubtitles	6.1M	13.3M	22.3M
SETimes	/	/	200K
Ubuntu	557	86K	51K
Training Data	**Sl-Hr**	**Sl-Sr**	**Hr-Sr**
L1 words:	39M	90M	137M
L2 words:	40M	94M	139M
unique L1 w.:	468K	775K	1.22M
unique L2 w.:	579K	966K	1.24M
Par. sentences:	5.5M	12.6M	19.4M

Table 1: Statistics on parallel corpora used to build the translation models (explanation: Slovene-Croatian → L1=Slovene, L2=Croatian).

Such data sets are usual for evaluation and comparing SMT systems, however, they are not optimal for comparing an SMT and an RBMT system since they originate from the same text type as the SMT training corpus – the results would probably be biased. Therefore, additional test sets were created for this comparison:

- 1000 Croatian source sentences were extracted from the hrenWaC and DGT part of the OPUS data and translated by both systems into Serbian; about 300 segments from each of the translation outputs were post-edited by native speakers.

- 3000 Serbian source sentences were extracted from a corpus containing language course material and translated by both systems into Croatian; about 450 segments from each of the translation outputs were post-edited by native speakers.

In addition, a subset of the Slovenian-to-Serbian SMT translation output containing about 350 sentences was post-edited as well.
The test sets were post-edited for two reasons:

1. post-edited data are generally more convenient for analysis and identifying prominent errors and issues;

2. the OpenSubtitles contain translations from English the as original source so that the obtained translations are often too different and do not fully reflect the language closeness.

Although it was not the motivation for post-editing, it should be noted that there were no available reference translations for Croatian-Serbian additional test sets.

3.3 Evaluation

For all test sets and MT systems, BLEU scores (Papineni et al., 2002) and character n-gram F-scores CHRF3 (Popović, 2015) are reported. BLEU is a well-known and widely used metric, and CHRF3 is shown to correlate very well with human judgments for morphologically rich languages (Stanojević et al., 2015). Besides, it seems convenient for closely related languages since a large portion of differences is on the character level.

In order to better understand the overall evaluation scores and differences between the MT systems, five error classes, produced by the automatic error analysis tool Hjerson (Popović, 2011), are reported.

Finally, in order to determine most prominent language related issues for the MT systems, a manual inspection of the errors and their causes is carried out, predominantly on the post-edited data.

	BLEU	CHRF3
Serbian→Croatian	70.1 (64.9)	80.9 (78.6)
Croatian→Serbian	67.4 (59.9)	78.0 (73.8)
Serbian→Slovenian	29.2 (14.1)	47.4 (37.2)
Slovenian→Serbian	23.5 (12.3)	43.2 (34.3)
Croatian→Slovenian	38.6 (16.1)	55.0 (39.5)
Slovenian→Croatian	34.6 (13.5)	51.0 (37.4)

Table 2: Automatic translation scores BLEU and CHRF3 for the SMT system (together with the *Google Translate* system in parentheses) on the in-domain test set.

	inflection	order	omission	addition	lexical	ΣERR
Serbian→Croatian	1.8	1.3	3.6	4.9	12.0	23.5
Croatian→Serbian	2.0	1.4	5.0	3.9	14.9	27.7
Serbian→Slovenian	3.7	4.5	10.1	12.1	27.6	58.0
Slovenian→Serbian	3.4	3.9	14.6	9.1	30.1	62.0
Croatian→Slovenian	3.1	4.2	8.8	11.4	24.2	51.7
Slovenian→Croatian	3.1	3.8	12.4	8.0	28.2	55.6

Table 3: Translation error classes of the SMT system identified by the Hjerson tool on the in-domain test set.

4 Evaluation results on standard in-domain test sets

Table 2 presents the automatic scores for standard test sets for all SMT systems together with the scores for translations[7] by the publicly available Google translate[8] system.

The obtained scores are rather high for translation between Serbian and Croatian and lower for translations involving Slovenian. Nevertheless, considering the language closeness, the scores are not particularly high – the most probable reason are the "unnecessary" differences introduced by human translation from a third language, namely English. It can be noted that translation into Serbian is worse than into the other two languages and that translation into Slovenian is better than into the other two languages.

Table 3 gives details on the translation error classes. For the Serbian-Croatian language pair most errors are lexical, whereas there is a rather low number of inflectional and ordering errors. This can be expected considering that the main differences between the languages are on the lexical level, as described in Section 2.2. As for translating from and into Slovenian, lexical errors are also predominant and much more frequent. Furthermore, the amount of ordering and inflectional errors is not negligible. These results are consistent with the language differences described in Section 2.3, however, they are not giving precise information of which phenomena are causing which errors. For this purpose, a shallow manual inspection of errors is carried out. It has been noted that the structural differences often result in different error types. Nevertheless it was not easy to isolate specific phenomena due to the described suboptimal test sets. Therefore the manual inspection of errors has been carried out thoroughly on the post-edited data and the results are reported in the next section.

5 Evaluation results on post-edited test sets

The first evaluation step of post-edited test sets was performed to calculate automatic evaluation metrics and class error rates. After that, a detailed manual inspection of language related phenomena leading to particular errors is carried out. Finally, the most problematic phenomena were isolated from test sets and evaluated separately.

---

[7] generated in September 2016

[8] https://translate.google.com/

	BLEU		CHRF3	
	SMT	RBMT	SMT	RBMT
Serbian→Croatian overall	91.0	89.6	95.4	95.1
trebati	52.4	54.8	77.5	78.5
Croatian→Serbian overall	86.2	82.9	93.4	92.2
trebati	58.8	62.5	83.4	84.4

		SMT		RBMT	
Serbian→Croatian		overall	*trebati*	overall	*trebati*
	ΣERR	4.3	29.6	4.8	27.6
	inflection	1.2	13.7	1.3	13.0
	order	0.3	0.2	0.4	0.0
	omission	0.4	0.0	0.0	0.0
	addition	0.9	5.5	0.9	5.5
	lexical	1.4	10.2	2.2	8.9
Croatian→Serbian		overall	*trebati*	overall	*trebati*
	ΣERR	6.3	21.5	7.8	20.3
	inflection	2.1	10.4	2.7	10.0
	order	0.3	0.9	0.2	1.2
	omission	0.8	1.6	0.3	1.7
	addition	0.4	3.0	0.2	2.9
	lexical	2.7	5.7	4.5	4.5

Table 4: Automatic evaluation scores BLEU and CHRF3 and classified edit operations on Serbian↔Croatian post-edited data.

5.1 Croatian-Serbian translation

The manual analysis revealed that for the Croatian-Serbian translation in both directions, constructions involving the verb *trebati* pose the most problems, both for the SMT as well as the RBMT system. Therefore, the segments containing this verb were isolated and analysed separately. The automatic evaluation scores are presented in Table 4, both for the whole test set as well as for the segments containing *trebati*.

- the overall performance is better for the SMT system, mainly due to less lexical errors;

- the RBMT system handles better the constructions with *trebati* producing less inflectional and lexical errors which are the predominant error types produced in these constructions

- both systems perform slightly better for translation into Croatian, but *trebati* constructions are better translated into Serbian by both systems. A probable reason for this is the different nature of the used test texts.

Especially problematic structures for both systems are long range dependencies where the main verb(s) is/are separated from the verb *trebati*. Furthermore, mistranslations were detected because of impersonal constructions and conditional forms, which are more problematic for the RBMT system. In addition, the meaning *to need* is often incorrectly translated by both systems, especially from Serbian into Croatian.

All in all, there is no significant difference between the performance of the SMT and the RBMT approach. Nevertheless, the systems do not always fail in the same way of the same segment, which indicates that a hybrid approach for this language pair could be beneficial.

5.2 Slovenian-to-Serbian translation

Manual evaluation has shown that the most frequent problems in Slovenian→Serbian post-edited translations are the future tense and the structures involving the Slovenian conjunction *tudi* (*also/too*). There-

Slovenian→Serbian	BLEU		CHRF3	
	sl→sr	sl→hr→hr	sl→sr	sl→hr→sr
standard test	23.5	25.4	43.2	44.4
overall	70.3	71.7	81.6	82.8
future+*tudi*	67.8	73.8	78.3	84.0

Slovenian→Serbian	standard		post-edited		pe future+*tudi*	
	sl-sr	sl-hr-sr	sl-sr	sl-hr-sr	sl-sr	sl-hr-sr
ΣERR	62.8	62.1	14.3	15.8	16.8	15.2
inflection	3.5	3.6	2.3	2.1	3.6	2.3
order	4.0	4.9	0.8	3.2	1.4	1.9
omission	14.4	12.3	4.3	2.6	3.8	2.6
addition	9.1	9.6	1.1	1.6	0.9	2.3
lexical	31.8	31.8	5.9	6.2	7.1	6.2

Table 5: Automatic evaluation scores BLEU and CHRF3 and classified edit operations on Slovenian→Serbian post-edited data.

fore, sentences containing these two structures were identified and analysed separately.

For this translation direction, an additional preliminary experiment has been carried out, namely an attempt to improve the translation quality by two-stage (bridge, pivot) translation via Croatian.

Table 5 shows the overall post-edited results as well as the results on segments containing future tense and *tudi* both for direct as well as for two-stage SMT system. In addition, results for the overall standard test set are also shown for both systems. The following can be observed from the presented results:

- as expected, the automatic scores on post-edited test are lower than for Croatian-Serbian translation, but not so much lower as for the standard (suboptimal) test sets;

- scores on segments containing future tense and *tudi* are lower than overall scores;

- two-stage translation via Croatian generally helps, especially for the *problematic* segments – it reduces the number of inflectional edits, omissions and lexical edits;

- main disadvantage of two-stage translation is the increased amount of reordering errors.

The results show that two-stage translation has a good potential and should be further investigated. Further investigation should also include other translation directions from and into Slovenian, using different types of data sets.

6 Summary and outlook

This work represents a first step in the systematic evaluation of MT results between Croatian, Serbian and Slovenian and it has already shown several interesting results.

The analysis has revealed that the differences between the structural properties represent the most prominent issue for all translation directions. For translation between Croatian and Serbian, the constructions involving the verb *trebati* (*should/need*) definitely represent the larger obstacle for both translation directions and for both MT approaches, statistical as well as rule-based. However, the systems do not fail in the same way on the same segments, therefore hybrid systems should be investigated in future work.

For translations from Slovenian into Serbian, future tense represents one of the dominant issues followed by conjunction/adverb *tudi*. Other translation directions involving Slovenian have to be explored in future work. Two-stage translation via Croatian improves significantly the performance of the segments containing those problematic structures, the rest of the segments, however, are partially improved and partially deteriorated by introducing reordering errors and should be further investigated.

Future work should also include working on the identified issues, namely improving the systems by targeting the verb *trebati* and the Slovenian future tense. Also, other MT methods, such as hierarchical phrase-based and neural approach, should be investigated.

Acknowledgments

This work has emerged from research supported by TRAMOOC project (Translation for Massive Open Online Courses) partially funded by the European Commission under H2020-ICT-2014/H2020-ICT-2014-1 under grant agreement number 644333 and by the Science Foundation Ireland (SFI) under Grant Number SFI/12/RC/2289 (Insight). The research leading to these results has also received funding from the European Union Seventh Framework Programme FP7/2007-2013 under grant agreement PIAP-GA-2012-324414 (Abu-MaTran) and the Swiss National Science Foundation grant IZ74Z0_160501 (ReLDI).

References

Mihael Arčan, Maja Popović, and Paul Buitelaar. 2016. Asistent – a machine translation system for Slovene, Serbian and Croatian. In *Proceedings of the 10th Conference on Language Technologies and Digital Humanities*, Ljubljana, Slovenia, September.

Bogdan Babych, Anthony Hartley, and Serge Sharoff. 2007. Translating from under-resourced languages: comparing direct transfer against pivot translation. In *Proceedings of the MT Summit XI*, pages 412–418, Copenhagen.

Nicola Bertoldi and Marcello Federico. 2009. Domain adaptation for statistical machine translation with monolingual resources. In *Proceedings of the Fourth Workshop on Statistical Machine Translation*. Association for Computational Linguistics.

Thierry Etchegoyhen, Lindsay Bywood, Mark Fishel, Panayota Georgakopoulou, Jie Jiang, Gerard Van Loenhout, Arantza Del Pozo, Mirjam Sepesy Maučec, Anja Turner, and Martin Volk. 2014. Machine Translation for Subtitling: A Large-Scale Evaluation. In *Proceedings of the Ninth International Conference on Language Resources and Evaluation (LREC14)*, Reykjavik, Iceland, May.

Mikel L. Forcada, Mireia Ginestí-Rosell, Jacob Nordfalk, Jim O'Regan, Sergio Ortiz-Rojas, Juan Antonio Pérez-Ortiz, Gema Ramírez-Sánchez Felipe Sánchez-Martínez, and Francis M. Tyers. 2011. Apertium: a free/open-source platform for rule-based machine translation. *Machine Translation*, 25(2):127–144. Special Issue: Free/Open-Source Machine Translation.

Kenneth Heafield. 2011. KenLM: faster and smaller language model queries. In *Proceedings of the EMNLP 2011 Sixth Workshop on Statistical Machine Translation*, pages 187–197, Edinburgh, Scotland, United Kingdom, July.

Filip Klubička, Gema Ramírez-Sánchez, and Nikola Ljubešić. 2016. Collaborative development of a rule-based machine translator between Croatian and Serbian. In *Proceedings of the 19th Annual Conference of the European Association for Machine Translation (EAMT)*, volume 4, Riga, Latvia. Baltic Journal of Modern Computing.

Philipp Koehn, Hieu Hoang, Alexandra Birch, Chris Callison-Burch, Marcello Federico, Nicola Bertoldi, Brooke Cowan, Wade Shen, Christine Moran, Richard Zens, Chris Dyer, Ondřej Bojar, Alexandra Constantin, and Evan Herbst. 2007. Moses: Open source toolkit for statistical machine translation. In *Proceedings of the 45th Annual Meeting of the ACL on Interactive Poster and Demonstration Sessions*, Stroudsburg, PA, USA.

Philipp Koehn. 2004. Pharaoh: a beam search decoder for phrase-based statistical machine translation models. Washington DC.

David Kolovratník, Natalia Klyueva, and Ondřej Bojar. 2009. Statistical Machine Translation Between Related and Unrelated Languages. In *Proceedings of the Conference on Theory and Practice of Information Technologies (ITAT-09)*, Kralova Studna, Slovakia, September.

Vladislav Kubon and Jernej Vičič. 2014. A comparison of mt methods for closely related languages: a case study on czech - slovak language pair. In *Proceedings of the EMNLP'2014 Workshop on Language Technology for Closely Related Languages and Language Variants*, pages 92–98, Doha, Qatar, October. Association for Computational Linguistics.

Franz Josef Och and Hermann Ney. 2003. A systematic comparison of various statistical alignment models. *Computational Linguistics*, 29.

Kishore Papineni, Salim Roukos, Todd Ward, and Wei-Jing Zhu. 2002. Bleu: a method for automatic evaluation of machine translation. In *Proceedings of the 40th annual meeting on association for computational linguistics*, pages 311–318. Association for Computational Linguistics.

Hrvoje Peradin, Filip Petkovski, and Francis Tyers. 2014. Shallow-transfer rule-based machine translation for the Western group of South Slavic languages. In *Proceedings of the 9th SaLTMiL Workshop on Free/open-Source Language Resources for the Machine Translation of Less-Resourced Languages*, pages 25–30, Reykjavik, Iceland, May.

Maja Popović and Mihael Arčan. 2015. Identifying main obstacles for statistical machine translation of morphologically rich South Slavic languages. In *18th Annual Conference of the European Association for Machine Translation (EAMT-15)*, Antalya, Turkey, May.

Maja Popović and Nikola Ljubešić. 2014. Exploring cross-language statistical machine translation for closely related South Slavic languages. In *Proceedings of the EMNLP14 Workshop on Language Technology for Closely Related Languages and Language Variants*, pages 76–84, Doha, Qatar, October.

Maja Popović. 2011. Hjerson: An Open Source Tool for Automatic Error Classification of Machine Translation Output. *The Prague Bulletin of Mathematical Linguistics*, (96):59–68, October.

Maja Popović. 2015. chrF: character n-gram F-score for automatic MT evaluation. In *Proceedings of the 10th Workshop on Statistical Machine Translation (WMT-15)*, pages 392–395, Lisbon, Portugal, September.

Víctor Manuel Sánchez-Cartagena, Juan Antonio Pérez-Ortiz, and Felipe Sánchez-Martínez. 2015. A generalised alignment template formalism and its application to the inference of shallow-transfer machine translation rules from scarce bilingual corpora. *Computer Speech & Language*, 32(1):46–90.

Miloš Stanojević, Amir Kamran, Philipp Koehn, and Ondřej Bojar. 2015. Results of the WMT15 Metrics Shared Task. In *Proceedings of the 10th Workshop on Statistical Machine Translation (WMT-15)*, pages 256–273, Lisbon, Portugal, September.

Jorg Tiedemann. 2009. News from OPUS – A Collection of Multilingual Parallel Corpora with Tools and Interfaces. In *Advances in Natural Language Processing*, volume V, chapter V, pages 237–248. Borovets, Bulgaria.

Antonio Toral, Raphael Rubino, and Gema Ramírez-Sánchez. 2016. Re-assessing the Impact of SMT Techniques with Human Evaluation: a Case Study on English-Croatian. In *Proceedings of the 19th Annual Conference of the European Association for Machine Translation (EAMT)*, volume 4, Riga, Latvia. Baltic Journal of Modern Computing.

Francis M. Tyers and Murat Alperen. 2010. South-East European Times: A parallel corpus of the Balkan languages. In *Proceedings of the LREC Workshop on Exploitation of Multilingual Resources and Tools for Central and (South-) Eastern European Languages*, pages 49–53, Valetta, Malta, May.

Jernej Vičič. 2008. Rapid development of data for shallow transfer RBMT translation systems for highly inflective languages. In *Proceedings of the 6th Conference on Language Technologies*, Ljubljana, Slovenia, October.

Romanized Berber and Romanized Arabic Automatic Language Identification Using Machine Learning

Wafia Adouane[1], Nasredine Semmar[2], Richard Johansson[3]
Department of FLoV, University of Gothenburg, Sweden[1]
CEA Saclay – Nano-INNOV, Institut CARNOT CEA LIST, France[2]
Department of CSE, University of Gothenburg, Sweden[3]
`wafia.gu@gmail.com, nasredine.semmar@cea.fr`
`richard.johansson@gu.se`

Abstract

The identification of the language of text/speech input is the first step to be able to properly do any language-dependent natural language processing. The task is called Automatic Language Identification (ALI). Being a well-studied field since early 1960's, various methods have been applied to many standard languages. The ALI standard methods require datasets for training and use character/word-based n-gram models. However, social media and new technologies have contributed to the rise of informal and minority languages on the Web. The state-of-the-art automatic language identifiers fail to properly identify many of them. Romanized Arabic (RA) and Romanized Berber (RB) are cases of these informal languages which are under-resourced. The goal of this paper is twofold: detect RA and RB, at a document level, as separate languages and distinguish between them as they coexist in North Africa. We consider the task as a classification problem and use supervised machine learning to solve it. For both languages, character-based 5-grams combined with additional lexicons score the best, F-score of 99.75% and 97.77% for RB and RA respectively.

1 Introduction

Social media and new technology devices have facilitated the emergence of new languages on the Web which are mainly written forms of colloquial languages. Most of these languages are under-resourced and do not adhere to any standard grammar or orthography. Romanized Arabic (RA) or Arabic written in Latin script (called often Arabizi) is an informal language. However, Romanized Berber (RB) is one of the Berber or Tamazight[1] standard forms. Both RA and RB are under-resourced and unknown languages to the available language identification tools [2]. To be able to automatically process and analyze content in RA and RB, it is necessary to properly recognize the languages. Otherwise, there is a large risk of getting misleading information. Moreover, it is crucial to be able to distinguish between them. The reason is that RA and RB coexist in North Africa, which is a rich multilingual region, and they share a considerable amount of vocabulary due to the close contact between them. Undoubtedly, this type of tool will help to build NLP applications for both. There is some work done to automatically transliterate RA into Arabic script (Al-Badrashiny et al., 2014). However, this is very limited because RA perfectly adheres to the principle 'write as you speak', i.e. there is no standardized orthography. Furthermore, the Arabic Chat Alphabet (ACA), designed for Romanized Arabic used in social media, is just a suggested writing system and not necessarily a Natural Language Processing (NLP) tool for RA. To overcome the various challenges faced when dealing with RA automatic processing, namely the use of non-standardized orthography, spelling errors and the lack of linguistic resources, we believe that it is better to consider RA as a stand-alone language and try to find better ways to deal with it instead of using only transliteration. RB is already a stand-alone language. It is important to clarify that considering both

---

[1]An Afro-Asiatic language widely spoken in North Africa. It is a minority language compared to Arabic.

[2]Among the freely available language identification tools, we tried Google Language Identifier, Open Xerox language, langid.py (M. Lui and T. Baldwin, 2012) and Translated labs at http://labs.translated.net.

Proceedings of the Third Workshop on NLP for Similar Languages, Varieties and Dialects,
pages 53–61, Osaka, Japan, December 12 2016.

RA and RB as a stand-alone languages does not suggest, at any point, that the use of the Latin alphabet is a sufficient criteria to define them as such. Our main motivation is to make their automatic processing easier.

We start the paper with a general overview about the work done for informal Arabic NLP in Section 2. We then give some brief information about RA and RB in Section 3. Next, in Section 4, we describe how we proceed to build the linguistic resources used to build our system. In Section 5, we explain the used methods and describe the experiments and discuss the results. We conclude by general findings and future directions.

2 Related Work

Arabic NLP is mainly Modern Standard Arabic (MSA) based. Recently, the automatic processing of informal Arabic or dialectal Arabic in general has attracted more attention from the research community and industry. However, the main issue is the absence of freely available linguistic resources[3] which allow for automatic processing. The deficiency of linguistic resources for dialectal Arabic written in Arabic script (DA) is caused by two factors "a lack of orthographic standards for the dialects, and a lack of overall Arabic content on the web, let alone DA content. These lead to a severe deficiency in the availability of computational annotations for DA data" (Diab et al., 2010). This is applied only to the written DA because there are available resources for spoken DA or at least it is easy to create them, for instance by recording TV-shows. However, for dialectal Arabic written in Latin script or RA, the only available resources are a few datasets that have been individually built for specific projects.

In general, only some work has been done for dialectal Arabic written in Arabic script, among others, automatic identification of some Arabic dialects (Egyptian, Gulf and Levantine) using word and character n-gram[4] models (Cavnar and Trenkle, 1994) and automatic identification of Maghrebi Arabic (Algerian, Moroccan and Tunisian) using morpho-syntactic information (Saâdane, 2015), Arabic dialect identification using a parallel multidialectal corpus (Malmasi et al., 2015) and identification of the most popular Arabic dialects using various automatic language identification methods (Adouane, 2016). However, the work done so far for RA deals mainly with Egyptian Arabic. For instance, Eskander et al., (2014) presented a system for automatic processing of Arabic social media text written in Arabizi by detecting Arabic tokens, Egyptian words, and non-Arabic words, mainly English words. They used a supervised machine learning approach to detect the label of each input token (sounds, punctuation marks, names, foreign words or Arabic words) and transliterated it into Arabic script. Darwish (2014) also presented an Arabizi identification system using word and sequence-level features to identify Arabizi that is mixed with English and reported an identification accuracy of 98.5%. This does not generalize to other RA content since it did not consider a broader range of data, i.e. there are many other Arabic dialects which are considerably different from Egyptian Arabic, for instance Arabic dialects used in North Africa, Levant region, Gulf countries and Iraq. Moreover, the mixed language used with Romanized Arabic is not always English[5].

To our knowledge, there has not been much work done to process RA (NLP applications like language identification, sentiment analysis/opinion mining, machine translation, Part-of-Speech tagging, etc.) as a stand-alone language. Furthermore, none of the automatic language identification standard methods have been applied to a wide range of Arabic dialects written in Latin script. As mentioned, the main challenge is the absence of data. RB is also unknown to the current language identifiers. It is an under-resourced language and a minority language compared to Arabic. There has been some work done for Berber automatic language identification, for instance Chelali et al. (2015) created a Berber speaker identification system using some speech signal information as features. Also Halimouche et al. (2014) have used prosodic information to discriminate between affirmative and interrogative sentences in Berber. Both sets of work were done at the speaker level. There are also some other applications which assume

---

[3]For dialectal Arabic written in Arabic script, there are some collections by individuals but unfortunately not digitalized or do not respect corpus linguistics annotation conventions (Behnstdt and Woidich, 2013).

[4]A sequence of n characters from a given sequence of text where n is an integer.

[5]We collected a dataset written in Romanized Arabic (including various Arabic dialects) and found various mixed languages, namely Berber, French, German, Italian, Spanish, Swedish and English.

that the input is always in RB. Both RA and RB are unknown languages to the available automatic language identifiers. The main motivation of this paper is to create an automatic language identifier which is able to detect RA and RB and at the same time is able to distinguish between them.

3   Characteristics of RA and RB

By informal languages, we mean the kind of written or spoken languages that do not adhere strictly to some standard spelling and grammar. The informality can be manifested in the form of ungrammatical sentences, misspellings, newly created words and abbreviations or even using unusual scripts as in the case of RA which has existed since the 20th century in North Africa. During the French colonialism period, educated people mastered Latin alphabet which was also used, for pedagogical purpose, to transcribe Arabic texts based on some phonological criteria (Souag, 2004).

RA is mainly dialectal Arabic which uses non-standard spellings, no fixed grammar and regional vocabulary-sense usage, i.e. the meaning of words depends on the area it is spoken in. Moreover, the use of the Latin script has increased the number of possible spellings per word at both vowels and consonants levels. With consonants, the main issue is the non-existence of some Arabic sounds in the Latin alphabet. Consequently, people use different characters to express those sounds. Unfortunately, the spellings are inconsistent even inside a group of people of the same area. RB also uses different national standardized orthography where each country has created its own standard spelling which is not necessarily used by another.

There are many false friends between RA and RB. For instance, each word in the Romanized Berber sentence 'AHml sAqwl mA$y dwl kAn'[6] which means 'love is from heart and not just a word' has a false friend in MSA and all Arabic dialects, namely when written in Latin script. In MSA, the sentence means literally 'I carry I will say going countries was' which does not mean anything. Both RA and RB share the use of mix-languages depending on the country or the region they are spoken in. In North Africa, RA is mixed mostly with Berber, French or English[7] and in the Middle East, it is mixed with English and some other languages. The same is applicable for Berber where some dialects use lots of French and Maghrebi Arabic words whereas others use only Maghrebi Arabic words for historical reasons.

4   Linguistic Resources

The main challenge in automatically processing any under-resourced natural language, using supervised machine learning approaches, is the lack of human annotated data. To overcome this serious hindrance, we created linguistic resources, namely corpora, for both RA and RB which are commonly used in social media. They are also used for commenting on events/news published on news agencies websites. In its standard form, RB is also used in media. We compiled a list of websites and platforms (micro-blogs, forums, blogs and online newspapers from all over the Arab world to ensure that many Arabic dialects are included) where RA and RB are used. Both manually and using a script, we collected content roughly published between 2013 and 2016. We collected 20,000 documents (144,535 words)[8] for RA and 7,000 documents for RB (31,274 words) from North Africa including various dialects[9] as well. Data collection and cleaning took us two months. We made sure to include various word spellings for both languages.

The included documents are short, between 2 and 236 words, basically product reviews, comments and opinions on quite varied topics. In terms of data source distribution, for RA, the majority of the content is comments collected from popular TV-show YouTube channels (9,800 documents, 49% of the data), content of blogs and forums (3,600 documents, 18% of the data), news websites (2,800 documents, 14 % of the data), the rest comes from Twitter (2,400 documents, 12% of the data) and Facebook (1,000 documents, 5% of the data). For RB, most content comes from Berber websites promoting Berber

---

[6]We use Buckwalter Arabic transliteration scheme. For the complete chart see: http://www.qamus.org/transliteration.htm.

[7]Based on the data used in this paper.

[8]By document, we mean a piece of text containing between 1 to 5 sentences; approximately 2 - 236 words. It is hard to precisely say how many sentences there are in each document because users use punctuation inconsistently in micro-blogs.

[9]Berber has 13 distinguished varieties. Here, we include only the six most popular dialects, namely Kabyle, Tachelhit, Tarifit, Tachawit, Tachenwit and Tamzabit.

culture and language (4,900 documents, 70%), YouTube (910 documents, 13%), news websites (700 documents, 10%) and Facebook (490 documents, 7%). With the help of two Arabic native speakers (Algerian and Lebanese) who are familiar with other Arabic dialects, we cleaned the collected data and manually checked that all the documents are written in RA. The same for RB, the platforms from which we collected data are 100% Berber and a Berber native speaker (Algerian) checked the data. For Romanized Arabic, it is hard for an Arabic speaker not to recognize Arabic and the task is easy (is a text written in Arabic or not) compared to classifying Arabic dialects (finding which Arabic variety a text is written in). The same is applicable for RB. Therefore, we consider the inter-annotator agreement (IAA) to be satisfactory. We are expending the RA and RB corpora and planning to use human annotators to compute the IAA using Cohen's kappa coefficient[10].

RA and RB use lots of mix-languages[11]. Consequently, we allowed mix-language documents[12] given that they contain clearly Arabic/Berber words in Latin script and a native speaker can understand/produce the same (sounds very natural for a native speaker). A preliminary study of the collected corpus showed that Berber (only for data collected from North Africa), French and English are the most commonly used languages with RA. Berber uses lots of French words and many Arabic words for some dialects like Tamzabit and Tachawit. It is also important to mention that in the entire Romanized Arabic corpus, only four (4) documents (0.02%) were actually written in Modern Standard Arabic (MSA) and the rest of documents were written in different Arabic dialects[13]. This indicates clearly that RA is commonly used to write dialectal Arabic. In terms of the dialectal distribution of the collected data, we noticed that most of the content in RA comes from North Africa (Maghrebi and Egyptian Arabic) and less from Levantine Arabic (mainly from Lebanon) and even less in Gulf and Kuwaiti/Iraqi Arabic.

Our corpora contain a mixture of languages (Arabic, Berber, English and French words all in Latin script). Also some German, Italian, Spanish and Swedish content is found, but not that frequent compared to English and French. This has motivated our choice to build a system which is able to distinguish between all these co-existing languages. In addition, we thought it would be good to add Maltese and Romanized Persian languages. The decision of adding Maltese language is based on the fact that Maltese is the only Semitic language written in Latin script in its standard form. This means that it has lots of common vocabulary with Arabic, namely Tunisian dialect[14]. We would like to add the Cypriot Arabic[15] variety written in Latin (not the variety using the Greek script), but unfortunately we could not collect enough data. We hardly collected 53 documents (287 words). We also added Romanized Persian (RP) language since Persian is one of the few non-Semitic languages that uses the Arabic script in its standard form. It has many false friends with Arabic, i.e. sharing the same word forms (spelling) but having different meanings. This causes an automatic language identifier to get confused easily when dealing with short texts. In addition, we would like to add Romanized Pashto[16] to the collection, but as with Cypriot Arabic we found it hard to collect enough data and find a native speaker to check it.

In addition to the data collected for RA and RB, we have collected, from social media platforms and news websites, 1,000 documents (6,000 - 10,000 words) for each of the mentioned languages (English (EN), French (FR), Maltese (ML), Romanized Persian (RP)) with the help of a native speaker of each language. From the entire data set, we removed 500 documents (around 6,000 words) for each language to be used in training and evaluating our system. We used the rest of the data to compile lexicons, for each language, by extracting the unique vocabulary using a script. We also used external lexicon for RB.

---

[10] A standard metric used to evaluate the quality of a set of annotations in classification tasks.

[11] This term refers to the use of more than one language in a single interaction. The classic code-switching framework does not always apply to Arabic for many complex reasons which are out of our scope. Researchers like D. Sankoff (1998) suggested to classify the use of mixed languages in Arabic as a separate phenomenon and not code-switching. Others like Davies et al. (2013) called it 'mixed Arabic'. We will use 'language mixing' to refer to both code-switching and borrowing.

[12] Documents containing vocabulary of different languages. In our case, Arabic written in Latin script plus Berber, English, French, German, Spanish and Swedish words.

[13] Including Algerian, Egyptian, Gulf, Kuwaiti/Iraqi, Levantine, Moroccan and Tunisian Arabic.

[14] Being familiar with north African Arabic dialects, we have noticed that Maltese is much closer to Tunisian Arabic.

[15] An Arabic dialect spoken in Cyprus by the Maronite community and which is too close to Levantine Arabic for historical reasons and when written in Latin script, it is easily confused with Romanized Arabic.

[16] Pashto, an Easter Iranian language belonging to Indo-European family, is an official language of Pakistan. It has its own script but when written in Latin script, it has many false friends with Romanized Arabic.

We manually cleaned the word lists and kept only the clearly vocabulary in one of the corresponding mentioned languages (this took us almost two months). We were left with clean lexicons of more than 46,000 unique words for RA, 35,100 for RB and 2,700 for RP. Still RA and RB lexicons contain various spellings for the same word. In the absence of a reference orthography, we allowed all possible spellings (as found in the data) and introduce some normalization rules, namely lower-casing of all characters and the reduction of all the repeated adjacent characters to a maximum of two. For instance, all the words *'kbir', 'kbiiir' and 'kbiiiiiir'* refer to the same Arabic word 'big' with different emphasis. We should have reduced all the repeated characters to one occurrence as the doubling does not add much meaning to the word. This would be aggressive for EN, FR and ML which allow two consecutive repeated characters. For RB, we simply included all the possible spellings for each word as found in our corpus. The normalized lexicons contain 42,000 unique words for RA and 35,100 for RB. We added extra lexicons for both EN and FR (containing 14,000 and 8,400 unique words respectively). The same for ML, we used an extra list including 4,516,286 words. The added extra lexicons include different morphological inflections of the same word.

5 Methods and Experiments

Various methods have been applied to Automatic Language Identification since early 1960's. In this paper, we use two techniques of supervised machine learning, namely Cavnar's method and Support Vector Machines (SVM). As features, we experiment with both character-based and word based n-grams of different lengths. We use the term frequency-inverse document frequency[17] (TF-IFD) scheme to weight the importance of the features. Both methods require training data which we pre-processed to filter unimportant tokens such as punctuation, emoticons, etc. We also want to build an automatic language identifier which learns linguistic information rather than learning topical and country specific words. Therefore, we remove all Named Entities (NE) such as names of people, organizations and locations using a large NE database which includes both RA and RB NEs we compiled for an ongoing project. For experiments, we use a balanced dataset of 500 documents (between 4,506 - 117,000 words) for each language (total of 3,000 documents or 640,207 words) divided into 1,800 documents or 420,300 words (300 documents for each language) for training and the remaining 1,200 documents or 219,907 words for evaluation. As mentioned before, a document is an entire user's comment which may contain between 2 to 5 sentences depending on the social media platform.

5.1 Cavnar's Method

Cavnar's Text Categorization Character-based n-gram method is one of the automatic language identification (ALI) statistical standard methods. It is a collection of the most common character-based n-grams used as a language profile (Cavnar and Trenkle, 1994). For each language, we create a character-based n-gram profile (including different lengths of n-gram where the value of n ranges between 2-5), sort it and consider only the most common 300 n-grams. This choice is for practical reasons which which are explained by the fact that at some point, the frequency of some n-grams is more or less the same for all languages. Therefore, they are no longer informative, i.e. do not really represent a given language or cannot be used as distinctive features to distinguish each language from others. The distance between language models is defined as the sum of all the out-of-place scores[18]. At the end, the language with the minimum distance from the source text will be the identified language.

We implement the Cavnar's classifier as described above. We experimented with different text and n-gram lengths. We found that bigrams outperform the rest of the character-based n-grams. Also increasing the text length increases the accuracy of the Cavnar's classifier. Table 1 shows the performance of the Cavnar's classifier per language for maximum text length of 140 characters (the maximum length of a Tweet) using character-based bigrams as features. The text length limitation to 140 characters means that we consider only the 140 first characters of each document. The purpose of doing this is to build a

---

[17]A statistical measure used to filter stop-words and keep only important words for each document.

[18]Computing the distance between the ranking of the n-gram lists. The out-of-place score of an n-gram which keeps its ranking is zero. Otherwise, the out-of-place score is the difference between the two rankings.

language identifier which is able to identify RA and RB regardless of the platform length restriction.

Language	Precision (%)	Recall (%)	F-score (%)
RA	**88.73**	**94.50**	**91.53**
RB	**97.50**	**97.50**	**97.50**
EN	94.29	99.00	96.56
FR	97.01	97.50	97.26
ML	97.50	97.50	97.50
RP	96.59	85.00	90.43

Table 1: Cavnar's classification per language using character-based bigrams.

For these settings, the macro-average F-score of the classifier is 95.13%. Overall, the results show that Cavnar's method is better at detecting text written in RB (F-score of 97.50%) compared to those written in RA. It performs slightly less for RA (F-score of 91.53%). An error analysis shows that the classifier is confused between RA and RP (21 times) and between RB and RP (3 times). The confusion is mainly caused by false friends and the use of the same vocabulary. Our purpose in using the Cavnar's method is to set its classification results as our baseline.

5.2 Support Vector Machines Classifier

We use the LinearSVC classifier (SVM) as implemented in Scikit-learn package (?)[19] with the default parameters. We experiment with both character and word n-grams as features. In both cases, we use the binary classification setting[20] as opposed to the 6-class classification. For instance, 'is a document written in RB or something else (other language)?' as opposed to 'is a document written in RB, EN, FR, ML, RA or RP?'.

5.2.1 Experiment 1

We use text maximum length of 140 characters when using character-based n-gram and text maximum length of 15 words[21] for word-based n-grams. The classification results are shown in Table 2.

	Accuracy (%)	
Features	**Character-based**	**Word-based**
Unigram	95.33	**95.91**
Bigrams	98.41	73.41
Trigrams	98.49	41.91
4-grams	98.66	27.91
5-grams	**98.75**	21.41
1+2-grams	98.25	94.66
1+3-grams	98.57	94.58

Table 2: SVM performance using different features.

For character-based n-grams, increasing the length of the n-gram improves the classification, 5-grams outperform all the rest of the n-gram lengths (5-grams have access to more information compared to shorter n-grams), giving 98.75% accuracy. Also, combining character-based unigram with trigrams has a positive effect on the classification; the accuracy has slightly increased to 98.57% compared to using only unigram or trigrams, 95.33% and 98.49% respectively. However, increasing the length of the word-based n-gram decreases the classifier's performance. This is caused by the data sparsity where it is

---

[19]For more information see: http://scikit-learn.org/stable/.

[20]We also experimented with the 6-class classification setting, and we found that the results were close to the binary classification.

[21]The choice of maximum 15 words is arbitrary for the sake of illustration. Still the focus is on short texts.

unlikely for long matches to occur frequently by chance. The word-based unigram scores the best, with an accuracy of 95.91%. Table 3 shows the performance of the SVM classifier per language using the combination of character-based unigram and trigrams for text with a maximum length of 140 characters.

Language	Precision (%)	Recall (%)	F-score (%)
RA	**98.98**	**97.50**	**98.24**
RB	**99.01**	**100**	**99.50**
EN	98.51	99.00	98.75
FR	99.00	99.00	99.00
ML	99.50	99.00	99.25
RP	97.51	98.00	97.76

Table 3: SVM classification using the combination of character-based unigram and trigrams.

The macro-average F-score of the SVM is 98.75%. Overall, the classifier identifies accurately RB (F-score of 99.50%) as well as RA (F-score of 98.24%). The SVM method performs better than the Cavnar's classifier (the baseline). The top-3 classification errors of the SVM are confusions between RA and RP (3 times), RA and FR (2 times) and between RP and RA (2 times). All the confused documents are very short (less than 10 words in our case).

5.2.2 Experiment 2

In another experiment, we use the same previous experimental setup but this time we combine the word-based unigram with the entries of the compiled lexicons as features. The SVM classifier accuracy has slightly improved to 97.50% compared to using only the word unigram 95.91%. This indicates that combining the word unigram with the lexicon entries (language-specific word) has a positive effect on the classification. Still there is confusion between RP and RA caused mainly by false friends. Furthermore, we combine character-based 5-grams with the entries of the compiled lexicons using the same experimental setup. The SVM accuracy has increased to 99.02%. Table 4 summarizes the SVM performance using the combination of character-based 5-grams and the entries of the compiled lexicons as features.

Language	Precision (%)	Recall (%)	F-score (%)
RA	97.04	98.50	**97.77**
RB	100	99.50	**99.75**
EN	99.00	99.50	99.25
FR	99.01	100	99.50
ML	99.50	99.50	99.50
RP	99.49	97.00	98.23

Table 4: SVM classification using the combination of character-based 5-grams and lexicons.

The classifier's macro-average F-score is 99.00%. Using the combination of the character-based 5-grams and the entries of the compiled lexicons as features has improved the overall accuracy of the SVM 99.02% compared to 98.75% using only character-based 5-grams. It has also positive effect on each language except for RA where the F-score has slightly decreased to 97.77% compared to 98.24%.

5.2.3 Experiment 3

To be able to compare the word-based n-grams and character-based n-grams, we rerun the same experiment using text full length. Still, the character-based 5-grams outperform the word-based n-grams, F-score of 99.77% and 97.89% respectively.

There are a few misclassifications between different languages as shown in Table 5. The few errors are caused by false friends between close/similar languages such as RA and RP and also in case of mix-languages, for instance between RA and FR where the former uses lots of words from the latter. An error analysis of the sample shows that most errors occurred in very short documents (less than 10 words in our case).

<table>
<tr><td rowspan="2"></td><td rowspan="2"></td><td colspan="6" align="center">Misclassified languages</td></tr>
<tr><td>RA</td><td>RB</td><td>EN</td><td>FR</td><td>ML</td><td>RP</td></tr>
<tr><td rowspan="6">Correct languages</td><td>RA</td><td>196</td><td>0</td><td>0</td><td>2</td><td>0</td><td>2</td></tr>
<tr><td>RB</td><td>0</td><td>199</td><td>0</td><td>0</td><td>0</td><td>1</td></tr>
<tr><td>EN</td><td>0</td><td>0</td><td>198</td><td>0</td><td>1</td><td>1</td></tr>
<tr><td>FR</td><td>0</td><td>0</td><td>0</td><td>200</td><td>0</td><td>0</td></tr>
<tr><td>ML</td><td>0</td><td>0</td><td>1</td><td>0</td><td>199</td><td>0</td></tr>
<tr><td>RP</td><td>5</td><td>0</td><td>1</td><td>0</td><td>0</td><td>194</td></tr>
</table>

Table 5: The confusion matrix of the system for the same settings as in Table 4.

6   Conclusion

We have described the linguistic resources built and used to train and evaluate our Romanized Arabic (RA) and Romanized Berber (RB) Automatic Language Identification (ALI) tool. We used supervised machine learning techniques, using various features. The focus is on short documents (social media domain) maximum text length of 140 characters or 15 words approximately, and the language identification is done at the document level. We assume that if the system works well for short documents, it should work better for longer ones since it will have access to more information. We found that using character based 5-grams perform reasonably well in detecting both RA and RB and slightly better than word-based unigram. Combining both character-based 5-grams and word-based unigram with the compiled lexicons has improved the SVM overall performance. In all cases, the SVM classifier outperformed our baseline (Cavnar's classifier). Our main purpose in this paper is to apply some ALI standard methods to Romanized Berber (RB) and Romanized Arabic (RA) rather than proposing new methods. Our motivation is that the existing ALI methods have not been not applied to neither RA or RB.

In this paper, we used a small sample of the data for training and testing. The limited text length allowed in social medial platforms, using very short documents (2-250 tokens), can be seen as distinguishing between the included languages at a sentence level especially that punctuation is mostly ignored. As a future work, we are planning to test our system on large dataset. We want to identify each RA and RB varieties. We want also to transliterate the compiled RA lexicon into the Arabic script, both dialectal Arabic and Modern Standard Arabic (MSA) equivalents. We believe that this will help in adapting the existing Arabic Natural Language Processing tools. The collected corpora are valuable for the Automated Identification of RA and RB, but also for linguistic and sociolinguistic research, as well as further applications in both language groups. Therefore, the datasets are freely available for research from the first author.

References

Cyril Goutte, Serge Léger and Marine Carpuat. 2014. The NRC System for Discriminating Similar Languages. *In the Proceedings of the VarDial Workshop.*

David Sankoff. 1998. The production of code-mixed discourse. *In Proceedings of the 36th Annual Meeting of the Association for Computational Linguistics and the 17th International Conference on Computational Linguistics, New Brunswick*, NJ: ACL Press, pages 8–21.

Eirlys Davies, Abdelâli Bentahila and Jonathan Owens. 2013. Codeswitching and related issues involving Arabic. *Oxford Handbook of Arabic Linguistics, Sociolinguistics*, pages 326–348.

Fabian Pedregosa, Gaël Varoquaux, Alexandre Gramfort, Vincent Michel, Bertrand Thirion, Olivier Grisel, Mathieu Blondel, Peter Prettenhofer, Ron Weiss, Vincent Dubourg, Jake VanderPlas, Alexandre Passos, David Cournapeau, Matthieu Brucher, Matthieu Perrot and Edouard Duchesnay. 2011. Scikit-learn: Machine learning in Python. *Machine learning in Python. Journal of Machine Learning Research*, 12, pages 2825–2830.

Fatma Zohra Chelali, Khadidja Sadeddine and Amar Djeradi. 2015. Speaker identification system using LPC-Application on Berber language. *HDSKD journal*, 1(2):29–46.

Houda Saâdane. 2015. *Le traitement automatique de l'arabe dialectalisé: aspects méthodologiques et algorithmiques*. PhD thesis, Université Grenoble Alpes.

Kareem Darwish. 2014. Arabizi Detection and Conversion to Arabic. *In the Proceedings of the EMNLP 2014 Workshop on Arabic Natural Language Processing (ANLP).Doha, Qatar*, pages 217–224.

Lameen Souag. 2004. Writing Berber Languages: a quick summary. L. Souag. Archived from http://goo.gl/ooA4uZ. Retrieved on April 8th, 2016.

Mohamed Al-Badrashiny, Ramy Eskander, Nizar Habash and Owen Rambow. 2014. Automatic Transliteration of Romanized Dialectal Arabic. *In the Proceedings of the Eighteenth Conference on Computational Language Learning, Baltimore, Maryland USA*, pages 30–38.

Marco Lui and Timothy Baldwin. 2012. langid. py: An Off-the-shelf Language Identification Tool. *In Proceedings of the ACL.*

Mona Diab, Nizar Habash, Owen Rambow, Mohamed Altantawy and Yassine Benajiba. 2010. COLABA: Arabic dialect annotation and processing. *In Proceedings of the LREC Workshop on Semitic Language Processing*, pages 66–74.

Omar F. Zaidan and Chris Callison-Burch. 2011. The Arabic online commentary dataset: an annotated dataset of informal Arabic with high dialectal content. *In the Proceedings of the Association for Computational Linguistics (ACL)*, pages 37–41.

Peter Behnstadt and Manfred Woidich. 2013. Diactology. *In the Oxford Handbook of Arabic Linguistics.*

Ramy Eskander, Mohamed Al-Badrashiny, Nizar Habash and Owen Rambow. 2014. Foreign Words and the Automatic Processing of Arabic Social Media Text Written in Roman Script. *In the Proceedings of The First Workshop on Computational Approaches to Code Switching. Doha, Qatar*, pages 1–12.

Ramzi Halimouche, Hocine Teffahi and Leila Falek. 2014. Detecting Sentences Types in Berber Language. *International Conference on Multimedia Computing and Systems (ICMCS)*, pages 197–200.

Shervin Malmasi, Eshrag Refaee and Mark Dras. 2015. Arabic Dialect Identification using a Parallel Multidialectal Corpus. *In the Proceedings of the 14th Conference of the Pacific Association for Computational Linguistics (PACLING 2015)*, pages 209–217, Bali, Indonesia.

Wafia Adouane. 2016. *Automatic Detection of Under-resourced Languages: The case of Arabic Short Texts*. Master's thesis, University of Gothenburg.

William B. Cavnar and John M. Trenkle. 1994. N-Gram-Based Text Categorization. *In the Proceedings of SDAIR-94, 3rd Annual Symposium on Document Analysis and Information Retrieval, University of Nevada, Las Vegas.*

How Many Languages Can a Language Model Model?
(invited talk)

Robert Östling
Department of Modern Languages
University of Helsinki
`robert.ostling@helsinki.fi`

Abstract

One of the purposes of the VarDial workshop series is to encourage research into NLP methods that treat human languages as a continuum, by designing models that exploit the similarities between languages and variants. In my work, I am using a continuous vector representation of languages that allows modeling and exploring the language continuum in a very direct way. The basic tool for this is a character-based recurrent neural network language model conditioned on language vectors whose values are learned during training. By feeding the model Bible translations in a thousand languages, not only does the learned vector space capture language similarity, but by interpolating between the learned vectors it is possible to generate text in unattested intermediate forms between the training languages.

Biography

Robert Östling is working on ways to use parallel corpora in computational linguistics, including machine translation, cross-language learning and language typology.

Proceedings of the Third Workshop on NLP for Similar Languages, Varieties and Dialects,
page 62, Osaka, Japan, December 12 2016.

Automatic Detection of Arabicized Berber and Arabic Varieties

Wafia Adouane[1], Nasredine Semmar[2], Richard Johansson[3], Victoria Bobicev[4]
Department of FLoV, University of Gothenburg, Sweden[1]
CEA Saclay – Nano-INNOV, Institut CARNOT CEA LIST, France[2]
Department of CSE, University of Gothenburg, Sweden[3]
Technical University of Moldova[4]
wafia.gu@gmail.com, nasredine.semmar@cea.fr
richard.johansson@gu.se, vika@rol.md

Abstract

Automatic Language Identification (ALI) is the detection of the natural language of an input text by a machine. It is the first necessary step to do any language-dependent natural language processing task. Various methods have been successfully applied to a wide range of languages, and the state-of-the-art automatic language identifiers are mainly based on character n-gram models trained on huge corpora. However, there are many languages which are not yet automatically processed, for instance minority and informal languages. Many of these languages are only spoken and do not exist in a written format. Social media platforms and new technologies have facilitated the emergence of written format for these spoken languages based on pronunciation. The latter are not well represented on the Web, commonly referred to as under-resourced languages, and the current available ALI tools fail to properly recognize them. In this paper, we revisit the problem of ALI with the focus on Arabicized Berber and dialectal Arabic short texts. We introduce new resources and evaluate the existing methods. The results show that machine learning models combined with lexicons are well suited for detecting Arabicized Berber and different Arabic varieties and distinguishing between them, giving a macro-average F-score of 92.94%.

1 Introduction

Automatic Language Identification (ALI) is a well-studied field in computational linguistics, since early 1960's, where various methods achieved successful results for many languages. ALI is commonly framed as a categorization.[1] problem. However, the rapid growth and wide dissemination of social media platforms and new technologies have contributed to the emergence of written forms of some varieties which are either minority or colloquial languages. These languages were not written before social media and mobile phone messaging services, and they are typically under-resourced. The state-of-the-art available ALI tools fail to recognize them and represent them by a unique category; standard language. For instance, whatever is written in Arabic script, and is clearly not Persian, Pashto or Urdu, is considered as Arabic, Modern Standard Arabic (MSA) precisely, even though there are many Arabic varieties which are considerably different from each other.

There are also other less known languages written in Arabic script but which are completely different from all Arabic varieties. In North Africa, for instance, Berber or Tamazight[2], which is widely used, is also written in Arabic script mainly in Algeria, Libya and Morocco. Arabicized Berber (BER) or Berber written in Arabic script is an under-resourced language and unknown to all available ALI tools which misclassify it as Arabic (MSA).[3] Arabicized Berber does not use special characters and it coexists with Maghrebi Arabic where the dialectal contact has made it hard for non-Maghrebi people to distinguish

---

[1] Assigning a predefined category to a given text based on the presence or absence of some features.

[2] An Afro-Asiatic language widely spoken in North Africa and different from Arabic. It has 13 varieties and each has formal and informal forms. It has its unique script called Tifinagh but for convenience Latin and Arabic scripts are also used. Using Arabic script to transliterate Berber has existed since the beginning of the Islamic Era (L. Souag, 2004).

[3] Among the freely available language identification tools, we tried Google Translator, Open Xerox language and Translated labs at http://labs.translated.net.

Proceedings of the Third Workshop on NLP for Similar Languages, Varieties and Dialects,
pages 63–72, Osaka, Japan, December 12 2016.

it from local Arabic dialects.[4] For instance each word in the Arabicized Berber sentence 'AHml sAqwl mA$y dwl kAn' [5] which means 'love is from heart and not just a word' has a false friend in MSA and all Arabic dialects. In MSA, the sentence means literally 'I carry I will say going countries was' which does not mean anything.

In this study, we deal with the automatic detection of Arabicized Berber and distinguishing it from the most popular Arabic varieties. We consider only the seven most popular Arabic dialects, based on the geographical classification, plus MSA. There are many local dialects due to the linguistic richness of the Arab world, but it is hard to deal with all of them for two reasons: it is hard to get enough data, and it is hard to find reliable linguistic features as these local dialects are very hard to describe and full of unpredictability and hybridization (Hassan R.S., 1992). We start the paper by a brief overview about the related work done for Arabicized Berber and dialectal Arabic ALI in Section 2. We then describe the process of building the linguistic resources (dataset and lexicons) used in this paper and motivate the adopted classification in Section 3. We next describe the experiments and analyze the results in Sections 4 and 5, and finally conclude with the findings and future plans.

2 Related Work

Current available automatic language identifiers rely on character n-gram models and statistics using large training corpora to identify the language of an input text (Zampieri and Gebre, 2012). They are mainly trained on standard languages and not on the varieties of each language, for instance available language identification tools can easily distinguish Arabic from Persian, Pashto and Urdu based on character sets and topology. However, they fail to properly distinguish between languages which use the same character set. Goutte et al., (2016) and Malmasi et al., (2016) give a comprehensive bibliography of the recently published work dealing with discriminating between similar languages and language varieties for different languages. There is some work done to identify spoken Berber. For instance Halimouche et al., (2014) discriminated between affirmative and interrogative Berber sentences using prosodic information, and Chelali et al., (2015) used speech signal information to automatically identify Berber speaker. We are not aware of any work which deals with automatic identification of written Arabicized Berber.

Recently, there is an increasing interest in processing Arabic informal varieties (Arabic dialects) using various methods. The main challenge is the lack of freely available data (Benajiba and Diab, 2010). Most of the work focuses on distinguishing between Modern Standard Arabic (MSA) and dialectal Arabic (DA) where the latter is regarded as one class which consists mainly of Egyptian Arabic (Elfardy and Diab 2013). Further, Zaidan and Callison-Burch (2014) distinguished between four Arabic varieties (MSA, Egyptian, Gulf and Levantine dialects) using n-gram models. The system is trained on a large dataset and achieved an accuracy of 85.7%. However, the performance of the system can not be generalized to other domains and topics, especially that the data comes from the same domain (users' comments on selected newspapers websites). Sadat et al., (2014) distinguished between eighteen[6] Arabic varieties using probabilistic models (character n-gram Markov language model and Naive Bayes classifiers) across social media datasets. The system was tested on 1,800 sentences (100 sentences for each Arabic variety) and the authors reported an overall accuracy of 98%. The small size of the used test dataset makes it hard to generalize the performance of the system to all dialectal Arabic content. Also Saâdane (2015) in her PhD classified Maghrebi Arabic (Algerian, Moroccan and Tunisian dialects) using morphosyntactic information. Furthermore, Malmasi et al., (2015) distinguished between six Arabic varieties, namely MSA, Egyptian, Tunisian, Syrian, Jordanian and Palestinian, on sentence-level, using a Parallel Multidialectal Corpus (Bouamor et al., 2014).

It is hard to compare the performance of the proposed systems, among others, namely that all of them were trained and tested on different datasets (different domains, topics and sizes). To the best of our

---

[4] In all polls about the hardest Arabic dialect to learn, Arabic speakers mention Maghrebi Arabic which has Berber, French and words of unknown origins unlike other Arabic dialects.

[5] We use Buckwalter Arabic transliteration scheme. For the complete chart see: http://www.qamus.org/transliteration.htm.

[6] Egypt; Iraq; Gulf including Bahrein, Emirates, Kuwait, Qatar, Oman and Saudi Arabia; Maghrebi including Algeria, Tunisia, Morocco, Libya, Mauritania; Levantine including Jordan, Lebanon, Palestine, Syria; and Sudan.

knowledge, there is no single work done to evaluate the systems on one large multi-domain dataset. Hence, it is wrong to consider the automatic identification of Arabic varieties as a solved task, especially that there is no available tool which can be used to deal with further NLP tasks for dialectal Arabic.

In this paper, we propose an automatic language identifier which distinguishes between Arabicized Berber and the eight most popular high level Arabic variants (Algerian, Egyptian, Gulf, Levantine, Iraqi (Mesopotamian), Moroccan, Tunisian dialects and MSA). We also present the dataset and the lexicons which were newly built as part of a Masters thesis project in Language Technology (Adouane, 2016). Both the dataset and the lexicons are freely available for research from the first author.

3   Building Linguistic Resources

Arabicized Berber (BER) has been officially used only in online newspapers and official institutions in North African countries like Algeria and Libya. It has been also used recently on social media by people who do not master the Berber script or Tifinagh and by those who do not master French.[7] An important question to answer when dealing with Arabic varieties is whether these variants are dialects or languages. There is no linguistically well-motivated answer since these varieties are different with their own regional/local varieties and are spoken in different countries. However, modern Arabic dialectology considers each Arabic variety as a stand-alone language (Hassan R.S., 1992). In this paper, we use the terms variety, dialect and language interchangeably.

It is necessary to decide how to cluster Arabic variants in order to be able to properly analyze and process them automatically. Nonetheless, it is not easy to distinguish each variant from another, particularly for short texts, because of the considerable lexical overlap and similarities between them. Moreover, it is very hard and expensive to collect data for each single variant given that some are rarely used on the Web. Based on the fact that people of the same region tend to use the same vocabulary and have the same pronunciation, Habash (2010) suggested to group Arabic dialects in six main groups, namely Egyptian (which includes Egyptian, Libyan and Sudanese), Levantine (which includes Lebanese, Jordanian, Palestinian and Syrian), Gulf (including Gulf Cooperation Council Countries), Iraqi, Maghrebi (which includes Algerian, Moroccan and Tunisian) and the rest is grouped in one class called 'Other'.

We use slightly different division where we count each Maghrebi variant as a stand-alone language. Moreover, we differently cluster Gulf/Mesopotamian[8] dialect group. We base our dialect clustering on common linguistic features, for instance the use of 'ch' instead of 'k' (Palva, 2006). So for the Mesopotamian Arabic, we include many local variants of Iraqi, Kuwaiti, Qatari and Emirati spoken Arabic. We group the rest of regions in the Gulf Arabic.[9] Our motivation is that these two broad regional dialectal groups (Maghrebi and Gulf/Mesopotamian) include a wide variety of languages which are easily distinguished by humans. Therefore, machines should be also able to discriminate between these varieties. In this study, we consider eight high level dialectal groups which are: Algerian (ALG), Egyptian (EGY), Gulf (GUL), Levantine (LEV), Mesopotamian (KUI), Moroccan (MOR), Tunisian (TUN) dialects plus MSA. In all cases, we focus on the language of the indigenous populations and not on the Pidgin Arabic.[10]

The use of Arabic dialects (in written format) on the Web is a quite recent phenomenon which started with the emergence of social media platforms and new technology devices. These Arabic variants, which use non-standardized orthography based on pronunciation or what is called 'write as you speak' principle, are still not well represented on the Web. This makes it hard to automatically process and analyze them (Diab et al., 2010). To overcome the deficiency of linguistic resources,[11] we built from scratch

---

[7]It is wrong to assume that all people from North Africa master French and use it in social media instead of Berber.

[8]There is no clear-cut dialectal borderlines between the Arabic varieties spoken in the Arabian Peninsula, namely between Gulf Arabic and Mesopotamian Arabic. Qafisheh (1977) gave a thorough morpho-syntactic analysis of the Gulf Arabic including Bahraini, Emirati, Qatari, Kuwaiti and regions of Saudi Arabia and excluding the Arabic dialects spoken in the rest of the Gulf countries. However, we do not have any morpho-syntactic parser, if it exists at all, to take all the grammars into account.

[9]Recent works consider all spoken Arabic in Gulf Cooperation Council Countries as Gulf Arabic.

[10]Simplified language varieties created by foreigners living in Arabic-speaking countries to make communication easier.

[11]There are collections by individuals but unfortunately not digitalized or which do not respect corpus linguistics annotation conventions.

linguistic resources consisting of dataset and lexicon for each Arabic variety considered in this study and Arabicized Berber.

3.1 Dataset

For Arabicized Berber, two Berber native speakers collected 503 documents (5,801 words) from north African countries mainly from forums, blogs and Facebook. For more data, we have selected varied texts from Algerian newspapers and segmented them. Originally the news texts are short, around 1,500 words each, so we considered each paragraph as a document (maximum 178 words). The selected newspapers use various Berber standard varieties written in Arabic script.

For each Arabic variety, two native speakers have manually collected content from various social media platforms (forums, blogs and micro-blogs) where each user's comment is counted as a single document/text. We gave instructions, for instance 'Collect only what is clearly written in your dialect, i.e. texts containing at least one clear dialectal word and you can easily understand it and reproduce the same in your daily interactions'. We have also compiled a list of dialectal words for each Arabic variety based on our knowledge. We then used a script with the compiled words as keywords to collect more data. Likewise, we collected 1,000 documents (around 54,150 words) for each dialect, roughly published between 2012-2016 in various platforms (micro-blogs, forums, blogs and online newspapers) from all over the Arab world. The same native speakers have been asked to clean the data following the same set of instructions.

We ended up with an unbalanced corpus of between 2,430 documents (64,027 words) and 6,000 documents or (170,000 words) for each dialect. In total, the collected dataset contains 579,285 words. In terms of data source distribution, the majority of the content comes from blogs and forums where users are trying to promote their dialects; roughly 50%, around 30% of the data comes from popular YouTube channels and the rest is collected from micro-blogs. The selection of the data sources is based on the quality of the dialectal content, i.e. we know that the content of the selected forums and blogs is dialectal which is used to teach or promote dialects between users. Ideally we would have looked at just some data resources and harvest content as much as possible either manually or using a script. But given the fact that data depends on the platform it is used in[12] and our goal that is to build a general system which will be able to handle various domain/topic independent data, we have used various data domains dealing with quite varied topics like cartoons, cooking, health/body care, movies, music, politics and social issues. We labeled each document with the corresponding Arabic variety.

We introduced necessary pre-processing rules such as tokenization, normalization and removal of non-discriminative words including punctuation, emoticons, any word occurring in the MSA data more than 100 times (prepositions, verbs, common nouns, proper nouns, adverbs, etc.) and Named Entities (NE). Removing non-discriminative words is motivated by the fact that these words are either prevalent in all Arabic varieties or they do not carry any important linguistic information like emoticons and punctuation. The choice of removing NE is motivated by the fact that NE are either dialect (region) specific or prevalent; i.e. they exist in many regions, so they are weak discriminants. Moreover, we want the system to be robust and effective by learning the language variety and not heuristics about a given region. The pre-processing step was done manually because of the absence of the appropriate tools.

To assess the reliability of the annotated data, we have conducted a human evaluation. As a sample, we have picked up randomly 100 documents for each language from the collection, removed the labels, shuffled and put all in one file (900 unlabeled documents in total). We asked two native speakers for each language, not the same ones who collected the original data, to pick out what s/he thinks is written in his/her dialect, i.e. can understand easily and can produce the same in his/her daily life. All the annotators are educated, either have already finished their university or are still students. This means that all of them are expected to properly distinguish between MSA and dialectal Arabic. To interpret the results, we computed the inter-annotator agreement for each language to see how often the annotators agree. Since we have two annotators per language, we computed the Cohen's kappa coefficient which is

---

[12]For instance the use of special markers in some platforms and the allowed length of the texts where shorter text means more abbreviations.

a standard metric used to evaluate the quality of a set of annotations in classification tasks by assessing the annotators' agreement (Carletta, 1996). Overall, the data quality is 'satisfactory' for Algerian, Gulf and Tunisian dialects by interpreting the kappa metric which is between 0.6–0.8. The quality of the rest of the dialectal data is 'really good', kappa 0.8–1.

3.2 Lexicons

We removed 18,000 documents (2,000 documents, between 60,000 and 170,000 words, for each Arabic variety and Arabicized Berber) to be used for training and evaluation. We extracted from the rest of the data all the unique vocabulary, using a script, to build lexicons. We have also added dialectal words collected from exchange forums where users were trying to promote their culture and dialects. The reason we have done so is the desperate lack of digitalized dialectal lexicons[13] and the few available ones are outdated word lists in paper format. For MSA, we have used the content of two freely available books. We would have also used an MSA dictionary, but this would need more effort as the freely available dictionaries are not designed to be easily used for any computational purpose.

In order to have even more refined lexicons, we used Term Frequency-Inverse document Frequency (TF-IDF)[14] to measure the importance of each word to each dialect. Table 1 shows the number of unique words (types) of the compiled lexicons for each language after applying TF-IDF and removing non-informative words. The specific vocabulary of each Arabicized Berber and Arabic variety is stored in a separate .txt file, one word per line.

Language	ALG	BER	EGY	GUL	KUI	LEV	MSA	MOR	TUN
#Types	9 172	21 786	5 979	10 349	10 272	9 969	88 361	11 879	13 101

Table 1: The size (total number of unique vocabulary) of the compiled lexicons.

4   Methods and Experiments

We use supervised machine learning, namely Cavnar's Text classification, support vector machines (SVM) and Prediction by Partial Matching (PPM) methods. For features, we use both character-based n-gram[15] and word-based n-gram[16] models, then we combine them. We also use the words of the compiled lexicons as features. We focus more on social media short texts, so we limit the text maximum length to 140 characters (which is the maximum length of a tweet) assuming that if a method works for short texts, it should work better for longer texts as there will be access to more information. We use a balanced dataset containing 18,000 documents (2,000 documents, between 60,000 and 170,000 words, for each language) where we used 80% (total of 14,400 documents or 1,600 for each language) for training and 20%, total of 3,600 documents or 131,412 words (400 documents for each language), for evaluation.

4.1   Cavnar's Text Classification Method

Cavnar's Text Classification Method is one of the automatic language identification (ALI) statistical standard methods. It is a ranked collection of the most common character-based n-grams for each language used as its profile (Cavnar and Trenkle, 1994). The distance between language profiles is defined as the sum of all distances between the ranking of the n-gram profiles, and the language with the minimum distance from the source text will be returned. We experimented with different character-based n-grams and combinations and found that 3-grams performed the best with a macro-average F-score of 52.41%. Table 2 shows the performance of the Cavnar's method per language.

---

[13]"For many regions, no substantial dictionaries are available. We have reasonable dictionaries for Levantine, Algerian and Iraqi, but these are sometimes outdated and need to be replaced or updated" (Behnstdt and Woidich, 2013).

[14]A weighting scheme used to measure the importance of each word in a document and a other documents based on its frequency.

[15]A sequence of n characters from a given sequence of text where n is an integer.

[16]A sequence of n words from a given sequence of text where n is an integer.

Language	Precision (%)	Recall (%)	F-score (%)
ALG	41.34	37.00	39.05
BER	98.43	94.00	**96.16**
EGY	56.20	38.50	45.70
GUL	32.69	50.50	39.69
KUI	47.05	53.75	50.18
LEV	46.23	36.75	40.95
MOR	57.14	48.00	52.17
MSA	63.28	81.00	**71.05**
TUN	39.71	34.25	36.78

Table 2: Cavnar's method performance using character 3-grams.

The results show that except for Arabicized Berber (BER) which is properly identified, Cavnar's classifier finds it hard to distinguish Arabic varieties from each other even though it performs better in distinguishing MSA from dialectal Arabic. Our main purpose in using Cavnar's method is to set its performance as our baseline.

4.2 Support Vector Machines (SVM)

We use the LinearSVC classifier (method) as implemented in Scikit-learn package (Pedregosa et al., 2011)[17] with the default parameters.[18] Furthermore, we use the binary classification setting as opposed to the 9-class classification, for instance 'is a document written in BER or something else (Arabic varieties)' as opposed to 'is a document written in BER, MSA, ALG, EGY, GUL, LEV, KUI, MOR or TUN.' Both classification settings return only one label or category as an output because each classifier is implemented as a group of classifiers, and the label with the highest prediction score is returned. We experimented with various features (character and word based n-grams of different lengths and combinations) and found that combining character-based 5-grams and 6-grams with the words of the compiled lexicons performed the best with a macro-average F-score of 92.94%. Table 3 shows the performance of the SVM method per language.

Language	Precision (%)	Recall (%)	F-score (%)
ALG	91.79	92.25	92.02
BER	100	100	**100**
EGY	95.63	82.00	88.29
GUL	86.92	89.75	88.31
KUI	91.20	93.25	92.21
LEV	91.71	88.50	90.08
MOR	93.84	95.25	94.54
MSA	93.46	100	**96.62**
TUN	92.98	96.00	94.46

Table 3: SVM performance combining character-based 5-grams and 6-grams with lexicons.

SVM classifier performs very well for BER and even better than the Cavnar's classifier. It also performs very well in distinguishing Arabic varieties. It identifiers MOR and TUN better than ALG. Likewise, it recognizes KUI better than GUL. MSA is also well distinguished from other varieties.

---

[17]For more information see: `http://scikit-learn.org/stable/`.

[18]The default parameters for each classifier are detailed in `http://scikit-learn.org/stable/`.

4.3 Prediction by Partial Matching (PPM)

A lossless compression algorithm which has been successfully applied to language identification (Bobicev, 2015) as well as other tasks. PPM encodes all the symbols (characters or words) of a training data within their context where a context of each symbol is a sequence of preceding symbols of different lengths.[19] PPM is a simple method which does not require feature selection as it considers the entire text as a single string and computes the probability distribution for each symbol using a blending mechanism. We implemented a simple version of the PPM method as explained in (Moffat, 1990; Bobicev, 2015) where we used the context of 5 characters for each symbol and the benchmark escape method called C. Hence, we implemented the PPMC5 version of PPM. Here, we use the entire text length. The method reaches a macro-average F-score of 87.55%.

At the end, we validated our three models using the 10-fold cross-validation technique. Each time, we preserve one fold for validation and train on the rest 9 folds. This gives us an idea on how a model is dataset independent. For each method, we used the same settings above and found that the accuracy values are close to each other for all cross-validation folds, and close to the overall accuracy. This means that the models are not an overfit.

It is unfair to compare the results of the three methods as we limited the maximum text length to 140 characters for both SVM and Cavnar's methods and used full-length text for the PPM method. Now, we use the full-length text for all methods using the same experimental setups. The results are shown in Table 4 where 'DV' is short for 'dialectal vocabulary' and it refers to the words of the compiled lexicons.

Method	Features	Maximum Text Length	Macro-average F-score (%)
Cavnar	Character 3-grams	140 characters	52.41
Cavnar	Character 3-grams	Full length	81.57
SVM	Character 5-6-grams + DV	140 characters	**92.94**
SVM	Character 5-6-grams + DV	Full length	**93.40**
PPMC5	No features	Full length	87.55

Table 4: Performance of the three methods with full-length text.

The results show that increasing the length of the text improves the performance of both Cavnar's and SVM methods. Cavnar's method performs poorly for short texts (maximum length of 140 characters). It is true that SVM outperforms the Cavnar's method because it has access to extra data (lexicons). However, even with the same experimental setup (using character-based 3-grams as features with text maximum length of 140 characters), SVM still outperforms the Cavnar's method which is taken as our baseline.

5 Error Analysis

Analyzing the confusion matrix of each method shows that the confusions are of the same type with different frequencies. For illustration, we show in Table 5 the confusion matrix of the SVM method using the combination of character-based 5-6-grams and the dialectal vocabulary as features and text maximum length of 140 characters.

Most confusions are between very close Arabic varieties, namely Maghrebi dialects (ALG, MOR, TUN) and between GUL and KUI dialects. This is expected and accepted because, as mentioned above, there are no dialectal clear-cut borderlines between neighboring dialects. In more details, there are more MOR and TUN documents confused with ALG ones compared to the ALG documents confused with MOR or TUN documents. The same is applicable for KUI documents confused with GUL ones. This may be related to the fact that in practice it is impossible to draw the dialectal borderlines, especially for very short texts as in our case. Moreover, there are confusions between Maghrebi, Egyptian and Levantine varieties. This is explained by the fact that some Levantine dialects (southern Syria and some

---

[19]Previous works reported that taking the context of 5 characters is the best maximum context length. This makes a perfect sense because long matches are less frequent to occur by chance.

<table>
<tr><td rowspan="2"></td><td rowspan="2"></td><td colspan="9" align="center">Misclassified languages</td></tr>
<tr><td>ALG</td><td>BER</td><td>EGY</td><td>GUL</td><td>KUI</td><td>LEV</td><td>MSA</td><td>MOR</td><td>TUN</td></tr>
<tr><td rowspan="9">Correct languages</td><td>ALG</td><td>369</td><td>0</td><td>1</td><td>0</td><td>0</td><td>1</td><td>2</td><td>12</td><td>15</td></tr>
<tr><td>BER</td><td>0</td><td>400</td><td>0</td><td>0</td><td>0</td><td>0</td><td>0</td><td>0</td><td>0</td></tr>
<tr><td>EGY</td><td>6</td><td>0</td><td>328</td><td>15</td><td>6</td><td>19</td><td>10</td><td>8</td><td>8</td></tr>
<tr><td>GUL</td><td>1</td><td>0</td><td>5</td><td>359</td><td>24</td><td>7</td><td>3</td><td>0</td><td>1</td></tr>
<tr><td>KUI</td><td>1</td><td>0</td><td>1</td><td>21</td><td>373</td><td>4</td><td>0</td><td>0</td><td>0</td></tr>
<tr><td>LEV</td><td>7</td><td>0</td><td>7</td><td>16</td><td>3</td><td>354</td><td>10</td><td>1</td><td>2</td></tr>
<tr><td>MSA</td><td>0</td><td>0</td><td>0</td><td>0</td><td>0</td><td>0</td><td>400</td><td>0</td><td>0</td></tr>
<tr><td>MOR</td><td>9</td><td>0</td><td>0</td><td>2</td><td>1</td><td>1</td><td>3</td><td>381</td><td>3</td></tr>
<tr><td>TUN</td><td>9</td><td>0</td><td>1</td><td>0</td><td>2</td><td>0</td><td>0</td><td>4</td><td>384</td></tr>
</table>

Table 5: SVM confusion matrix using character-based 5-6-grams and dialectal vocabulary.

parts of Lebanon, including Beirut) share the use of split-morpheme negations with Egyptian and north African dialects (Palva, 2006). It is also important to notice that while BER is rarely confused, MSA is often confused with the rest of Arabic varieties.

6 Conclusion and Future Directions

In this study, we dealt with both tasks of identifying Arabicized Berber and different Arabic varieties as well as discriminating between all of them. For Arabic, we considered eight high level varieties (Algerian (ALG), Egyptian (EGY), Gulf (GUL), Levantine (LEV), Mesopotamian (KUI), Moroccan (MOR), Tunisian (TUN) dialects plus Modern Standard Arabic (MSA)) which are the most popular Arabic variants. The task is challenging at many levels. First, Arabicized Berber and Arabic varieties, except MSA, are under-resourced and undocumented. Second, dialectal Arabic is mostly used in social media and mobile phone messages. This makes the task harder since this genre allows only short texts.

To overcome these challenges, we created the necessary linguistic resources (dataset and lexicons). We framed the task as a categorization problem for short texts written in very similar languages. We applied one of the automatic language identification standard methods, namely supervised machine learning including Cavnar's text classification, support vector machines (SVM) and the Prediction by Partial Matching methods. We set the performance of the Cavnar's method as our baseline. All in all, for short texts of 140 characters or less, Cavnar's character-based method is not efficient in distinguishing Arabic varieties from each other, particularly the very close ones like Maghrebi dialects. The reason is that all the varieties use the same character set with almost the same distribution. Nevertheless, it performs better in discriminating between MSA and dialectal Arabic. Also, it distinguishes Arabicized Berber fairly well from Arabic. SVM combining the character-based 5-6-grams with the words of the compiled lexicons performs fairly well for short texts, and increasing the text length performs even better. Likewise, the PPM (precisely PPMC5) method is good at distinguishing Arabicized Berber from Arabic and MSA from dialectal Arabic. Error analysis shows that all the errors, whatever the method, are of the same type; confusion between very similar languages.

So far, we have applied the automatic language identification standard methods to discriminate between Arabicized Berber and Arabic varieties which are under-resourced languages, and we found that supervised machine learning using character-based n-gram models are well suited for our task to a large extent. This should be a good start to automatically process dialectal Arabic. For now, we find it hard to compare our system to other reported results of related work because the datasets used in evaluation are different. We would like to test our system on larger and multi-domain/topic datasets to see how it performs as well as test it on some newly collected corpora, for instance (Salama et al., 2014). This will allow us to improve the system and generalize the results.

Still, there are other points we want to explore further in future work like distinguishing between varieties of Arabicized Berber, and applying the two step classification process which consists in first identifying the regional dialectal group, for instance Maghrebi Arabic, then apply some different feature weighting to identify the dialect itself. It would be also possible to analyze the misspellings which seem to be consistent within the same variant because the orthography is based on the pronunciation. This could help improving the dialectal Arabic identification. Another way worth exploring is to include user metadata (extralinguistic information) like the location.

Acknowledgments

The authors would like to thank all anonymous reviewers for their comments that over time have substantially improved the paper.

References

Ahmed Salama, Houda Bouamor, Behrang Mohit and Kemal Oflazer. 2014. YouDACC: the Youtube Dialectal Arabic Comment Corpus. *In the Proceedings of the Ninth International Conference on Language Resources and Evaluation (LREC'14)*, pages 1246–1251, Reykjavik, Iceland.

Alistair Moffat. 1990. Implementing the PPM data compression scheme. *IEEE Transactions on Communications*, 38(11), pages 1917–1921.

Abd-El-Jawad, Hassan R.S. 1992. Is Arabic a pluricentric language?. *In Clyne, Michael G. Pluricentric Languages: Differing Norms in Different Nations. Contributions to the sociology of language 62.* Berlin & New York: Mouton de Gruyter. pages 261–303.

Cyril Goutte , Serge Léger, Shervin Malmasi and Marcos Zampieri. 2016. Discriminating Similar Languages: Evaluations and Explorations. *In the Proceedings of Language Resources and Evaluation (LREC).* Portoroz, Slovenia.

Fabian Pedregosa, Gaël Varoquaux, Alexandre Gramfort, Vincent Michel, Bertrand Thirion, Olivier Grisel, Mathieu Blondel, Peter Prettenhofer, Ron Weiss, Vincent Dubourg, Jake VanderPlas, Alexandre Passos, David Cournapeau, Matthieu Brucher, Matthieu Perrot and Edouard Duchesnay. 2011. Scikit-learn: Machine learning in Python. *Machine learning in Python. Journal of Machine Learning Research*, 12, pages 2825–2830.

Fatma Zohra Chelali, Khadidja Sadeddine and Amar Djeradi. 2015. Speaker identification system using LPC-Application on Berber language. *HDSKD journal*, 1(2):29–46.

Fatiha Sadat, Farnazeh Kazemi and Atefeh Farzindar. 2014. Automatic Identification of Arabic Language Varieties and Dialects in Social Media. *In the Proceedings of the Second Workshop on Natural Language Processing for Social Media (SocialNLP)*, pages 22–27, Dublin, Ireland.

Hamdi A. Qafisheh. 1977. A short reference grammar of Gulf Arabic. *Tucson: University of Arizona Press.*

Heba Elfardy and Mona Diab. 2013. Sentence-Level Dialect Identification in Arabic. *In the Proceedings of the 51st Annual Meeting of the Association for Computational Linguistics, ACL 2013*, Sofia, Bulgaria.

Heikki Palva. 2006. *Encyclopedia of Arabic languages and linguistics, v.1, A-Ed..* Leiden: Brill, pages 604–613.

Houda Bouamor, Nizar Habash and Kemal Oflazer. 2014. A Multidialectal Parallel Corpus of Arabic. *In the Proceedings of the Ninth International Conference on Language Resources and Evaluation (LREC'14)*, pages 1240–1245, Reykjavik, Iceland.

Houda Saâdane. 2015. Le traitement automatique de l'arabe dialectalise: aspects methodologiques et algorithmiques. *PhD thesis*, Université Grenoble Alpes.

Jean Carletta. 1996. Assessing agreement on classification tasks: The kappa statistic. *Computational Linguistics, 22(2)*, pages 249–254.

Lameen Souag. 2004. Writing Berber Languages: a quick summary. *L. Souag. Archived from* `http://goo.gl/ooA4uZ`, Retrieved on April 8th, 2016.

Marcos Zampieri and Binyam Gebrekidan Gebre. 2012. Automatic Identification of Language Varieties: The Case of Portuguese. *In the Proceedings of KONVENS 2012 (Main track: poster presentations)*, Vienna.

Mona Diab, Nizar Habash, Owen Rambow, Mohamed Altantawy and Yassine Benajiba 2010. COLABA: Arabic dialect annotation and processing. *In the Proceedings of the LREC Workshop on Semitic Language Processing*, pages 66–74.

Nizar Habash. 2010. Introduction to Arabic Natural Language Processing. *Morgan & Claypool Publishers*.

Omar F. Zaidan. 2012. Crowdsourcing Annotation for Machine Learning in Natural Language Processing Tasks. *PhD thesis*, Johns Hopkins University.

Omar F. Zaidan and Chris Callison-Burch. 2014. Arabic dialect identification. *Computational Linguistics, 40(1)*, pages 171–202.

Peter Behnstadt and Manfred Woidich. 2013. Dialectology. *In the Oxford Handbook of Arabic Linguistics, Dialectology*, pages 300–323.

Ramzi Halimouche, Hocine Teffahi and Leila Falek. 2014. Detecting Sentences Types in Berber Language. *International Conference on Multimedia Computing and Systems (ICMCS)*, pages 197–200.

Shervin Malmasi, Eshrag Refaee and Mark Dras. 2015. Arabic Dialect Identification using a Parallel Multidialectal Corpus *In the Proceedings of the 14th Conference of the Pacific Association for Computational Linguistics (PACLING 2015)*, pages 209–217, Bali, Indonesia.

Shervin Malmasi, Marcos Zampieri, Nikola Ljubešić, Preslav Nakov , Ahmed Ali and Jörg Tiedemann. 2016. Discriminating between Similar Languages and Arabic Dialect Identification: A Report on the Third DSL Shared Task. *In the Proceedings of the 3rd Workshop on Language Technology for Closely Related Languages, Varieties and Dialects (VarDial)*, Osaka, Japan.

Victoria Bobicev. 2015. Discriminating between similar languages using ppm. *In the Proceedings of the LT4VarDial Workshop*, Hissar, Bulgaria.

Wafia Adouane. 2016. *Automatic Detection of Under-resourced Languages: The case of Arabic Short Texts*. Master's thesis, University of Gothenburg.

William B. Cavnar and John M. Trenkle. 1994. N-gram-based text categorization. *In the Proceedings of SDAIR-94, 3rd Annual Symposium on Document Analysis and Information Retrieval*, pages 161–175, Las Vegas, US.

Yassine Benajiba and Mona Diab. 2010. A web application for dialectal Arabic text annotation. *In the Proceedings of the LREC Workshop for Language Resources (LRs) and Human Language Technologies (HLT) for Semitic Languages: Status, Up-dates, and Prospects*.

Automatic Verification and Augmentation of Multilingual Lexicons

Maryam Aminian, Mohamed Al-Badrashiny, Mona Diab
Department of Computer Science
The George Washington University
Washington, DC
{aminian,badrashiny,mtdiab}@gwu.edu

Abstract

We present an approach for automatic verification and augmentation of multilingual lexica. We exploit existing parallel and monolingual corpora to extract multilingual correspondents via triangulation. We demonstrate the efficacy of our approach on two publicly available resources: Tharwa, a three-way lexicon comprising Dialectal Arabic, Modern Standard Arabic and English lemmas among other information (Diab et al., 2014); and BabelNet, a multilingual thesaurus comprising over 276 languages including Arabic variant entries (Navigli and Ponzetto, 2012). Our automated approach yields an F1-score of 71.71% in generating correct multilingual correspondents against gold Tharwa, and 54.46% against gold BabelNet without any human intervention.

1 Introduction

Machine readable multilingual lexica are typically created by a combination of manual and automatic (semi-automatic) techniques. This illustrates the need for continuous verification of the quality of the lexica during the development process. Approaches exploited for lexicon evaluation and verification mainly comprise manual assessment and human verification. This process is expensive and poses several limitations in terms of domain coverage as well as the amount of data that can be manually evaluated. Hence, efforts to automate the evaluation process and reduce manual annotation expenses are quite desireable.

Researchers have mainly resorted to using manual evaluation to verify coverage, automatically extend and measure accuracy of different lexical resources such as multilingual lexica and WordNets (Sagot and Fišer, 2011a; Sagot and Fišer, 2011b; Sagot and Fišer, 2012; Saleh and Habash, 2009). For example, Saleh and Habash (2009) propose an approach for extracting an Arabic-English dictionary while exploiting different human annotated samples to measure accuracy of the extracted dictionary. De Melo and Weikum (2009) use human annotated samples to measure accuracy of the multilingual dictionary they extract. More recently, Navigli and Ponzetto (2012) benefit from manual evaluation by expert annotators to assess coverage of additional lexicalizations provided by their resource and not covered in existing lexical knowledge bases.

In this paper, we devise a framework for automatic verification and augmentation of multilingual lexica using evidence leveraging parallel and monolingual corpora. The proposed method is capable of detecting inconsistencies in the lexicon entries and possibly providing/suggesting candidates to replace them. Accordingly, one can exploit this method to automatically augment multilingual lexica with partially or completely new entries. Naturally the method lends itself to also bootstrapping multilingual lexica from scratch, however, this is outside the scope of the present work.

We demonstrate the efficacy of our proposed framework in the context of verifying and augmenting a publicly available lexicon that is manually created Tharwa (Diab et al., 2014). Tharwa is an electronic three-way lexicon comprising Egyptian Dialectal Arabic (EGY), Modern Standard Arabic (MSA) and English correspondents (EN). The entries in Tharwa are in lemma form. We show that our approach obtains F1-score of 71.71% in generating multilingual correspondents which match with a gold Tharwa set. We further evaluate our approach against the Arabic entries in BabelNet (Navigli and Ponzetto, 2012).

Proceedings of the Third Workshop on NLP for Similar Languages, Varieties and Dialects,
pages 73–81, Osaka, Japan, December 12 2016.

We show that our automated approach reaches F1-score of 54.46% in generating correct correspondents for BabelNet Arabic entries.

2   Approach

Let L denote a multilingual lexicon that covers three languages l_1, l_2, l_3. Each row in L contains correspondents from l_1, l_2, l_3 and can be written as a tuple in the form $(w^{l_1}, w^{l_2}, w^{l_3})$ where w^{l_i} refers to a word from language l_i. We call $(w^{l_1}, w^{l_2}, w^{l_3})$ multilingual correspondents when w^{l_i} is translation of w^{l_j}, for all $i, j \in \{1, 2, 3\}$. Here, we consider the case that we have three languages in L but the following approach can be generalized to lexica with more than three languages. Our main objective is to develop a fully automated approach to verify the quality of multilingual correspondents in L, while detecting erroneous ones, and possibly providing candidates to replace them. Moreover, adding more entries to the lexicon.

2.1   Multilingual Correspondent Expansion

We exploit parallel corpora to generate the initial set of multilingual correspondents. This set is further expanded with correspondents extracted from monolingual resources such as WordNet (Fellbaum, 1998) and word clusters induced over monolingual corpora.

2.1.1   Leveraging Parallel corpora

We assume we have access to two parallel corpora $P_{1,2}$ and $P_{3,2}$, where $P_{i,j}$ is set of aligned sentences in the source language l_i and target language l_j. Thus, we need two parallel corpora with a common target side (in this case l_2) to generate word-level correspondents. We assume word alignment technology to automatically induce word correspondents from $P_{1,2}$ and $P_{3,2}$.

Given word alignment output, we extract a function $t(w, i, j)$ for all $w \in l_i$. This function returns a list of all $w' \in l_j$ which have been aligned to w. We derive the initial set of multilingual correspondents using Eq. 1:

$$T = \{(w^{l_1}, w^{l_2}, w^{l_3}) | w^{l_1} \in t(w^{l_2}, 2, 1), w^{l_3} \in t(w^{l_2}, 2, 3)\} \tag{1}$$

In other words, T comprises tuples which are obtained by *pivoting* through the common language (here l_2). This is a process of lexical triangulation and refer to the generated multilingual word level correspondents as *multilingual tuples* or simply *tuples* hereafter.

Nevertheless, there is always some noise in the automatic word alignment process. But we prune a large portion of the noise by applying constraints on part-of-speech tags (POS) correspondence, thereby accepting tuples in T with a certain mapping between POS tag categories. We call the pruned set T' as shown in Eq. 2 and refer to the POS mapping function as $M(pos(w^{l_i}))$, in which $pos(w^{l_i})$ refers to the POS tag of w^{l_i} of either source languages (l_1, l_3). This mapping function lets us account for some language-dependent functional divergences that happens when translating a word with certain POS tag from source to target language. For instance, word *jmylp*[1] as an adjective in EGY could end up being aligned through pivoting on English to the same word in MSA but functioning in context as a noun.

$$T' = \{(w^{l_1}, w^{l_2}, w^{l_3}) \in T | M(pos(w^{l_1})) = pos(w^{l_3})\} \tag{2}$$

2.1.2   Leveraging Monolingual Resources

Parallel corpora pose several limitations in size and coverage for the extracted multilingual correspondents due to domain and genres variation of naturally available data. Accordingly to mitigate these limitations we propose expanding a target word with all its synonyms. We use the following methods that leverage different monolingual resources to expand T':

WordNet   One can use synonyms that WordNet generates to expand a word. Before expanding monolingual correspondents in T', we perform word sense disambiguation using (Pedersen et al., 2005). If a

---

[1]Arabic characters are shown using Buckwalter transliteration scheme throughout this paper. Transliteration table can be found in http://www.qamus.org/transliteration.htm

	EGY	EN	MSA
Tharwa	OaSAb	strike	sadad
1	OaSAb	collide	sadad
2	OaSAb	strike	TAr

Table 1: Examples of partially-matched tuples generated by T' compared to a Tharwa entry.

word belongs to more than one WordNet synset, word sense is used to disambiguate the correct synset to expand. We additionally use POS tags to filter returned synonyms.

Word clusters Not all languages have an extensively developed WordNet. Therefore, we leverage monolingual corpora to expand words to their semantically similar correspondents. Thereby, having large monolingual corpora in any of the languages present in our lexicon, we can generate high quality word clusters. Accordingly, we exploit existing methods to obtain vector-space word embeddings. Word vectors are then clustered using a hard clustering technique such as K-means. Namely, we expand each correspondent in T' with all the words from the same cluster that the correspondent belongs to. We also use POS tags to skip irrelevant words. This can be done for any language in our lexicon conditioned on the fact that the language has enough monolingual data to induce word clusters. We acknowledge, however, that induced clusters do not necessarily contain exclusively semantically similar synonym words. There might be related and irrelevant words altogether.

2.1.3 Leveraging Cross Lingual Resources

Cross-lingual embedding We further incorporate multilingual evidence into monolingual vectors-space word embeddings. Cross-lingual CCA model proposed by (Faruqui and Dyer, 2014) projects vectors of two different languages into a shared space where they are maximally correlated. Correlation is inferred from an existing bilingual dictionary for the languages. Having projected vectors of a particular language, we expect the synonyms of a word to be found amongst the most similar words in the projected space. Each word is then expanded with the k most similar words acquired from the projected vector-space model.

2.2 Automatic Verification and Augmentation

We compare the set of multilingual correspondents acquired in Section 2.1 (T') with set of correspondents in L. This comparison leads to the following disjoint partitions:

Fully-matched tuples: This set contains $(w^{l_1}, w^{l_2}, w^{l_3}) \in L \cap T'$. The number of entries in this set can be used to measure lexicon coverage in comparison to gold data;

Partially-matched tuples: This set contains correspondents from L which have been matched with T' in a subset of languages but correspondents of at least one language are not matched. These partially matched correspondents are useful for lexicon verification purposes. The mismatches might reveal some existing errors in the correspondents. In addition to providing clues for lexicon verification, partially matched entries can be useful for lexical augmentation as some of the mismatches occur due to some unseen correspondents discovered from bilingual data. In other words, phenomena such as polysemy and homonymy may cause the partial match;

Fully-unmatched tuples: This set contains entries from L where none of the correspondents matched with T'. Hence, this set can provide correspondents for lexicon augmentation and boost the manual augmentation of the lexicon. The first row of Table 1 shows a tuple from Tharwa comprising correspondents from EGY, MSA and EN. The first example in the Table shows a tuple from T' that has matched in EGY and MSA but the EN correspondent does not match with gold Tharwa EN. Nevertheless, EN (collide) is in fact a synonym of the gold Tharwa EN (strike) and can be used for lexicon augmentation. Example number 2 is also a partially matched example where the EGY and EN match but the MSA does not match. However, the MSA word *TAr* is a synonym of the Tharwa MSA *sadad*, thereby, it can be used for Tharwa augmentation.

3 Experimental Setup

3.1 Data Resources

We use Bolt-ARZ v3+v4 for EGY-EN parallel data. This data comprises 3.5 million EGY words. For MSA-EN parallel data, we use GALE phase4 data which contains approx. 60 million MSA words.[2]

Additionally, we use multiple monolingual EGY corpora collected from Bolt and ATB data sets with approx. 260 million words (EGY_{mono}) to generate monolingual word clusters described in Section 2.1.2. We furthermore acquire a collection of several MSA LDC data sets[3] from several years with 833 million words (MSA_{mono}) to induce monolingual MSA word clusters. We use EGY_{mono} and English Gigaword 5th Edition (Parker et al., 2011) to train the the cross-lingual CCA embedding model.

We carry out a set of preprocessing steps in order to clean, lemmatize and diacritize the Arabic side of both parallel data sets and render the resources compatible. For the sake of consistency, the lemmatization step is replicated on the English data. The tool we use for processing Arabic is MADAMIRA v1.0 (Pasha et al., 2014), and for English we use TreeTagger (Schmid, 1995). Hence, all the entries in our resources are rendered in lemma form, with the Arabic components being additionally fully diacritized.

3.2 Data Processing

The lemmatized-diacritized corpora with the corresponding EN translations are word aligned using GIZA++ (Och and Ney, 2000) producing pairwise EGY-EN and MSA-EN lemma word type alignment files, respectively. We intersected the word alignments on the token level to the type level resulting in a cleaner list of lemma word type alignments per parallel corpus.

All correspondents in the form of EGY-EN-MSA are extracted from both alignment files by pivoting on the EN correspondent following Eq. 1 and 2. We refer to this set of tuples as *TransDict*.

We obtain monolingual vector space models using word2vec (Mikolov et al., 2013). We use the Skip-gram model to build word vectors of size 300 from EGY_{mono} and MSA_{mono} corpora using a word window of size 8 for both left and right. The number of negative samples for logistic regression is set to 25 and the threshold used for sub-sampling of frequent words is set to 10^5 in the model with 15 iterations. We also use full softmax to obtain the probability distribution. Word clusters are obtained from word2vec K-means word clustering tool with k=500. We additionally induce clusters with k=9228 corresponding to the number of synsets in the Arabic WordNet (Black et al., 2006).

Word2vec is further used to generate vectors of size 300 using a continuous bag of word model from English Gigaword. The generated vectors of a) EGY_{mono}-English Gigaword, and b) MSA_{mono}-English Gigaword are then used to train the Cross-lingual CCA model. Projected EGY and MSA vector space models are used to get a list of synonyms for the EGY and MSA words in TransDic. For EN expansion, we initially expand all the EN correspondents in *TransDict* using synonyms extracted from WordNet3. We further expand *TransDict* EGY and MSA correspondents using either word clusters or cross-lingual synonyms obtained from cross-lingual CCA model.

3.3 Evaluation Data

We measure quality of the correspondents generated by our approach represented in *TransDict* via two multilingual resources. BabelNet (Navigli and Ponzetto, 2012), a multilingual semantic network comprising concepts and named entities lexicalized in different languages including MSA, EGY and EN; and, Tharwa, a three-way lexicon containing MSA, EGY and EN correspondents. All entries in both resources are in lemma form and marked with a POS tag.

BabelNet is comprised of multilingual synsets. Each synset consists of multilingual senses including MSA, EGY and EN. First, we iterate over all synsets of type **CONCEPT**[4] and extract tuples in the form MSA-EN-EGY from each synset which satisfy the following conditions:

- None of MSA, EN and EGY words are out of vocabulary with respect to our MSA, EN and MSA corpora *independently*;

---

[2] MSA and EGY parallel data are collected from 41 LDC catalogs including data prepared for DARPA GALE and BOLT projects.

[3] This data is collected from 70 LDC catalogs including Gale, ATB and Arabic Gigawords4 projects.

[4] Named entities are excluded from the comparison.

Extraction Method	BabelNet			Tharwa		
	Precision	Recall	F1-Score	Precision	Recall	F1-Score
PARL	84.9%	21.26%	34.01%	77.63%	49.74%	60.63%
PARL+EGY-WC	90.00%	22.54%	36.05%	83.32%	53.38%	65.07%
PARL+EGY-SYN	86.61%	21.69%	34.69%	79.19%	50.74%	61.85%
PARL+MSA-WC	77.68%	23.79%	36.43%	74.14%	51.87%	61.03%
PARL+MSA-SYN	81.08%	22.65%	35.4%	76.66%	51.10%	61.33%
PARL+EN-WSD	87.16%	34.34%	49.27%	77.54%	56.40%	65.3%
PARL+EN-WSD+EGY-WC+MSA-WC	87.82%	39.47%	**54.46%**	81.63%	63.94%	**71.71%**
PARL+EN-WSD+EGY-SYN+MSA-SYN	86.26%	36.05%	50.85%	78.16%	58.07%	66.63%

Table 2: Precision, recall and F-score of different correspondence learning methods against BabelNet and Tharwa, respectively.

- MSA, EN and EGY, each, are not composed of more than a single word.

We acquired 8381 BabelNet tuples applying the above constraints. It is worth emphasizing that this evaluation is limited to measuring *quality* of the generated multilingual correspondents in *TransDict*. First constraint ensures that no mismatch happens due to domain divergence. Also since *TransDict* contains only single-word correspondents, we limit the set of extracted BabelNet tuples to the singletons.

Tharwa We define a particular subset of the Tharwa lexicon as the gold standard to measure performance of generated correspondents. Similar to BabelNet, gold Tharwa contains MSA-EN-EGY tuples from original Tharwa where none of their correspondent words is out of vocabulary with respect to all the MSA, EN and MSA corpora, respectively. Gold Tharwa obtained according to above conditions contains 19459 rows. We focus on the three main fields in Tharwa, namely: EGY lemma, MSA lemma, and EN lemma equivalents and their corresponding POS tags. This condition ensures that none of the mismatches is caused by domain divergence between Tharwa and *TransDict*.

3.4 Experimental conditions

We have devised the following settings:

PARL Only parallel data is used to generate correspondents in *TransDict*. We consider this to be our baseline.

WC This is where we expand the lemmas in a source language (MSA or EGY) using lemma clusters induced over word2vec vectors in addition to PARL.

SYN This is where we expand the lemmas in a source language (MSA or EGY) using cross-lingual synonyms by leveraging cross-lingual CCA (SYN) together with PARL.

EN-WSD This the condition where we expand English lemmas using word sense disambiguation to generate WordNet synsets for the pivot language EN. Accordingly, we present results for the following experimental conditions corresponding to the various extraction methods: (a) baseline PARL; (b) PARL+EGY-WC where we expand the EGY lemmas using WC clusters; (c) PARL+EGY-SYN where we expand EGY lemmas using the SYN expansion method; (d) PARL+MSA-WC where we expand the MSA lemmas using WC clusters; (e) PARL+EGY-SYN where we expand MSA lemmas using the SYN expansion method; (f) PARL+EN-WSD where we are only expanding the English lemmas using WSD; (g) PARL+EN-WSD+EGY-WC+MSA-WC where all three languages are expanded: EN using WSD, EGY and MSA are expanded using WC; and, (i) PARL+EN-WSD+EGY-SYN+MSA-SYN, similar to condition (g) but EGY and MSA are expanded using SYN.

3.5 Evaluation Metrics

We present the results in terms of Precision, Recall and the harmonic mean F1-score.

4 Results

Table 2 shows precision, recall and F1-score of different correspondent extraction setups (as described in Section 2) against BabelNet and Tharwa. The results reflect full exact match, where *TransDict* entries

Extraction Method	Precision	Recall	F1-score
PARL	79.15%	65.14%	71.46%
PARL+EGY-WC	84.51%	69.55%	76.3%
PARL+EGY-SYN	80.65%	66.37%	72.79%
PARL+MSA-WC	76.00%	67.9%	71.72%
PARL+MSA-SYN	78.31%	66.9%	72.19%
PARL+EN-WSD	79.30%	73.97%	76.54%
PARL+EN-WSD+EGY-WC+MSA-WC	82.99%	82.99%	**82.99%**
PARL+EN-WSD+EGY-SYN+MSA-SYN	79.95%	76.09%	77.97%

Table 3: Precision, Recall and F1-score of *TransDict* **dialectal component EGY** against Tharwa.

fully matched BabelNet/Tharwa entries including POS tag match. This is the harshest metric to evaluate against. We note the following observations. We note similar trends across the two evaluation data sets. In general recall is quite low for BabelNet compared to Tharwa which might be relegated to some domain divergence between our corpora and BabelNet resources where a word might not be out of vocabulary but a sense of a word is hence it is not found in *TransDict*. It should be noted that we only constrained the entries in the gold by being in vocabulary for our corpora without checking if the senses were in vocabulary. We don't observe this effect in Tharwa as much due to the relative sizes of BabelNet (almost 9K entries) and Tharwa (almost 20K entries). Expanding EN with WSD significantly improves the results (PARL F1-score is 34.01% vs. 49.27% for PARL+EN-WSD for BabelNet, and 60.63% for PARL vs. 65.3% for PARL+EN-WSD for Tharwa). This is the impact of significant increase in recall with little impact on precision. Expansion for MSA and EGY in general yield better results over the baseline in terms of overall F1-score. However expanding MSA negatively affects precision compared to recall. In general, WC expansion yields better results than SYN for EGY across both evaluation data sets. However we note that for MSA expansion, for Tharwa, SYN outperforms WC, contrasting with WC outperforming WC for MSA against BabelNet data. For both BabelNet and Tharwa evaluation sets, we note that the same condition PARL+EN-WSD+EGY-WC+MSA-WC yields the highest results of (54.46% and 71.71% F1-score, respectively).

5 Analysis and Discussion

5.1 Evaluating Dialectal Extraction Component

Most multilingual lexica are bilingual lexica, but in the current research atmosphere, many researchers would like to have true multilingual resources that go beyond a pair of languages at a time. Hence we evaluate the quality of adding a third language to an already existing bilingual resource. The method can be extended beyond 3 languages, but for sake of exposition we focus on adding a third language in the scope of this paper. Accordingly, we specifically measure the quality of the extracted EGY correspondents compared to a subset of the Tharwa lexicon. This reference subset must contain EGY-EN-MSA correspondents from our gold Tharwa that satisfy these constraints: 1) EGY correspondent is found in the EGY monolingual corpora, 2) MSA-EN correspondents match with at least one row in *TransDict* and 3) POS tag of the Tharwa row matches the POS tag of *TransDict* correspondents. Here, the first constraint avoids domain divergence between Tharwa and *TransDict*. Second constraint is applied because we focus on measuring quality of the EGY extraction component, thus fixing MSA-EN. Additionally, the POS constraint is meant to strengthen the match.

Table 3 demonstrates results of comparing *TransDict* dialectal extraction component with Tharwa. Results are assuring that performance of dialectal extraction component is persistently higher than quality of entire *TransDict* yielding highest F1-score of 82.99%. Similar to the trends observed in the overall evaluation, PARL+EN-WSD+EGY-WC+MSA-WC yields the highest performance.

5.2 POS Mapping Constraints and Number of Word Clusters

As mentioned in Section 2.1.1, we can prune noisy correspondents by applying POS constraints in the process of creating *TransDict*. Results demonstrated in Table 2 are obtained when exact POS match constraint is used, meaning only MSA-EN-EGY correspondents are included in *TransDict* that their MSA and EGY have exactly the same POS tags.

POS constraint	k=500			k=9228		
	Precision	Recall	F1-Score	Precision	Recall	F1-Score
No POS constraint	81.05%	66.52%	73.07%	79.04%	61.56%	69.21%
Relaxed POS match	82.13%	65.36%	72.79%	79.84%	61.51%	69.49%
Exact POS match	81.63%	63.94%	71.71%	79.61%	60.37%	68.67%

Table 4: Precision, Recall and F1-score of PARL+EN-WSD+EGY-WC+MSA-WC for different number of word clusters (k=500 and k=9228) and different POS constraints.

Tharwa Tuple			EGY variants generated by TransDict
EGY	MSA	EN	
		boy	cabAb, libon, Aibon, cAb, Tifol wAdiy, cab, bunay, waliyd, **wAd** EiyAl, fataY, janotalap, wilod, Eayil, walad
		child	**wAd,**daloE**, binot, bin, Aibon, Libon, IinojAb** xalof, Tifol, EiyAl, Tufuwlap, xilofap
wAd	walad		SaEobAn, mutoEib, Easiyr
		hard	qAsiy, qawiy, EaSiyb, **SAfiy**, taEobAn
jAmid	Sulob	solid	Sulob, qawiy
Oatiyliyh	macogal	operator	maSonaE, warocap

Table 5: Examples of EGY candidates generated by *TransDict* for some Tharwa entries.

In this section, we pick the best-performing setup from Table 2 (PARL+EN-WSD+EGY-WC+MSA-WC) and study effects of different POS matching constraints and also number of word clusters on the results. First row of Table 4 shows Precision, Recall and F1-score of evaluating PARL+EN-WSD+EGY-WC+MSA-WC against Tharwa when no constraint is applied on POS tags. Second row shows relaxed POS match results when we accept certain POS divergence patterns between MSA and EGY as a valid POS match.[5] Finally, the last row shows the match results for the case where only exactly the same POS tags on both EGY and MSA is included in *TransDict*.

In addition to different POS constraints, Table 4 shows results when different cluster sizes are exploited for monolingual expansion. The reason we choose k=9228 in addition to k=500 (which has been frequently used for clustering in the literature) is that it encodes total number of synsets in Arabic WordNet.

As shown in Table 4, F1-score generally decreases when POS match constraints increases. This mainly happens because system recall gradually drops when stricter POS constraints are applied. Therefore, we might dismiss some of the correct correspondents but we expect correspondents with higher purity in this case. Nonetheless, we notice precision increases in the relaxed mode as we are allowing for more divergence accommodation. On the other hand, we observe that the F1-score drops when number of clusters increases from 500 to 9228 (regardless of the POS constraint used). This suggests that despite getting purer clusters in the case of the 9228 setting, we are losing significant numbers of synonyms by fragmenting the semantic space too much potentially.

In order to measure the quality of EGY candidates generated by *TransDict* and also assess the feasibility of using this component to augment Tharwa with other dialects, we perform two manual assessments of the generated *TransDict* lexicon, assuming a partial match.

First, we compile a random sample of size 1000 from the matched *TransDict* entries with gold Tharwa rows, i.e. whose MSA-EN-EGY are found in *TransDict* Tharwa. We also have the corresponding list of other potential EGY candidates generated by *TransDict* for each row of this sample as augmented candidates. We obtain this augmented candidate list from two different setups: a) PARL+EN-WSD+EGY-WC+MSA+WC with 500 clusters, and b) PARL+EN-WSD+EGY-WC+MSA-WC with 9228 clusters.

An expert annotator is asked to manually assess the list of augmented EGY candidates and decide how many candidates in the list are actual synonyms of the gold EGY word. Manual annotation shows that on average 6.6% of EGY candidates provided by *TransDict* in each row are actual synonyms of the gold EGY word in the 500 cluster setup (a). The match percentage increases to **21.6%** for the second

---

[5]Mapping table is provided as supplementary material.

setup, the 9228 clusters case (b). This shows that increasing the number of clusters makes the matched clusters more pure. The remaining irrelevant (non-synonym) candidates are caused by either erroneous word alignments or lack of efficient pruning criteria in the correspondence learning algorithm.

Second, we carry out an analysis to assess the potential for augmenting Tharwa with generated EGY correspondents. We create a random sample of size 1000 from Tharwa rows where their MSA-EN is found in *TransDict* (EN expansion setup) but none of *TransDict* EGY candidates matches with Tharwa gold EGY (non-matched rows, i.e. our errors). Here, the annotator was asked to mark EGY candidates (generated by *TransDict*) that are synonyms of the *TransDict* generated EGY word. According to our manual assessment by an expert, **78.1%** of the rows in the given sample contained at least one synonym of the gold EGY word. Hence, we expect that the actual matching accuracy over the entire gold Tharwa is 93.8%.

Table 5 shows list of EGY candidates generated by *TransDict* for different EN senses of two MSA-EGY tuples in Tharwa.[6] For the first tuple, where we found a match with Tharwa, wAd (EGY)-walad (MSA), we show the list of words that were found in *TransDict*. We note that we for both the EN corresponding senses *boy* and *child*, the EGY word wAd is listed and highlighted in boldface. We also note the correspondents yielded in *TransDict* rendered in red in the Table to indicate that they are different senses that are not correct for the triple. For example the word *janotalap* is slang for *polite* which is could be pragmatically related to *boy* as in not a polite way to call on a man for example. The highlighted words in the Table show incorrect sense correspondences given the entire tuple. These could have resulted from sense variations in the pivot EN word such as correspondents of *child* in the case of *binot*, meaning *girl/child/daughter* and that given our techniques would naturally cluster with *wAd* as in the female of *boy/child/son*. We also see related words such as *daloE* meaning *pampering*. For example, *wAdiy* is a synonym of *wAd* meaning *valley* however, not *child*. Accordingly, errors observed are a result of various sources of noise: misalignments, sense divergences for any of the three languages, differences in vowelization between the EGY resources. The second tuple in Table 5 shows cases where no matches are found with Tharwa in *TransDict*, yet the resulting *TransDict* entries comprise correct correspondents but they are not covered in Tharwa hence they are viable candidates for augmention. The third tuple in the Table shows cases where the entry in Tharwa is incorrect and would need to be corrected. For example, the English word should have been *workshop* not *operator*. Thereby highlighting these partial matches allows for a faster turn around in fixing the underlying lexicon Tharwa.

We finally attempt to assess the amount of possible augmentation of whole entries to Tharwa for completely unseen triplets and verify their validity. We compile a list of a 1000 triplets generated in *TransDict* where none of the word types (EN, EGY, MSA) is seen in any entry in Tharwa. 85% of these entries are considered correct by the expert lexicographer.

6 Conclusion

We presented a new approach for automatic verification and augmentation of multilingual lexica leveraging evidence extracted from parallel and monolingual corpora. Extracted multilingual correspondents can be used to verify lexicon converge and detect errors. We showed that our approach reaches F1-score of 71.71% in generating correct correspondents for a gold subset of a three way lexicon (Tharwa) without any human intervention in the cycle. We also demonstrated that our approach reaches F1-score of 54.46% in generating correct correspondents for Arabic entries in BabelNet.

Acknowledgements

This work was supported by the Google Faculty Award 2015-2016. We would like to acknowledge the useful comments by two anonymous reviewers who helped in making this publication more concise and better presented.

---

[6]Arabic examples in Table 5 are shown according to safe Buckwalter scheme to avoid some of the special characters in the original Buckwalter encoding.

References

William Black, Sabri Elkateb, Horacio Rodriguez, Musa Alkhalifa, Piek Vossen, Adam Pease, and Christiane Fellbaum. 2006. Introducing the arabic wordnet project. In *Proceedings of the third international WordNet conference*, pages 295–300. Citeseer.

G. De Melo and G. Weikum. 2009. Towards a universal wordnet by learning from combined evidence. In *Proceedings of the 18th ACM conference on Information and knowledge management*, pages 513–522. ACM.

Mona Diab, Mohamed Al-Badrashiny, Maryam Aminian, Mohammed Attia, Pradeep Dasigi, Heba Elfardy, Ramy Eskander, Nizar Habash, Abdelati Hawwari, and Wael Salloum. 2014. Tharwa: A Large Scale Dialectal Arabic-Standard Arabic-English Lexicon. In *LREC*.

Manaal Faruqui and Chris Dyer. 2014. Improving vector space word representations using multilingual correlation. In *Proceedings of EACL*.

Christiane Fellbaum. 1998. *WordNet*. Wiley Online Library.

Tomas Mikolov, Kai Chen, Greg Corrado, and Jeffrey Dean. 2013. Efficient estimation of word representations in vector space. *arXiv preprint arXiv:1301.3781*.

Roberto Navigli and Simone Paolo Ponzetto. 2012. Babelnet: The automatic construction, evaluation and application of a wide-coverage multilingual semantic network. *Artificial Intelligence*, 193:217–250.

Franz Josef Och and Hermann Ney. 2000. Improved statistical alignment models. In *Proceedings of the 38th Annual Meeting on Association for Computational Linguistics*, pages 440–447. Association for Computational Linguistics.

Robert Parker, David Graff, Junbo Kong, Ke Chen, and Kazuaki Maeda. 2011. English gigaword fifth edition.

Arfath Pasha, Mohamed Al-Badrashiny, Mona Diab, Ahmed El Kholy, Ramy Eskander, Nizar Habash, Manoj Pooleery, Owen Rambow, and Ryan M. Roth. 2014. MADAMIRA: A Fast, Comprehensive Tool for Morphological Analysis and Disambiguation of Arabic. In *Proceedings of LREC*, Reykjavik, Iceland.

Ted Pedersen, Satanjeev Banerjee, and Siddharth Patwardhan. 2005. Maximizing semantic relatedness to perform word sense disambiguation. *University of Minnesota supercomputing institute research report UMSI*, 25:2005.

Benoît Sagot and Darja Fišer. 2011a. Classification-based extension of wordnets from heterogeneous resources. In *Human Language Technology Challenges for Computer Science and Linguistics*, pages 396–407. Springer.

Benoît Sagot and Darja Fišer. 2011b. Extending wordnets by learning from multiple resources. In *LTC'11: 5th Language and Technology Conference*.

Benoît Sagot and Darja Fišer. 2012. Automatic extension of wolf. In *GWC2012-6th International Global Wordnet Conference*.

I. Saleh and N. Habash. 2009. Automatic extraction of lemma-based bilingual dictionaries for morphologically rich languages. In *Third Workshop on Computational Approaches to Arabic Script-based Languages at the MT Summit XII*, Ottawa, Canada.

Helmut Schmid. 1995. Treetagger— a language independent part-of-speech tagger. *Institut für Maschinelle Sprachverarbeitung, Universität Stuttgart*, 43:28.

Faster decoding for subword level Phrase-based SMT between related languages

Anoop Kunchukuttan, Pushpak Bhattacharyya
Center For Indian Language Technology,
Department of Computer Science & Engineering
Indian Institute of Technology Bombay
{anoopk,pb}@cse.iitb.ac.in

Abstract

A common and effective way to train translation systems between related languages is to consider sub-word level basic units. However, this increases the length of the sentences resulting in increased decoding time. The increase in length is also impacted by the specific choice of data format for representing the sentences as subwords. In a phrase-based SMT framework, we investigate different choices of *decoder parameters* as well as *data format* and their impact on decoding time and translation accuracy. We suggest best options for these settings that significantly improve decoding time with little impact on the translation accuracy.

1 Introduction

Related languages are those that exhibit lexical and structural similarities on account of sharing a **common ancestry** or being in **contact for a long period of time** (Bhattacharyya et al., 2016). Examples of languages related by common ancestry are Slavic and Indo-Aryan languages. Prolonged contact leads to convergence of linguistic properties even if the languages are not related by ancestry and could lead to the formation of *linguistic areas* (Thomason, 2000). Examples of such linguistic areas are the Indian subcontinent (Emeneau, 1956), Balkan (Trubetzkoy, 1928) and Standard Average European (Haspelmath, 2001) linguistic areas. Both forms of language relatedness lead to related languages sharing vocabulary and structural features.

There is substantial government, commercial and cultural communication among people speaking related languages (Europe, India and South-East Asia being prominent examples and linguistic regions in Africa possibly in the future). As these regions integrate more closely and move to a digital society, translation between *related* languages is becoming an important requirement. In addition, translation to/from related languages to a *lingua franca* like English is also very important. However, in spite of significant communication between people speaking related languages, most of these languages have few parallel corpora resources. It is therefore important to leverage the relatedness of these languages to build good-quality statistical machine translation (SMT) systems given the lack of parallel corpora.

Modelling the lexical similarity among related languages is the key to building good-quality SMT systems with limited parallel corpora. **Lexical similarity** implies that the languages share many words with the similar form (spelling/pronunciation) and meaning *e.g.* blindness is andhapana in Hindi, aandhaLepaNaa in Marathi. These words could be cognates, lateral borrowings or loan words from other languages.

Sub-word level transformations are an effective way for translation of such shared words. Using subwords as basic units of translation has been shown to be effective in improving translation quality with limited parallel corpora. Subword units like character (Vilar et al., 2007; Tiedemann, 2009a), character n-gram (Tiedemann and Nakov, 2013) and orthographic syllables (Kunchukuttan and Bhattacharyya, 2016) have been explored and have been shown to improve translation quality to varying degrees.

Proceedings of the Third Workshop on NLP for Similar Languages, Varieties and Dialects,
pages 82–88, Osaka, Japan, December 12 2016.

Original	this is an example of data formats for segmentation
Subword units	thi s i s a n e xa m p le o f da ta fo rma t s fo r se gme n ta tio n
Internal Marker	thi_ s i_ s a_ n e_ xa_ m_ p_ le o_ f da_ ta fo_ rma_ t_ s fo_ r se_ gme_ n_ ta_ tio_ n
Boundary Marker	thi s_ i s_ a n_ e xa m p le_ o f_ da ta_ fo rma t s_ fo r_ se gme n ta tio n_
Space Marker	thi s _ i s _ a n _ e xa m p le _ o f _ da ta _ fo rma t s _ fo r _ se gme n ta tio n

Table 1: Formats for sentence representation with subword units (example of orthographic syllables)

However, the use of subword units increases the sentence length. This increases the training, tuning and decoding time for phrase-based SMT systems by an order of magnitude. This makes experimentation costly and time-consuming and impedes faster feedback which is important for machine translation research. Higher decoding time also makes deployment of MT systems based on subword units impractical.

In this work, we systematically study the choice of data format for representing sentences and various decoder parameters which affect decoding time. Our studies show that the use of cube-pruning during tuning as well as testing with a lower value of the stack pop limit parameter improves decoding time substantially with minimal change in translation quality.

The rest of the paper is organized as follows. Section 2 discusses the factors that affect decoding time which have been studied in this paper. Section 3 discusses our experimental setup. Section 4 discusses the results of our experiments with decoder parameters. Section 5 discusses the results of our experiments with corpus formats. Section 6 discusses prior work related to optimizing decoders for phrase-based SMT. Section 7 concludes the paper.

2 Factors affecting decoding time

This section describes the factors affecting the decoding time that have been studied in this paper.

2.1 Unit of translation

The decoding time for a sentence is proportional to length of the sentence (in terms of the basic units). Use of subword units will obviously result in increased sentence length. Various units have been proposed for translation (character, character n-gram, orthographic syllable, morpheme, etc.). We analysed the average length of the input sentence on four language pairs (Hindi-Malayalam, Malayalam-Hindi, Bengali-Hindi, Telugu-Malayalam) on the ILCI corpus (Jha, 2012). The average length of an input sentence for character-level representation is 7 times of the word-level input, while it is 4 times the word-level input for orthographic syllable level representation. So, the decoding time will increase substantially.

2.2 Format for sentence representation

The length of the sentence to be decoded also depends on how the subword units are represented. We compare three popular formats for representation, which are illustrated in Table 1:

- **Boundary Marker**: The subword at the boundary of a word is augmented with a marker character. There is one boundary subword, either the first or the last chosen as per convention. Such a representation has been used in previous work, mostly related to morpheme level representation.

- **Internal Marker**: Every subword internal to the word is augmented with a marker character. This representation has been used rarely, one example being the Byte Code Encoding representation used by University of Edinburgh's Neural Machine Translation system (Williams et al., 2016; Sennrich et al., 2016).

- **Space Marker**: The subword units are not altered, but inter-word boundary is represented by a space marker. Most work on translation between related languages has used this format.

For boundary and internal markers, the addition of the marker character does not change the sentence length, but can create two representations for some subwords (corresponding to internal and boundary positions), thus introducing some data sparsity. On the other hand, space marker doubles the sentence length (in terms in words), but each subword has a unique representation.

2.3 Decoder Parameters

Given the basic unit and the data format, some important decoder parameters used to control the search space can affect decoding time. The decoder is essentially a search algorithm, and we investigated important settings related to two search algorithms used in the *Moses* SMT system: (i) stack decoding, (ii) cube-pruning (Chiang, 2007). We investigated the following parameters:

- **Beam Size**: This parameter controls the size of beam which maintains the best partial translation hypotheses generated at any point during stack decoding.

- **Table Limit**: Every source phrase in the phrase table can have multiple translation options. This parameter controls how many of these options are considered during stack decoding.

- **Cube Pruning Pop Limit**: In the case of cube pruning, the parameter limits the number of hypotheses created for each stack .

Having a lower value for each of these parameters reduces the search space, thus reducing the decoding time. However, reducing the search space may increase search errors and decrease translation quality. Our work studies this time-quality trade-off.

3 Experimental Setup

In this section, we describe the language pairs and datasets used, the details of our experiments and evaluation methodology.

3.1 Languages and Dataset

We experimented with four language pairs (Bengali-Hindi, Malayalam-Hindi, Hindi-Malayalam and Telugu-Malayalam). Telugu and Malayalam belong to the Dravidian language family which are agglutinative. Bengali and Hindi are Indo-Aryan languages with a relatively poor morphology. The language pairs chosen cover different combinations of morphological complexity between source and target languages.

We used the multilingual ILCI corpus for our experiments (Jha, 2012), consisting of sentences from tourism and health domains. The data split is as follows – *training: 44,777, tuning: 1000, test: 500* sentences.

3.2 System details

As an example of subword level representation unit, we have studied the orthographic syllable (OS) (Kunchukuttan and Bhattacharyya, 2016) in our experiments. The OS is a linguistically motivated, variable length unit of translation, which consists of one or more consonants followed by a vowel (a $C^{+}V$ unit). But our methodology is not specific to any subword unit. Hence, the results and observations should hold for other subword units also. We used the *Indic NLP Library*[1] for orthographic syllabification.

Phrase-based SMT systems were trained with OS as the basic unit. We used the *Moses* system (Koehn et al., 2007), with *mgiza*[2] for alignment, the *grow-diag-final-and* heuristic for symmetrization of word alignments, and Batch MIRA (Cherry and Foster, 2012) for tuning. Since data sparsity is a lesser concern due to small vocabulary size and higher order n-grams are generally trained for translation using subword units (Vilar et al., 2007), we trained 10-gram language models. The language model was trained on the training split of the target language corpus.

---

[1] http://anoopkunchukuttan.github.io/indic_nlp_library
[2] https://github.com/moses-smt/mgiza

	Translation Accuracy				Relative Decoding Time			
	ben-hin	hin-mal	mal-hin	tel-mal	ben-hin	hin-mal	mal-hin	tel-mal
default (stack, tl=20,ss=100)	33.10	11.68	19.86	9.39	46.44	65.98	87.98	76.68
Stack								
tl=10	32.84	11.24	19.21	9.47	35.49	48.37	67.32	80.51
tl=5	32.54	11.01	18.39	9.29	15.05	21.46	30.60	41.52
ss=50	33.10	11.69	19.89	9.36	17.33	25.81	35.76	43.45
ss=10	33.04	11.52	19.51	9.38	4.49	7.32	10.18	11.75
+tuning	32.83	11.01	19.57	9.23	5.24	8.85	11.60	9.31
Cube Pruning								
pl=1000	33.05	11.47	19.66	9.42	5.67	9.29	12.38	17.85
+tuning	33.12	11.3	19.77	9.35	7.68	13.06	15.18	14.56
pl=100	32.86	10.97	18.74	9.15	2.00	4.22	5.41	5.29
pl=10	31.93	9.42	15.26	8.5	1.51	3.64	4.57	3.84
Word-level	31.62	9.67	15.69	7.54	100.56 ms	65.12 ms	50.72 ms	42.4 ms

Table 2: Translation accuracy and Relative decoding time for orthographic syllable level translation using different decoding methods and parameters. Relative decoding time is indicated as a multiple of word-level decoding time. The following methods & parameters in *Moses* have been experimented with: (i) *normal stack decoding* - vary ss: stack-size, tt: table-limit; (ii) *cube pruning*: vary pl:cube-pruning-pop-limit. +tuning indicates that the decoder settings mentioned on previous row were used for tuning too. Translation accuracy and decode time per sentence for word-level decoding (in milliseconds) is shown on the last line for comparison.

The PBSMT systems were trained and decoded on a server with Intel Xeon processors (2.5 GHz) and 256 GB RAM.

3.3 Evaluation

We use BLEU (Papineni et al., 2002) for evaluating translation accuracy. We use the sum of user and system time minus the time for loading the phrase table (all reported by Moses) to determine the time taken for decoding the test set.

4 Effect of decoder parameters

We observed that the decoding time for OS-level models is approximately 70 times of the word-level model. This explosion in the decoding time makes translation highly compute intensive and difficult to perform in real-time. It also makes tuning MT systems very slow since tuning typically requires multiple decoding runs over the tuning set. Hence, we experimented with some heuristics to speed up decoding.

For normal stack decoding, two decoder parameters which impact the decode time are: (1) *beam size* of the hypothesis stack, and (2) *table-limit*: the number of translation options for each source phrase considered by the decoder. Since the vocabulary of the OS-level model is far less than that of the word-level model, we hypothesize that lower values for these parameters can reduce the decoding time without significantly affecting the accuracy. Table 2 shows the results of varying these parameters. We can see that with a beam size of 10, the decoding time is now about 9 times that of word-level decoding. This is a 7x improvement in decoding time over the default parameters, while the translation accuracy drops by less than 1%. If a beam size of 10 is used while decoding too, the drop in translation accuracy is larger (2.5%). Using this beam size during decoding also slightly reduces the translation accuracy. On the other hand, reducing the table-limit significantly reduces the translation accuracy, while resulting in lesser gains in decoding time.

We also experimented with *cube-pruning* (Chiang, 2007), a faster decoding method first proposed for use with hierarchical PBSMT. The decoding time is controlled by the pop-limit parameter in the Moses implementation of cube-pruning. With a pop-limit of 1000, the decoding time is about 12 times

	Translation Accuracy				Relative Decoding Time			
	ben-hin	hin-mal	mal-hin	tel-mal	ben-hin	hin-mal	mal-hin	tel-mal
default (stack, tl=20,ss=100)	27.29	6.72	12.69	6.06	206.98	391.00	471.96	561.00
Cube Pruning pl=1000	26.98	6.57	11.94	5.99	10.23	19.57	24.59	26.20
Word-level	31.62	9.67	15.69	7.54	100.56 ms	65.12 ms	50.72 ms	42.4 ms

Table 3: Translation accuracy and Relative decoding time for character level translation using different decoding methods and parameters. Relative decoding time is indicated as a multiple of word-level decoding time. Translation accuracy and decode time per sentence for word-level decoding (in milliseconds) is shown on the last line for comparison.

	Translation Accuracy				Relative Decoding Time			
	ben-hin	hin-mal	mal-hin	tel-mal	ben-hin	hin-mal	mal-hin	tel-mal
Boundary Marker	32.83	**12.00**	**20.88**	9.02	**7.44**	11.80	17.08	18.98
Internal Marker	30.10	10.53	19.08	7.53	7.82	**10.81**	**14.43**	17.06
Space Marker	**33.12**	11.30	19.77	**9.35**	7.68	13.06	15.18	**14.56**
Word-level	31.62	9.67	15.69	7.54	100.56 ms	65.12 ms	50.72 ms	42.4 ms

Table 4: Translation accuracy and Relative decoding time for orthographic syllable level translation using different data formats. Relative decoding time is indicated as a multiple of word-level decoding time. Translation accuracy and decode time per sentence (in milliseconds) for word-level decoding is shown on the last line for comparison.

that of word-level decoding. The drop in translation accuracy is about 1% with a 6x improvement over default stack decoding, even when the model is tuned with a pop-limit of 1000. Using this pop-limit during tuning also hardly impacts the translation accuracy. However, lower values of pop-limit reduce the translation accuracy.

While our experiments primarily concentrated on OS as the unit of translation, we also compared the performance of stack decoding and cube pruning for character lavel models. The results are shown in Table 3. We see that character level models are 4-5 times slower than OS level models and hundreds of time slower than word level models with the default stack decoding. In the case of character based models also, the use of cube pruning (with `pop-limit=1000`) substantially speeds up decoding (20x speedup) with only a small drop in BLEU score.

To summarize, we show that reducing the beam size for stack decoding as well as using cube pruning help to improve decoding speed significantly, with only a marginal drop in translation accuracy. Using cube-pruning while tuning only marginally impacts translation accuracy.

5   Effect of corpus format

For these experiments, we used the following decoder parameters: cube-pruning with cube-pruning-pop-limit=1000 for tuning as well as testing. Table 4 shows the results of our experiments with different corpus formats.

The internal boundary marker format has a lower translation accuracy compared to the other two formats whose translation accuracies are comparable. In terms of decoding time, no single format is better than the others across all languages. Hence, it is recommended to use the space or boundary marker format for phrase-based SMT systems. Neural MT systems based on encoder decoder architectures, particularly without attention mechanism, are more sensitive to sentence length, so we presume that the boundary marker format may be more appropriate.

6 Related Work

It has been recognized in the past literature on translation between related languages that the increased length of subword level translation is challenge for training as well as decoding (Vilar et al., 2007). Aligning long sentences is computationally expensive, hence most work has concentrated on corpora with short sentences (*e.g.* OPUS (Tiedemann, 2009b)) (Tiedemann, 2009a; Nakov and Tiedemann, 2012; Tiedemann, 2012). To make alignment feasible, Vilar et al. (2007) used the phrase table learnt from word-level alignment, which will have shorter parallel segments, as parallel corpus for training subword-level models. Tiedemann and Nakov (2013) also investigated reducing the size of the phrase table by pruning, which actually improved translation quality for character level models. The authors have not reported the decoding speed, but it is possible that pruning may also improve decoding speed since fewer hypothesis may have to be looked up in the phrase table, and smaller phrase tables can be loaded into memory.

There has been a lot of work looking at optimizing specific components of SMT decoders in a general setting. Hoang et al. (2016) provide a good overview of various approaches to optimizing decoders. Some of the prominent efforts include efficient language models (Heafield, 2011), lazy loading (Zens and Ney, 2007), phrase-table design (Junczys-Dowmunt, 2012), multi-core environment issues (Fernández et al., 2016), efficient memory allocation (Hoang et al., 2016), alternative stack configurations (Hoang et al., 2016) and alternative decoding algorithms like cube pruning (Chiang, 2007).

In this work, we have investigated stack decoding configurations and cube pruning as a way of optimizing decoder performance for the translation between related languages (with subword units and monotone decoding). Prior work on comparing stack decoding and cube-pruning has been limited to word-level models (Huang and Chiang, 2007; Heafield et al., 2014).

7 Conclusion and Future Work

We systematically study the choice of data format for representing subword units in sentences and various decoder parameters which affect decoding time in a phrase-based SMT setting. Our studies (using OS and character as basic units) show that the **use of cube-pruning during tuning as well as testing with a lower value of the stack pop limit parameter** improves decoding time substantially with minimal change in translation quality. Two data formats, the space marker and the boundary marker, perform roughly equivalently in terms of translation accuracy as well as decoding time. Since the tuning step contains a decoder in the loop, these settings also reduce the tuning time. We plan to investigate reduction of the time required for alignment.

Acknowledgments

We thank the Technology Development for Indian Languages (TDIL) Programme and the Department of Electronics & Information Technology, Govt. of India for their support. We also thank the anonymous reviewers for their feedback.

References

Pushpak Bhattacharyya, Mitesh Khapra, and Anoop Kunchukuttan. 2016. Statistical machine translation between related languages. In *NAACL Tutorials*.

Colin Cherry and George Foster. 2012. Batch tuning strategies for statistical machine translation. In *Proceedings of the 2012 Conference of the North American Chapter of the Association for Computational Linguistics: Human Language Technologies*.

David Chiang. 2007. Hierarchical phrase-based translation. *Computational Linguistics*, June.

Murray B Emeneau. 1956. India as a lingustic area. *Language*.

M Fernández, Juan C Pichel, José C Cabaleiro, and Tomás F Pena. 2016. Boosting performance of a statistical machine translation system using dynamic parallelism. *Journal of Computational Science*.

Martin Haspelmath. 2001. The european linguistic area: Standard average european. In *Language Typology and Language Universals*.

Kenneth Heafield, Michael Kayser, and Christopher D Manning. 2014. Faster phrase-based decoding by refining feature state. In *Annual Meeting-Association For Computational Linguistics*, pages 130–135.

Kenneth Heafield. 2011. Kenlm: Faster and smaller language model queries. In *Proceedings of the Sixth Workshop on Statistical Machine Translation*.

Hieu Hoang, Nikolay Bogoychev, Lane Schwartz, and Marcin Junczys-Dowmunt. 2016. Fast, scalable phrase-based smt decoding. In *arXiv Pre-print arXiv:1610.04265*.

Liang Huang and David Chiang. 2007. Forest rescoring: Faster decoding with integrated language models. In *Annual Meeting-Association For Computational Linguistics*.

Girish Nath Jha. 2012. The TDIL program and the Indian Language Corpora Initiative. In *Language Resources and Evaluation Conference*.

Marcin Junczys-Dowmunt. 2012. A space-efficient phrase table implementation using minimal perfect hash functions. In *International Conference on Text, Speech and Dialogue*.

Philipp Koehn, Hieu Hoang, Alexandra Birch, Chris Callison-Burch, Marcello Federico, Nicola Bertoldi, Brooke Cowan, Wade Shen, Christine Moran, Richard Zens, et al. 2007. Moses: Open source toolkit for statistical machine translation. In *Proceedings of the 45th Annual Meeting of the ACL on Interactive Poster and Demonstration Sessions*.

Anoop Kunchukuttan and Pushpak Bhattacharyya. 2016. Orthographic syllable as basic unit for smt between related languages. In *Empirical Methods in Natural Language Processing*.

Preslav Nakov and Jörg Tiedemann. 2012. Combining word-level and character-level models for machine translation between closely-related languages. In *Proceedings of the 50th Annual Meeting of the Association for Computational Linguistics: Short Papers-Volume 2*.

Kishore Papineni, Salim Roukos, Todd Ward, and Wei-Jing Zhu. 2002. Bleu: a method for automatic evaluation of machine translation. In *Proceedings of the 40th annual meeting on association for computational linguistics*, pages 311–318. Association for Computational Linguistics.

Rico Sennrich, Barry Haddow, and Alexandra Birch. 2016. Neural machine translation of rare words with subword units. In *ACL*.

Sarah Thomason. 2000. Linguistic areas and language history. In *lLanguages in Contact*.

Jörg Tiedemann and Preslav Nakov. 2013. Analyzing the use of character-level translation with sparse and noisy datasets. In *RANLP*.

Jörg Tiedemann. 2009a. Character-based psmt for closely related languages. In *Proceedings of the 13th Conference of the European Association for Machine Translation (EAMT 2009)*.

Jörg Tiedemann. 2009b. News from opus-a collection of multilingual parallel corpora with tools and interfaces. In *Recent advances in natural language processing*.

Jörg Tiedemann. 2012. Character-based pivot translation for under-resourced languages and domains. In *Proceedings of the 13th Conference of the European Chapter of the Association for Computational Linguistics*.

Nikolai Trubetzkoy. 1928. Proposition 16. In *Actes du premier congres international des linguistes La Haye*.

David Vilar, Jan-T Peter, and Hermann Ney. 2007. Can we translate letters? In *Proceedings of the Second Workshop on Statistical Machine Translation*.

Philip Williams, Rico Sennrich, Maria Nadejde, Matthias Huck, Barry Haddow, and Ondrej Bojar. 2016. Edinburghs statistical machine translation systems for wmt16. In *Proceedings of the First Conference on Machine Translation*.

Richard Zens and Hermann Ney. 2007. Efficient phrase-table representation for machine translation with applications to online mt and speech translation. In *HLT-NAACL*.

Subdialectal Differences in Sorani Kurdish

Shervin Malmasi[1,2]
[1] Harvard Medical School, Boston, MA 02115, USA
[2] Macquarie University, Sydney, NSW, Australia
`shervin.malmasi@mq.edu.au`

Abstract

In this study we apply classification methods for detecting subdialectal differences in Sorani Kurdish texts produced in different regions, namely Iran and Iraq. As Sorani is a low-resource language, no corpus including texts from different regions was readily available. To this end, we identified data sources that could be leveraged for this task to create a dataset of 200,000 sentences. Using surface features, we attempted to classify Sorani subdialects, showing that sentences from news sources in Iraq and Iran are distinguishable with 96% accuracy. This is the first preliminary study for a dialect that has not been widely studied in computational linguistics, evidencing the possible existence of distinct subdialects.

1 Introduction

Language Identification (LID) is the task of determining the language of a given text, which may be at the document, sub-document or even sentence level. Recently, attention has turned to discriminating between close languages, such as Malay-Indonesian and Croatian-Serbian (Ljubešić et al., 2007), or even dialects or varieties of one language (British *vs.* American English). LID has several useful applications including lexicography, authorship profiling, machine translation and Information Retrieval. Another example is the application of the output from these LID methods to adapt NLP tools that require annotated data, such as part-of-speech taggers, for resource-poor languages. This will be further discussed in §2.2.

The primary aim of this work is to apply classification methods to regional variants of Central Kurdish, also known as Sorani. Kurdish is a low-resourced but important language. It is classified within a group of "non-Western European languages critical to U.S. national security".[1] In recent years there has been increasing research interest in processing Kurdish (Aliabadi, 2014; Esmaili et al., 2014).

As we will outline in §3, Kurdish is spoken in a number of countries and has several dialects. Sorani is one of these dialects and is spoken in several regions. The main objective of this study is to determine whether subdialectal variations in Sorani can be identified in texts produced from different regions. More specifically, we consider the two main areas where Sorani is spoken, Iran and Iraq.

As the first such study, we identify the relevant data sources and attempt to establish the performance of currently used classification methods on this dialect. We also make available a dataset of 200,000 Sorani sentences to facilitate future research. We approach this task at the sentence-level by developing a corpus of sentences from different regions in §4 and applying classification methods.

2 Related Work and Background

2.1 Language and Variety Identification

Work in language identification (LID) dates back to the seminal work of Beesley (1988), Dunning (1994) and Cavnar and Trenkle (1994). Automatic LID methods have since been widely used in NLP. Although LID can be extremely accurate in distinguishing languages that use distinct character sets (e.g. Chinese or Japanese) or are very dissimilar (e.g. Spanish and Swedish), performance is degraded when it is used for discriminating similar languages or dialects.

[1] `https://www.nsep.gov/content/critical-languages`

Proceedings of the Third Workshop on NLP for Similar Languages, Varieties and Dialects,
pages 89–96, Osaka, Japan, December 12 2016.

This has led to researchers turning their attention to the sub-problem of discriminating between closely-related languages and varieties. This issue has been investigated in the context of confusable languages/dialects, including Malay-Indonesian (Bali, 2006), Croatian-Slovene-Serbian (Ljubešić et al., 2007), Bosnian-Croatian-Serbian (Tiedemann and Ljubešić, 2012), Farsi-Dari (Malmasi and Dras, 2015a) and Chinese varieties (Huang and Lee, 2008).

This issue was also the focus of the recent "Discriminating Similar Language" (DSL) shared task.[2] The shared task used data from 13 different languages and varieties divided into 6 sub-groups and teams needed to build systems for distinguishing these classes. They were provided with a training and development dataset comprised of 20,000 sentences from each language and an unlabelled test set of 1,000 sentences per language was used for evaluation. Most entries used surface features and many applied hierarchical classifiers, taking advantage of the structure provided by the language family memberships of the 13 classes. More details can be found in the shared task report (Zampieri et al., 2014).[3]

Although LID has been investigated using data from many languages, to our knowledge, the present study is the first treatment of Sorani within this context.

2.2 Applications of LID

Further to determining the language of documents, LID has applications in statistical machine translation, lexicography (e.g. inducing dialect-to-dialect lexicons) and authorship profiling in the forensic linguistics domain. In an Information Retrieval context it can help filter documents (e.g. news articles or search results) by language and even dialect; one such example is presented by (Bergsma et al., 2012) where LID is used for creating language-specific Twitter collections.

LID serves as an important preprocessing method for other NLP tasks. This includes selecting appropriate models for machine translation, sentiment analysis or other types of text analysis, *e.g.* Native Language Identification (Malmasi et al., 2013; Malmasi and Dras, 2015b).

LID can also be used in the adaptation of NLP tools, such as part-of-speech taggers for low-resourced languages (Feldman et al., 2006). If Sorani subdialects are too different to directly share the same resources and statistical models, the distinguishing features identified through LID can assist in adapting existing resources for one subdialect to another.

3   Kurdish Language Overview

Spoken by twenty to thirty million Kurds (Haig and Matras, 2002; Esmaili and Salavati, 2013; Salih, 2014; Blau, 2016; Kurdish Academy of Language, 2016), "Kurdish" as a language is nonetheless not easily defined, producing both difficulty and debate for many scholars and researchers (Haig and Matras, 2002; Hassani and Medjedovic, 2016; Paul, 2008). Kurdish, spoken in "Kurdistan" (a region split primarily among Turkey, Iran, Iraq and Syria (Esmaili and Salavati, 2013; Haig and Matras, 2002)), has been embroiled in conflict, so the question of Kurdish linguistic boundaries is complicated by political, cultural and historical factors (Paul, 2008).

One reason for disagreement about the Kurdish language is that Kurdish ethnic identity plays a large role in shaping who claims to speak "Kurdish" (Paul, 2008), and Kurdish ethnic identity is highly politicized (Nerwiy, 2012), especially with regards to a singular "Kurdish language" or plural "Kurdish languages" (Kurdish Academy of Language, 2016; Paul, 2008). While being described as a "dialect-rich language, sometimes referred to as a dialect continuum" (Esmaili and Salavati, 2013), the very act of categorizing a "Kurdish" dialect as a separate language or a separate language as a "Kurdish" dialect is contentious. Further complicating the Kurdish language is its precarious situation in recent history: Kurdish is recognized as an official language in Iraq (Hassani and Medjedovic, 2016), but its pedagogy and use have also been banned in Turkey and Syria (Blau, 2016; Nerwiy, 2012; Salih, 2014).

---

[2]Held at the Workshop on Applying NLP Tools to Similar Languages, Varieties and Dialects, co-located w/ COLING 2014.
[3]The task was also expanded and held in 2015 and 2016.

3.1 Geography

Historically, Kurdistan was divided into North and South by the Byzantine and Islamic empires and into Northwest and East by the Ottoman and Persian empires (Nerwiy, 2012). After World War I, Kurdistan was divided among Turkey, Persia, Iraq and Syria (Blau, 2009). Kurds have also lived in Armenia, Lebanon and Egypt for centuries and have formed strong diasporic communities in Europe and North America (Haig and Matras, 2002; Hassani and Medjedovic, 2016).

Most Kurds are bilingual or multilingual, speaking other languages like Arabic, Turkish or Farsi in addition to Kurdish (Salih, 2014). Having been immersed in multilingual contexts for centuries, Kurds—presumably Kurdish speakers—have interacted closely with speakers of Arabic, Armenian, Persian, New Aramaic and Turkish, which have all left traces in the Kurdish language (Haig and Matras, 2002).

3.2 Language Family

Kurdish belongs to the Indo-European family of languages within the northwestern Iranian group (Kurdish Academy of Language, 2016; Nerwiy, 2012; Paul, 2008), though it may also be described as only solidly belonging to a western subgroup of Iranian languages encompassing Persian, Kurdish, Balōči and the other Iranian languages of present-day Iran (Paul, 2008). An important isogloss shared among Persian, Kurdish and Balōči in contrast with many northwestern Iranian languages is the past stem of many verbs formed with the vowel i (Paul, 2008).

Still, relations of borrowing and influence within the western Iranian languages—that is, between Kurdish, Persian and Balōči (and Zazaki and Gurani as different from Kurdish, dependent upon the classification system)—are complex and not always straightforward based upon phonological and morphological evidence (Paul, 2008).

3.3 Dialects

Kurdish dialects are highly differentiated and are not mutually intelligible (Paul, 2008). It has even been suggested that the two main dialects (the Northern and Central dialects) of Kurdish can be treated as separate languages (Haig and Matras, 2002).

For both political and linguistic reasons, both Kurds and scholars have disagreed as to how Kurdish dialects should best be taxonomized (Kurdish Academy of Language, 2016; Paul, 2008; Zahedi and Mehrazmay, 2011). The broadest classifications of the Kurdish language include the Northern, Central and Southern dialects as well as Zazaki and Gurani. Other classifications typically disqualify Zazaki and Gurani based upon linguistic evidence and mainly focus upon the Northern and Central dialects (Zahedi and Mehrazmay, 2011), which account for over 75% of native Kurdish speakers (Esmaili and Salavati, 2013). A study put forth by D. N. Mackenzie in 1961—which treats Zazaki and Gurani as separate languages—remains standard in linguistic research and considers "Kurdish" to be a language divisible into the Northern, Central and Southern Kurdish dialects (Haig and Matras, 2002; Paul, 2008).

Of the Northern, Central and Southern dialects, Kurdish dialects differ morphologically in terms of case and gender (Haig and Matras, 2002; Paul, 2008; Zahedi and Mehrazmay, 2011), though researchers have found exceptions to these rules (Esmaili and Salavati, 2013; Haig and Matras, 2002; Hassani and Medjedovic, 2016). Northern Kurdish dialects distinguish gender and retain an inflectional system for masculine nouns (Haig and Matras, 2002; Paul, 2008). Some Central Kurdish dialects also have a case system, but some have also dropped case distinction entirely; all Central Kurdish dialects do not distinguish gender (Haig and Matras, 2002; Paul, 2008). South Kurdish dialects do not distinguish gender, and some show different forms of plural endings (Paul, 2008).

Ezafe in Kurdish dialects are more complex in the Northern dialects, which distinguish a masculine/feminine -$\bar{e}$ / -$\bar{a}$ and plural -$\bar{e}t$, and simplifies toward the Southern dialects, which have one general form of the Ezafe, -$\bar{\imath}$. Ezafe in the Central dialects can be considered intermediate (Paul, 2008).

Central and Southern Kurdish dialects utilize suffix pronouns, while the Northern dialects do not (Paul, 2008). Central and Southern Kurdish dialects also have a secondary passive conjugation which does not exist in the Northern dialects (Paul, 2008).

3.3.1 Northern Kurdish Dialects

Most Kurds in Turkey, Iraqi Kurdistan, northeastern Syria and the former Soviet Union (especially Georgia and Armenia) speak the Northern Kurdish dialects (also referred to as Kurmanji, Northern Kurmanji or Badinani (Kurdish Academy of Language, 2016; Paul, 2008; Nerwiy, 2012)). The Northern Kurdish dialects encompass around 20 million speakers (Hassani and Medjedovic, 2016) and primarily use a Latin-based alphabet (Esmaili and Salavati, 2013), as we will describe below.

3.3.2 Central Kurdish Dialects

Most Kurds located around Arbil, Suleymaniyeh and Kirkuk in Iraq as well as those in Iranian Kurdistan speak the Central Kurdish dialects (also referred to as Sorani (Kurdish Academy of Language, 2016; Paul, 2008; Nerwiy, 2012)). Speakers of the Central Kurdish dialects number around seven million (Hassani and Medjedovic, 2016) and use an Arabic-based alphabet (Esmaili and Salavati, 2013).

Regarding verb morphology, Central Kurdish dialects employ clitics with verb stems as concord markers, a feature that distinguishes them from the Northern dialects. In the Central dialects, the positions of these markers vary according to negation, auxiliary usage, valency and thematic roles; in the Northern dialects, concord markers are fixed, following the verb stem (Haig and Matras, 2002).

For verbal agreement and alignment, Central Kurdish dialects use pronominal enclitics that attach to the direct object for past-tense transitive constructions, whereas the Northern dialects use ergative constructions (Esmaili and Salavati, 2013; Haig and Matras, 2002).

A further point of distinction is that the Central (and Southern) Kurdish dialects use the definite marker *-aka*, which is absent in the Northern dialects (Esmaili and Salavati, 2013; Zahedi and Mehrazmay, 2011).

This is the dialect being investigated in this study. We're interested in identifying subdialectal differences in Sorani texts sourced from different regions, namely Iran and Iraq.

3.3.3 Southern Kurdish Dialects

The Southern Kurdish dialects (also referred to as Pehlewani, Pahlawanik (Kurdish Academy of Language, 2016; Paul, 2008) or Hawramani (Salih, 2014)) are spoken primarily in the Khanaqin and Mandalin districts of Iraqi Kurdistan and in the Kermanshah region of Iran (Nerwiy, 2012).

3.4 Orthography

Kurdish utilizes four scripts for writing (Latin, Perso-Arabic, Cyrillic and Yekgirtú) dependent upon geographical, political and cultural factors; it lacks a standard, formalized orthographic system (Hassani and Medjedovic, 2016). Nevertheless, there have been efforts at standardization (Haig and Matras, 2002), and most research recognizes the Latin and Arabic scripts as being the most prominent, earning Kurdish the title of being a bi-standard language (Esmaili and Salavati, 2013; Zahedi and Mehrazmay, 2011).

The Central dialects adapted the Perso-Arabic script in the city of Suleymaniya in Iraqi Kurdistan in the nineteenth century, and this script has been used in the Kurdish regions of Iraq and Iran that speak the Central dialects (Haig and Matras, 2002). For the Northern dialects, Kurdish nationalists adapted Arabic script in the nineteenth century; later in the 1930s, Celadet Bedir-Khan introduced a Latin script for Kurdish that has been used in Turkish and Syrian Kurdistan as well as in the European diaspora (Haig and Matras, 2002; Hassani and Medjedovic, 2016). In 1940, the Cyrillic script for Kurdish was converted from a Roman script developed in the Soviet Union and is mainly based upon the Northern dialects (Haig and Matras, 2002). As compared to the Perso-Arabic script and the Cyrillic script, usage of the Latin script is growing (Hassani and Medjedovic, 2016). Additionally, the Kurdish Academy of Language recently proposed Yekgirtú as a unified alphabetic system for Kurdish (Zahedi and Mehrazmay, 2011).

Mapping the Kurdish Latin-based alphabet (used by the Northern dialects) to the Kurdish Arabic-based alphabet (used by the Central dialects) yields twenty-four one-to-one mappings, four one-to-two mappings and five one-to-zero mappings (Esmaili and Salavati, 2013). The one-to-two and one-to-zero mappings attest respectively to the ambiguities of the alphabets and to the differences between the Northern and Central dialects (Esmaili and Salavati, 2013; Hassani and Medjedovic, 2016). Both orthographies are alphabetic, meaning that vowels must be written (Esmaili and Salavati, 2013).[4]

---

[4]This is in contrast with other abjad writing systems that use the Perso-Arabic script.

4 Data

As Sorani is a low-resourced language, no corpus including texts from different regions was readily available. However, the amount of Sorani language content on the web has been increasing and this provides a good source of data for building corpora.

Similar to the recent work in this area, we approach this task at the sentence-level. Sentence length, measured by the number of tokens, is an important factor to consider when creating the dataset. There may not be enough distinguishing features if a sentence is too short, and conversely, very long texts will likely have more features that facilitate correct classification. This assumption is supported by recent evidence from related work suggesting that shorter sentences are more difficult to classify (Malmasi and Dras,). Bearing this in mind, we limited our dataset to sentences in the range of 5–55 tokens in order to maintain a balance between short and long sentences.

For this study we opted to extract data from news providers based in Iran and Iraq as the source of our data. For Iraq we chose Rudaw and Sharpress, while for Iran we used Sahar TV and Kurdpress. Using articles from these news sources, a total of 100,000 sentences matching our length requirements were extracted for each class, resulting in a corpus of 200,000 sentences. We also make this data freely available to other researchers.[5]

5 Experimental Methodology

We approach this task as a binary classification problem, splitting our data into two classes representing Sorani texts from Iran and Iraq.

5.1 Features

We employ two lexical surface feature types for this task, as described below. The sentences are tokenized based on whitespace and punctuation prior to feature extraction.

Character n-grams This is a sub-word feature that uses the constituent characters that make up the whole text. When used as n-grams, the features are n-character slices of the text. From a linguistic point of view, the substrings captured by this feature, depending on the order, can implicitly capture various sub-lexical features including single letters, phonemes, syllables, morphemes and suffixes. In this study we examine n-grams of order 2–4.

Word n-grams The surface forms of words can be used as a feature for classification. Each unique word may be used as a feature (i.e. unigrams), but the use of bigram distributions is also common. In this scenario, the n-grams are extracted along with their frequency distributions. For this study we evaluate unigram features.

5.2 Named Entity Masking

Our dataset is not controlled for topic and it is possible implicitly capture topical cues and are thus susceptible to *topic bias*. *Topic bias* can occur as a result of the themes or topics of the texts to be classified not being evenly distributed across the classes, leading to correlations between classes and topics (Brooke and Hirst, 2012; Malmasi and Dras, 2014a; Malmasi and Dras, 2015c). More specifically for the current work, the topics can refer to regional toponyms and location names.

One way to counter this issue is to create a balanced or parallel corpus (Malmasi and Dras,). This is a non-trivial task that requires time and resources, and so was not considered for this preliminary study. Another approach is based on named entity masking, which aims to identify and remove named entities such as location names to minimize their influence on the classification models. This approach requires the identification of such tokens through Named Entity Recognition (NER) or some other method. The 2015 DSL Shared Task included evaluation using such masked texts where this was achieved using a heuristic method that masked all capitalized tokens (Zampieri et al., 2015). However, given the lack of NER systems for Sorani and the absence of capitalization info in the Perso-Arabic script, it was not

---

[5]http://web.science.mq.edu.au/%7Esmalmasi/resources/sorani

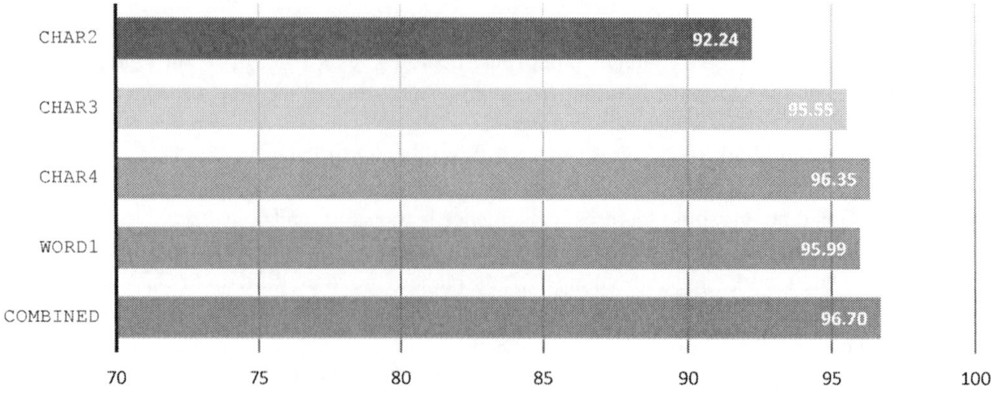

Figure 1: Accuracy for our individual features and their combination.

possible to use either approach. Therefore, in this study we limited our entity masking to the names of the websites and news agencies that we chose as our data sources.[6] More sophisticated entity masking approaches will be considered in future work.

5.3 Classifier

We use a linear Support Vector Machine to perform multi-class classification in our experiments. In particular, we use the LIBLINEAR[7] SVM package (Fan et al., 2008) which has been shown to be efficient for text classification problems with large numbers of features and documents.[8]

5.4 Evaluation

Consistent with most previous studies, we report our results as classification accuracy under k-fold cross-validation, with $k = 10$. For creating our folds, we employ stratified cross-validation which aims to ensure that the proportion of classes within each partition is equal (Kohavi, 1995).

We use a *random baseline* for comparison purposes. This is commonly employed in classification tasks where it is calculated by randomly assigning labels to documents. It is a good measure of overall performance in instances where the training data is evenly distributed across the classes, as is the case here. Since our data is equally distributed across both classes, this baseline is 50%.

6 Results

Our experiment explores the classification of Sorani sentences within our corpus using 10-fold cross-validation. We experiment with the different features discussed in the previous section and their combination. The results are shown in Figure 1. All of our features surpass the random baseline of 50% by a large margin. We observe that character n-grams, particularly 4-grams, are very useful here with 96.4% accuracy using a single feature type. Word unigrams are also very informative here with 96.0% accuracy. These results indicate that important lexical and orthographic differences may exist between the Sorani texts from different regions.

We also tested combinations of the features types into a single feature vector, showing that this can yield slightly improved results, with 96.7% accuracy.

It is interesting that character n-grams are a slightly better feature than words. These results also suggest that, at least for this dataset, character n-grams generalize the most. However, it may be the case that word unigrams may perform better with a sufficiently large dataset.

---

[6]For example: رووداو

[7]http://www.csie.ntu.edu.tw/%7Ecjlin/liblinear/

[8]SVM has proven to perform well for large text classification tasks (Malmasi and Dras, 2014c; Malmasi and Dras, 2014b).

7 Discussion and Conclusion

In this study we explored methods for the automatic identification of Sorani subdialects, showing that sentences from news sources in Iraq and Iran are distinguishable with 96% accuracy. This is a new result for dialect that has not previously been experimented with. To this end, we also identified data sources that could be leveraged for this task.

Future work can be directed in several directions. First, detailed analysis of the most discriminative features can provide useful insights about the subdialectal differences. They may reveal interesting sources of influence from Arabic and Persian. A preliminary analysis of the discriminative features showed such differences, but a detailed analysis will be left for future research. While we did not observe a disproportionate amount of named entities in these distinguishing features, methods to eliminate their influence will be important for future work.

Expanding the dataset with additional data from different sources could also be helpful. Further refinement of the dataset to create a topic-balanced corpus can also help conduct more robust experiments in the future. From a machine learning perspective, classifier ensembles have been shown to improve classification performance for numerous NLP tasks. Their application here could also increase system accuracy. Finally, conducting an error analysis on the data could also help better understand the subdialectal differences. Feedback from native speakers would be of assistance here in better documenting the distinguishing features of each dialect, as learned by our models.

Acknowledgements

A special thanks to the reviewers for their helpful comments and feedback.

References

Purya Aliabadi. 2014. Semi-Automatic Development of KurdNet, The Kurdish WordNet. In *ACL (Student Research Workshop)*, pages 94–99.

Ranaivo-Malançon Bali. 2006. Automatic Identification of Close Languages–Case Study: Malay and Indonesian. *ECTI Transaction on Computer and Information Technology*, 2(2):126–133.

Kenneth R Beesley. 1988. Language identifier: A computer program for automatic natural-language identification of on-line text. In *Proceedings of the 29th Annual Conference of the American Translators Association*, volume 47, page 54. Citeseer.

Shane Bergsma, Paul McNamee, Mossaab Bagdouri, Clayton Fink, and Theresa Wilson. 2012. Language identification for creating language-specific Twitter collections. In *Proceedings of the Second Workshop on Language in Social Media*, pages 65–74. Association for Computational Linguistics.

Joyce Blau. 2009. Kurdish Language ii. History of Kurdish. *Encyclopaedia Iranica*.

Joyce Blau. 2016. The Kurdish Language and Literature. Accessed: 2016-09-20.

Julian Brooke and Graeme Hirst. 2012. Measuring interlanguage: Native language identification with L1-influence metrics. In *Proceedings of the Eight International Conference on Language Resources and Evaluation (LREC'12)*, pages 779–784, Istanbul, Turkey, May.

William B. Cavnar and John M. Trenkle. 1994. N-Gram-Based Text Categorization. In *Proceedings of SDAIR-94, 3rd Annual Symposium on Document Analysis and Information Retrieval*, pages 161–175, Las Vegas, US.

Ted Dunning. 1994. *Statistical identification of language*. Computing Research Laboratory, New Mexico State University.

Kyumars Sheykh Esmaili and Shahin Salavati. 2013. Sorani Kurdish versus Kurmanji Kurdish: An Empirical Comparison. In *ACL*, pages 300–305.

Kyumars Sheykh Esmaili, Shahin Salavati, and Anwitaman Datta. 2014. Towards Kurdish information retrieval. *ACM Transactions on Asian Language Information Processing (TALIP)*, 13(2):7.

Rong-En Fan, Kai-Wei Chang, Cho-Jui Hsieh, Xiang-Rui Wang, and Chih-Jen Lin. 2008. LIBLINEAR: A Library for Large Linear Classification. *Journal of Machine Learning Research*, 9:1871–1874.

Anna Feldman, Jirka Hana, and Chris Brew. 2006. A cross-language approach to rapid creation of new morpho-syntactically annotated resources. In *Proceedings of LREC*, pages 549–554.

Geoffrey Haig and Yaron Matras. 2002. Kurdish linguistics: a brief overview. *STUF-Language Typology and Universals*, 55(1):3–14.

Hossein Hassani and Dzejla Medjedovic. 2016. Automatic Kurdish Dialects Identification. *Computer Science & Information Technology*.

Chu-Ren Huang and Lung-Hao Lee. 2008. Contrastive Approach towards Text Source Classification based on Top-Bag-Word Similarity.

Ron Kohavi. 1995. A study of cross-validation and bootstrap for accuracy estimation and model selection. In *IJCAI*, volume 14, pages 1137–1145.

Kurdish Academy of Language. 2016. Kurdish Language. Accessed: 2016-09-20.

Nikola Ljubešić, Nives Mikelić, and Damir Boras. 2007. Language indentification: How to distinguish similar languages? In *Information Technology Interfaces, 2007. ITI 2007. 29th International Conference on*, pages 541–546. IEEE.

Shervin Malmasi and Mark Dras. Arabic Dialect Identification using a Parallel Multidialectal Corpus. In *PACLING 2015*.

Shervin Malmasi and Mark Dras. 2014a. Arabic Native Language Identification. In *Proceedings of the Arabic Natural Language Processing Workshop (EMNLP 2014)*, pages 180–186, Doha, Qatar. Association for Computational Linguistics.

Shervin Malmasi and Mark Dras. 2014b. Chinese Native Language Identification. In *Proceedings of the 14th Conference of the European Chapter of the Association for Computational Linguistics (EACL-14)*, pages 95–99, Gothenburg, Sweden. Association for Computational Linguistics.

Shervin Malmasi and Mark Dras. 2014c. Language Transfer Hypotheses with Linear SVM Weights. In *Proceedings of the 2014 Conference on Empirical Methods in Natural Language Processing (EMNLP)*, pages 1385–1390, Doha, Qatar, October. Association for Computational Linguistics.

Shervin Malmasi and Mark Dras. 2015a. Automatic Language Identification for Persian and Dari texts. In *Proceedings of the 14th Conference of the Pacific Association for Computational Linguistics (PACLING 2015)*, pages 59–64, Bali, Indonesia, May.

Shervin Malmasi and Mark Dras. 2015b. Large-scale Native Language Identification with Cross-Corpus Evaluation. In *Proceedings of NAACL-HLT 2015*, Denver, Colorado, June. Association for Computational Linguistics.

Shervin Malmasi and Mark Dras. 2015c. Multilingual Native Language Identification. In *Natural Language Engineering*.

Shervin Malmasi, Sze-Meng Jojo Wong, and Mark Dras. 2013. NLI Shared Task 2013: MQ Submission. In *Proceedings of the Eighth Workshop on Innovative Use of NLP for Building Educational Applications*, pages 124–133, Atlanta, Georgia, June. Association for Computational Linguistics.

Hawar Khalil Taher Nerwiy. 2012. *The Republic of Kurdistan, 1946*. Ph.D. thesis, Faculty of the Humanities, Leiden University.

Ludwig Paul. 2008. Kurdish language. i. History of the Kurdish language. *Encyclopaedia Iranica*.

Rashwan Ramadan Salih. 2014. *A comparative study of English and Kurdish connectives in newspaper opinion articles*. Ph.D. thesis, Department of English, University of Leicester.

Jörg Tiedemann and Nikola Ljubešić. 2012. Efficient discrimination between closely related languages. In *Proceedings of COLING 2012*, pages 2619–2634.

Keivan Zahedi and Roghayeh Mehrazmay. 2011. Definiteness in sorani Kurdish and English. *Dialectologia: revista electrònica*, (7):129–157.

Marcos Zampieri, Liling Tan, Nikola Ljubešić, and Jörg Tiedemann. 2014. A report on the DSL shared task 2014. *COLING 2014*, page 58.

Marcos Zampieri, Liling Tan, Nikola Ljubešić, Jörg Tiedemann, and Preslav Nakov. 2015. Overview of the dsl shared task 2015. In *Proceedings of the Joint Workshop on Language Technology for Closely Related Languages, Varieties and Dialects*, LT4VarDial '15, pages 1–9, Hissar, Bulgaria.

Enlarging scarce in-domain English-Croatian corpus for SMT of MOOCs using Serbian

Maja Popović, Kostadin Cholakov, Valia Kordoni, Nikola Ljubešić*

Humboldt University of Berlin, Germany
`name.surname@hu-berlin.de`

* Dept. of Knowledge Technologies, Jožef Stefan Institute, Slovenia
`nikola.ljubesic@ijs.si`

Abstract

Massive Open Online Courses have been growing rapidly in size and impact. Yet the language barrier constitutes a major growth impediment in reaching out all people and educating all citizens. A vast majority of educational material is available only in English, and state-of-the-art machine translation systems still have not been tailored for this peculiar genre. In addition, a mere collection of appropriate in-domain training material is a challenging task. In this work, we investigate statistical machine translation of lecture subtitles from English into Croatian, which is morphologically rich and generally weakly supported, especially for the educational domain. We show that results comparable with publicly available systems trained on much larger data can be achieved if a small in-domain training set is used in combination with additional in-domain corpus originating from the closely related Serbian language.

1 Introduction

Massive Open Online Courses (MOOCs) have been growing rapidly in size and importance, but the language barrier constitutes a major obstacle in reaching out all people and educating all citizens. A vast majority of materials is available only in English, and state-of-the-art machine translation (MT) systems still have not been tailored for this type of texts: the specific type of spoken language used in lectures, ungrammatical and/or incomplete segments in subtitles, slides and assignments, a number of distinct courses i.e. domains such as various natural sciences, computer science, engineering, philosophy, history, music, etc.

Machine translation of this genre into an under-resourced morphologically rich target language represents an additional challenge – in this work, we investigate translation into Croatian. Croatian has recently become the third official South Slavic language in the EU,[1] but it is still rather under-resourced in terms of free/open-source language resources and tools, especially in terms of parallel bilingual corpora. Finding appropriate parallel educational data is even more difficult. Therefore, we based our experiments on a small in-domain parallel corpus containing about 12k parallel segments. We then investigate in what way the translation quality can be improved by an additional in-domain corpus of about 50k segments containing a closely related language, namely Serbian. In addition, we explore the impact of adding a relatively large (200k) out-of-domain news corpus.

Croatian and Serbian are rather close languages, so one option could be to directly use additional English-Serbian data. However, previous work has shown a significant drop in translation quality for a similar cross-language translation scenario (Popović and Ljubešić, 2014). Therefore we also investigate a high-quality Serbian-to-Croatian rule-based MT system for creating additional artificial English-Croatian data.

[1]together with Slovenian and Bulgarian

Proceedings of the Third Workshop on NLP for Similar Languages, Varieties and Dialects,
pages 97–105, Osaka, Japan, December 12 2016.

1.1 Related work

In the last decade, several SMT systems have been built for various South Slavic languages and English. Through the transLectures project,[2] transcriptions and translation technologies for automatic generation of multilingual subtitles for online educational data were provided for a set of language pairs. Through this project, one of the South Slavic languages, namely Slovenian, became an optional language pair in the 2013 evaluation campaign of IWSLT (International Workshop on Spoken Language Translation) (Cettolo et al., 2013). The SUMAT project[3] included translation between Serbian and Slovenian subtitles (Etchegoyhen et al., 2014), however translation from English was not explored and no educational subtitles were used.

For Croatian-English language pair, first results are reported in (Ljubešić et al., 2010) on a small weather forecast corpus. Translation between Croatian and English has become one of the focuses of the AbuMatran project:[4] an SMT system for the tourist domain is presented in (Toral et al., 2014), the use of morpho-syntactic information by means of factored models is investigated in (Sánchez-Cartagena et al., 2016) and several scenarios with different models and data-sets are explored in (Toral et al., 2016). Furthermore, SMT systems for the news domain for Croatian and Serbian are described in (Popović and Ljubešić, 2014).

To the best of our knowledge, no systematic investigation on English-to-Croatian educational data has been carried out yet.

2 Challenges for machine translation of MOOCs

As already mentioned, machine translation of MOOCs induces several challenging tasks. A first step for building a statistical machine translation (SMT) is collection of parallel data. For educational genre, already this step is a challenge due to the following reasons:

- crawling: the structure of the web resource containing desired material is complex and does not allow for large-scale automatic crawling;

- data extraction and alignment: a large portion of materials is in pdf format, which can lead to misalignments during conversion into plain text;

- the size of extracted data: the available data is often very small, so that machine translation with scarce resources has to take place;

- target languages: majority of materials is available in English, meaning that machine translation into morphologically rich languages has to take place;

- representativeness: majority of available materials are lecture subtitles; slides, notes and assignments are unfortunately rarely translated.

- copyright issues are often not clear and are difficult to define.

Once the parallel data is extracted from some source, segmentation can be a challenging task itself. The platforms used for translation are primarily designed for subtitles so that the translators are encouraged to use short segments which often represent incomplete and/or ungrammatical sentences. Another peculiarity is the fact that the lecturers often do not finish a sentence properly or change the subject in the middle of a utterance.

3 Challenges for English-Croatian machine translation and getting help from Serbian

Croatian, as a Slavic language, has a very rich inflectional morphology for all word classes. There are six distinct cases, three genders and a number of verb inflections since person and many tenses are expressed

---

[2]https://www.translectures.eu/
[3]http://www.sumat-project.eu/
[4]http://www.abumatran.eu/

by the suffix. In addition, negation of three important verbs is formed by adding the negative particle to the verb as a prefix. As for syntax, the language has a quite free word order, and there are no articles, neither indefinite nor definite. In addition, multiple negation is always used.

All these morpho-syntactic peculiarities are even more difficult to generate correctly if the available resources are scarce, especially for spoken language style used in lectures as well as for ungrammatical and/or unfinished sentences.

Differences between Croatian and Serbian Both languages belong to the South-Western Slavic branch. Although they exibit a large overlap in vocabulary and a strong morpho-syntactic similarity so that the speakers can understand each other without difficulties, there is a number of small but notable and frequently occurring differences between them.

The largest differences between the two languages are in vocabulary: some words are completely different, some however differ only by one or two letters. In addition, Serbian language usually phonetically transcribes foreign names and words although both transcription and transliteration are allowed, whereas the Croatian standard only transliterates.

Apart from lexical differences, there are also structural differences, mainly concerning verbs: constructions involving modal verbs, especially those with the verb "trebati" (to need, should), future tense, conditional.

4   Research questions

Taking into account the facts described in previous sections, i.e. peculiarities of educational genre, difficulties regarding characteristics of the Croatian language and scarceness of available resources, as well as similarities and differences between Croatian and Serbian, our main questions are:

- how does the translation performance for a small in-domain training data compare with the performance for a larger out-of-domain data?

- is it possible to increase the performance by adding Serbian in-domain data and what is the optimal way?

Our work is to certain extent related to the experiments described in (Popović and Ljubešić, 2014). They explored adaptation of the in-domain news test data to the desired language by applying a set of simple rules or a Serbian-Croatian SMT system, whereas the training data for the English-Serbian/Croatian system were fixed. We investigate different combinations of training data for the challenging genre i.e. educational material in order to build a ready SMT so that the test data once translated do not require any further intervention. In addition, we use a recently developed high quality rule-based Serbian-to-Croatian system (Klubička et al., 2016) which performs better than SMT systems used in (Popović and Ljubešić, 2014).

5   Experimental set-up

Parallel texts

The data used in our experiments are collaboratively translated subtitles from Coursera[5] and contain several types of courses/domains: biology, computer science, philosophy, nutrition, music, etc. The translations are produced by course participants who usually translate into their native languages. Translations are done via a collaborative platform which is usually used for translation of movie subtitles, thus not designed with large-scale crawling in mind. In order to crawl the relevant data, we first had to construct manually a list of the Coursera courses available there. Once the list of translated Coursera courses was constructed, Python scripts were used to download the original English data and the corresponding translations. However, this process was not fully automatic because there were some issues with the format of the URLs of some of the courses as well as the data format of the translations.

---

[5]https://www.coursera.org/

The parallel data collected is of a relatively good quality. The texts are mostly properly aligned, however the sentence segmentation is not optimal. As mentioned in Section 2, the extracted parallel segments often contain incomplete sentences or parts of two different sentences. Of course, one can think of automated correction of segmentation. However, for bilingually aligned texts this represents a peculiar task for several reasons:

- there are no apparent punctuation rules which are consistent in both languages: some sentences end with "." i one language but with "," or ";" or conjunction or even nothing in the other;

- some consecutive English source segments are only partially translated (Table 1) – if these segments were merged in both languages, a proper English sentence aligned with an incorrect and/or ungrammatical translation would be generated.

English	Croatian
Five years ago	Pre pet godina
I was told specifically	(no translation)
this is his name	da mu je to ime.

Table 1: Example of English successive segments and their Croatian translations: the middle of the sentence is not translated at all.

For these reasons, and also taking into account the fact that the test set is in the same format, no resegmentation attempts were performed and the texts are used directly in the format they were extracted. Nevertheless, since the data are not completely clean, certain filtering steps had to be performed. First of all, there was a large number of short redundant segments such as "Mhm", "Hello", "Welcome back", etc. These segments were separated from the rest according to the sentence length and only a unique occurrences were kept. The rest of the corpus was then cleaned from incorrect translations on the base of sentence length: if the proportion of source and target sentence length was too high or too small, the segment was removed. As a final step, the two cleaned parts of the corpus were merged. The same procedure was carried out for both for English-Croatian as well as for English-Serbian data sets. For English-Croatian, about 12k parallel segments were extracted, and for English-Serbian about 50k. An interesting observation is that although Croatian is generally better supported in terms of publicly available parallel data,[6] Serbian is currently better supported for educational parallel texts.

As for the out-of-domain corpus, we used the SETimes news corpus (Tyers and Alperen, 2010) since it is relatively large (200k parallel sentences) and clean.

Moses set-ups

We trained the statistical phrase-based systems using the Moses toolkit (Koehn et al., 2007) with MERT tuning. The word alignments were built with GIZA++ (Och and Ney, 2003) and a 5-gram language model was built with SRILM (Stolcke, 2002).

The investigated bilingual training set-ups are:

1. en-hr SEtimes (relatively large clean out-of-domain corpus)

2. en-hr Coursera (small in-domain corpus)

3. en-hr Coursera (small in-domain corpus) + en-sr Coursera (larger in-domain corpus)

4. en-hr Coursera + en-hr' Coursera

5. en-hr SEtimes + en-hr Coursera + en-hr' Coursera

---

[6]http://opus.lingfil.uu.se/

		sentences	running words		voc		oov (%) (dev/test)	
			en	hr	en	hr	en	hr
Training	1) setimes	206k	4.9M	4.6M	68k	137k	2.7/2.4	10.9/7.4
	2) coursera	12k	148k	118k	8k	17k	5.5/5.5	8.2/8.8
	3) 2+coursera_en-sr	62k	782k	659k	21k	54k	1.5/1.2	5.3/5.7
	4) 2+coursera_en-hr'	62k	782k	696k	21k	52k	1.5/1.2	4.9/5.2
	5) 1+4	268k	5.7M	5.3M	76k	162k	0.8/0.6	2.9/2.9
Dev	coursera	2935	28k	23k	3.8k	6.3k		
Test	coursera	2091	25k	20k	3.4k	5.5k		

Table 2: Data statistics.

where hr' denotes Serbian part of the corpus translated by a rule-based machine translation system into Croatian. For each set-up, the language model was trained on the target part of the used bilingual corpus. For set-ups including combined parallel corpora (3, 4 and 5), the corpora were merged by simple concatenation and the interpolated language model was used. Data statistics for all set-ups can be seen in Table 2.

Serbian-to-Croatian RBMT system

The MT system (Klubička et al., 2016) used for creating additional artificial Croatian data from Serbian is a bidirectional rule-based system based on the open-source Apertium platform (Forcada et al., 2011). Considering the fact that differences between Croatian and Serbian occur mostly at the lexical and orthography, using a rule-based system makes the most sense. The system tested on newspaper texts achieves 83.0% BLEU for translation into Croatian, whereas the BLEU score is 72.7% if the Serbian source is directly compared to the Croatian reference translation.

Evaluation

For all set-ups, BLEU scores (Papineni et al., 2002) and character n-gram F-scores i.e. CHRF3 scores (Popović, 2015) are reported. In addition, five Hjerson error classes (Popović, 2011) are reported in order to get a better insight into differences between the systems: inflectional errors, ordering errors, missing words, additions and lexical errors.

6 Results

6.1 Automatic evaluation scores

Table 3 presents the obtained automatic scores for all Moses training set-ups described in Section 5 together with the scores for translations generated[7] by two publicly available SMT systems for English-to-Croatian: Asistent[8] (Arčan et al., 2016) and Google translate[9].

It can be seen that the most promising set-up according to automatic evaluation metrics is the set-up 5, i.e merging both domains and adding artificial in-domain English-Croatian parallel text where the target Croatian part is generated from Serbian by the rule-based MT system. This set-up even outperforms the Asistent system which is trained on much larger parallel texts, albeit none of them from educational domain.

Furthermore, it can be seen that both SETimes and original Coursera set produce the same percentage of lexical errors – the first one due to the domain discrepance and the other due to data sparsity. Adding in-domain Serbian data reduces the number of lexical errors, which is further reduced by translating Serbian into Croatian. Merging of two data-sets reduces lexical errors even more, however their number is still larger than for Asistent and Google systems.

---

[7] in June 2016

[8] http://server1.nlp.insight-centre.org/asistent/

[9] https://translate.google.com/

101

system	overall scores		Hjerson error rates					
	BLEU	CHRF3	infl	order	miss	add	lex	Σer
1) setimes	8.1	38.5	10.6	5.0	6.4	10.5	40.8	73.2
2) coursera	12.7	38.9	7.5	4.2	4.0	14.6	40.8	71.1
3) 2+coursera-sr	13.2	41.1	8.8	4.7	5.3	11.8	38.4	69.2
4) 2+coursera-hr'	14.1	42.6	9.4	4.8	5.3	11.8	37.0	68.4
5) 1+4	**15.5**	**44.9**	10.2	5.0	6.5	9.9	35.5	**67.1**
asistent	14.7	43.5	9.9	5.2	8.1	9.4	34.7	67.4
google	17.1	49.4	8.2	4.5	4.4	13.8	30.1	61.0

Table 3: Automatic evaluation scores (%) for each of the systems: BLEU score, CHRF3 score and five Hjerson error rates: inflectional, ordering, omission, addition and lexical error rate together with their sum.

Ordering errors and omissions are lower for the set-ups without SEtimes, most probably due to different sentence (i.e. segment) structure in two genres/domains.

Morphological errors are also lower without SEtimes, however they are high in all set-ups which should be generally addressed in future work by using morpho-syntactic analysers and/or generators.

Apart from this, it can be observed that the main advantage of the Google system is the low number of lexical errors which is probably achieved by using very large training corpora.

6.2 Translation examples

In order to illustrate advantages and disadvantages of different SMT systems, Table 4 shows six English source segments and their translations by each of the systems. Erroneous parts of the obtained translations are annotated by parentheses: {} stands for lexical errors, additions, omissions and inflections (where only part of the word is in parenthesis), // stands for ordering errors and <> for stylistic variants.

segment 1: A completely correct sentence is produced only by the set-up 5, as well as by the publicly available systems. The other systems generate ungrammatical sentences, en-hr Coursera alone generates stylistically questionable translation.

segment 2: None of the systems produces a perfect translation – however, the most accurate translation containing only two minor morphological errors is produced by set-up 5, i.e. combination of all Coursera data and SETimes.

segment 3: Spoken lecture language issues: SEtimes produces the worst translation, followed by Google and then Asistent; all set-ups with Coursera data produce correct translations.

segment 4: The translation of the incomplete segment is difficult for all systems. Both SETimes and Croatian Coursera alone generate very bad translations – the first one because of domain discrepancy, the second one because of data sparsity; the other set-ups generate ungrammatical segments where the meaning still can be captured. Asistent produces the best translation containing only one inflectional error which does not change the meaning.

segment 5: The best translation (without any error) of another incomplete sentence is generated by set-up 4, i.e. Coursera with additional artificial data; the worst translation is generated by SEtimes, which also introduces morphological errors when combined with Coursera in set-up 5. This example illustrates that in-domain data are important not only for vocabulary and lexical errors but also for morpho-syntactic properties.

segment 6: Spoken language and incomplete sentence: SETimes, Google and Asistent produce a number of errors; using Serbian instead of Croatian induces some errors mainly due to differences in verb structures; the best option is the use of Croatian Coursera with or without additional data.

1)	Is this a problem?
setimes	Je {} to problem{a}?
coursera	Da li <bi> to <bio> problem?
coursera+sr	Je {} <bi> to <bio> problem?
coursera+hr'	/Li/ <bi> to <bio> problem?
all	Je li to problem?
asistent	Je li to problem?
google	Je li to problem?
2)	Then the next thing we need, is energy.
setimes	{Tada} sljedeća stvar {} nam treba, je energija.
coursera	{Onda} sljedeće {} trebamo je energije.
coursera+sr	Sljedeća stvar koju {moramo}, je energije.
coursera+hr'	Sljedeća stvar koju {moramo} je energije.
all	Sljedeća stvar koj{u} nam treba, je energij{e}.
asistent	{onda} sljedeća stvar koju trebamo, je energija.
google	{onda je} sljedeća stvar koju trebamo, je energija.
3)	Now on an Android device, of course yeah, there is no mouse.
setimes	{Sada} {o} Android <naprava>, naravno {yeah}, nema miša.
coursera	Na Android uredjaju, naravno, nema miša.
coursera+sr	Na Android uredjaju, naravno, nema miša.
coursera+hr'	Na Android uredjaju, naravno, nema miša.
all	Na Android uredjaju, naravno, nema miša.
asistent	{Sada} Android uredjaj, naravno, nema miša.
google	{Sada} na Android uredjaju, naravno da{,} nema miš{}.
4)	but the number of insects flying in the
setimes	ali broj {insects} {} lete{nja} u
coursera	ali broj insek{ti} {} {flying} u
coursera+sr	ali broj insek{ti} {} lete{ći} u
coursera+hr'	ali broj insek{ti} {} lete{ći} u
all	ali broj insek{ti} {} lete{ći} u
asistent	ali broj insek{tima} koji lete u
google	ali broj insekata {} let{i} u
5)	that he learned French and English later in life.
setimes	{kako} nauči{la} francusk{e} i englesk{e} kasnije u životu.
coursera	da je naučio francu{zi} i {jezikom} {later} u {life}.
coursera+sr	da je naučio francuski i engleski kasnije u životu.
coursera+hr'	da je naučio francuski i engleski kasnije u životu.
all	da je naučio francusk{e} i englesk{e} kasnije u životu.
asistent	{to} je naučio francuski i engleski kasnije u životu.
google	{koji} je kasnije u životu naučio francuski i engleski.
6)	Now you can see up here that I need to select Android mode, so these are the
setimes	{Sada} možete vidjeti {iz} ovdje {kako} trebam izabrati android način, tako {} to /su/
coursera	Ovdje gore možete vidjeti da trebam odabrati android način rada. dakle, ovo
coursera+sr	Ovdje gore možete videti {koji} <ja> treba da izabere{te} android način rada. znači ovo su
coursera+hr'	Ovdje gore možete vidjeti da trebam odabrati android način rada. dakle, ovo
all	Ovdje gore možete vidjeti da trebam odabrati android način rada. dakle, ovo
asistent	{Sada} možeš vidjeti {što} ja moram odabrati android {}, {} ovo su
google	{Sada} možete vidjeti ovdje da moram odabrati android mod{u}, tako da su to

Table 4: Examples of six English source sentences and their translations by different SMT system set-ups; erroneous parts are annotated by {} (mistranslations, additions, omissions, inflections), // (order) and <> (style).

It can be noted that the additional Serbian data does not help only in the first example – only when a larger out-of-domain data is added, a correct translation is obtained. For segment 2), the baseline English-Croatian corpus already yielded a correct translation and there is no change when any of additional corpora is used. In example 3) both the direct use of Serbian and translating into Croatian help to some extent but some errors are still present. For segments 4) and 5) both untranslated and translated Serbian texts result in the same correct translation. For the example 6) using the translated additional data significantly improves the performance in comparison with the "raw" Serbian data.

7   Summary and outlook

This work has shown that a small amount of in-domain training data is very important for the English-to-Croatian statistical machine translation of the specific genre of Massive Open Online Courses, especially for capturing appropriate morpho-syntactic structure. Adding in-domain data containing the closely related Serbian language improves the performance, especially when the Serbian part is translated into Croatian thus producing an artificial English-Croatian in-domain corpus. The improvements consist mainly from reducing the number of lexical errors. Further improvements have been achieved by adding a relatively large out-of-domain news corpus reaching performance comparable with systems trained on much larger (out-of-domain) parallel texts. Adding this corpus reduces the number of additions and lexical errors, nevertheless it introduces more morphological and ordering errors due to the different nature and structure of the segments.

Future work should include investigating better ways of combining and extracting relevant information from original (in-domain) and additional (out-of-domain and/or "out-of-language") data. In addition, the use of morpho-syntactic information should be explored, especially since this also represents a challenging task for the peculiar genre such as educational material.

Acknowledgments

This work has emerged from research supported by TRaMOOC project (Translation for Massive Open Online Courses) partially funded by the European Commission under H2020-ICT-2014/H2020-ICT-2014-1 under grant agreement number 644333. The research leading to these results has also received funding from the European Union Seventh Framework Programme FP7/2007-2013 under grant agreement PIAP-GA-2012-324414 (Abu-MaTran).

References

Mihael Arčan, Maja Popović, and Paul Buitelaar. 2016. Asistent – a machine translation system for Slovene, Serbian and Croati an. In *Proceedings of the 10th Conference on Language Technologies and Digit al Humanities*, Ljubljana, Slovenia, September.

Mauro Cettolo, Jan Niehues, Sebastian Stüker, Luisa Bentivogli, and Marcello Federico. 2013. Report on the 10th IWSLT evaluation campaign. In *Proceedings of the International Workshop on Spoken Language Translation (IWSLT)*, Heidelberg, Germany, December.

Thierry Etchegoyhen, Lindsay Bywood, Mark Fishel, Panayota Georgakopoulou, Jie Jiang, Gerard Van Loenhout, Arantza Del Pozo, Mirjam Sepesy Maučec, Anja Turner, and Martin Volk. 2014. Machine Translation for Subtitling: A Large-Scale Evaluation. In *Proceedings of the Ninth International Conference on Language Resources and Evaluation (LREC14)*, Reykjavik, Iceland, May.

Mikel L. Forcada, Mireia Ginestí-Rosell, Jacob Nordfalk, Jim O'Regan, Sergio Ortiz-Rojas, Juan Antonio Pérez-Ortiz, Gema Ramírez-Sánchez Felipe Sánchez-Martínez, and Francis M. Tyers. 2011. Apertium: a free/open-source platform for rule-based machine translation. *Machine Translation*, 25(2):127–144. Special Issue: Free/Open-Source Machine Translation.

Filip Klubička, Gema Ramírez-Sánchez, and Nikola Ljubešić. 2016. Collaborative development of a rule-based machine translator between Croatian and Serbian. In *Proceedings of the 19th Annual Conference of the European Association for Machine Translation (EAMT)*, volume 4, Riga, Latvia. Baltic Journal of Modern Computing.

Philipp Koehn, Hieu Hoang, Alexandra Birch, Chris Callison-Burch, Marcello Federico, Nicola Bertoldi, Brooke Cowan, Wade Shen, Christine Moran, Richard Zens, Chris Dyer, Ondřej Bojar, Alexandra Constantin, and Evan Herbst. 2007. Moses: Open source toolkit for statistical machine translation. In *Proceedings of the 45th Annual Meeting of the ACL on Interactive Poster and Demonstration Sessions*, Stroudsburg, PA, USA.

Nikola Ljubešić, Petra Bago, and Damir Boras. 2010. Statistical machine translation of Croatian weather forecast: How much data do we need? In Vesna Lužar-Stiffler, Iva Jarec, and Zoran Bekić, editors, *Proceedings of the ITI 2010 32nd International Conference on Information Technology Interfaces*, pages 91–96, Zagreb. SRCE University Computing Centre.

Franz Josef Och and Hermann Ney. 2003. A systematic comparison of various statistical alignment models. *Computational Linguistics*, 29.

Kishore Papineni, Salim Roukos, Todd Ward, and Wei-Jing Zhu. 2002. Bleu: a method for automatic evaluation of machine translation. In *Proceedings of the 40th annual meeting on association for computational linguistics*, pages 311–318. Association for Computational Linguistics.

Maja Popović and Nikola Ljubešić. 2014. Exploring cross-language statistical machine translation for closely related South Slavic languages. In *Proceedings of the EMNLP14 Workshop on Language Technology for Closely Related Languages and Language Variants*, pages 76–84, Doha, Qatar, October.

Maja Popović. 2011. Hjerson: An Open Source Tool for Automatic Error Classification of Machine Translation Output. *The Prague Bulletin of Mathematical Linguistics*, (96):59–68, October.

Maja Popović. 2015. chrF: character n-gram F-score for automatic MT evaluation. In *Proceedings of the 10th Workshop on Statistical Machine Translation (WMT-15)*, pages 392–395, Lisbon, Portugal, September.

Víctor M. Sánchez-Cartagena, Nikola Ljubešić, and Filip Klubička. 2016. Dealing with data sparseness in SMT with factored models and morphological expansion: a Case Study on Croatian. In *Proceedings of the 19th Annual Conference of the European Association for Machine Translation (EAMT)*, volume 4, Riga, Latvia. Baltic Journal of Modern Computing.

Andreas Stolcke. 2002. SRILM – an extensible language modeling toolkit. volume 2, pages 901–904, Denver, CO, September.

Antonio Toral, Raphael Rubino, Miquel Esplà-Gomis, Tommi Pirinen, Andy Way, and Gema Ramirez-Sanchez. 2014. Extrinsic Evaluation of Web-Crawlers in Machine Translation: a Case Study on CroatianEnglish for the Tourism Domain. In *Proceedings of the 17th Conference of the European Association for Machine Translation (EAMT)*, pages 221–224, Dubrovnik, Croatia, June.

Antonio Toral, Raphael Rubino, and Gema Ramírez-Sánchez. 2016. Re-assessing the Impact of SMT Techniques with Human Evaluation: a Case Study on English-Croatian. In *Proceedings of the 19th Annual Conference of the European Association for Machine Translation (EAMT)*, volume 4, Riga, Latvia. Baltic Journal of Modern Computing.

Francis M. Tyers and Murat Alperen. 2010. South-East European Times: A parallel corpus of the Balkan languages. In *Proceedings of the LREC Workshop on Exploitation of Multilingual Resources and Tools for Central and (South-) Eastern European Languages*, pages 49–53, Valetta, Malta, May.

Arabic Dialect Identification in Speech Transcripts

Shervin Malmasi[1,2]   **Marcos Zampieri[3]**

[1] Harvard Medical School, Boston, MA 02115, USA
[2] Macquarie University, Sydney, NSW, Australia
[3] University of Cologne, Germany

`shervin.malmasi@mq.edu.au, marcos.zampieri@uni-koeln.de`

Abstract

In this paper we describe a system developed to identify a set of four regional Arabic dialects (Egyptian, Gulf, Levantine, North African) and Modern Standard Arabic (MSA) in a transcribed speech corpus. We competed under the team name MAZA in the Arabic Dialect Identification sub-task of the 2016 Discriminating between Similar Languages (DSL) shared task. Our system achieved an F1-score of 0.51 in the closed training track, ranking first among the 18 teams that participated in the sub-task. Our system utilizes a classifier ensemble with a set of linear models as base classifiers. We experimented with three different ensemble fusion strategies, with the mean probability approach providing the best performance.

1   Introduction

The interest in processing Arabic texts and speech data has grown substantially in the last decade.[1] Due to its intrinsic variation, research has been carried out not only on Modern Standard Arabic (MSA), but also on the various Arabic dialects spoken in North Africa and in the Middle East. Research in NLP and Arabic dialects includes, most notably, machine translation of Arabic dialects (Zbib et al., 2012), corpus compilation for Arabic dialects (Al-Sabbagh and Girju, 2012; Cotterell and Callison-Burch, 2014), parsing (Chiang et al., 2006), and Arabic dialect identification (Zaidan and Callison-Burch, 2014). The latter has become a vibrant research topic with several papers published in the last few years (Sadat et al., 2014; Malmasi et al., 2015).

In this paper we revisit the task of Arabic dialect identification proposing an ensemble method applied to a corpus of broadcast speeches transcribed from MSA and four Arabic dialects: Egyptian, Gulf, Levantine, and North African (Ali et al., 2016). The system competed in the Arabic dialect identification sub-task of the 2016 edition of the DSL shared task (Malmasi et al., 2016b)[2] under the team name MAZA. The system achieved very good performance and was ranked first among the 18 teams that participated in the closed submission track.

2   Related Work

There have been several studies published on Arabic dialect identification. Shoufan and Al-Ameri (2015) presents a survey on NLP methods for processing Arabic dialectal data with a comprehensive section on Arabic dialect identification.

Two studies on Arabic dialect identification use the Arabic online commentary dataset (Zaidan and Callison-Burch, 2011), namely the one by Elfardy and Diab (2013) and the one by Tillmann et al. (2014) who developed systems to discriminate between MSA and Egyptian Arabic at the sentence level. The first study reports results of 85.5% accuracy and the latter reports 89.1% accuracy using a linear SVM classifier.

[1]See Habash (2010) for an overview on Arabic NLP.

[2]`http://ttg.uni-saarland.de/vardial2016/dsl2016.html`

Proceedings of the Third Workshop on NLP for Similar Languages, Varieties and Dialects,
pages 106–113, Osaka, Japan, December 12 2016.

Malmasi et al. (2015) evaluates the performance of different methods and features to discriminate between MSA and five Arabic dialects: Egyptian, Jordanian, Palestinian, Syrian, and Tunisian using the Multidialectal Parallel Corpus of Arabic (MPCA) (Bouamor et al., 2014). Malmasi et al. (2015) report results of 74.0% accuracy using a meta-classifier. Darwish et al. (2014) identified important lexical, morphological, and syntactic features to discriminate between MSA and Egyptian Arabic *tweets* reporting 94.4% accuracy.

Using the same dataset as the DSL 2016 Arabic dialect identification sub-task, Ali et al. (2016) propose an SVM method to discriminate between MSA and dialectal Arabic achieving perfect performance. Ali et al. (2016) proposes the same method to identify the four aforementioned Arabic dialects and MSA and reports 59.2% accuracy.

The work on Arabic dialect identification is related to several studies published on computational methods to discriminate between pairs or groups of similar languages, language varieties and dialects. This includes South Slavic languages (Ljubešić et al., 2007), Portuguese varieties (Zampieri and Gebre, 2012), English varieties (Lui and Cook, 2013), Persian and Dari (Malmasi and Dras, 2015a), Romanian dialects (Ciobanu and Dinu, 2016), and the two editions of the DSL shared task organized in 2014 and 2015 which included several groups of closely-related languages and language varieties such as Bosnian, Croatian and Serbian, Bulgarian and Macedonian, Czech and Slovak, and Mexican and Peninsular Spanish (Zampieri et al., 2014; Zampieri et al., 2015).

3 Methods

3.1 Data

For the first time, the DSL challenge includes a sub-task on Arabic dialect identification. The data for this sub-task was provided by the DSL shared task organizers and it is described in the aforementioned study by Ali et al. (2016). The corpus contains transcribed speech from Egyptian (EGY), Gulf (GLF), Levantine (LAV), North African (NOR), and MSA.

The training corpus contains a total of 7,619 sentences. An additional unlabelled test set containing 1,540 sentences was released one month later for the official evaluation. A breakdown of the number of training sentences for each of these classes is listed in Table 1.

Dialect	Class	Sentences
Egyptian	EGY	1,578
Gulf	GLF	1,672
Levantine	LAV	1,758
Modern Standard	MSA	999
North African	NOR	1,612
Total		7,619

Table 1: The breakdown of the dialectal training data provided (Ali et al., 2016).

3.2 Approach

There have been various methods proposed for dialect identification in recent years. Given its success in previous work, we decided to use an ensemble classifier for our entry. We follow the methodology described by Malmasi and Dras (2015b): we extract a number of different feature types and train a single linear model using each feature type. We extract the following feature types, each of them used to train a single classification model:

- Character n-grams ($n = 1$–6): these substrings, depending on the order, can implicitly capture various sub-lexical features including single letters, phonemes, syllables, morphemes and suffixes. They could capture interesting inter-dialectal differences that generalize better than word n-grams.

- Word unigrams: entire words can capture lexical differences between dialects.

We did not perform any pre-processing[3] on the data prior to feature extraction. This was not needed as the data are machine-generated ASR transcripts.[4]

For our base classifier we utilize a linear Support Vector Machine (SVM). SVMs have proven to deliver very good performance in discriminating between language varieties and in other text classification problems, SVMs achieved first place in both the 2015 (Malmasi and Dras, 2015b) and 2014 (Goutte et al., 2014) editions of the DSL shared task.[5]

The best performing system in the 2015 edition of the DSL challenge (Malmasi and Dras, 2015b) used SVM ensembles evidencing the adequacy of this approach for the task of discriminating between similar languages and language varieties. In light of this, we decided to test three ensemble methods described next.

- **System 1 - Plurality Ensemble**

  In this system each classifier votes for a single class label. The votes are tallied and the label with the highest number[6] of votes wins. Ties are broken arbitrarily. This voting method is very simple and does not have any parameters to tune. An extensive analysis of this method and its theoretical underpinnings can be found in the work of (Kuncheva, 2004, p. 112). We submitted this system as run 1.

- **System 2 - Median Probability Ensemble**

  In this ensemble method the probabilities assigned to each class by each classifier are ordered, and the median probability for each label is selected. Among these, the label with the highest median is selected (Kittler et al., 1998). As with the mean probability combiner, which we describe in the next section, this method measures the central tendency of support for each label as a means of reaching a consensus decision. We submitted this system as run 2.

- **System 3 - Mean Probability Ensemble**

  The probability estimates for each class are added together and the class label with the highest average probability is the winner. An important aspect of using probability outputs in this way is that a classifier's support for the true class label is taken in to account, even when it is not the predicted label (*e.g.* it could have the second highest probability). This method has been shown to work well on a wide range of problems and, in general, it is considered to be simple, intuitive, stable (Kuncheva, 2014, p. 155) and resilient to estimation errors (Kittler et al., 1998) making it one of the most robust combiners discussed in the literature. We submitted this system as run 3.

4 Cross-validation Results

In this section we investigate the impact of three variables in the classification performance: the features used, the data, and the type of ensemble used in our system.

We used the training data provided by the shared task organizers and performance cross-validation experiments testing 1) the performance of each individual feature in dialect identification (described in Section 4.1); 2) the impact of the amount of training data on the classification performance (presented in Section 4.2); and 3) the accuracy of each proposed ensemble method (discussed in Section 4.3).

4.1 Feature Performance

We first report our cross-validation results on the training data. We began by testing individual feature types, with results displayed in Figure 1.

As expected we observe that most character n-grams outperform word features. Character 4-grams, 5-grams, and 6-grams obtained higher results than those obtained using word uni-grams. The best results were obtained with character 4-grams achieving 65.95% accuracy and character 5-grams obtaining 65.70% accuracy.

---

[3]For example, case folding or tokenization.

[4]The data was transliterated using the Buckwalter scheme: http://www.qamus.org/transliteration.htm

[5]See Goutte et al. (2016) for a comprehensive evaluation.

[6]This differs with a *majority* voting combiner where a label must obtain over 50% of the votes to win. However, the names are sometimes used interchangeably.

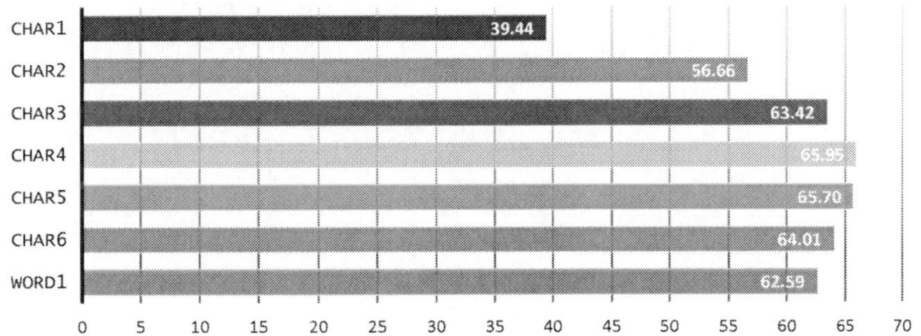

Figure 1: Cross-validation performance for each of our individual feature types.

4.2 Influence of Training Data

Next we look at the influence of the amount of training data in the Arabic dialect identification task. As the size of the training corpus provided by the shared task organizers is relatively small, we are interested in evaluating how this affects performance. A learning curve for a classifier trained on character 4-grams is shown in Figure 2. We observe that accuracy continues to increase, demonstrating potential for even better performance given a larger training corpus.[7]

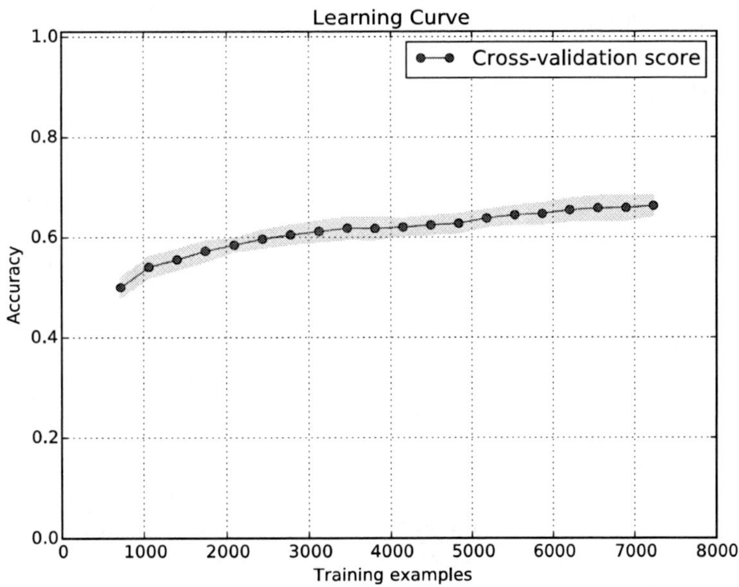

Figure 2: Learning curve for a classifier trained on character 4-grams using the training data.

4.3 Ensemble Methods

In this section we test our three ensemble configurations on the training data. Results are shown in Table 2. We note that all of the ensembles outperform individual features, with the mean probability combiner achieving the best result of 68%. For the voting ensemble, 344 of the 7619 samples (4.52%) resulted in ties which were broken arbitrarily.

---

[7]Due to lack of available comparable data, we only participated in the closed submission track.

System	Accuracy
Majority Class Baseline	0.2307
Voting Ensemble (System 1)	0.6755
Median Ensemble (System 2)	0.6782
Mean Probability Ensemble (System 3)	**0.6800**

Table 2: Cross-validation results for the Arabic training data.

5 Test Set Results

Finally, in this section we report the results of our three submissions generated from the unlabelled test data. The samples in the test set were slightly unbalanced with a majority class baseline of 22.79%. Shared task performance was evaluated and teams ranked according to the weighted F1-score which provides a balance between precision and recall. Accuracy, along with macro- and micro-averaged F1-scores were also reported.

Run	Accuracy	F1 (micro)	F1 (macro)	F1 (weighted)
Baseline	0.2279	—	—	—
System 1 (run1)	0.4916	0.4916	0.4888	0.4924
System 2 (run2)	0.4929	0.4929	0.4908	0.4937
System 3 (run3)	0.5117	0.5117	0.5088	**0.5132**

Table 3: Results for test set C (closed training).

Results for our three submissions are listed in Table 3. While Systems 1 and 2 achieved similar performance, System 3 outperformed them by approximately 2%, ranking first among the 18 teams who competed in the sub-task.

A confusion matrix for our best performing system is shown in Figure 3. We note that MSA is the most distinguishable dialect, while the Gulf dialect has the most misclassifications. Table 4 also shows per-class performance for our best system.

Class	Precision	Recall	F1-score	Sentences
EGY	0.50	0.56	0.53	315
GLF	0.33	0.36	0.35	256
LAV	0.51	0.48	0.49	344
MSA	0.60	0.63	0.61	274
NOR	0.62	0.52	0.56	351
Average/Total	0.52	0.51	0.51	1,540

Table 4: Per-class performance for our best system.

The results for all of our systems are much lower than the cross-validation results. This was a trend noted by other teams in the task. It is likely related to the sampling of the test set; it may have not been drawn from the same source as the training data.

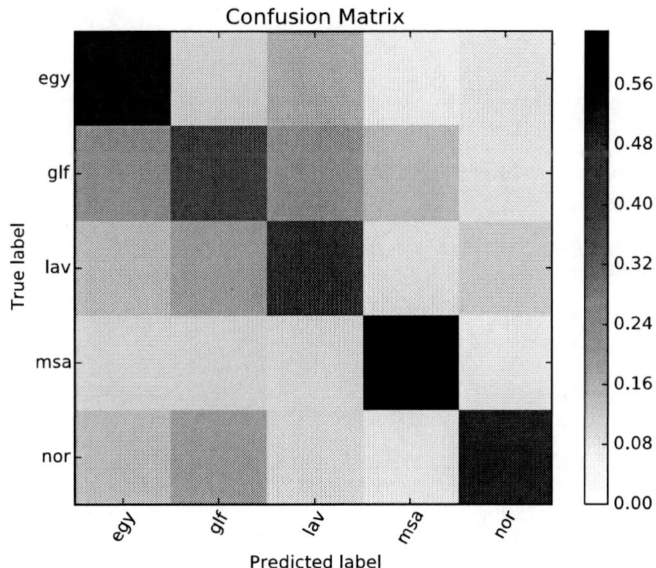

Figure 3: Confusion matrix for our top performing system on the test set.

5.1 Discussion

An important highlight from this work goes beyond Arabic dialect identification. Our work confirms the utility of ensemble methods for different text classification tasks. These methods have proven to perform well in similar shared tasks such as the recent Complex Word Identification (CWI) task at SemEval-2016 (Paetzold and Specia, 2016). A description of the ensemble system applied to CWI is presented in Malmasi et al. (2016a).

Regarding the task itself, this initial experiment shows that accurate dialect identification using ASR transcripts is not a trivial task. An interesting extension is the creation of joint audio-transcript classification models where transcript-based features like the ones used here are combined with acoustic features to capture phonological variation.

6 Conclusion

We presented three robust ensemble methods trained to discriminate between four Arabic dialects and MSA in speech transcripts. The best results were obtained by the Mean Probability Ensemble system (run 3) achieving 0.51 F1-score in the test data. The system outperformed all the 18 teams that participated in the Arabic dialect identification task of the DSL shared task 2016. A comprehensive overview of the 2016 DSL challenge including the results obtained by all participants is presented in Malmasi et al. (2016b).

Our paper also discusses two important variables in Arabic dialect identification, namely the performance of individual character- and word-based features for this task, highlighting that character 4-grams were the features which performed best using this dataset, and the influence of the amount of training data in the classifiers' performance.

As discussed in Section 2, Arabic dialect identification methods are related to methods developed to discriminate between similar languages and language varieties. In future work we would like to evaluate whether our system also achieves good performance discriminating between the languages and language varieties available in the DSL corpus collection (DSLCC) (Tan et al., 2014).

References

Rania Al-Sabbagh and Roxana Girju. 2012. YADAC: Yet another Dialectal Arabic Corpus. In *Proceedings of LREC*.

Ahmed Ali, Najim Dehak, Patrick Cardinal, Sameer Khurana, Sree Harsha Yella, James Glass, Peter Bell, and Steve Renals. 2016. Automatic Dialect Detection in Arabic Broadcast Speech. In *Proceedings of Interspeech*.

Houda Bouamor, Nizar Habash, and Kemal Oflazer. 2014. A Multidialectal Parallel Corpus of Arabic. In *Proceedings of LREC*.

David Chiang, Mona T Diab, Nizar Habash, Owen Rambow, and Safiullah Shareef. 2006. Parsing Arabic Dialects. In *Proceedings of EACL*.

Alina Maria Ciobanu and Liviu P. Dinu. 2016. A Computational Perspective on Romanian Dialects. In *Proceedings of LREC*.

Ryan Cotterell and Chris Callison-Burch. 2014. A Multi-dialect, Multi-genre Corpus of Informal Written Arabic. In *Proceedings LREC*.

Kareem Darwish, Hassan Sajjad, and Hamdy Mubarak. 2014. Verifiably Effective Arabic Dialect Identification. In *Proceedings of EMNLP*.

Heba Elfardy and Mona T Diab. 2013. Sentence Level Dialect Identification in Arabic. In *Proceedings of ACL*.

Cyril Goutte, Serge Léger, and Marine Carpuat. 2014. The NRC System for Discriminating Similar Languages. In *Proceedings of the VarDial Workshop*.

Cyril Goutte, Serge Léger, Shervin Malmasi, and Marcos Zampieri. 2016. Discriminating Similar Languages: Evaluations and Explorations. In *Proceedings of LREC*.

Nizar Y Habash. 2010. Introduction to Arabic Natural Language Processing. *Synthesis Lectures on Human Language Technologies*, 3(1):1–187.

Josef Kittler, Mohamad Hatef, Robert PW Duin, and Jiri Matas. 1998. On combining classifiers. *IEEE Transactions on Pattern Analysis and Machine Intelligence*, 20(3):226–239.

Ludmila I Kuncheva. 2004. *Combining Pattern Classifiers: Methods and Algorithms*. John Wiley & Sons.

Ludmila I Kuncheva. 2014. *Combining Pattern Classifiers: Methods and Algorithms*. Wiley, second edition.

Nikola Ljubešić, Nives Mikelic, and Damir Boras. 2007. Language Identification: How to Distinguish Similar Languages? In *Proceedings of the International Conference on Information Technology Interfaces*.

Marco Lui and Paul Cook. 2013. Classifying English Documents by National Dialect. In *Proceedings of ALTW*.

Shervin Malmasi and Mark Dras. 2015a. Automatic Language Identification for Persian and Dari Texts. In *Proceedings PACLING*.

Shervin Malmasi and Mark Dras. 2015b. Language Identification using Classifier Ensembles. In *Proceedings of the LT4VarDial workshop*.

Shervin Malmasi, Eshrag Refaee, and Mark Dras. 2015. Arabic Dialect Identification using a Parallel Multidialectal Corpus. In *Proceedings of PACLING*.

Shervin Malmasi, Mark Dras, and Marcos Zampieri. 2016a. LTG at SemEval-2016 Task 11: Complex Word Identification with Classifier Ensembles. In *Proceedings of SemEval*.

Shervin Malmasi, Marcos Zampieri, Nikola Ljubešić, Preslav Nakov, Ahmed Ali, and Jörg Tiedemann. 2016b. Discriminating between Similar Languages and Arabic Dialect Identification: A Report on the Third DSL Shared Task. In *Proceedings of the VarDial Workshop*.

Gustavo Henrique Paetzold and Lucia Specia. 2016. Semeval 2016 task 11: Complex Word Identification. *Proceedings of SemEval*, pages 560–569.

Fatiha Sadat, Farnazeh Kazemi, and Atefeh Farzindar. 2014. Automatic Identification of Arabic Language Varieties and Dialects in Social Media. In *Proceedings of the SocialNLP Workshop*.

Abdulhadi Shoufan and Sumaya Al-Ameri. 2015. Natural Language Processing for Dialectical Arabic: A Survey. In *Proceedings of the Arabic NLP Workshop*.

Liling Tan, Marcos Zampieri, Nikola Ljubešic, and Jörg Tiedemann. 2014. Merging Comparable Data Sources for the Discrimination of Similar Languages: The DSL Corpus Collection. In *Proceedings of the BUCC Workshop*.

Christoph Tillmann, Saab Mansour, and Yaser Al-Onaizan. 2014. Improved Sentence-Level Arabic Dialect Classification. In *Proceedings of the VarDial Workshop*.

Omar F Zaidan and Chris Callison-Burch. 2011. The Arabic Online Commentary Dataset: An Annotated Dataset of Informal Arabic with High Dialectal Content. In *Proceedings of ACL*.

Omar F Zaidan and Chris Callison-Burch. 2014. Arabic Dialect Identification. *Computational Linguistics*.

Marcos Zampieri and Binyam Gebrekidan Gebre. 2012. Automatic Identification of Language Varieties: The Case of Portuguese. In *Proceedings of KONVENS*.

Marcos Zampieri, Liling Tan, Nikola Ljubešić, and Jörg Tiedemann. 2014. A Report on the DSL Shared Task 2014. In *Proceedings of the VarDial Workshop*.

Marcos Zampieri, Liling Tan, Nikola Ljubešić, Jörg Tiedemann, and Preslav Nakov. 2015. Overview of the DSL Shared Task 2015. In *Proceedings of the LT4VarDial Workshop*.

Rabih Zbib, Erika Malchiodi, Jacob Devlin, David Stallard, Spyros Matsoukas, Richard Schwartz, John Makhoul, Omar F Zaidan, and Chris Callison-Burch. 2012. Machine translation of Arabic Dialects. In *Proceedings of NAACL-HLT*.

DSL Shared task 2016: Perfect Is The Enemy of Good
Language Discrimination Through Expectation-Maximization and Chunk-based Language Model

Ondřej Herman and **Vít Suchomel** and **Vít Baisa** and **Pavel Rychlý**
Natural Language Processing Centre
Faculty of Informatics, Masaryk University, Brno, Czech Republic
{xherman1, xsuchom2, xbaisa, pary}@fi.muni.cz

Abstract

We investigate two approaches to automatic discrimination of similar languages: Expectation-maximization algorithm for estimating conditional probability $P(word|language)$ and a series of byte level language models. The accuracy of these methods reached 86.6 % and 88.3 %, respectively, on set A of the DSL Shared task 2016 competition.

1 Introduction

Discriminating similar languages is a very important step in building monolingual text corpora. Given a focus language, the aim is to get rid of all documents in languages other than the focus language. Our goal is to implement language-independent and efficient algorithms able to process billion-word corpora with sufficient accuracy and at a reasonable speed.

Organizers of the DSL shared task in 2016 provided three datasets for 2 subtasks: discrimination of a) similar languages and language varieties in newspaper texts (Bosnian, Croatian, and Serbian; Malay and Indonesian; Portuguese: Brazil and Portugal; Spanish: Argentina, Mexico, and Spain; French: France and Canada), b) in social media "texts" and c) Arabic dialects. Participants could submit closed or open variants: whether using only training and development data provided by organizers or using any additional language resources. Details are available at the website of the task.[1]

2 Related Work

The previous DSL tasks were organised in 2014 (Zampieri et al., 2014) and 2015 (Zampieri et al., 2015).

Unlike the two stage statistical classifier trained on character and word ngram features (Goutte and Leger, 2015) which performed the best in 2015 we wanted to try the EM algorithm in the steps of (Nigam et al., 2000) who used the EM to improve accuracy of a classifier trained on a small number of documents by adding a large number of unlabelled instances (aiming on the open submission). We also did not implement a separate classification stage for identifying the language group. Neither we implemented a special algorithm to discriminate Arabic dialects. The same approaches were used for all subtasks.

This year's competition (Malmasi et al., 2016) introduced languages harder to discriminate while Czech/Slovak which is easy to distinguish because of differences in high frequency words was abandoned.

3 Expectation-Maximization of $P(word|language)$

This method is an implementation of the EM algorithm for all sentence words. Given a sentence of words $w_1, w_2, \ldots, w_n$, the aim is to find the language with the highest probability "the sentence is in the language". That can be reduced to maximizing probabilities of separate words belonging to the language.

[1]http://ttg.uni-saarland.de/vardial2016/dsl2016.html

Proceedings of the Third Workshop on NLP for Similar Languages, Varieties and Dialects,
pages 114–118, Osaka, Japan, December 12 2016.

$$P(lang|sentence) = P(lang|w_1, w_2, \ldots, w_n) = \prod_{i=1}^{n} P(lang|w_i)$$

That can be decomposed by applying the Bayes' theorem:

$$P(lang|word) = \frac{P(word|lang) \cdot P(lang)}{P(word)}$$

$P(lang)$ is determined by the distribution of samples in the training data. A uniform distribution was used in the case of the competition. The value can be adjusted accordingly for other uses, e.g. separating a minority dialect represented by less text from a standard text in a language. $P(word)$ can also be obtained from the training data (closed submission) or from a large text corpus (open submission).

$$P(lang) = \frac{1}{\text{language count}}, \quad P(word) = \frac{\text{count}_{\text{all data}}(word)}{\text{count}_{\text{all data}}(\text{any word})}$$

The iterative algorithm is initialized with relative counts of words in texts in the language from the training set (closed submission) or from our own big web corpora (open submission) (Jakubíček et al., 2013).

$$P(word|lang) = \frac{\text{count}_{\text{language data}}(word)}{\text{count}_{\text{language data}}(\text{any word})}$$

It can be observed that some words occur quite frequently in a single language (and significantly infrequently in other languages) while other words occur in multiple languages. To represent the ratio of words in a language within a sentence, $\lambda_{lang}(sent)$ is introduced. This enables the algorithm to learn the weight of words from more relevant sentences with regards to the language.[2]

$$\lambda_{lang}(sent) = \frac{P(lang|sent)}{\sum_{lang}^{languages} P(lang|sent)}$$

$\lambda_{lang}(sent)$ is raised to the power of α to give even more weight to words occurring in sentences with a high probability of belonging to the language. We experimented with $\alpha \in \{0, 1, 2, 3\}$. The best results were obtained with $\alpha \in \{0, 1\}$. $\alpha = n + 1$ always performed a bit worse than $\alpha = n$ for $n \geq 1$. Therefore it seems this kind of weight adjustment does not help in the case of the uniformly distributed classes in the datasets.

Then, in each iteration $\lambda_{lang}(sent)$ and $P'(lang|sentence)$ is re-calculated for each language and each sentence.

The higher the probability $lang$ is the language of a sentence, the higher the probability $word$ is in language $lang$ for each word in the sentence.

$$P'(word|lang) = \frac{\sum_{sent}^{sentences} \lambda_{lang}^{\alpha}(sent) \cdot \frac{\lambda_{lang}(sent) \cdot P(word|lang) \cdot \text{count}_{sent}(word)}{\sum_{lang}^{languages} \lambda_{lang}(sent) \cdot P(word|lang)}}{\sum_{sent}^{sentences} \lambda_{lang}^{\alpha+1}(sent) \cdot |sent|}$$

Results after the initialization step (zero iterations) and after the first iteration were submitted. Calculating more iterations did not contribute to accuracy improvement. It would be interesting to repeat the experiment with unevenly distributed data.

---

[2] Let $sent =$ "w1 w1 w1 w2" be a sentence comprised of words w1 appearing only in language L1 and word w2 appearing only in language L2. Then $\lambda_{L1}(sent) = 0.25$ and $\lambda_{L2}(sent) = 0.75$.

4 Chunk-based Language Model

Chunk-based language model (Baisa, 2016), CBLM, is a byte level model similar to prediction-by-partial-match compression language models (Teahan and Harper, 2003). It stores all sufficiently frequent sequences of bytes from training data in a prefix tree. A following byte is predicted using the longest prefix stored in the model which ends with that byte. The length of prefixes is variable and is not limited by their length as in n-gram models. Instead, a threshold—the number of occurrence of prefixes in training data—is used (usually 2 or 3).

The model can assign scores[3] $M(s)$ to any unseen byte sequence s. We built models M_i for each language in the training data separately. The language of an unknown sentence (byte sequence) $LANG(s)$ is then determined by the model which assigns it the highest score:

$$LANG(s) = \arg\max_i M_i(s).$$

CBLM is robust because it operates on byte level. The only preprocessing used for building and evaluation of the models was lowercasing all data. The models have one main parameter: the threshold for the minimum frequency of byte sequences stored in the prefix tree. Using the development part of the dataset we found out that threshold 3 performed the best, so the parameter was set to 3 in all runs. It means that all byte sequences occurring at least $3\times$ in training data were stored and used in language prediction.

5 Results

The DSL competition dataset (Tan et al., 2014) was used for training and evaluation. Frequency word lists extracted from several big web corpora described in (Jakubíček et al., 2013) were used for the open submission.

Two variants of the EM algorithm based method and one run of the chunk-based language model were submitted. The results are summarised in Tables 1–6.

Test set A had 12 classes while test sets B1 and B2 had 5 classes. The samples were evenly distributed across the classes and so a random baseline is used. The samples in test set C were slightly unbalanced, so a majority class baseline of 22.79 % is used. The baselines for each data set were: A—Random baseline: 0.083, B1/B2—Random baseline: 0.20, C—Majority class baseline: 0.2279.

Run	Accuracy	F1 (micro)	F1 (macro)	F1 (weighted)
EM, 0 iter	0.8651	0.8651	0.8643	0.8643
EM, 1 iter	0.8659	0.8659	0.865	0.865
CBLM	0.8827	0.8827	0.8829	0.8829

Table 1: Results for test set A (closed training).

Run	Accuracy	F1 (micro)	F1 (macro)	F1 (weighted)
E–M, 0 iter	0.8	0.8	0.5663	0.7929
E–M, 1 iter	0.712	0.712	0.528	0.7392
CBLM	0.424	0.424	0.1899	0.4557

Table 2: Results for test set B1 (closed training).

As can be seen, the EM algorithm performed better on datasets B and C while CBLM proved better on dataset A. By checking the errors made by our classifiers we found that in some cases one method deals with the sample well while the other not, for example EM cannot make use of n-grams of characters in suffixes of words characteristic for certain languages but not seen in the training data. Combining both approaches could result in further improving the accuracy.

---

[3]For our purpose we do not need models to provide true probability distributions.

Run	Accuracy	F1 (micro)	F1 (macro)	F1 (weighted)
E–M, 0 iter	0.8	0.8	0.5093	0.8149
E–M, 1 iter	0.51	0.51	0.4632	0.6484

Table 3: Results for test set B1 (open training).

Run	Accuracy	F1 (micro)	F1 (macro)	F1 (weighted)
E–M, 0 iter	0.76	0.76	0.5404	0.7565
E–M, 1 iter	0.692	0.692	0.5155	0.7216
CBLM	0.602	0.602	0.3052	0.6103

Table 4: Results for test set B2 (closed training).

Run	Accuracy	F1 (micro)	F1 (macro)	F1 (weighted)
E–M, 0 iter	0.728	0.728	0.5418	0.7586
E–M, 1 iter	0.54	0.54	0.4207	0.6731

Table 5: Results for test set B2 (open training).

Run	Accuracy	F1 (micro)	F1 (macro)	F1 (weighted)
E–M, 0 iter	0.3961	0.3961	0.3622	0.3666
E–M, 1 iter	0.461	0.461	0.4481	0.4516
CBLM	0.4474	0.4474	0.4459	0.4473

Table 6: Results for test set C (closed training).

6 Discussion

Our main motivation is to clean big monolingual corpora built from web documents used for lexicography or language studies. For example, we are dealing with separation of Bokmal and Nynorsk from Norwegian texts or removing Danish and Swedish from the same data. Our methods were devised for processing larger texts, e.g. paragraphs or documents rather than sentences, yet the results show they can be applied to the competition data as well.

According to our inspection of the competition data a large part seems not to contain linguistically rich sentences or even continuous text. Some samples looked like sports results or rows from tabular data. We believe both methods would yield better results when trained and evaluated on longer samples of fluent language.

Furthermore, all datasets were balanced in the sense that all languages and dialects were evenly represented (or almost evenly in some cases). This fact might help some machine learning techniques and also could be exploited explicitly but we believe that this is not the case for real scenarios and thus our methods do not exploit this knowledge at all.

Both methods presented in this paper will be applied to cleaning big web corpora. We also plan to combine the methods by applying CBLM to cases where EM is not sure.

References

Vít Baisa. 2016. *Byte level language models*. Ph.D. thesis, Masaryk University.

Cyril Goutte and Serge Leger. 2015. Experiments in discriminating similar languages. In *Proceedings of the Joint Workshop on Language Technology for Closely Related Languages, Varieties and Dialects (LT4VarDial)*, pages 78–84, Hissar, Bulgaria.

Miloš Jakubíček, Adam Kilgarriff, Vojtěch Kovář, Pavel Rychlý, Vít Suchomel, et al. 2013. The tenten corpus family. In *7th International Corpus Linguistics Conference CL*, pages 125–127.

Shervin Malmasi, Marcos Zampieri, Nikola Ljubešić, Preslav Nakov, Ahmed Ali, and Jörg Tiedemann. 2016. Discriminating between similar languages and arabic dialect identification: A report on the third dsl shared task. In *Proceedings of the 3rd Workshop on Language Technology for Closely Related Languages, Varieties and Dialects (VarDial)*, Osaka, Japan.

Kamal Nigam, Andrew Kachites McCallum, Sebastian Thrun, and Tom Mitchell. 2000. Text classification from labeled and unlabeled documents using EM. *Machine learning*, 39(2-3):103–134.

Liling Tan, Marcos Zampieri, Nikola Ljubešic, and Jörg Tiedemann. 2014. Merging comparable data sources for the discrimination of similar languages: The dsl corpus collection. In *Proceedings of the 7th Workshop on Building and Using Comparable Corpora (BUCC)*, pages 11–15, Reykjavik, Iceland.

William J Teahan and David J Harper. 2003. Using compression-based language models for text categorization. In *Language modeling for information retrieval*, pages 141–165. Springer.

Marcos Zampieri, Liling Tan, Nikola Ljubešić, and Jörg Tiedemann. 2014. A report on the dsl shared task 2014. In *Proceedings of the First Workshop on Applying NLP Tools to Similar Languages, Varieties and Dialects (VarDial)*, pages 58–67, Dublin, Ireland.

Marcos Zampieri, Liling Tan, Nikola Ljubešić, Jörg Tiedemann, and Preslav Nakov. 2015. Overview of the dsl shared task 2015. In *Proceedings of the Joint Workshop on Language Technology for Closely Related Languages, Varieties and Dialects (LT4VarDial)*, pages 1–9, Hissar, Bulgaria.

Byte-based Language Identification with Deep Convolutional Networks

Johannes Bjerva
University of Groningen
The Netherlands
`j.bjerva@rug.nl`

Abstract

We report on our system for the shared task on discrimination of similar languages (DSL 2016). The system uses only byte representations in a deep residual network (ResNet). The system, named ResIdent, is trained only on the data released with the task (closed training). We obtain 84.88% accuracy on subtask A, 68.80% accuracy on subtask B1, and 69.80% accuracy on subtask B2. A large difference in accuracy on development data can be observed with relatively minor changes in our network's architecture and hyperparameters. We therefore expect fine-tuning of these parameters to yield higher accuracies.

1 Introduction

Language identification is an unsolved problem, certainly in the context of discriminating between very similar languages (Baldwin and Lui, 2010). This problem is tackled in the Discriminating between Similar Languages (DSL) series of shared tasks (Zampieri et al., 2014; Zampieri et al., 2015). Most successful approaches to the DSL shared task in previous years have relied on settings containing ensembles of classifiers (Goutte et al., 2016). These classifiers often use various combinations of features, mostly based on word, character, and/or byte n-grams (see, e.g., Cavnar et al. (1994), Lui and Baldwin (2012)).

We are interested in exploring a single methodological aspect in the current edition of this shared task (Malmasi et al., 2016). We aim to investigate whether reasonable results for this task could be obtained by applying recently emerged neural network architectures, coupled with sub-token input representations. To address this question, we explore convolutional neural networks (CNNs) and recurrent neural networks (RNNs). Deep residual networks (ResNets) are a recent building block for CNNs which have yielded promising results in, e.g., image classification tasks (He et al., 2015; He et al., 2016). ResNets are constructed by stacking so-called residual units. These units can be viewed as a series of convolutional layers with a 'shortcut' which facilitates signal propagation in the neural network. This, in turn, allows for training deeper networks more easily (He et al., 2016). In Natural Language Processing (NLP), ResNets have shown state-of-the-art performance for Semantic and Part-of-Speech tagging (Bjerva et al., 2016). However, no previous work has attempted to apply ResNets to language identification.

2 Method

Several previous approaches in the DSL shared tasks have formulated the task as a two-step classification, first identifying the language group, and then the specific language (Zampieri et al., 2015). Instead of taking this approach, we formulate the task as a multi-class classification problem, with each language / dialect representing a separate class. Our system is a deep neural network consisting of a bidirectional Gated Recurrent Unit (GRU) network at the upper level, and a Deep Residual Network (ResNet) at the lower level (Figure 1). The inputs of our system are byte-level representations of each input sentence, with byte embeddings which are learnt during training. Using byte-level representations differs from character-level representations in that UTF-8 encodes non-ascii symbols with more than one byte, which

Proceedings of the Third Workshop on NLP for Similar Languages, Varieties and Dialects,
pages 119–125, Osaka, Japan, December 12 2016.

potentially allows for more disambiguating power. A concrete example can be found when considering the relatively similar languages Norwegian and Swedish. Here, there are two pairs of letters which are interchangeable: where Swedish uses 'ä' (C3 A4) and 'ö' (C3 B6), Norwegian uses 'æ' (C3 A6) and 'ø' (C3 B8). Hence, using the lower-level byte representation, we allow the model to take advantage of the first shared byte between these characters. The architecture used in this work is based on the sequence-to-sequence labelling architecture used in Bjerva et al. (2016), modified for the task of language identification. Our system is implemented in Keras using the Tensorflow backend (Chollet, 2015; Abadi et al., 2016).

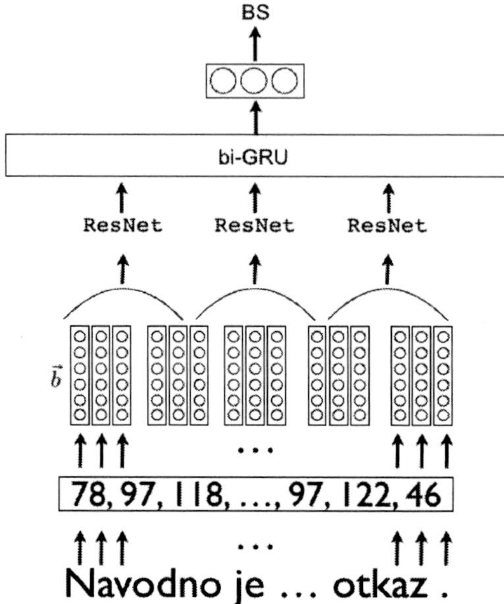

Figure 1: Model architecture: ResNet with byte representations $(\vec{b})$, with a bi-GRU at the upper level. The input example sequence is converted to a sequence of byte identifiers (one integer per byte, rather than one integer per character), which are converted to a byte embedding representation. This input is treated by the ResNet, followed by the bi-GRU, finally yielding the language id *BS* (Bosnian).

2.1 Gated Recurrent Unit Networks

GRUs (Cho et al., 2014) are a recently introduced variant of RNNs, and are designed to prevent vanishing gradients, thus being able to cope with longer input sequences than vanilla RNNs. GRUs are similar to the more commonly-used Long Short-Term Memory networks (LSTMs), both in purpose and implementation (Chung et al., 2014). A bi-directional GRU makes both forward and backward passes over sequences, and can therefore use both preceding and succeeding contexts to predict a tag (Graves and Schmidhuber, 2005; Goldberg, 2015). Bi-directional GRUs and LSTMs have been shown to yield high performance on several NLP tasks, such as POS and semantic tagging, named entity tagging, and chunking (Wang et al., 2015; Yang et al., 2016; Plank et al., 2016; Bjerva et al., 2016).

2.2 Deep Residual Networks

Deep Residual Networks (ResNets) are built up by stacking residual units. A residual unit can be expressed as:

$$y_l = h(x_l) + \mathcal{F}(x_l, \mathcal{W}_l),$$
$$x_{l+1} = f(y_l),$$

$$(1)$$

where x_l and x_{l+1} are the input and output of the l-th layer, $\mathcal{W}_l$ is the weights for the l-th layer, and $\mathcal{F}$ is a residual function (He et al., 2016), e.g., the identity function (He et al., 2015), which we also use in our experiments. ResNets can be intuitively understood by thinking of residual functions as paths through which information can propagate easily. This means that, in every layer, a ResNet learns more complex feature combinations, which it combines with the shallower representation from the previous layer. This architecture allows for the construction of much deeper networks. ResNets have recently been found to yield impressive performance in both image recognition and NLP tasks (He et al., 2015; He et al., 2016; Östling, 2016; Conneau et al., 2016), and are an interesting and effective alternative to simply stacking layers. In this paper we use the *assymetric* variant of ResNets as described in Equation 9 in He et al. (2016):

$$x_{l+1} = x_l + \mathcal{F}(\hat{f}(x_l), \mathcal{W}_l). \tag{2}$$

Our residual block, using dropout and batch normalization (Srivastava et al., 2014; Ioffe and Szegedy, 2015), is defined in Table 1. In the table, *merge* indicates the concatenation of the input of the residual block, with the output of the final convolutional layer.

type	patch/pool size
Batch normalization + ReLu + Dropout ($p = 0.5$)	
Convolution	8
Batch normalization + ReLu + Dropout ($p = 0.5$)	
Convolution	4
Merge	
Maximum pooling	2

Table 1: Residual block overview.

2.3 System Description

We represent each sentence using a byte-based representation (S_b). This representation is a 2-dimensional matrix $S_b \in \mathbb{R}^{s \times d_b}$, where s is the zero-padded sentence length and d_b is the dimensionality of the byte embeddings. Byte embeddings are first passed through a ResNet in order to obtain a representation which captures something akin to byte n-gram features.[1] The size of n is determined by the convolutional window size used. We use a convolutional window size with length 8, meaning that for each byte in the input, the ResNet can learn a suitable representation incorporating up to 8 bytes of context information. These overlapping byte-based n-gram features are then passed through to the bi-GRU, which yields a *sentence level* representation. The softmax layer applied to the bi-GRU output is then used in order to obtain the network's predicted class per input.

2.3.1 Hyperparameters

The hyperparameters used by the system were tuned on an altogether different task (semantic tagging), and adapted for the current task. The dimensionality of our byte embeddings, d_b, is set to 64. Our residual block is defined in Section 2.2. We use rectified linear units (ReLUs) for all activation functions (Nair and Hinton, 2010), and apply dropout with $p = 0.1$ to both input weights and recurrent weights in the bi-GRU. All GRU layers have 100 hidden units.

All experiments were run with early stopping monitoring validation set loss, using a maximum of 50 epochs, and a batch size of 100. Optimisation is done using the ADAM algorithm (Kingma and Ba, 2015), with the categorical cross-entropy loss function as training objective.

For the B tasks, we train the model in the same way as for the A tasks. Only a handful of instances ($n \approx 5$) per B run are classified as belonging to a language which the B group does not contain. These cases are automatically converted to being in the class *hr*. For the B tasks, we also perform a simple clean-up of the data. We first remove all hyperlinks, hashtags and usernames from the text with a simple regex-based script. We then remove all tweets classified as English. We submitted three runs for each subtask. The system used for runs 1, 2 and 3 contain five, four and three residual blocks respectively.

---

[1] Note that bytes are passed through the ResNet *one by one*, yielding one representation per byte, rather than as a whole sequence, which would yield a single representation per sentence.

3   Results

Test Set	Track	Run	Accuracy	F1 (micro)	F1 (macro)	F1 (weighted)
A	closed	Baseline	0.083			
A	closed	run1	0.8462	0.8462	0.8415	0.8415
A	closed	run2	0.8324	0.8324	0.8272	0.8272
A	closed	run3	**0.8488**	0.8488	0.8467	0.8467
B1	closed	Baseline	0.020			
B1	closed	run1	0.682	0.682	0.6802	0.6802
B1	closed	run2	0.676	0.676	0.6708	0.6708
B1	closed	run3	**0.688**	0.688	0.6868	0.6868
B2	closed	Baseline	0.020			
B2	closed	run1	0.684	0.684	0.6788	0.6788
B2	closed	run2	**0.698**	0.698	0.6942	0.6942
B2	closed	run3	0.664	0.664	0.6524	0.6524

Table 2: Results for all runs in subtasks A, B1 and B2 (closed training).

	es-ar	es-es	es-mx	fr-ca	fr-fr	id	my	pt-br	pt-pt	hr	bs	sr
es-ar	824	77	94	0	1	1	0	2	1	0	0	0
es-es	90	778	127	0	1	0	0	1	2	0	1	0
es-mx	210	269	520	0	0	0	0	1	0	0	0	0
fr-ca	0	0	0	956	44	0	0	0	0	0	0	0
fr-fr	0	0	0	93	905	0	0	1	0	1	0	0
id	0	0	0	0	0	951	48	0	0	0	0	1
my	0	0	0	0	0	30	970	0	0	0	0	0
pt-br	0	0	1	0	0	0	0	891	107	1	0	0
pt-pt	0	1	0	0	0	0	0	78	920	0	1	0
hr	0	0	0	0	0	0	0	0	0	823	150	27
bs	0	0	0	0	1	0	0	1	0	143	730	125
sr	0	0	0	0	1	0	0	0	0	15	67	917

Table 3: Confusion matrix, closed run 3, on test set A. The x-axis indicates predicted labels, and the y-axis indicates true labels.

We evaluate our system in subtasks A, B1 and B2. Subtask A contains data for five language groups, with two to three languages in each group (Tan et al., 2014). Subtask B1 and B2 contain data for a subset of the languages in subtask A, compiled from Twitter. Subtask B1 contains the amount of tweets necessary for a human annotator to make reliable judgements, whereas B2 contains the maximum amount of data available per tweet.

For subtasks A and B1, run 3 results in the best accuracy on test, whereas run 2 results in the best accuracy on B2. The results are shown in Table 2. Table 3 and Table 4 contain confusion matrices for the results in subtask A and B respectively.

4   Discussion

Judging from the confusion matrices in Section 3, our system has very low confusion between language groups. However, confusion can be observed within all groups. Although the system achieves reasonable

	B1					**B2**				
	pt-br	pt-pt	hr	bs	sr	pt-br	pt-pt	hr	bs	sr
pt-br	74	24	1	0	1	54	40	3	2	1
pt-pt	31	67	1	0	1	15	80	5	0	0
bs	0	0	60	31	9	0	0	75	20	5
hr	1	0	20	62	17	0	0	31	56	13
sr	4	0	5	10	81	2	0	8	6	84

Table 4: Confusion matrix, closed run 3 on test set B1 (left) and closed run 2 on test set B2 (right). The x-axis indicates predicted labels, and the y-axis indicates true labels.

performance, there is a large gap between our system and the best performing systems (e.g. Çöltekin and Rama (2016), who obtain 89.38% accuracy on task A, 86.2% on B1, and 82.2% on B2). This can to some extent be explained by limitations caused by our implementation.

The largest limiting factor can be found in the fact that we only allowed our system to use the first ca. 384 bytes of each training/testing instance. For the training and development set, and subtask A, this was no major limitation, as this allowed us to use more than 90% of the available data. However, for subtasks B1 and B2, this may have seriously affected the system's performance. Additionally, we restricted our system to using only byte embeddings as input. Adding word-level representations into the mix, would likely increase system performance.

We also observed considerable differences in development accuracy when changing hyperparameters of our network in relatively minor ways. For instance, altering the patch sizes used in our CNNs had a noticeable impact on validation loss. However, altering the amount of residual blocks used, did not have a large effect on results. The neural network architecture, as well as most of the hyperparameters, were tuned on an altogether different task (semantic tagging), and adapted for the current task. Further fine tuning of the network architecture and hyperparameters for this task would therefore likely lead to narrowing the performance gap.

5   Conclusions

We implemented a language identification system using deep residual networks (ResNets) coupled with a bidirectional Gated Recurrent Unit network (bi-GRU), using only byte-level representations. In the DSL 2016 shared task, we achieved reasonable performance, with 84.88% accuracy on subtask A, 68.80% accuracy on subtask B1, and 69.80% accuracy on subtask B2. Although acceptable performance was achieved, further fine tuning of input representations and system architecture would likely improve performance.

Acknowledgements

We would like to thank the Center for Information Technology of the University of Groningen for their support and for providing access to the Peregrine high performance computing cluster, as well as the anonymous reviewers for their valuable feedback.

References

Martín Abadi, Ashish Agarwal, Paul Barham, Eugene Brevdo, Zhifeng Chen, Craig Citro, Gregory S. Corrado, Andy Davis, Jeffrey Dean, Matthieu Devin, Sanjay Ghemawat, Ian J. Goodfellow, Andrew Harp, Geoffrey Irving, Michael Isard, Yangqing Jia, Rafal Józefowicz, Lukasz Kaiser, Manjunath Kudlur, Josh Levenberg, Dan Mane, Rajat Monga, Sherry Moore, Derek Gordon Murray, Chris Olah, Mike Schuster, Jonathon Shlens,

Benoit Steiner, Ilya Sutskever, Kunal Talwar, Paul A. Tucker, Vincent Vanhoucke, Vijay Vasudevan, Fernanda B. Viégas, Oriol Vinyals, Pete Warden, Martin Wattenberg, Martin Wicke, Yuan Yu, and Xiaoqiang Zheng. 2016. Tensorflow: Large-scale machine learning on heterogeneous distributed systems. *arXiv preprint arXiv:1603.04467*.

Timothy Baldwin and Marco Lui. 2010. Language identification: The long and the short of the matter. In *Human Language Technologies: The 2010 Annual Conference of the North American Chapter of the Association for Computational Linguistics*, pages 229–237. Association for Computational Linguistics.

Johannes Bjerva, Barbara Plank, and Johan Bos. 2016. Semantic Tagging with Deep Residual Networks. In *Proceedings of COLING 2016*, Osaka, Japan, December.

William B Cavnar, John M Trenkle, et al. 1994. N-gram-based text categorization. *Ann Arbor MI*, 48113(2):161–175.

Çağrı Çöltekin and Taraka Rama. 2016. Discriminating similar languages: experiments with linear SVMs and neural networks. In *Proceedings of the 3rd Workshop on Language Technology for Closely Related Languages, Varieties and Dialects (VarDial)*, Osaka, Japan.

Kyunghyun Cho, Bart Van Merriënboer, Caglar Gulcehre, Dzmitry Bahdanau, Fethi Bougares, Holger Schwenk, and Yoshua Bengio. 2014. Learning phrase representations using RNN encoder-decoder for statistical machine translation. In *Proceedings of EMNLP 2014*, Doha, Qatar.

François Chollet. 2015. Keras. https://github.com/fchollet/keras.

Junyoung Chung, Caglar Gulcehre, KyungHyun Cho, and Yoshua Bengio. 2014. Empirical evaluation of gated recurrent neural networks on sequence modeling. *arXiv preprint arXiv:1412.3555*.

Alexis Conneau, Holger Schwenk, Loïc Barrault, and Yann Lecun. 2016. Very Deep Convolutional Networks for Natural Language Processing. *arXiv preprint arXiv:1606.01781*.

Yoav Goldberg. 2015. A primer on neural network models for natural language processing. *arXiv preprint arXiv:1510.00726*.

Cyril Goutte, Serge Léger, Shervin Malmasi, and Marcos Zampieri. 2016. Discriminating Similar Languages: Evaluations and Explorations. In *Proceedings of the 10th International Conference on Language Resources and Evaluation (LREC 2016)*.

Alex Graves and Jürgen Schmidhuber. 2005. Framewise phoneme classification with bidirectional LSTM and other neural network architectures. *Neural Networks*, 18(5):602–610.

Kaiming He, Xiangyu Zhang, Shaoqing Ren, and Jian Sun. 2015. Deep residual learning for image recognition. *arXiv preprint arXiv:1512.03385*.

Kaiming He, Xiangyu Zhang, Shaoqing Ren, and Jian Sun. 2016. Identity mappings in deep residual networks. *arXiv preprint arXiv:1603.05027*.

Sergey Ioffe and Christian Szegedy. 2015. Batch Normalization: Accelerating Deep Network Training by Reducing Internal Covariate Shift. In *Proceedings of The 32nd International Conference on Machine Learning*, pages 448–456.

Diederik Kingma and Jimmy Ba. 2015. Adam: A method for stochastic optimization. In *Proceedings of ICLR 2015*, San Diego, USA.

Marco Lui and Timothy Baldwin. 2012. langid.py: An off-the-shelf language identification tool. In *Proceedings of the ACL 2012 system demonstrations*, pages 25–30. Association for Computational Linguistics.

Shervin Malmasi, Marcos Zampieri, Nikola Ljubešić, Preslav Nakov, Ahmed Ali, and Jörg Tiedemann. 2016. Discriminating between Similar Languages and Arabic Dialect Identification: A Report on the Third DSL Shared Task. In *Proceedings of the 3rd Workshop on Language Technology for Closely Related Languages, Varieties and Dialects (VarDial)*, Osaka, Japan.

Vinod Nair and Geoffrey E Hinton. 2010. Rectified linear units improve restricted boltzmann machines. In *Proceedings of the 27th International Conference on Machine Learning (ICML-10)*, pages 807–814.

Robert Östling. 2016. Morphological reinflection with convolutional neural networks. In *Proceedings of the 2016 Meeting of SIGMORPHON*, Berlin, Germany. Association for Computational Linguistics.

Barbara Plank, Anders Søgaard, and Yoav Goldberg. 2016. Multilingual Part-of-Speech Tagging with Bidirectional Long Short-Term Memory Models and Auxiliary Loss. In *Proceedings of ACL 2016.*

Nitish Srivastava, Geoffrey E Hinton, Alex Krizhevsky, Ilya Sutskever, and Ruslan Salakhutdinov. 2014. Dropout: a simple way to prevent neural networks from overfitting. *Journal of Machine Learning Research*, 15(1):1929–1958.

Liling Tan, Marcos Zampieri, Nikola Ljubešic, and Jörg Tiedemann. 2014. Merging Comparable Data Sources for the Discrimination of Similar Languages: The DSL Corpus Collection. In *Proceedings of the 7th Workshop on Building and Using Comparable Corpora (BUCC)*, pages 11–15, Reykjavik, Iceland.

Peilu Wang, Yao Qian, Frank K Soong, Lei He, and Hai Zhao. 2015. A Unified Tagging Solution: Bidirectional LSTM Recurrent Neural Network with Word Embedding. *arXiv preprint arXiv:1511.00215.*

Zhilin Yang, Ruslan Salakhutdinov, and William Cohen. 2016. Multi-Task Cross-Lingual Sequence Tagging from Scratch. *arXiv preprint arXiv:1603.06270.*

Marcos Zampieri, Liling Tan, Nikola Ljubešić, and Jörg Tiedemann. 2014. A Report on the DSL Shared Task 2014. In *Proceedings of the First Workshop on Applying NLP Tools to Similar Languages, Varieties and Dialects (VarDial)*, pages 58–67, Dublin, Ireland.

Marcos Zampieri, Liling Tan, Nikola Ljubešić, Jörg Tiedemann, and Preslav Nakov. 2015. Overview of the DSL Shared Task 2015. In *Proceedings of the Joint Workshop on Language Technology for Closely Related Languages, Varieties and Dialects (LT4VarDial)*, pages 1–9, Hissar, Bulgaria.

Classifying ASR Transcriptions According to Arabic Dialect

Abualsoud Hanani, Aziz Qaroush
Electrical & Computer Engineering Dept
Birzeit University
West Bank, Palestine
{ahanani,qaroush}@birzeit.edu

Stephen Taylor
Computer Science Dept
Fitchburg State University
Fitchburg, MA, USA
staylor@fitchburgstate.edu

Abstract

We describe several systems for identifying short samples of Arabic dialects, which were prepared for the shared task of the 2016 DSL Workshop (Malmasi et al., 2016). Our best system, an SVM using character tri-gram features, achieved an accuracy on the test data for the task of 0.4279, compared to a baseline of 0.20 for chance guesses or 0.2279 if we had always chosen the same most frequent class in the test set. This compares with the results of the team with the best weighted F1 score, which was an accuracy of 0.5117. The team entries seem to fall into cohorts, with the all the teams in a cohort within a standard-deviation of each other, and our three entries are in the third cohort, which is about seven standard deviations from the top.

1 Introduction

In 2016 the Distinguishing Similar Languages workshop (Malmasi et al., 2016) added a shared task to classify short segments of text as one of five Arabic dialects. The workshop organizers provided a training file and a schedule. After allowing the participants development time, they distributed a test file, and evaluated the success of participating systems.

We built several systems for dialect classification, and submitted runs from three of them. Interestingly, our results on the workshop test data were not consistent with our tests on reserved training data.

Our accuracy rates cluster around 40%; the rates of the best systems were a little better than 50%. If we take the raw scores as drawn from a binomial distribution, the standard deviation is $\sqrt{p(1-p)n}$. With $n = 1540$, and $p = 0.5$ or $p = 0.4$ the standard deviation is 19.2 or 19.6 correct answers respectively, corresponding to a difference in accuracy of about 1.25%. Since the best overall accuracy score is 51.33%, our best score is 6.9 standard deviations below it. (The scores of the top three teams don't seem to be significantly different from each other.)

On reserved training data, our systems all scored much better than they did on the test data, with our best system achieving an accuracy rate of 57%. No doubt the best systems in the trial also scored better in training. In addition to describing our systems, we speculate what factors might account for the difference in training and test results.

2 Related Work

The Arabic dialects have a common written form and unified literary tradition, so it seems most logical to distinguish dialects on the basis of acoustics, and there is a fair amount of work there, including (Hanani et al., 2013; Hanani et al., 2015; Ali et al., 2016). Determining the contents of a transcript, i.e. what word that sound sequence is most likely to be, is easier if you know what language model and what dictionary to apply. (Najafian et al., 2014)

Language modeling of Arabic dialects has been held back by an absence of appropriate corpora. Work has been done by Al-Haj et al. (2009; Ali et al. (2008; Elmahdy et al. (2012; Elmahdy et al. (2010; Novotney et al. (2011; Elmahdy et al. (2013; Vergyri et al. (2005; Zaidan and Callison-Burch (2011) and

Proceedings of the Third Workshop on NLP for Similar Languages, Varieties and Dialects,
pages 126–134, Osaka, Japan, December 12 2016.

EGY	Egyptian	The dialect most often called Egyptian is an urban dialect used in Cairo and Alexandria. The next largest Egyptian dialect, Sa'idi, with 20 million speakers, is said to be incomprehensible to Cairene speakers.
GLF	Gulf	The dialects from the Arabic Gulf countries of Bahrain, Kuwait, Oman, Saudi Arabia, United Arab Emirates, and sometimes Iraq are often grouped together.
LAV	Levantine	This group may include dialects from Jordan, Palestine, Syria. (The label *LAV* is used consistently in this corpus.)
MSA	Modern Standard Arabic	This includes most Arabic literature and most formal speech, including television news.
NOR	North African	Dialects from north Africa including the countries of Algeria, Libya, Morocco, Tunisia.

Table 1: Dialect Labels

Ali et al. (2016), most of whom developed corpora for the purpose, several of which are now publicly available.

Ali et al. (2016) developed the corpus on which the DSL Arabic shared task is based. Their own dialect detection efforts depended largely on acoustical cues. Malmasi et al. (2015) do Arabic dialect identification from text corpora, including the Multi-Dialect Parallel Corpus of Arabic (Bouamor et al., 2014) and the Arabic Online Commentary database (Zaidan and Callison-Burch, 2011). Zaidan and Callison-Burch (2014) builds on their own corpus to do dialect identification. ElFardy and Diab (2013) also build a classifier based on the Zaidan and Callison-Burch (2011) corpus.

Most of the work identifying Arabic dialects from text uses character features; many also use word features. Many use Support Vector Machines (SVM.) We investigated building SVM models using character n-gram features.

In the 2014 DSL workshop shared task, the second place entry (Porta and Sancho, 2014) used a *whitelisted words* feature, the 10,000 most frequent words in each language, which is slightly similar to the idea we implement in Section 4.3. However, given the substantial overlap in vocabulary between Arabic dialects, our approach is to look for unusual frequencies, both excesses and scarcities.

3 Methodology and Data

3.1 Training and Test Data

The training data is drawn from the speech corpus collected by Ali et al. (2016). The text is provided in the Buckwalter transcription (Buckwalter, 2002). There are no vowels, and no punctuation, except for the space character.

The training data comprises 7619 segments, ranging in size from one to 18017 characters each. Each segment is labeled with one of five Arabic dialects as shown in table 3.1. The labels are broad and imprecise. For example rural and urban dialects in a single country are likely to differ a great deal, and both accents and vocabulary might have big differences between countries. For another example, urban Palestinian and urban Syrian are both Levantine, but are easily distinguished by pronunciation, vocabulary, and the grammar of negation.

Many of the very short segments appear more than once, with different dialect labels. For example, لا lA "no" appears three times, labelled Gulf, Levantine, and North African. This reflects vocabulary overlap between dialects, as well as a small sample bias (less than 300 of the segments are only a single word) since this word could also appear in Egyptian and MSA.

The number of segments of various sizes is shown in table 2. Notice that almost 20% of the segments are less than 40 characters long, but less than 2% of the data is in these segments. Similarly only 10% of the segments are greater than 520 characters, but 38% of the training data is in these segments, with 18017 characters, 1% of the data, in a single segment.

The most common segment size is seven characters, with 61 occurences, slightly less than 1% of the segments. Three and five character segments are in second and third place, with 3.4% of all segments less than eight characters in length. One might expect that segmental structure would be an unreliable feature for small segments.

In contrast, the test data for the shared task, also shown in Table 2, has less than 8% of the segments less than 40 characters in size. The largest segment is 2454 characters, the mean is 239 characters. There are only 21 segments, or 1.4% less than 10 characters in length. The twenty commonest sizes are all larger than 90 characters. This is much more suitable for discovering features in segments, but doesn't perfectly match the training data.

segment size	number of segments		total characters in all in this range	
	training	test	training	test
1 - 40	1510	119	30027	2576
41 - 80	1063	169	64032	10593
81 - 120	898	224	89242	23002
121 - 160	702	227	98197	31975
161 - 200	556	219	99443	39220
201 - 240	512	145	112377	31748
241 - 280	387	110	100655	28418
181 - 320	327	60	98136	18192
321 - 360	251	51	85298	17276
360 - 400	215	23	81505	8759
401 - 440	167	21	70047	8724
441 - 480	155	15	71291	6904
481 - 520	114	14	57125	7012
521 - ∞	762	143	651156	132073
sums	7619	1540	1708531	366472

Table 2: Training and Test data by segment size

3.2 Character N-gram feature vectors

The N-gram components of the sequence of characters generated from a sentence S can be represented as a D-dimensional vector p where, D is the number of all N-grams, C_j is the jth N-gram and the probability p_j of Cj is estimated using counts of N-grams,

$$p_j = \frac{count(C_j)}{\sum_i count(C_i)} \tag{1}$$

Where the sum in (1) is performed over all N-grams and $Count(C_j)$ is the number of times the N-gram component C_j occurs in the produced sequence of tokens.

Assuming p^{tar} and p^{bkg} are probability vectors of the target and background Arabic dialects respectively, the SVM can be applied to find a separating hyperplane h by using different kinds of kernel functions. The most commonly used SVM kernels are the Gaussian and the polynomial. The simple linear dot-product kernel is used in this system because other kernels gave no improvement.

3.3 Weighting

Before applying SVM, the generated probabilities vectors, p_j, are weighted to emphasize the most discriminative components (i.e. those which occur frequently in one dialect and infrequently in others). The

N-gram components which are common in most dialects, such as common characters or words, contain little discriminative information and are de-emphasized. Numerous weighting techniques are available for this purpose, such as the Inverse Document Frequency (IDF) from Information Retrieval (IR), Usefulness from Topic Spotting and Identification, and the Log-Likelihood Ratio (LLR) weighting technique proposed in (Campbell et al., 2007).

The LLR weighting w_j for component C_j is given by:

$$w_j = g\left(\frac{1}{P(C_j/all)}\right) \tag{2}$$

Here $g()$ is a function used to smooth and compress the dynamic range (for example, $g(x) = \sqrt{x}$, or $g(x) = \log(x) + 1$). $p(C_j/all)$ is the probability of N-gram component C_j across all dialects.

The components which have zero occupancy in all dialects are removed since they do not carry any useful information. A benefit of discarding these non-visited components is that it reduces the feature dimension dramatically, particularly for the high order N-gram system as the dimension of the N-gram increases exponentially (M^n), where M is the number of distinct Buckwalter Arabic transcription characters in the data set ($M = 51$ for the training data.)

Those N-gram components which have a very small probability have a very high weighting, allowing a minority of components to dominate the scores. To prevent this, a minimum threshold T1 on the weighting w_j was applied. According to Zipfs law, the rank-frequency distribution of words in a typical document follows a decaying exponential. The high ranking words with high probability are not useful for discrimination because they appear in most of the documents. Conversely, the low-rank words are too rare to gather useful statistical information. The area of interest is somewhere in the middle. To address this we apply a second, maximum, threshold T2 on the weighting vector to deemphasize the common components. The values of T1 and T2 were determined empirically on the training data set.

3.4 Feature Selection

In addition to the weighting and thresholds described in the above sub-section, a feature selection technique is needed to minimize the number of N-gram components by keeping only those which are most discriminative. This is particularly necessary in high-order N-gram systems because the dimension is increased exponentially. Consequently, reducing the number of N-gram components decreases the computational cost and the required amount of memory.

A powerful feature selection technique based on the information entropy is applied to all n-gram feature vectors.

4 The systems

Six different systems were investigated during development; test runs were submitted for three of these. In addition, after the testing was completed, we ran some experiments on three additional SVM variants.

- Two of the systems, discussed in section 4.1, are based on the same set of extracted character n-grams. One run was submitted from these two systems, an SVM based on a subset of 3-gram character sequences.

- Our second run is the output of a system based on word frequencies (section 4.3.)

- Two neural network models were built (section 4.2.) Neither appears as a stand-alone run, but their output is incorporated into into the input for the system used for our final run.

- A neural network system (section 4.4) was built to combine the word and neural-network models, and this system was used for our third run.

4.1 Characteristics of the SVM systems

In developing these system, the provided training data was split, with 70% going into a training set, and 30% retained for validation and testing.

For the submitted system, the model was built using the WEKA tool (Hall et al., 2009).

The model was trained on all training tri-gram data set using 10-fold cross validation on SVM classifier after doing feature selection using information gain.

This system gave our best run on the test data, with an accuracy of 0.4279220779 and a weighted F1 score of 0.4264282701. It performed much better against the reserved test data, achieving an accuracy rate on that set of 57% with character trigram features.

4.2 LSTM systems

For the LSTM and word-feature systems, we chose a different split of the training data, into 90% training, 5% validation, and 5% test.

Our LSTM system is based on the char_rnn software described in (Karpathy et al., 2016). This is a character-based language model for text, built with a neural net.

The char_rnn software implements a Long Short Term Memory recurrent neural network (LSTM RNN) which reads the test or training data one character at a time. In training, the error function is effectively the entropy of the next character; in testing, the same network is repeatedly used to predict the most likely next character, resulting in excerpts in the style of the training data.

We modified the program[1], which is written in the Torch language (Collobert et al., 2011) so that it classifies text samples, instead of predicting the next character.

We developed two LSTM RNN models. Both have one-of-48 character inputs, and the hidden (LSTM) layers have forget gates, etc. at each node. As in other RNN models, the state of each node in a hidden layer is an input to the next input step, so that at each character input, not only the current input character, but the past input history affects the output.

We specify a maximum sequence length n in training, and at each training step the past states of the neural net are *unrolled*, so that internal states of the hidden layers for past states are considered while adjusting the parameters being trained.

Our better-performing LSTM has two hidden layers of 128 nodes each. This amounts to 223877 parameters to train. It was trained with a maximum sequence length of 520 characters, so during training up to 520 complete past states of the neural net need to be retained. (520 was chosen as the 90th percentile of sizes from the training data.) In addition, Karpathy's code was built to take advantage of parallel processing in a graphics controller, and handles batches of sequences at a time. Typically, at each training step a batch of sequences, all the same length, would be processed through a single character of input, and the single set of parameters used by all batches would be adjusted to optimize the loss function for the current character, given that changes in the parameters would have affected previous states.

Although we did not use a graphics controller, we kept the batch structure, which averages out the parameter changes, and reduces the training time per segment, since all the segments in a batch contribute to the training step.

We trained with a maximum batch size of 50, but given the training data, such large batches occurred only for small sequence sizes.

Our training technique was to check the loss function for the validation set every thousand training steps, roughly seven times an epoch. When the validation loss began to diverge, we'd reduce the learning rate and continue to train from the last good point. Our best loss function is 1.3176 (compare below.) This gave us an accuracy rate on the reserved test data of 0.4368.

We also experimented with a three hidden layer LSTM, again with 128 nodes in each hidden layer. The number of parameters in this LSTM is 355973, and this proved to be an issue. For longer sequences, there was not enough memory available to keep copies of the state for each character in the sequence for modest batch sizes. It proved necessary to train with a smaller batch size (25) and a smaller sequence

---

[1]Our changes are available at https://github.com/StephenETaylor/varDialNN

length (420.) For whatever reason, this network did not converge as well. We achieved a best loss function of 1.4369.

4.3 Outlier unigram system

This system uses word features, in the hope that they would be independent of the character features other models were using. It goes through the training data, and builds frequencies for uni-grams, bi-grams, and tri-grams for the whole set and for each dialect.

For n-grams which occur five or more times in the training set, it estimates by how many standard deviations the count in each dialect diverges from the expected mean, assuming a binomial distribution.

An advantage feature of this model is that it gives an intermediate result which is easily interpretable. The list of common and uncommon words is interesting, and probably forms a big part of how a human would make the distinction between dialect samples. Of course, many of the most-divergent words are named entities. The commonness of place names in language samples supposedly tied to geographic areas isn't surprising, but there's no reason that a discussion of Casablanca shouldn't be carried out in Gulf Arabic, so the fact that it happens not to have been doesn't convey deep information about the dialect.

Tallying standard deviations of words in a sample as positive and negative votes for whether the sample is in a dialect turns out to be very effective.

Using unigrams alone, it gave an accuracy rate on the 5% reserved test data of 0.5103.

Before considering how to merge in bigram and trigram data, we turned to attempting to combine the results from this program with the output of our two LSTM models.

4.4 System Combiners

As soon as it became clear that the two-layer LSTM was nearing a local if not global maximum performance, we looked for models with independent errors which could be combined with it (or replace it.)

The three-layer LSTM and two-layer LSTM use a soft-max function to determine the dialect; we arranged to normalize and output the assigned probabilities for each dialect from the two LSTMs and the unigram frequency model. A Python script was written to combine the probabilities from each model with addition. This is the plurality model of Malmasi and Dras (2015).

However, the normalized output of the section 4.3 model was too extreme. The rankings were not probabilities and after normalization, "probabilities" came out to either almost zero or almost one. We tried various rescaling functions to get the "probabilities" better distributed, without hurting the accuracy rate. This helped the voting work better, but not significantly. And it seemed logical that the two LSTMs, which have lower accuracy, should be down-weighted somehow.

Therefore we trained a simple neural network on the validation data. This combiner network has 15 inputs – the dialect weights from each system, one hidden layer of 10 nodes, and 5 softmax outputs. This system accepted the outputs from the two LSTM systems and the outlier system, and gave us an accuracy rate of 0.57 on our reserved training data.

4.5 Post-test experiments

After the results of the test runs came back, we conducted some experiments to see whether using all 7619 segments of the training data would have made any difference to our SVM models.

Three different orders of n-grams, 2, 3 and 4-gram, are used to model the sentences of training and testing data set. The n-gram feature vectors produced from training data are used to train Multi-class SVM model. This results in three SVMs; 2, 3 and 4-gram based models.

After removing the n-gram components with zero counts over all training data, the dimensions of resulted feature vectors are 2601, 13656 and 82790 for 2-gram, 3-gram and 4-gram, respectively.

Three SVM systems were trained on bigram features, trigram features and 4-gram features respectively, and evaluated on testing data (1540 sentences.) The bigram system achieved a score of 515 out of 1540 correct, or 0.3344. The trigram system's score was 597 out of 1540, or 0.3877. The 4-gram system's score was 649 out of 1540 or 0.4214, essentially the same as our best submitted system.

5　Results

The results are rather modest – substantially above the baseline, but significantly below the best systems.

In the discussion below, we attempt to address why our test results in the shared task were so far below our test results during development.

Herewith the judgement on our runs:

Run	Accuracy	F1 (micro)	F1 (macro)	F1 (weighted)
SVM	0.4279	0.4279	0.4257	0.4264
unigram outliers	0.3948	0.3948	0.3462	0.3409
combined unigram and LSTMs	0.4091	0.4091	0.4112	0.4117

Table 3: Results for test set C (closed training).

6　Discussion and ideas for future work

There are a few possible reasons our results on the training data were better than our results on the test data. Dealing with some of them might have made our systems not only more robust, but perform better in both contexts.

For the two SVM systems, we split the training data into 70% training data, 30% evaluation data. For the LSTM and word-feature systems, we chose a different split of the training data, into 90% training, 5% validation, and 5% test. A consequence of the small amount of validation and testing data is a fairly large standard deviation in the test results, not observed during our testing, but perhaps apparent in the difference between results with the reserved training data (380 samples) and the workshop test data (1540 samples.) With accuracy/error rates about 0.50 we'd expect standard deviations of 8.5 out of 380 or 2.2% and 20 out of 1540 or 1.2%, respectively. While a jack-knife approach to cross-validation might have given us a better judgement for the mean accuracy achieved by this technique, the time involved in re-training the LSTM would have been substantial.

There are numerous experiments that we did not carry out, which might also have improved our development.

- Experimenting with shorter sequence lengths *should* have sped up training our LSTM systems. This would have let us experiment more with different configurations.

- Seeking out a system or cloud system with a graphics coprocessor could have also sped up neural network development.

- In general, we did not experiment with many constants, but chose them based on plausibility.

- Our word and neural net systems are both attentive to segment size, and the distribution of segment sizes in the test data is different than the training data.

- In spite of its surprising effectiveness on the reserved training data, our unigram word system isn't well-thought-out. A better mathematical foundation for combining standard deviations of words is the cumulative probability distribution of the normal curve. Adding logs of the cpdf is equivalent to multiplying probabilities, and seems mathematically justified, whereas adding positive and negative deviations is very ad-hoc.

  Even using the cpdf will over-emphasize variability in common words, however. Reviewing the standard deviations of words, we see that, for example, يعني yEny "that is", which occurs in MSA in the training data 16 standard deviations less frequently than might be expected from its occurrence in the whole corpus, still has 190 occurrences in 917 MSA training segments, and a frequency of $190/44932 = 0.004$ in MSA data. So the presence of *yEny* in a test segment, while interesting, is nowhere near as exciting for ruling out MSA as its standard deviation indicates.

In fact, the second and fourth 'most unusually frequent' words in the MSA training data, respectively 18.2 and 16.3 standard deviations more common than expected, are الفلسطينية AlflsTynyp "female Palestinian" and الإسرائيلية Al<srA}ylyp "female Israeli". These words are probably topical, rather than typical of MSA. The frequency of *AlflsTynyp* in the MSA training data is about 0.002 (87 occurences) – and once in EGY, twice in GLF, eleven times in LAV. Judging from the metadata labels in the original dataset, it is used in six or more different stories in MSA. *AlflsTynyp* occurs twice in the training data we reserved for testing. In the test data, it occurs twice in EGY, seven times in LAV, and seven times in MSA.

Similarly, *Al<srA}ylyp* occurs 45 times in the MSA training data and five times in all other dialects, and occurs three times in the reserved testing data. In the test data it occurs once in EGY, 8 times in LAV, 6 times in MSA.

It seems plausible that this story-topic effect may apply to other words in the training data, and that this alone might be sufficient to account for a fall-off in the performance of our software on the test task.

- Our procedure for splitting the training data was non-random, so that evaluation, verification and test data may have shared common prefixes, since the training sentences were sorted.

- We should have used a common split of the training data for all systems, so that the SVM systems could be combined with the others. As things stand, testing data reserved for one set of systems overlaps training data for others.

In the months to come, we hope to use the training and test data from the workshop to carry out some of the experiments we did not do in time to present. We owe a big 'thank you' to the organizers for giving us this opportunity!

References

Hassan Al-Haj, Roger Hsiao, Ian Lane, Alan W. Black, and Alex Waibel. 2009. Pronunciation modeling for dialectal Arabic speech recognition. In *Automatic Speech Recognition and Understanding Conference.*

Mohammed Ali, Moustafa Elshafei, Mansour Al-Ghamdi, Husni Al-Muhtaseb, and Atef Al-Najjar. 2008. Generation of Arabic phonetic dictionaries for speech recognition. In *International Conference on Innovations in Information Technology, 2008.*, pages 59–63. IEEE.

Ahmed Ali, Najim Dehak, Patrick Cardinal, Sameer Khurana, Sree Harsha Yella, James Glass, Peter Bell, and Steve Renals. 2016. Automatic dialect detection in Arabic broadcast speech. In *Proceedings of Interspeech 2016*, pages 2934–2938.

Houda Bouamor, Nizar Habash, and Kemal Oflazer. 2014. A multidialectal parallel corpus of Arabic. In *Proceedings of the Ninth International Conference on Language Resources and Evaluation (LREC14)*. European Language Resources Association (ELRA), May.

Tim Buckwalter. 2002. Aramorph 1.0 program.

William M. Campbell, Joseph P. Campbell, Terry P. Gleason, Douglas A. Reynolds, and Wade Shen. 2007. Speaker verification using support vector machines and high-level features. *IEEE Transactions on Audio, Speech, and Language Processing*, 15(7):2085–2094.

Ronan Collobert, Koray Kavukcuoglu, and Clément Farabet. 2011. Torch7: A MATLAB-like environment for machine learning. In *BigLearn, Neural Information Processing Systems Workshop*.

Heba ElFardy and Mona Diab. 2013. Sentence level dialect identification in Arabic. In *Proceedings of the 51st Annual Meeting of the Association for Computational Linguistics (ACL)*, pages 456–461.

Mohamed Elmahdy, Rainer Gruhn, Wolfgang Minker, and S. Abdennadher. 2010. Cross-Lingual Acoustic Modeling for Dialectal Arabic Speech Recognition. In *International Conference on Speech and Language Processing (Interspeech)*, September.

Mohamed Elmahdy, Mark Hasegawa-Johnson, and Eiman Mustafawi. 2012. A baseline speech recognition system for Levantine colloquial Arabic. In *12th ESOLEC conference on Language Engineering*.

Mohamed Elmahdy, Mark Hasegawa-Johnson, and Eiman Mustafawi. 2013. A transfer learning approach for under-resourced Arabic dialects speech recognition. In *The 6th Language and Technology Conference*.

Mark Hall, Eibe Frank, Geoffrey Holmes, Bernhard Pfahringer, Peter Reutemann, and Ian H. Witten. 2009. The WEKA data mining software: An update. *SIGKDD Explorations*, 11(1).

Abualsoud Hanani, Martin J. Russell, and Michael J. Carey. 2013. Human and computer recognition of regional accents and ethnic groups from British english speech. *Computer Speech and Language*, 27(1):5974.

Abualsoud Hanani, Hanna Basha, Yasmeen Sharaf, and Stephen Taylor. 2015. Palestinian Arabic regional accent recognition. In *The 8th International Conference on Speech Technology and Human-Computer Dialogue*.

Andrej Karpathy, Justin Johnson, and Li Fei-Fei. 2016. Visualizing and understanding recurrent networks. In *5th International Conference on Learning Representations*.

Shervin Malmasi and Mark Dras. 2015. Language identification using classifier ensembles. In *Proceedings of the Joint Workshop on Language Technology for Closely Related Languages, Varieties and Dialects (LT4VarDial)*, pages 35–43, Hissar, Bulgaria.

Shervin Malmasi, Eshrag Refaee, and Mark Dras. 2015. Arabic dialect identification using a parallel multidialectal corpus. In *Proceedings of the 14th Conference of the Pacific Association for Computational Linguistics (PACLING 2015)*, pages 209–217, Bali, Indonesia, May.

Shervin Malmasi, Marcos Zampieri, Nikola Ljubešić, Preslav Nakov, Ahmed Ali, and Jörg Tiedemann. 2016. Discriminating between similar languages and Arabic dialect identification: A report on the third DSL shared task. In *Proceedings of the 3rd Workshop on Language Technology for Closely Related Languages, Varieties and Dialects (VarDial)*, Osaka, Japan.

Maryam Najafian, Andrea DeMarco, Stephen Cox, and Martin Russell. 2014. Unsupervised model selection for recognition of regional accented speech. In *Proceedings of Interspeech 2014*.

Scott Novotney, Rich Schwartz, and Sanjeev Khudanpur. 2011. Unsupervised Arabic dialect adaptation with self-training. In *Proceedings of Interspeech 2011*, pages 1–4.

Jordi Porta and José-Luis Sancho. 2014. Using maximum entropy models to discriminate between similar languages and varieties. In *Proceedings of the First Workshop on Applying NLP Tools to Similar Languages, Varieties and Dialects (VarDial)*, pages 120–128, Dublin, Ireland.

Dimitra Vergyri, Katrin Kirchhoff, Venkata Raman Rao Gadde, Andreas Stolcke, and Jing Zheng. 2005. Development of a conversational telephone speech recognizer for Levantine Arabic. In *Proceedings of Interspeech 2005*, pages 1613–1616.

Omar F. Zaidan and Chris Callison-Burch. 2011. The Arabic Online Commentary dataset: An annotated dataset of informal Arabic with high dialectal content. In *Proceedings of ACL*, pages 37–41.

Omar F. Zaidan and Chris Callison-Burch. 2014. Arabic dialect identification. *Computational Linguistics*, 40(1):171–202.

UnibucKernel: An Approach for Arabic Dialect Identification based on Multiple String Kernels

Radu Tudor Ionescu and **Marius Popescu**
University of Bucharest
Department of Computer Science
14 Academiei, Bucharest, Romania
raducu.ionescu@gmail.com
popescunmarius@gmail.com

Abstract

The most common approach in text mining classification tasks is to rely on features like words, part-of-speech tags, stems, or some other high-level linguistic features. Unlike the common approach, we present a method that uses only character p-grams (also known as n-grams) as features for the Arabic Dialect Identification (ADI) Closed Shared Task of the DSL 2016 Challenge. The proposed approach combines several string kernels using multiple kernel learning. In the learning stage, we try both Kernel Discriminant Analysis (KDA) and Kernel Ridge Regression (KRR), and we choose KDA as it gives better results in a 10-fold cross-validation carried out on the training set. Our approach is shallow and simple, but the empirical results obtained in the ADI Shared Task prove that it achieves very good results. Indeed, we ranked on the second place with an accuracy of 50.91% and a weighted F_1 score of 51.31%. We also present improved results in this paper, which we obtained after the competition ended. Simply by adding more regularization into our model to make it more suitable for test data that comes from a different distribution than training data, we obtain an accuracy of 51.82% and a weighted F_1 score of 52.18%. Furthermore, the proposed approach has an important advantage in that it is language independent and linguistic theory neutral, as it does not require any NLP tools.

1 Introduction

It seems natural to use words as basic units in text categorization, authorship identification, plagiarism detection or similar text mining tasks. Perhaps surprisingly, recent results indicate that methods handling the text at the character level can also be very effective (Lodhi et al., 2002; Sanderson and Guenter, 2006; Kate and Mooney, 2006; Popescu and Dinu, 2007; Grozea et al., 2009; Popescu, 2011; Escalante et al., 2011; Popescu and Grozea, 2012; Ionescu et al., 2014; Ionescu et al., 2016). By avoiding to explicitly consider features of natural language such as words, phrases, or meaning, an approach that works at the character level has an important advantage in that it is language independent and linguistic theory neutral. In this context, we present a method based on character p-grams that we designed for the Arabic Dialect Identification (ADI) Shared Task of the DSL 2016 Challenge (Malmasi et al., 2016). In this task, the participants had to discriminate between Modern Standard Arabic (MSA) and 4 Arabic dialects, in a 5-way classification setting. A number of 18 teams have submitted their results on the final test set, and our team (UnibucKernel) ranked on the second place with an accuracy of 50.91% and a weighted F_1 score of 51.31%. Our best scoring system is based on combining three different string kernels via multiple kernel learning (MKL) (Gonen and Alpaydin, 2011). The first kernel that we considered is the p-grams presence bits kernel[1], which takes into account only the presence of p-grams instead of their frequency. The second kernel is the (histogram) intersection string kernel[2], which was first used in a text mining task by Ionescu et al. (2014), although it is much more popular in computer vision (Maji et al., 2008; Vedaldi and Zisserman, 2010). The third kernel is derrived from Local Rank Distance[3], a distance measure that

---

[1]We computed the p-grams presence bits kernel using the open source code provided at http://string-kernels.herokuapp.com

[2]We computed the intersection string kernel using the open source code provided at http://string-kernels.herokuapp.com

[3]We computed the Local Rank Distance using the open source code provided at http://lrd.herokuapp.com

Proceedings of the Third Workshop on NLP for Similar Languages, Varieties and Dialects,
pages 135–144, Osaka, Japan, December 12 2016.

was first introduced in computational biology (Ionescu, 2013; Dinu et al., 2014), but it has also shown its application in NLP (Popescu and Ionescu, 2013; Ionescu, 2015). Although character p-grams have been employed for ADI in several works (Darwish et al., 2014; Zaidan and Callison-Burch, 2014; Malmasi et al., 2015), to the best of our knowledge, none of these string kernels have been previously used for ADI. Interestingly, these kernels have also been used for native language identification (Popescu and Ionescu, 2013; Ionescu et al., 2014; Ionescu et al., 2016), obtaining state-of-the-art performance for several languages, including Arabic.

Two kernel classifiers (Shawe-Taylor and Cristianini, 2004) were considered for the learning task, namely Kernel Ridge Regression (KRR) and Kernel Discriminant Analysis (KDA). The KDA classifier is sometimes able to improve accuracy by avoiding the masking problem (Hastie and Tibshirani, 2003). In a set of preliminary experiments performed on the training set, we found that KDA gives slightly better results than KRR. Hence, all our submissions are based on learning with KDA. Before submitting our results, we have also tuned our string kernels for the task. First of all, we tried out p-grams of various lengths, including blended variants of string kernels as well. The best accuracy was obtained with blended kernels of 3 to 6 p-grams. Second of all, we have evaluated the individual kernels and various MKL combinations. The empirical results indicate that combining kernels via MKL can help to improve the accuracy by nearly 1%. All these choices played a significant role in obtaining the second place in the final ranking of the ADI Shared Task. After the challenge, as we learned that the test set comes from a different source, we further improved our models just by adding more regularization. Interestingly, our approach treats the text documents simply as strings, since it does not involve any linguistic processing of the text, not even tokenization. Therefore, our method is language independent and linguistic theory neutral. Furthermore, the proposed approach is simple and effective, as it is just based on shallow features (character p-grams).

The paper is organized as follows. Work related to Arabic dialect identification and to methods based on string kernels is presented in Section 2. Section 3 presents the string kernels that we used in our approach. The learning methods used in the experiments are described in Section 4. Section 5 presents details about experiments, including parameter tuning, combining kernels and results of submitted systems. Finally, we draw our conclusion in Section 6.

2 Related Work

2.1 Arabic Dialect Identification

Arabic dialect identification is a relatively new NLP task with only a handful of works to address it (Biadsy et al., 2009; Zaidan and Callison-Burch, 2011; Elfardy and Diab, 2013; Darwish et al., 2014; Zaidan and Callison-Burch, 2014; Malmasi et al., 2015). Although it did not received too much attention, the task is very important for Arabic NLP tools, as most of these tools have only been design for Modern Standard Arabic. Biadsy et al. (2009) describe a phonotactic approach that automatically identifies the Arabic dialect of a speaker given a sample of speech. While Biadsy et al. (2009) focus on spoken Arabic dialect identification, others have tried to identify the Arabic dialect of given texts (Zaidan and Callison-Burch, 2011; Elfardy and Diab, 2013; Darwish et al., 2014; Malmasi et al., 2015). Zaidan and Callison-Burch (2011) introduce the Arabic Online Commentary (AOC) data set of 108K labeled sentences, 41% of them having dialectal content. They employ a language model for automatic dialect identification on their collected data. A supervised approach for sentence-level dialect identification between Egyptian and MSA is proposed by Elfardy and Diab (2013). Their system outperforms the approach presented by Zaidan and Callison-Burch (2011) on the same data set. Zaidan and Callison-Burch (2014) extend their previous work (Zaidan and Callison-Burch, 2011) and conduct several ADI experiments using word and character p-grams. Different from most of the previous work, Darwish et al. (2014) have found that word unigram models do not generalize well to unseen topics. They suggest that lexical, morphological and phonological features can capture more relevant information for discriminating dialects. As the AOC corpus is not controlled for topic bias, Malmasi et al. (2015) also state that the models trained on this corpus may not generalize to other data as they implicitly capture topical cues. They perform ADI experiments on the Multidialectal Parallel Corpus of Arabic (MPCA) (Bouamor et al., 2014) using various word and character p-grams models in order to assess the influence of topic bias. Interestingly, Malmasi et al. (2015) find that character p-grams are "in most scenarios the best single feature for this task", even in a cross-corpus setting. Their findings are consistent with our results in the ADI Shared Task of the DSL 2016 Challenge (Malmasi et al., 2016), as we ranked on the second place using solely character p-grams. It is important to remark that the ADI Shared Task data set contains Automatic Speech Recognition (ASR) transcripts of Arabic speech collected from the Broadcast News domain (Ali et al., 2016). The fact that the data set may contain ASR errors (perhaps more in the dialectal speech segments) makes the ADI task much more difficult than in previous studies.

2.2 String Kernels

In recent years, methods of handling text at the character level have demonstrated impressive performance levels in various text analysis tasks (Lodhi et al., 2002; Sanderson and Guenter, 2006; Kate and Mooney, 2006; Popescu and Dinu, 2007; Grozea et al., 2009; Popescu, 2011; Escalante et al., 2011; Popescu and Grozea, 2012; Ionescu et al., 2014; Ionescu et al., 2016). String kernels are a common form of using information at the character level. They are a particular case of the more general convolution kernels (Haussler, 1999). Lodhi et al. (2002) used string kernels for document categorization with very good results. String kernels were also successfully used in authorship identification (Sanderson and Guenter, 2006; Popescu and Dinu, 2007; Popescu and Grozea, 2012). For example, the system described by Popescu and Grozea (2012) ranked first in most problems and overall in the PAN 2012 Traditional Authorship Attribution tasks. More recently, Ionescu et al. (2016) have used various blended string kernels to obtain state-of-the-art accuracy rates for native language identification.

3 Similarity Measures for Strings

3.1 String Kernels

The kernel function gives kernel methods the power to naturally handle input data that is not in the form of numerical vectors, for example strings. The kernel function captures the intuitive notion of similarity between objects in a specific domain and can be any function defined on the respective domain that is symmetric and positive definite. For strings, many such kernel functions exist with various applications in computational biology and computational linguistics (Shawe-Taylor and Cristianini, 2004). String kernels embed the texts in a very large feature space, given by all the substrings of length p, and leave it to the learning algorithm to select important features for the specific task, by highly weighting these features.

Perhaps one of the most natural ways to measure the similarity of two strings is to count how many substrings of length p the two strings have in common. This gives rise to the p-spectrum kernel. Formally, for two strings over an alphabet Σ, $s, t \in \Sigma^*$, the p-spectrum kernel is defined as:

$$k_p(s, t) = \sum_{v \in \Sigma^p} \text{num}_v(s) \cdot \text{num}_v(t),$$

where $\text{num}_v(s)$ is the number of occurrences of string v as a substring in s.[4] The feature map defined by this kernel associates a vector of dimension $|\Sigma|^p$ containing the histogram of frequencies of all its substrings of length p (p-grams) with each string.

A variant of this kernel can be obtained if the embedding feature map is modified to associate a vector of dimension $|\Sigma|^p$ containing the presence bits (instead of frequencies) of all its substrings of length p with each string. Thus, the character p-grams presence bits kernel is obtained:

$$k_p^{0/1}(s, t) = \sum_{v \in \Sigma^p} \text{in}_v(s) \cdot \text{in}_v(t),$$

where $\text{in}_v(s)$ is 1 if string v occurs as a substring in s, and 0 otherwise.

---

[4]Note that the notion of substring requires contiguity. Shawe-Taylor and Cristianini (2004) discuss the ambiguity between the terms *substring* and *subsequence* across different domains: biology, computer science.

In computer vision, the (histogram) intersection kernel has successfully been used for object class recognition from images (Maji et al., 2008; Vedaldi and Zisserman, 2010). Ionescu et al. (2014) have used the intersection kernel as a kernel for strings. The intersection string kernel is defined as follows:

$$k_p^{\cap}(s, t) = \sum_{v \in \Sigma^p} \min\{\text{num}_v(s), \text{num}_v(t)\},$$

where $\text{num}_v(s)$ is the number of occurrences of string v as a substring in s.

For the p-spectrum kernel, the frequency of a p-gram has a very significant contribution to the kernel, since it considers the product of such frequencies. On the other hand, the frequency of a p-gram is completely disregarded in the p-grams presence bits kernel. The intersection kernel lies somewhere in the middle between the p-grams presence bits kernel and p-spectrum kernel, in the sense that the frequency of a p-gram has a moderate contribution to the intersection kernel. In other words, the intersection kernel assigns a high score to a p-gram only if it has a high frequency in both strings, since it considers the minimum of the two frequencies. The p-spectrum kernel assigns a high score even when the p-gram has a high frequency in only one of the two strings. Thus, the intersection kernel captures something more about the correlation between the p-gram frequencies in the two strings. Based on these comments, we decided to use only the p-grams presence bits kernel and the intersection string kernel for ADI.

Data normalization helps to improve machine learning performance for various applications. Since the value range of raw data can have large variation, classifier objective functions will not work properly without normalization. After normalization, each feature has an approximately equal contribution to the similarity between two samples. To obtain a normalized kernel matrix of pairwise similarities between samples, each component is divided by the square root of the product of the two corresponding diagonal components:

$$\hat{K}_{ij} = \frac{K_{ij}}{\sqrt{K_{ii} \cdot K_{jj}}}.$$

This is equivalent to normalizing the kernel function as follows:

$$\hat{k}(s_i, s_j) = \frac{k(s_i, s_j)}{\sqrt{k(s_i, s_i) \cdot k(s_j, s_j)}}.$$

To ensure a fair comparison of strings of different lengths, normalized versions of the p-grams presence bits kernel and the intersection kernel are being used. Taking into account p-grams of different length and summing up the corresponding kernels, new kernels, termed *blended spectrum kernels*, can be obtained. We have used various blended spectrum kernels in the experiments in order to find the best combination.

3.2 Local Rank Distance

Local Rank Distance (Ionescu, 2013) is a recently introduced distance measure for strings that aims to provide a better similarity than rank distance (Dinu and Manea, 2006). Local Rank Distance (LRD) has already shown promising results in computational biology (Ionescu, 2013; Dinu et al., 2014) and native language identification (Popescu and Ionescu, 2013; Ionescu, 2015).

In order to describe LRD, we use the following notations. Given a string x over an alphabet Σ, the length of x is denoted by $|x|$. Strings are considered to be indexed starting from position 1, that is $x = x[1]x[2] \cdots x[|x|]$. Moreover, $x[i : j]$ denotes its substring $x[i]x[i + 1] \cdots x[j - 1]$.

Local Rank Distance is inspired by rank distance (Dinu and Manea, 2006), the main differences being that it uses p-grams instead of single characters, and that it matches each p-gram in the first string with the nearest equal p-gram in the second string. Given a fixed integer $p \geq 1$, a threshold $m \geq 1$, and two strings x and y over Σ, the *Local Rank Distance* between x and y, denoted by $\Delta_{LRD}(x, y)$, is defined through the following algorithmic process. For each position i in x ($1 \leq i \leq |x| - p + 1$), the algorithm searches for that position j in y ($1 \leq j \leq |y| - p + 1$) such that $x[i : i + p] = y[j : j + p]$ and $|i - j|$ is minimized. If j exists and $|i - j| < m$, then the offset $|i - j|$ is added to the Local Rank Distance. Otherwise, the maximal offset m is added to the Local Rank Distance. An important remark is that LRD does not impose any mathematically developed global constraints, such as matching the i-th occurrence of a p-gram in x with the i-th occurrence of that same p-gram in y. Instead, it is focused on the local phenomenon, and tries to pair equal p-grams at a minimum offset. To ensure that LRD is a (symmetric) distance function, the algorithm also has to sum up the offsets obtained from the above process by exchanging x and y. LRD is formally defined in (Ionescu, 2013; Dinu et al., 2014).

Interestingly, the search for matching p-grams is limited within a window of fixed size. The size of this window is determined by the maximum offset parameter m. This parameter must be set a priori and should be proportional to the average length of the strings. We set $m = 500$ in our experiments, which is about twice the average length of the ASR transcripts provided in the training set. In the experiments, the efficient algorithm of Ionescu (2015) is used to compute LRD. However, LRD needs to be used as a kernel function. We use the RBF kernel (Shawe-Taylor and Cristianini, 2004) to transform LRD into a similarity measure:

$$\hat{k}_p^{LRD}(s,t) = e^{-\frac{\Delta_{LRD}(s,t)}{2\sigma^2}},$$

where s and t are two strings and p is the p-grams length. The parameter σ is usually chosen so that values of $\hat{k}(s,t)$ are well scaled. In the above equation, Δ_{LRD} is already normalized to a value in the $[0,1]$ interval to ensure a fair comparison of strings of different length. Hence, we set $\sigma = 1$ in the experiments. The resulted similarity matrix is then squared in order to make sure it becomes a symmetric and positive definite kernel matrix.

4   Learning Methods

Kernel-based learning algorithms work by embedding the data into a Hilbert feature space, and searching for linear relations in that space. The embedding is performed implicitly, that is by specifying the inner product between each pair of points rather than by giving their coordinates explicitly. More precisely, a kernel matrix that contains the pairwise similarities between every pair of training samples is used in the learning stage to assign a vector of weights to the training samples. Let α denote this weight vector. In the test stage, the pairwise similarities between a test sample x and all the training samples are computed. Then, the following binary classification function assigns a positive or a negative label to the test sample:

$$g(x) = \sum_{i=1}^{n} \alpha_i \cdot k(x, x_i),$$

where x is the test sample, n is the number of training samples, $X = \{x_1, x_2, ..., x_n\}$ is the set of training samples, k is a kernel function, and α_i is the weight assigned to the training sample x_i.

The advantage of using the dual representation induced by the kernel function becomes clear if the dimension of the feature space m is taken into consideration. Since string kernels are based on character p-grams, the feature space is indeed very high. For instance, using 5-grams based only on the 28 letters of the basic Arabic alphabet will result in a feature space of $28^5 = 17,210,368$ features. However, our best model is based on a feature space that includes 3-grams, 4-grams, 5-grams and 6-grams. As long as the number of samples n is much lower than the number of features m, it can be more efficient to use the dual representation given by the kernel matrix. This fact is also known as the *kernel trick* (Shawe-Taylor and Cristianini, 2004).

Various kernel methods differ in the way they learn to separate the samples. In the case of binary classification problems, kernel-based learning algorithms look for a discriminant function, a function that assigns $+1$ to examples belonging to one class and -1 to examples belonging to the other class. For the ADI experiments, we used the Kernel Ridge Regression (KRR) binary classifier. Kernel Ridge Regression selects the vector of weights that simultaneously has small empirical error and small norm in the Reproducing Kernel Hilbert Space generated by the kernel function. KRR is a binary classifier, but Arabic dialect identification is usually a multi-class classification problem. There are many approaches for combining binary classifiers to solve multi-class problems. Typically, the multi-class problem is broken down into multiple binary classification problems using common decomposing schemes such as:

	EGY	GLF	LAV	NOR	MSA
Train set	1578	1672	1758	1612	999
Test set	315	256	344	351	274

Table 1: The sample distribution per class for the ADI Shared Task training and test sets.

one-versus-all and one-versus-one. We considered the one-versus-all scheme for our Arabic dialect classification task. There are also kernel methods that take the multi-class nature of the problem directly into account, for instance Kernel Discriminant Analysis. The KDA classifier is sometimes able to improve accuracy by avoiding the masking problem (Hastie and Tibshirani, 2003). In the case of multi-class ADI, the masking problem may appear, for instance, when an Arabic dialect A is somehow related to two other Arabic dialects B and C, in which case the samples that belong to class A can sit in the middle between the samples of classes B and C. In this case, the class in the middle is masked by the other two classes, as it never dominates. KDA can solve such unwanted situations automatically, without having to identify what dialects are related by any means, such as geographical position or quantitative linguistic analysis. More details about KRR and KDA are given in (Shawe-Taylor and Cristianini, 2004).

5 Experiments and Results

5.1 Data Set

The ADI Shared Task data set (Ali et al., 2016) contains Automatic Speech Recognition (ASR) transcripts of Arabic speech collected from the Broadcast News domain. The task is to discriminate between Modern Standard Arabic (MSA) and 4 Arabic dialects, namely Egyptian (EGY), Gulf (GLF), Levantine (LAV), and North-African or Maghrebi (NOR). Table 1 shows the sample distribution per class for the training and the test sets. As the samples are not evenly distributed, an accuracy of 22.79% can be obtained with a majority class baseline. Another important aspect is that the training and the test set are taken from different sources, and this could alter the performance of a classifier. However, we were unaware of this fact before the submission deadline.

5.2 Parameter Tuning and Implementation Choices

In our string kernels approach, ASR transcripts are treated as strings. Because the approach works at the character level, there is no need to split the texts into words, or to do any NLP-specific processing before computing the string kernels. The only editing done to the texts was the replacing of sequences of consecutive space characters (space, tab, and so on) with a single space character. This normalization was needed in order to prevent the artificial increase or decrease of the similarity between texts, as a result of different spacing.

In order to tune the parameters and to decide what kernel learning method works best, we fixed 10 folds in order to evaluate each option in a 10-fold cross-validation (CV) procedure on the training set. We first carried out a set of preliminary experiments to determine the range of p-grams that gives the most accurate results in the 10-fold CV procedure. We fixed the kernel method to KRR based on the Local Rank Distance kernel ($\hat{k}_p^{LRD}$) and we evaluated all the p-grams in the range 2-7. The results are illustrated in Figure 1. Interestingly, the best accuracy (64.97%) is obtained with 4-grams. Furthermore, experiments with different blended kernels were conducted to see whether combining p-grams of different lengths could improve the accuracy. More precisely, we evaluated combinations of p-grams in three ranges: 3-5, 4-6 and 3-6. In the end, the best accuracy (66.43%) was obtained when all the p-grams with the length in the range 3-6 were combined. Hence, we used blended kernels with p-grams in the range 3-6 in the subsequent experiments.

Further experiments were also performed to establish what type of kernel works better, namely the blended p-grams presence bits kernel ($\hat{k}_{3-6}^{0/1}$), the blended p-grams intersection kernel ($\hat{k}_{3-6}^{\cap}$), or the kernel based on LRD ($\hat{k}_{3-6}^{LRD}$). These different kernel representations are obtained from the same data. The idea of combining all these kernels is natural when one wants to improve the performance of a classifier. When multiple kernels are combined, the features are actually embedded in a higher-dimensional space. As a consequence, the search space of linear patterns grows, which helps the classifier to select a better

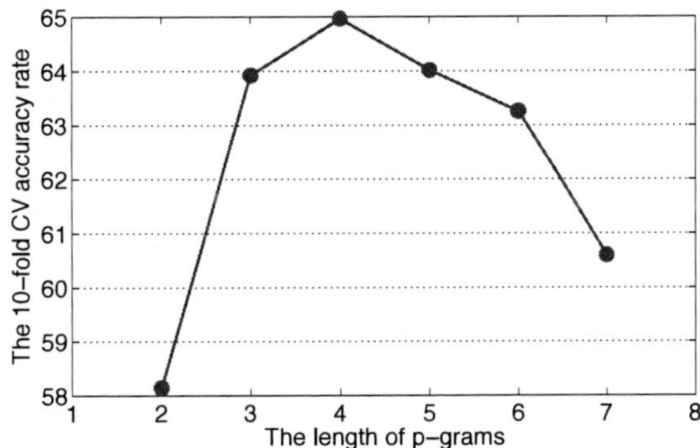

Figure 1: Accuracy rates of the KRR based on the LRD kernel with p-grams in the range 2-7. The results are obtained in a 10-fold cross-validation carried out on the training set.

Kernel	KRR	KDA
$\hat{k}_{3-6}^{0/1}$	65.89%	66.18%
$\hat{k}_{3-6}^{\cap}$	65.74%	66.28%
$\hat{k}_{3-6}^{LRD}$	66.43%	66.54%
$\hat{k}_{3-6}^{0/1} + \hat{k}_{3-6}^{\cap}$	65.96%	66.42%
$\hat{k}_{3-6}^{0/1} + \hat{k}_{3-6}^{LRD}$	66.64%	67.17%
$\hat{k}_{3-6}^{\cap} + \hat{k}_{3-6}^{LRD}$	66.81%	67.12%
$\hat{k}_{3-6}^{0/1} + \hat{k}_{3-6}^{\cap} + \hat{k}_{3-6}^{LRD}$	66.98%	**67.37%**

Table 2: Accuracy rates of different blended string kernels combined with either KRR or KDA. The results are obtained in a 10-fold cross-validation carried out on the training set. The best result is highlighted in bold.

Dialects	EGY	GLF	LAV	NOR	MSA
EGY	171	39	50	34	21
GLF	45	112	49	22	28
LAV	43	68	167	36	30
NOR	50	75	40	171	15
MSA	21	34	24	18	177

Table 3: Confusion matrix (on the test set) of KDA based on the sum of the blended p-grams presence bits kernel and the blended intersection kernel. The regularization parameter is set to 0.8, so the F_1 score of this model is 52.18%.

discriminant function. The most natural way of combining two kernels is to sum them up. Summing up kernels or kernel matrices is equivalent to feature vector concatenation. The kernels were evaluated alone and in various combinations, by employing either KRR or KDA for the learning task. All the results obtained in the 10-fold CV carried out on the training set are given in Table 2.

The empirical results presented in Table 2 reveal several interesting aspects about the proposed methods. Regarding the two kernel classifiers, it seems that KDA gives consistently better results, although the difference in terms of accuracy is almost always less than 0.5%. The individual kernels obtain fairly similar results. Perhaps surprisingly, the best individual kernel is the kernel based on Local Rank Distance with an accuracy of 66.43% when it is combined with KRR, and an accuracy of 66.54% when it is combined with KDA. Each and every kernel combination yields better results than each of its individual components alone. For both KRR and KDA, the best accuracy is actually obtained when all three kernels are combined together. Indeed, KRR reaches an accuracy of 66.98% when the blended p-grams presence bits kernel, the blended intersection kernel and the blended LRD kernel are summed up. With the same kernel combination, KDA yields an accuracy of 67.37%. As KDA gives consistently better results in the 10-fold CV procedure, we decided to submit three KDA models for the test set. The first submission (run1) is based on the LRD kernel, which seems to be the best one among the individual kernels, although previous works (Ionescu et al., 2014; Ionescu et al., 2016) indicate that the other two kernels obtain better results on native language identification. Influenced by these previous works, we also decided to give a fair chance to the blended p-grams presence bits kernel and the blended intersection kernel. Hence, the second submission (run2) is based on the sum between $\hat{k}_{3-6}^{0/1}$ and $\hat{k}_{3-6}^{\cap}$. Finally, our third submission (run3) is based on the sum of all three kernels, as this combination yields the best overall accuracy in the 10-fold CV procedure carried out on the training set.

Method	Reg.	Accuracy	F_1 (macro)	F_1 (weighted)	Submitted
KDA and $\hat{k}_{3-6}^{LRD}$	0.1	49.29%	49.43%	49.54%	Yes (run1)
KDA and $\hat{k}_{3-6}^{0/1} + \hat{k}_{3-6}^{\cap}$	0.4	50.84%	51.09%	51.23%	Yes (run2)
KDA and $\hat{k}_{3-6}^{0/1} + \hat{k}_{3-6}^{\cap} + \hat{k}_{3-6}^{LRD}$	0.2	50.91%	51.21%	51.31%	Yes (run3)
KDA and $\hat{k}_{3-6}^{LRD}$	0.2	49.35%	49.51%	49.59%	No
KDA and $\hat{k}_{3-6}^{0/1} + \hat{k}_{3-6}^{\cap}$	0.8	51.82%	52.00%	52.18%	No
KDA and $\hat{k}_{3-6}^{0/1} + \hat{k}_{3-6}^{\cap} + \hat{k}_{3-6}^{LRD}$	0.4	51.49%	51.52%	51.66%	No
KRR and $\hat{k}_{3-6}^{LRD}$	10^{-4}	50.19%	49.55%	49.72%	No
KRR and $\hat{k}_{3-6}^{0/1} + \hat{k}_{3-6}^{\cap}$	10^{-4}	52.21%	51.73%	51.99%	No
KRR and $\hat{k}_{3-6}^{0/1} + \hat{k}_{3-6}^{\cap} + \hat{k}_{3-6}^{LRD}$	10^{-4}	51.88%	51.39%	51.56%	No

Table 4: Results for test set C (closed training) of various models based on string kernels. Some models that have not been submitted for the challenge are also included. For each model, the regularization parameter used to control the trade-off between overfitting and underfitting is reported as well.

5.3 Results and Discussion

Table 4 presents our results for the Arabic Dialect Identification Closed Shared Task (test set C) of the DSL 2016 Challenge, along with a few systems that were not submitted for the task. Among the three submissions, the best performance is obtained when all three kernels are combined and KDA is used for learning. The submitted systems were ranked by their weighted F_1 score, and among the 18 participants, our best model obtained the second place with a weighted F_1 score of 51.31%. Nevertheless, the winning solution is marginally better, with a difference of 0.0078% in terms of the weighted F_1 score.

A very important remark is that all our submitted systems obtain significantly lower results on the test set than in the 10-fold CV procedure carried out on the training set. This could be explained by the fact that the test set comes from a different distribution. As described by Ali et al. (2016), it actually seems that the training and the test sets come from different sources. In this context, regularization plays an important role, as it can be used to reduce the overfitting of the training data. A straightforward experiment, in which we simply double the regularization parameter of KDA, proves that all our submitted models yield better results when they are forced to fit less of the training data. Our best weighted F_1 score (52.18%) on the test set is obtained by the KDA based on the sum of the blended p-grams presence bits kernel and the blended intersection kernel. The confusion matrix of this model is given in Table 3. For this model, it takes about 12 minutes to compute the two kernels, train the KDA classifier and predict the labels on a computer with Intel Core i7 2.3 GHz processor and 8 GB of RAM using a single Core.

Since the training and the test sets come from different distributions, the ADI task can also be regarded as a cross-corpus evaluation task. An interesting remark is that Ionescu et al. (2014) have used KRR and KDA in a cross-corpus setting for native language identification, and they have found that KRR is more robust in such a setting. Thus, we have also included results with KRR instead of KDA, while using the same kernels. The KRR based on the sum of the blended p-grams presence bits kernel and the blended intersection kernel is the best KRR model on the test set, with a weighted F_1 score of 51.99%.

6 Conclusion

We have presented a method based on character p-grams for the Arabic Dialect Identification (ADI) Shared Task of the DSL 2016 Challenge (Malmasi et al., 2016). Our team (UnibucKernel) ranked on the second place with a weighted F_1 score of 51.31%. As we learned that the training and the test sets come from different distributions (Ali et al., 2016), we were able to further improve our results after the challenge to a weighted F_1 score of 52.18%, which is better than the winning solution (51.32%). To improve the results even further, more advanced techniques suitable for the cross-corpus setting, such as semi-supervised or transfer learning, can be employed in future work.

Acknowledgments

The authors have equally contributed to this work. They thank the reviewers for helpful comments.

References

Ahmed Ali, Najim Dehak, Patrick Cardinal, Sameer Khurana, Sree Harsha Yella, James Glass, Peter Bell, and Steve Renals. 2016. Automatic dialect detection in arabic broadcast speech. *Proceedings of Interspeech*, pages 2934–2938.

Fadi Biadsy, Julia Hirschberg, and Nizar Habash. 2009. Spoken Arabic Dialect Identification Using Phonotactic Modeling. *Proceedings of the EACL 2009 Workshop on Computational Approaches to Semitic Languages*, pages 53–61.

Houda Bouamor, Nizar Habash, and Kemal Oflazer. 2014. A Multidialectal Parallel Corpus of Arabic. *Proceedings of LREC*, pages 1240–1245, may.

Kareem Darwish, Hassan Sajjad, and Hamdy Mubarak. 2014. Verifiably Effective Arabic Dialect Identification. *Proceedings of EMNLP*, pages 1465–1468.

Liviu P. Dinu and Florin Manea. 2006. An efficient approach for the rank aggregation problem. *Theoretical Computer Science*, 359(1–3):455–461.

Liviu P. Dinu, Radu Tudor Ionescu, and Alexandru I. Tomescu. 2014. A rank-based sequence aligner with applications in phylogenetic analysis. *PLoS ONE*, 9(8):e104006, 08.

Heba Elfardy and Mona T. Diab. 2013. Sentence Level Dialect Identification in Arabic. *Proceedings of ACL*, pages 456–461.

Hugo Jair Escalante, Thamar Solorio, and Manuel Montes-y-Gómez. 2011. Local histograms of character n-grams for authorship attribution. *Proceedings of ACL: HLT*, 1:288–298.

Mehmet Gonen and Ethem Alpaydin. 2011. Multiple Kernel Learning Algorithms. *Journal of Machine Learning Research*, 12:2211–2268, July.

Cristian Grozea, Christian Gehl, and Marius Popescu. 2009. ENCOPLOT: Pairwise Sequence Matching in Linear Time Applied to Plagiarism Detection. *Proceedings of 3rd PAN WORKSHOP*, page 10.

Trevor Hastie and Robert Tibshirani. 2003. *The Elements of Statistical Learning*. Springer, corrected edition, July.

David Haussler. 1999. Convolution Kernels on Discrete Structures. Technical Report UCS-CRL-99-10, University of California at Santa Cruz, Santa Cruz, CA, USA.

Radu Tudor Ionescu, Marius Popescu, and Aoife Cahill. 2014. Can characters reveal your native language? A language-independent approach to native language identification. *Proceedings of EMNLP*, pages 1363–1373, October.

Radu Tudor Ionescu, Marius Popescu, and Aoife Cahill. 2016. String kernels for native language identification: Insights from behind the curtains. *Computational Linguistics*, 42(3):491–525.

Radu Tudor Ionescu. 2013. Local Rank Distance. *Proceedings of SYNASC*, pages 221–228.

Radu Tudor Ionescu. 2015. A Fast Algorithm for Local Rank Distance: Application to Arabic Native Language Identification. *Proceedings of ICONIP*, 9490:390–400.

Rohit J. Kate and Raymond J. Mooney. 2006. Using String-kernels for Learning Semantic Parsers. *Proceedings of ACL*, pages 913–920.

Huma Lodhi, Craig Saunders, John Shawe-Taylor, Nello Cristianini, and Christopher J. C. H. Watkins. 2002. Text Classification using String Kernels. *Journal of Machine Learning Research*, 2:419–444.

Subhransu Maji, Alexander C. Berg, and Jitendra Malik. 2008. Classification using intersection kernel support vector machines is efficient. *Proceedings of CVPR*.

Shervin Malmasi, Eshrag Refaee, and Mark Dras. 2015. Arabic Dialect Identification using a Parallel Multidialectal Corpus. *Proceedings of PACLING*, pages 209–217, May.

Shervin Malmasi, Marcos Zampieri, Nikola Ljubešić, Preslav Nakov, Ahmed Ali, and Jörg Tiedemann. 2016. Discriminating between similar languages and arabic dialect identification: A report on the third dsl shared task. *Proceedings of the 3rd Workshop on Language Technology for Closely Related Languages, Varieties and Dialects (VarDial)*.

Marius Popescu and Liviu P. Dinu. 2007. Kernel methods and string kernels for authorship identification: The federalist papers case. *Proceedings of RANLP*, September.

Marius Popescu and Cristian Grozea. 2012. Kernel methods and string kernels for authorship analysis. *CLEF (Online Working Notes/Labs/Workshop)*, September.

Marius Popescu and Radu Tudor Ionescu. 2013. The Story of the Characters, the DNA and the Native Language. *Proceedings of the Eighth Workshop on Innovative Use of NLP for Building Educational Applications*, pages 270–278, June.

Marius Popescu. 2011. Studying translationese at the character level. *Proceedings of RANLP*, pages 634–639, September.

Conrad Sanderson and Simon Guenter. 2006. Short text authorship attribution via sequence kernels, markov chains and author unmasking: An investigation. *Proceedings of the 2006 Conference on Empirical Methods in Natural Language Processing*, pages 482–491, July.

John Shawe-Taylor and Nello Cristianini. 2004. *Kernel Methods for Pattern Analysis*. Cambridge University Press.

Andrea Vedaldi and Andrew Zisserman. 2010. Efficient additive kernels via explicit feature maps. *Proceedings of CVPR*, pages 3539–3546.

Omar F. Zaidan and Chris Callison-Burch. 2011. The Arabic Online Commentary Dataset: An Annotated Dataset of Informal Arabic with High Dialectal Content. *Proceedings of ACL: HLT*, 2:37–41.

Omar F. Zaidan and Chris Callison-Burch. 2014. Arabic dialect identification. *Computational Linguistics*, 40(1):171–202.

A Character-level Convolutional Neural Network
for Distinguishing Similar Languages and Dialects

Yonatan Belinkov and **James Glass**
MIT Computer Science and Artificial Intelligence Laboratory
Cambridge, MA 02139, USA
`{belinkov, glass}@mit.edu`

Abstract

Discriminating between closely-related language varieties is considered a challenging and important task. This paper describes our submission to the DSL 2016 shared-task, which included two sub-tasks: one on discriminating similar languages and one on identifying Arabic dialects. We developed a character-level neural network for this task. Given a sequence of characters, our model embeds each character in vector space, runs the sequence through multiple convolutions with different filter widths, and pools the convolutional representations to obtain a hidden vector representation of the text that is used for predicting the language or dialect. We primarily focused on the Arabic dialect identification task and obtained an F1 score of 0.4834, ranking 6th out of 18 participants. We also analyze errors made by our system on the Arabic data in some detail, and point to challenges such an approach is faced with.[1]

1 Introduction

Automatic language identification is an important first step in many applications. For many languages and texts, this is a fairly easy step that can be solved with familiar methods like n-gram language models. However, distinguishing between similar languages is not so easy. The shared-task on discriminating between similar languages (DSL) has offered a test bed for evaluating models on this task since 2014 (Tan et al., 2014; Zampieri et al., 2014; Zampieri et al., 2015). The 2016 shared-task included two sub-tasks: (1) discriminating between similar languages from several groups; and (2) discriminating between Arabic dialects (Malmasi et al., 2016). The following language varieties were considered in sub-task 1: Bosnian, Croatian, and Serbian; Malay and Indonesian; Portuguese of Brazil and Portugal; Spanish of Argentina, Mexico, and Spain; and French of France and Canada. In sub-task 2, the following Arabic varieties were considered: Levantine, Gulf, Egyptian, North African, and Modern Standard Arabic (MSA).

The training datasets released in the two sub-tasks were very different. Sub-task 1 was comprised of journalistic texts and included training and development sets. Sub-task 2 had automatic transcriptions of spoken recordings and included only a training set. This was the first time DSL has offered a task on Arabic dialects. The shared-task also included an open track that allows additional resources, but we have only participated in the closed track.

Previous DSL competitions attracted a variety of methods, achieving very high results with accuracies of over 95%. Most teams used character and word n-grams with various classifiers. One team in 2015 used vector embeddings of words and sentences (Franco-Salvador et al., 2015), achieving very good, though not state-of-the-art results. They trained unsupervised vectors and fed them as input to a classifier. Here we are interested in *character-level* neural network models. Such models showed recent success in other tasks (Kim et al., 2016, among many others). The basic question we ask is this: how well can a character-level neural network perform on this task without the notion of a word? To answer this, our model takes as input a sequence of characters, embeds them in vector space, and generates a high-level

---

[1]The code for this work is available at `https://github.com/boknilev/dsl-char-cnn`.
This work is licensed under a Creative Commons Attribution 4.0 International License. License details:
`http://creativecommons.org/licenses/by/4.0/`

Proceedings of the Third Workshop on NLP for Similar Languages, Varieties and Dialects,
pages 145–152, Osaka, Japan, December 12 2016.

representation of the sequence through multiple convolutional layers. At the top of the network, we output a probability distribution over labels and backpropagate errors, such that the entire network can be learned end-to-end.

We experimented with several configurations of convolutional layers, focusing on Arabic dialect identification (sub-task 2). We also participated in sub-task 1, but have not tuned our system to this scenario. Our best system obtained an F1 score of 0.4834 on the Arabic sub-task, ranking 6th out of 18 participants. The same system did not perform well on sub-task 1 (ranked 2nd to last), although we have not spent much time on adapting it to this task. In the next section, we discuss related work on identifying similar languages and dialects. We then present our methodology and results, and conclude with a discussion and a short error analysis for the Arabic system that sheds light on potential sources of errors.

2 Related Work

Discriminating similar languages and dialects has been the topic of two previous iterations of the DSL task (Zampieri et al., 2014; Zampieri et al., 2015). The previous competitions proved that despite very good performance (over 95% accuracy), it is still a non-trivial task that is considerably more difficult than identifying unrelated languages. Admittedly, even humans have a hard time identifying the correct language in certain cases, as observed by Goutte et al. (2016). The previous shared-task reports contain detailed information on the task, related work, and participating systems. Here we only highlight a few relevant trends.

In terms of features, the majority of the groups in previous years used sequences of characters and words. A notable exception is the use of word white-lists by Porta and Sancho (2014). Different learning algorithms were used for this task, most commonly linear SVMs or maximum entropy models. Some groups formulated a two-step classification model: first predicting the language group and then predicting an individual language. For simplicity, we only trained a single multi-class classification model, although we speculate that a two-step process could improve our results. For Arabic dialect identification (sub-task 2), one could first distinguish MSA from all the other dialects, and then identify the specific dialect.

Last year, Franco-Salvador et al. (2015) used vector embeddings of words and sentences, achieving very good results, though not state-of-the-art. They trained unsupervised word vectors and fed them as input to a classifier. In contrast, we build an end-to-end neural network over *character* sequences, and train character embeddings along with other parameters of the network. Using character embeddings is particularly appealing for this task given the importance of character n-gram features in previous work. In light of the recent success of character-level neural networks in various language processing and understanding tasks (Santos and Zadrozny, 2014; Zhang et al., 2015; Luong and Manning, 2016; Kim et al., 2016), we were interested to see how far one can go on this task without any word-level information.

Finally, this year's task offered a sub-task on Arabic dialect identification. It is unique in that the texts are automatic transcriptions generated by a speech recognizer. Previous work on Arabic dialect identification mostly used written texts (Zaidan and Callison-Burch, 2014; Malmasi et al., 2015) or speech recordings, with access to the acoustic signal (Biadsy et al., 2009; Ali et al., 2016). For example, Ali et al. (2016) exploited both acoustic and ASR-based features, finding that their combination works best. Working with automatic transcriptions obscures many dialectal differences (e.g. in phonology) and leads to inevitable errors. Still, we were interested to see how well a character-level neural network can perform on this task, without access to acoustic features.

3 Methodology

We formulate the task as a multi-class classification problem, where each language (or dialect) is a separate class. We do not consider two-step classification, although this was found useful in previous work (Zampieri et al., 2015). Formally, given a collection of texts and associated labels, $\{t^{(i)}, l^{(i)}\}$, we need to find a predictor $f : t \rightarrow l$. Our predictor is a neural network over character sequences. Let $t := \mathbf{c} = c_1, \cdots, c_L$ denote a sequence of characters, where L is a maximum length that we set empirically. Longer texts are truncated and shorter ones are padded with a special PAD symbol. Each character c in the alphabet is represented as a real-valued vector $x_c \in \mathbb{R}^{d_{emb}}$. This character embedding is learned during training.

Our neural network has the following structure:

- Input layer: mapping the character sequence $\mathbf{c}$ to a vector sequence $\mathbf{x}$. The embedding layer is followed by dropout.

- Convolutional layers: multiple parallel convolutional layers, mapping the vector sequence $\mathbf{x}$ to a hidden sequence $\mathbf{h}$. We use filters that slide over character vectors, similarly to Kim (2014)'s CNN over words. A single filter $k \in \mathbb{R}^{wd_{emb}}$ of width w creates a new feature $f_i \in \mathbb{R}$ by: $f_i = k \cdot \mathbf{x}_{i:i+w-1} + b$, where $\mathbf{x}_{i:i+w-1}$ is a concatenation of $x_i, \ldots x_{i+w-1}$ and $b \in \mathbb{R}$ is a bias term. Each convolution is followed by a Rectified Linear Unit (ReLU) non-linearity (Glorot et al., 2011). The outputs of all the convolutional layers are concatenated.

- Pooling layer: a max-over-time pooling layer, mapping the vector sequence $\mathbf{h}$ to a single hidden vector h representing the sequence. The size of h is $\Sigma_j n_j w_j$, where there are n_j filters of width w_j.

- Fully-connected layer: one hidden layer with a ReLU non-linearity and dropout, mapping h to the final vector representation of the text, h'.

- Output layer: a softmax layer, mapping h' to a probability distribution over labels l.

During training, each sequence is fed into this network to create label predictions. As errors are back-propagated down the network, the weights at each layer are updated, including the embedding layer. During testing, the learned weights are used in a forward step to compute a prediction over the labels. We always take the best predicted label for evaluation.

3.1 Training details and submitted runs

We train the entire network jointly, including the embedding layer. We use the Adam optimizer (Kingma and Ba, 2014) with the default original parameters to minimize the cross-entropy loss. Training is run with shuffled mini-batches of size 16 and stopped once the loss on the dev set stops improving; we allow a patience of 10 epochs. Our implementation is based on Keras (Chollet, 2015) with the TensorFlow backend (Abadi et al., 2015).

We mostly experimented with the sub-task 2 dataset of Arabic dialects. Since the official shared-task did not include a dedicated dev set, we randomly allocated 90% of the training set for development. We tuned the following hyperparameters on this split, shown in Table 1 (chosen parameters in bold): embedding layer dropout ρ_{emb}, fully-connected layer dropout ρ_{fc}, maximum text length L, character embedding size d_{emb}, and fully-connected layer output size d_{fc}. Note that removing the fully-connected layer led to a small drop in performance.

Param	Values
ρ_{emb}	**0.2**, 0.5
ρ_{fc}	0.2, **0.5**
L	200, **400**, 800
d_{emb}	25, **50**, 100
d_{fc}	100, **250**

Table 1: Tuned hyperparameters.

For the convolutional layers, we experimented with different combinations of filter widths and number of filters. We started with a single filter width and noticed that a width of 5 characters performs fairly well with enough filters (250). We then added multiple widths, similarly to a recent character-CNN used in language modeling (Kim et al., 2016). Using multiple widths led to a small improvement. Our best configuration was: $\{1*50, 2*50, 3*100, 4*100, 5*100, 6*100, 7*100\}$, where $w * n$ indicates n filters of width w.

Since the shared-task did not provide a dev set for sub-task 2, we explored several settings in our three submitted runs:

- **Run 1** used 90% of the training set for training and 10% for development.

- **Run 2** used 100% of the training for training, but stopped at the same epoch as Run 1.

- **Run 3** used 10 different models, each trained on a different random 90%/10% train/dev split, with a plurality vote among the 10 models to determine the final prediction.

Test Set	Track	Run	Accuracy	F1 (micro)	F1 (macro)	F1 (weighted)
A	closed	Baseline	0.083			
A	closed	run1	0.8042	0.8042	0.8017	0.8017
A	closed	run2	0.825	0.825	0.8249	0.8249
A	closed	run3	**0.8307**	**0.8307**	**0.8299**	**0.8299**
A	closed	Best	*0.8938*			*0.8938*
C	closed	Baseline	0.2279			
C	closed	run1	0.4487	0.4487	0.4442	0.4449
C	closed	run2	0.4357	0.4357	0.4178	0.4181
C	closed	run3	**0.4851**	**0.4851**	**0.4807**	**0.4834**
C	closed	Best	*0.5117*			*0.5132*

Table 2: Results for our submitted runs. Best results out of our runs are in **bold**; best overall systems shown in *italics* for reference. Refer to the text for a description of runs and baselines.

For the (larger) dataset of sub-task 1, we did not perform any tuning of hyperparameters and used the same setting as in sub-task 2, except for a larger mini-batch size (64) to speed up training. This was our **Run 1**, whereas in **Run 2** we used more filter maps, following the setting in (Kim et al., 2016): $\{1 * 50, 2 * 100, 3 * 150, 4 * 200, 5 * 200, 6 * 200, 7 * 200\}$. **Run 3** was the same as Run 2, but with more hidden units ($d_{fc} = 500$) and a higher dropout rate ($\rho_{fc} = 0.7$) in the fully-connected layer.

4 Results

Table 2 shows the results of our submitted runs, along with two baselines: a random baseline for sub-task 1, test set A (a balanced test set), and a majority baseline for sub-task 2, test set C (a slightly unbalanced test set). We also report results of the best performing systems in the shared-task.

In sub-task 2, test set C, we notice a fairly large difference between our runs. Our best result, with Run 3, used plurality voting among 10 different models trained on 90% of the training data. We chose this strategy in an effort to avoid overfitting. However, during development we obtained accuracy results of around 57-60% on a separate train/dev split, so we suspect there was still overfitting of the training set. With this run our team ranked 6th out of 18 teams according to the official evaluation.

For sub-task 1, test set A, larger models perform somewhat better, due to the larger training set. In this case we only have a small drop of about 2% in comparison to our performance on the dev set (not shown). Our system did not perform very well compared to other teams (we ranked 2nd to last), but this may be expected as we did not tune our system for this dataset.

Figure 1 shows confusion matrices for our best runs. Clearly, the vast majority of the confusion in sub-task 1 (test set A) comes from languages in the same group, whereas languages from different groups are rarely confused. The Spanish varieties are the most difficult to distinguish, with F1 scores between 0.57 (Mexican Spanish) and 0.75 (Argentinian Spanish). The South Slavic languages are less confused, with F1 scores of 0.75-0.83. French and Portuguese languages are easier to distinguish (F1 around 0.90), and Malay and Indonesian are the least confused (F1 of 0.96-0.97).

Turning to sub-task 2 (test set C), we see much more confusion, as also reflected in the final results (Table 2). Gulf is the most confusing dialect: true Gulf examples are often predicted as MSA, and true Levantine and North African examples are wrongly predicted as Gulf relatively frequently. This is also reflected in a low F1 score of 0.34 for Gulf. The other dialects have higher F1 scores ranging between 0.47 and 0.50, with MSA having an F1 of 0.60, making it the easiest variety to detect.

5 Discussion

In this section we focus on the Arabic dataset (sub-task 2, test set C) and consider some of our findings. The first issue that should be stressed is the nature of the data. As the texts are automatically generated speech transcriptions, they contain mistakes that depend on the training data used for the speech

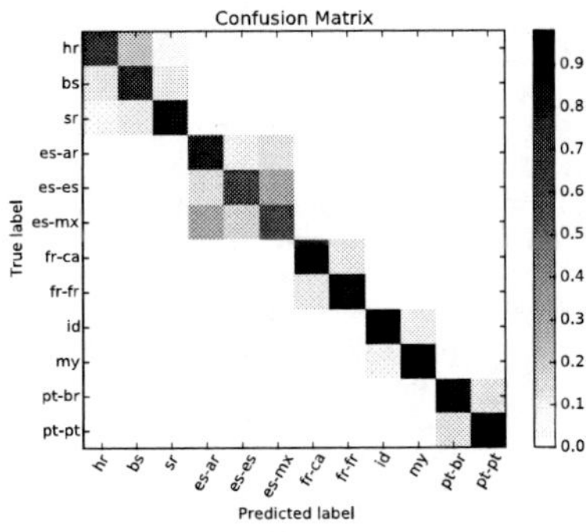
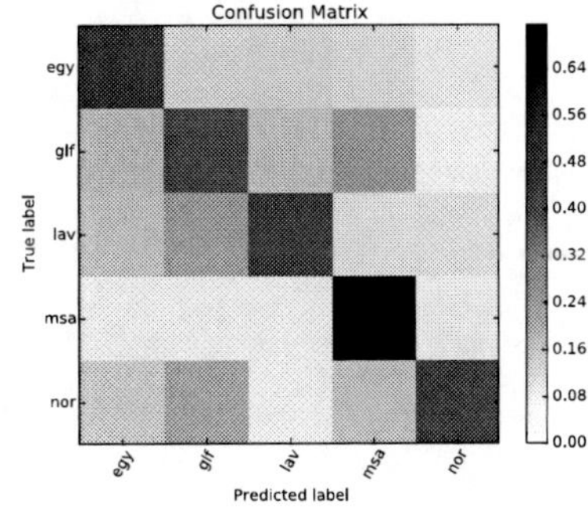

(a) Sub-task 1, test set A, Run 3.   (b) Sub-task 2, test set C, Run 3.

Figure 1: Confusion matrices for our best runs on test sets A and C. Best viewed in color.

recognizer. This might have a negative effect on the ability to correctly recognize the dialect just from the transcriptions. For comparison, previous work found that using acoustic features improves dialect recognition in a similar setting (Ali et al., 2016). Secondly, the transcribed texts use a transliteration system[2] that was designed for written MSA and obscures many dialectal features that are important for distinguishing Arabic dialects, especially phonological features.

The fact that MSA is confused with dialectal varieties at all may sound surprising at first. However, due to the writing scheme many of the known differences between MSA and the dialects are not accessible. In addition, MSA is often mixed with dialectal Arabic in many settings (e.g. news broadcasts), so it is reasonable to find MSA features in dialectal speech.

Levantine and Gulf dialects are relatively close geographically and linguistically, so confusing one with the other might be expected. The confusion between Gulf and North African dialects is more surprising, although there are always parallel innovations in dialects that stem from a mutual ancestor, as all Arabic dialects do.

Other factors that can play into similarities and differences are local foreign languages, religious terminology, and genre and domain. However, these are aspects that are difficult to tease apart without a more careful analysis, and they also depend on the data sources and the ASR system.

Error analysis We conclude this discussion with an analysis of several example errors made by our systems, as shown in Figure 2. These are examples from a dev set that we kept held out during the development of our system. In each case, we give the true and predicted labels, the text, and a rough translation. Note that the translations are often questionable due to ASR mistakes and the lack of context.

In the first example, an MSA text is predicted as Levantine, possibly due to the word *AllbnAnyp* "Lebanese", whose character sequence could be typical of Levantine texts. There are clear MSA features like the dual forms *hmA* and *-An*, but these are ambigious with dialectal forms that are found in the training data. Note also the Verb-Subject word order, typical of MSA – such a pattern requires syntactic knowledge and cannot be easily detected with simple character (or even word) features.

The second error shows an example of a mixed text, containing both dialectal (*>h HDrp* "yes the honorable", *bdy* "I want") and MSA features (*hl syHdv* "will it happen"). It is an example of mixing that is common in spoken data and can confuse the model.

In the third example, the form *Alm$kwk fyh* "doubtful" has a morphological construction that is typical of MSA. Such a feature is difficult to capture in a character model and might require morphological knowledge.

In the fourth example, the words *AlmAlky* and *AlhA$my* are actually seen most commonly in MSA in the training data, but they do not contain typical character-sequences. The phrase *Al Al*, which indicates

---

[2]`http://www.qamus.org/transliteration.htm`.

149

	True	Predicted	Text	Translation
1	MSA	Levantine	AndlEt AlHrb AllbnAnyp EAm 1975 >Syb bxybp >ml whmA yrwyAn kyf ynHArwn wqthA	The Lebanon war erupted in 1975, he was disappointed and they both tell how they deteriorated back then
2	MSA	Egyptian	>h HDrp AlEmyd AlAHtkAk bdy dm$q AlEASmp AlsyAdyp AlEASmp AlsyAsyp fy fy >kvr mn mrp wbEmlyp nwEyp kbyrp jdA hl syHdv AlmnErj fy h*h AlmwAjhp	Yes, the honorable general, the friction, I want Damascus the sovereign capitol the sovereign capitol more than once and in a very large high-quality operation, will the turn take place in this confrontation
3	MSA	Gulf	>mA xrjt ElY tlfzywn Aldwlp fy Alywm Al-tAly lvwrp wqlt lh HAfZ ElY tAryx >ql Al-wzArp Alywm Thr AlbrlmAn mn AlEDwyAt Alm$kwk fyh <dY msyrp Al<SlAH wbdA h*A qbl SlAp AljmEp	But (I) went on the state television the following day after the revolution and told him, keep the history at least the ministry today, cleanse the parliament from the doubtful memberships if(?) the course of reform and this started before the Friday prayer
4	MSA	North African	>wlA Al Al Alsyd AlmAlky ytmnY mn TArq AlhA$my Alxrwj wlA yEwd	First, mister Al-Maliki wants Tariq Al-Hashimi to exit and not return
5	Egyptian	Gulf	>nA bEmrnA ftrp mn HyAty snp Al>xyrp mtEwd ElY wqf Altfrd AHtlAly tEtbr llmsjd gryb mn mjls AlwzrA' wmjls Al$Eb wAl$wrY wnqAbp AlmHAmyn wxlAfh fkAn >y wAlAHtjAjyp byt>vr bhA Almsjd b$>n Al>wDAE	I in my life, time in my life, last year, used to stop being alone of occupation(?) that is considered for a mosque close to the cabinet and the parliament and the council and the bar association and behind it, and the protest, the mosque influences it because of the situation
6	Gulf	North African	lxwAtm Sgyrp fy AlHjm lkn tHtAj lEnAyp xASA $mAtp ksArp wHtY AlxSm ArtHnA ElyhA bn$wf h*A Altqryr wnErf mn xlAlh >kvr En tktlAt Alywm bfqr Aldm AlsyAsAt mE Alzmyl lwrA	The rings/stamps are of small size but they need special care malice(?) breaker(?) and even the discount, we are happy with it, we see this report and through it we know more about the blocks/fights of today in lack of blood, the policies with the colleague are backwards
7	North African	Gulf	"$Ahd tglb wAjb lxr mr Ebr EddA mn brnAmjh <HnA wyAhm lA ymnE xrwj bAlb$r ftzydh whlA Em lxrwqAt AlHq Al$yx xAld Hqq mEy lA yglq fyjb hdf AlnAtw bAlAxtyAr mn Altwqf lA tqAs bqyt Endk nsmH lkl $y' HtY tqrr trHb	See a must win last time through some of his programs, we are with them, will not prevent leaving with someone, and add more to it, and are now the violations, the truth the Sheikh Khalid interrogated me, he is not worried, and the goal of NATO must be to choose to stop, cannot be compared, still with you, I will permit everything until deciding to welcome

Figure 2: Example errors made by our system on the Arabic data set (sub-task 2). Some translations are questionable due to quality of transcription and lack of context.

some stuttering, is more common in some of the dialects than in MSA in the training data, but is about as common in NOR and MSA.

In the fifth example, the word *byt>vr* "influences" is likely misrecognized, as in Egyptian it would probably be *byt>tr*, but an Arabic language model with much MSA in it might push the ASR system towards the sequence *>vr*, which in turn is more common in Gulf.

In the seventh example, the phrase *<HnA wyAhm* "we're with them" might be more indicative of Gulf, but it is rare in the training set in both North African and Gulf. *bqyt* "remained" should have been a good clue for North African, and indeed it appears in training 5 times as North African and not at all as Gulf.

6 Conclusion

In this work, we explored character-level convolutional neural networks for discriminating between similar languages and dialects. We demonstrated that such a model can perform quite well on Arabic dialect identification, although it does not achieve state-of-the-art results. We also conducted a short analysis of errors made by our system on the Arabic dataset, pointing to challenges that such a model is faced with.

A natural extension of this work is to combine word-level features in the neural network. White-lists of words typical of certain dialects might also help, although in preliminary experiments we were not able to obtain performance gains by adding such features. We are also curious to see how our model would perform with access to the speech recordings, for example by running it on recognized phone sequences or by directly incorporating acoustic features. This, however, would require a different preparation of the dataset, which we hope would be made available in future DSL tasks.

Acknowledgments

The authors would like to thank Sergiu Nisioi and Noam Ordan for helpful discussions. This work was supported by the Qatar Computing Research Institute (QCRI). Any opinions, findings, conclusions, or recommendations expressed in this paper are those of the authors, and do not necessarily reflect the views of the funding organizations.

References

Martín Abadi, Ashish Agarwal, Paul Barham, Eugene Brevdo, Zhifeng Chen, Craig Citro, Greg S. Corrado, Andy Davis, Jeffrey Dean, Matthieu Devin, Sanjay Ghemawat, Ian Goodfellow, Andrew Harp, Geoffrey Irving, Michael Isard, Yangqing Jia, Rafal Jozefowicz, Lukasz Kaiser, Manjunath Kudlur, Josh Levenberg, Dan Mané, Rajat Monga, Sherry Moore, Derek Murray, Chris Olah, Mike Schuster, Jonathon Shlens, Benoit Steiner, Ilya Sutskever, Kunal Talwar, Paul Tucker, Vincent Vanhoucke, Vijay Vasudevan, Fernanda Viégas, Oriol Vinyals, Pete Warden, Martin Wattenberg, Martin Wicke, Yuan Yu, and Xiaoqiang Zheng. 2015. TensorFlow: Large-Scale Machine Learning on Heterogeneous Systems. Software available from tensorflow.org.

Ahmed Ali, Najim Dehak, Patrick Cardinal, Sameer Khurana, Sree Harsha Yella, James Glass, Peter Bell, and Steve Renals. 2016. Automatic Dialect Detection in Arabic Broadcast Speech. In *Interspeech 2016*, pages 2934–2938.

Fadi Biadsy, Julia Hirschberg, and Nizar Habash. 2009. Spoken Arabic Dialect Identification Using Phonotactic Modeling. In *Proceedings of the EACL 2009 Workshop on Computational Approaches to Semitic Languages*, pages 53–61, Athens, Greece.

François Chollet. 2015. Keras. https://github.com/fchollet/keras.

Marc Franco-Salvador, Paolo Rosso, and Francisco Rangel. 2015. Distributed Representations of Words and Documents for Discriminating Similar Languages. In *Proceedings of the Joint Workshop on Language Technology for Closely Related Languages, Varieties and Dialects (LT4VarDial)*, pages 11–16, Hissar, Bulgaria.

Xavier Glorot, Antoine Bordes, and Yoshua Bengio. 2011. Deep Sparse Rectifier Neural Networks. In *Proceedings of the Fourteenth International Conference on Artificial Intelligence and Statistics (AISTATS-11)*, volume 15, pages 315–323.

Cyril Goutte, Serge LÃľger, Shervin Malmasi, and Marcos Zampieri. 2016. Discriminating Similar Languages: Evaluations and Explorations. In *Proceedings of the Tenth International Conference on Language Resources and Evaluation (LREC 2016)*, Portorož, Slovenia.

Yoon Kim, Yacine Jernite, David Sontag, and Alexander Rush. 2016. Character-Aware Neural Language Models. In *AAAI Conference on Artificial Intelligence*.

Yoon Kim. 2014. Convolutional Neural Networks for Sentence Classification. In *Proceedings of the 2014 Conference on Empirical Methods in Natural Language Processing (EMNLP)*, pages 1746–1751, Doha, Qatar.

Diederik Kingma and Jimmy Ba. 2014. Adam: A method for stochastic optimization. *arXiv preprint arXiv:1412.6980*.

Minh-Thang Luong and Christopher D Manning. 2016. Achieving Open Vocabulary Neural Machine Translation with Hybrid Word-Character Models. *arXiv preprint arXiv:1604.00788*.

Shervin Malmasi, Eshrag Refaee, and Mark Dras. 2015. Arabic Dialect Identification using a Parallel Multidialectal Corpus. In *Proceedings of the 14th Conference of the Pacific Association for Computational Linguistics (PACLING 2015)*, pages 209–217, Bali, Indonesia.

Shervin Malmasi, Marcos Zampieri, Nikola Ljubešić, Preslav Nakov, Ahmed Ali, and Jörg Tiedemann. 2016. Discriminating between Similar Languages and Arabic Dialect Identification: A Report on the Third DSL Shared Task. In *Proceedings of the 3rd Workshop on Language Technology for Closely Related Languages, Varieties and Dialects (VarDial)*, Osaka, Japan.

Jordi Porta and José-Luis Sancho. 2014. Using Maximum Entropy Models to Discriminate between Similar Languages and Varieties. In *Proceedings of the First Workshop on Applying NLP Tools to Similar Languages, Varieties and Dialects (VarDial)*, pages 120–128, Dublin, Ireland.

Cicero D Santos and Bianca Zadrozny. 2014. Learning character-level representations for part-of-speech tagging. In *Proceedings of the 31st International Conference on Machine Learning (ICML-14)*, pages 1818–1826.

Liling Tan, Marcos Zampieri, Nikola Ljubešic, and Jörg Tiedemann. 2014. Merging Comparable Data Sources for the Discrimination of Similar Languages: The DSL Corpus Collection. In *Proceedings of the 7th Workshop on Building and Using Comparable Corpora (BUCC)*, pages 11–15, Reykjavik, Iceland.

Omar F. Zaidan and Chris Callison-Burch. 2014. Arabic Dialect Identification. *Comput. Linguist.*, 40(1):171–202.

Marcos Zampieri, Liling Tan, Nikola Ljubešić, and Jörg Tiedemann. 2014. A Report on the DSL Shared Task 2014. In *Proceedings of the First Workshop on Applying NLP Tools to Similar Languages, Varieties and Dialects (VarDial)*, pages 58–67, Dublin, Ireland.

Marcos Zampieri, Liling Tan, Nikola Ljubešić, Jörg Tiedemann, and Preslav Nakov. 2015. Overview of the DSL Shared Task 2015. In *Proceedings of the Joint Workshop on Language Technology for Closely Related Languages, Varieties and Dialects (LT4VarDial)*, pages 1–9, Hissar, Bulgaria.

Xiang Zhang, Junbo Zhao, and Yann LeCun. 2015. Character-level Convolutional Networks for Text Classification. In C. Cortes, N. D. Lawrence, D. D. Lee, M. Sugiyama, and R. Garnett, editors, *Advances in Neural Information Processing Systems 28*, pages 649–657. Curran Associates, Inc.

HeLI, a Word-Based Backoff Method for Language Identification

Tommi Jauhiainen
University of Helsinki
@helsinki.fi

Krister Lindén
University of Helsinki
@helsinki.fi

Heidi Jauhiainen
University of Helsinki
@helsinki.fi

Abstract

In this paper we describe the Helsinki language identification method, HeLI, and the resources we created for and used in the 3rd edition of the Discriminating between Similar Languages (DSL) shared task, which was organized as part of the VarDial 2016 workshop. The shared task comprised of a total of 8 tracks, of which we participated in 7. The shared task had a record number of participants, with 17 teams providing results for the closed track of the test set A. Our system reached the 2nd position in 4 tracks (A closed and open, B1 open and B2 open) and in this paper we are focusing on the methods and data used for those tracks. We describe our word-based backoff method in mathematical notation. We also describe how we selected the corpus we used in the open tracks.

1 Introduction

The 3rd edition of the Discriminating between Similar Languages (DSL) shared task, (Malmasi et al., 2016), was divided into two sub-tasks: "Similar Languages and Language Varieties" and "Arabic dialects". Furthermore, the first sub-task was divided into three test sets: A, B1 and B2. Each of the test sets for both tasks had a closed and an open track. On the closed track the participants were allowed to use only the training data provided by the organizers, whereas on the open track the participants could use any data source they had at their disposal.

The first sub-task had a language selection comparable to the 1st (Zampieri et al., 2014) and 2nd (Zampieri et al., 2015b) editions of the shared task. The languages and varieties of the sub-task 1 are listed in the Table 2. The differences from the previous year's shared task were the inclusion of the French language varieties and the Mexican Spanish, as well as the exclusion of Bulgarian, Macedonian, Czech, and Slovak. The four latter languages were practically 100% correct in most of the submissions to the 2nd edition of the shared task. On the other hand, discriminating between the two French varieties could be expected to be more difficult (Zampieri, 2013). Also the extra category "unknown language" introduced in 2015 was left out from the 3rd edition repertoire. These changes resulted in a drop of the best reported accuracy of any team (test set A) from the 95.54% of the 2nd edition closed track to the 89.38% of the 3rd edition closed track. The second sub-task comprised of discriminating between Modern Standard Arabic and four dialects: Egyptian, Gulf, Levantine, and North-African. The Arabic dialects were included in the shared task for the first time.

For the 2015 edition of the task, we used the word-based backoff language identification method first introduced in 2010 (Jauhiainen, 2010) and made several modifications to it in order to improve the method for the task of discriminating similar languages and to cope with the unknown language (Jauhiainen et al., 2015b). In the 3rd edition of the task, the unknown language was left out, which meant that the original method was directly applicable. We also felt that the modifications we made in 2015 complicated the system and did not really improve the results that much, so we decided to use the basic method out-of-the-box for the 3rd edition of the shared task. The word-based backoff method, now named HeLI, is a general purpose language identification method which we have used for collecting text

Proceedings of the Third Workshop on NLP for Similar Languages, Varieties and Dialects,
pages 153–162, Osaka, Japan, December 12 2016.

material written in Uralic languages in the Finno-Ugric Languages and the Internet project (Jauhiainen et al., 2015a) funded by the Kone foundation. We have also used the method as a language identifier part when developing a method for language set identification in multilingual documents (Jauhiainen et al., 2015c). The language identifier tool using the HeLI-method is available as open source from GitHub[1].

2   Related Work

Automatic language identification has been researched for more than 50 years. The first article on the subject was written by Mustonen (1965). For the history of automatic language identification (of textual material), as well as an excellent overview of the subject, the reader is suggested to take a look at the literature review chapter of Marco Lui's doctoral thesis (Lui, 2014). Recent surveys and overviews by Garg et al. (2014) and Shashirekha (2014) could also be of interest.

Automatic identification of Malay and Indonesian was studied by Ranaivo-Malançon (2006). Distinguishing between South-Slavic languages has been researched by Ljubešic et al. (2007), Tiedemann and Ljubešic (2012), Ljubešic and Kranjcic (2014), and Ljubešic and Kranjcic (2015). Automatic identification of Portuguese varieties was studied by Zampieri and Gebre (2012), whereas Zampieri et al. (2012), Zampieri (2013), Zampieri et al. (2013), and Maier and Gómez-Rodríguez (2014) researched language variety identification between Spanish dialects. Discriminating between French dialects was studied by Zampieri et al. (2012) and Zampieri (2013). Arabic dialect identification was researched by Elfardy and Diab (2013), Darwish et al. (2014), Elfardy et al. (2014), Sadat et al. (2014), Salloum et al. (2014), Tillmann et al. (2014), Zaidan and Callison-Burch (2014), Al-Badrashiny et al. (2015), Malmasi et al. (2015), and Ali et al. (2016).

The system description articles provided for the previous shared tasks are all relevant and references to them can be found in (Zampieri et al., 2014) and (Zampieri et al., 2015b). Detailed analysis of the previous shared task results was done by Goutte et al. (2016).

3   Methodology

The basic idea of the HeLI method was first introduced in (Jauhiainen, 2010). It was also described in the proceedings of the previous task (Jauhiainen et al., 2015b). In this paper, we present the complete description of the method for the first time. First we introduce the notation used in the description of the method.

3.1   On notation [2]

A corpus C consists of individual tokens u which may be words or characters. A corpus C is a finite sequence of individual tokens, $u_1, ..., u_l$. The total count of all individual tokens u in the corpus C is denoted by l_C. A feature f is some countable characteristic of the corpus C. When referring to all features F in a corpus C, we use C^F and the count of all features is denoted by l_{CF}. The count of a feature f in the corpus C is referred to as $c(C, f)$. An n-gram is a feature which consists of a sequence of n individual tokens. An n-gram starting at position i in a corpus is denoted $u_{i,...,i-1+n}$. If $n = 1$, u is an individual token. When referring to all n-grams of length n in a corpus C, we use C^n and the count of all such n-grams is denoted by l_{C^n}. The count of an n-gram u in a corpus C is referred to as $c(C, u)$ and is defined by Equation 1.

$$c(C, u) = \sum_{i=1}^{l_C + 1 - n} \begin{cases} 1 & \text{, if } u = u_{i,...,i-1+n} \\ 0 & \text{, otherwise} \end{cases} \tag{1}$$

The set of languages is G, and l_G denotes the number of languages. A corpus C in language g is denoted by C_g. A language model O based on C_g is denoted by $O(C_g)$. The features given values by the model $O(C_g)$ are the domain $dom(O(C_g))$ of the model. In a language model, a value v for the feature f is denoted by $v_{C_g}(f)$. For each potential language g of a corpus C in an unknown language, a resulting score $R_g(C)$ is calculated. A corpus in an unknown language is also referred to as a mystery text.

---

[1] https://github.com/tosaja/HeLI
[2] We would like to thank Kimmo Koskenniemi for many valuable discussions and comments.

3.2 HeLI method

The goal is to correctly guess the language $g \in G$ in which the monolingual mystery text M has been written, when all languages in the set G are known to the language identifier. In the method, each language $g \in G$ is represented by several different language models only one of which is used for every word t found in the mystery text M. The language models for each language are: a model based on words and one or more models based on character n-grams from one to n_{max}. Each model used is selected by its applicability to the word t under scrutiny. The basic problem with word-based models is that it is not really possible to have a model with all possible words. When we encounter an unknown word in the mystery text M, we back off to using the n-grams of the size n_{max}. The problem with high order n-grams is similar to the problem with words: there are simply too many of them to have statistics for all. If we are unable to apply the n-grams of the size n_{max}, we back off to lower order n-grams. We continue backing off until character unigrams, if needed.

A development set is used for finding the best values for the parameters of the method. The three parameters are the maximum length of the used character n-grams (n_{max}), the maximum number of features to be included in the language models (cut-off c), and the penalty value for those languages where the features being used are absent (penalty p). The penalty value has a smoothing effect in that it transfers some of the probability mass to unseen features in the language models.

3.3 Description of the method

The task is to select the most probable language g, given a mystery text M, as shown in Equation 2.

$$argmax_g P(g|M) \tag{2}$$

$P(g|M)$ can be calculated using the Bayes' rule, as in Equation 3.

$$P(g|M) = \frac{P(M|g)P(g)}{P(M)} \tag{3}$$

In Equation 3, $P(M)$ is equal for the languages $g \in G$ and can be omitted. Also, we assume that all languages have equal a priori probability, so that $P(g)$ can be omitted as well, leaving us with the Equation 4.

$$argmax_g P(g|M) = argmax_g P(M|g) \tag{4}$$

We approximate the probability $P(M|g)$ of the whole text through the probabilities of its words $P(t|g)$, which we assume to be independent as in Equation 5.

$$P(M|g) \approx P(t_1|g)P(t_2|g)...P(t_{l_M}|g) \tag{5}$$

We use the relative frequencies of words and character n-grams in the models for language g for estimating the probabilities $P(t|g)$.

3.3.1 Creating the language models

The training data is lowercased and tokenized into words using non-alphabetic and non-ideographic characters as delimiters. The relative frequencies of the words are calculated. Also the relative frequencies of character n-grams from 1 to n_{max} are calculated inside the words, so that the preceding and the following space-characters are included. The n-grams are overlapping, so that for example a word with three characters includes three character trigrams. Word n-grams are not used in this method, so all subsequent references to n-grams in this article refer to n-grams of characters.

The c most common n-grams of each length and the c most common words in the corpus of a language are included in the language models for that language. We estimate the probabilities using relative frequencies of the words and character n-grams in the language models, using only the relative frequencies of the retained tokens. Then we transform those frequencies into scores using 10-based logarithms.

The derived corpus containing only the word tokens retained in the language models is called C'. $dom(O(C'))$ is the set of all words found in the models of all languages $g \in G$. For each word $t \in dom(O(C'))$, the values $v_{C'_g}(t)$ for each language g are calculated, as in Equation 6

$$v_{C'_g}(t) = \begin{cases} -\log_{10}\left(\frac{c(C'_g, t)}{l_{C'_g}}\right) & \text{, if } c(C'_g, t) > 0 \\ p & \text{, if } c(C'_g, t) = 0 \end{cases} \tag{6}$$

where $c(C'_g, t)$ is the number of words t and $l_{C'_g}$ is the total number of all words in language g. If $c(C'_g, t)$ is zero, then $v_{C'_g}(t)$ gets the penalty value p.

The derived corpus containing only the n-grams retained in the language models is called C'^n. The domain $dom(O(C'^n))$ is the set of all character n-grams of length n found in the models of all languages $g \in G$. The values $v_{C'^n_g}(u)$ are calculated similarly for all n-grams $u \in dom(O(C'^n))$ for each language g, as shown in Equation 7

$$v_{C'^n_g}(u) = \begin{cases} -\log_{10}\left(\frac{c(C'^n_g, u)}{l_{C'^n_g}}\right) & \text{, if } c(C'^n_g, u) > 0 \\ p & \text{, if } c(C'^n_g, u) = 0 \end{cases} \tag{7}$$

where $c(C'^n_g, u)$ is the number of n-grams u found in the derived corpus of the language g and $l_{C'^n_g}$ is the total number of the n-grams of length n in the derived corpus of language g. These values are used when scoring the words while identifying the language of a text.

3.3.2 Scoring n-grams in the mystery text

When using n-grams, the word t is split into overlapping n-grams of characters u_i^n, where $i = 1, ..., l_t - n$, of the length n. Each of the n-grams u_i^n is then scored separately for each language g in the same way as the words.

If the n-gram u_i^n is found in $dom(O(C'^n_g))$, the values in the models are used. If the n-gram u_i^n is not found in any of the models, it is simply discarded. We define the function $d_g(t, n)$ for counting n-grams in t found in a model in Equation 8.

$$d_g(t, n) = \sum_{i=1}^{l_t - n} \begin{cases} 1 & \text{, if } u_i^n \in dom(O(C'^n)) \\ 0 & \text{, otherwise} \end{cases} \tag{8}$$

When all the n-grams of the size n in the word t have been processed, the word gets the value of the average of the scored n-grams u_i^n for each language, as in Equation 9

$$v_g(t, n) = \begin{cases} \frac{1}{d_g(t,n)} \sum_{i=1}^{l_t - n} v_{C'^n_g}(u_i^n) & \text{, if } d_g(t, n) > 0 \\ v_g(t, n-1) & \text{, otherwise} \end{cases} \tag{9}$$

where $d_g(t, n)$ is the number of n-grams u_i^n found in the domain $dom(O(C'^n_g))$. If all of the n-grams of the size n were discarded, $d_g(t, n) = 0$, the language identifier backs off to using n-grams of the size $n - 1$. If no values are found even for unigrams, a word gets the penalty value p for every language, as in Equation 10.

$$v_g(t, 0) = p \tag{10}$$

3.3.3 Language identification

The characters in the mystery text are lowercased, after which the text is tokenized into words using the non-alphabetic and non-ideographic characters as delimiters. After this, a score $v_g(t)$ is calculated for each word t in the mystery text for each language g. If the word t is found in the set of words $dom(O(C'_g))$, the corresponding value $v_{C'_g}(t)$ for each language g is assigned as the score $v_g(t)$, as shown in Equation 11.

$$v_g(t) = \begin{cases} v_{C'_g}(t) & \text{, if } t \in dom(O(C'_g)) \\ v_g(t, min(n_{max}, l_t + 2)) & \text{, if } t \notin dom(O(C'_g)) \end{cases} \tag{11}$$

If a word t is not found in the set of words $dom(O(C'_g))$ and the length of the word l_t is at least $n_{max} - 2$, the language identifier backs off to using character n-grams of the length n_{max}. In case the word t is shorter than $n_{max} - 2$ characters, $n = l_t + 2$.

The whole mystery text M gets the score $R_g(M)$ equal to the average of the scores of the words $v_g(t)$ for each language g, as in Equation 12

$$R_g(M) = \frac{\sum_{i=1}^{l_{T(M)}} v_g(t_i)}{l_{T(M)}} \tag{12}$$

where $T(M)$ is the sequence of words and $l_{T(M)}$ is the number of words in the mystery text M. Since we are using negative logarithms of probabilities, the language having the lowest score is returned as the language with the maximum probability for the mystery text.

4   Data

Creation of the earlier DSL corpora has been described by Tan et al. (2014). The training data for the test sets A and B consisted of 18,000 lines of text for each of 12 languages. The corresponding development set had 2,000 lines of text for each language. The training data for the test set C had 7,619 lines for all of the five varieties of the Arabic language and there was no separate development set available. The training and the tests sets for Arabic were produced using automatic speech recognition software (Ali et al., 2016). The amount of training data was different for each variety of Arabic as can be seen in Table 1.

Arabic variety	Number of lines
Modern Standard Arabic	999
Egyptian Arabic	1,578
Gulf Arabic	1,672
Levantine Arabic	1,758
North-African Arabic	1,612

Table 1: The number of lines of training material available for the Arabic varieties.

Test set A consisted of excerpts of journalistic texts similar to the training data provided for the task and the test sets B1 and B2 consisted of Bosnian, Croatian, Serbian, Brazilian Portuguese and European Portuguese tweets. Both the test sets B1 and B2 were formed out of tweets so that several tweets from the same user had been concatenated on one line, separated by a tab-character. The exact nature and format of the B1 and B2 test sets was revealed only a few days before the results were due to be returned. Before that the test set B had been characterized as an out-of-domain social media data. The test sets included a lot of material almost unique to the format of tweets. Without any prior experience on automatically handling tweets, it was very difficult to process them.

For the open tracks of test sets A, B1, and B2 we created a new corpus for each language. We collected from the Common Crawl [3] corpus all the web pages from the respective domains as in Table 2. When language models were created directly from the pages, the accuracy on the DSL development corpus was 49.86%, which was much lower than the 85.09% attained with the DSL training corpus. We used several ad-hoc techniques to improve the quality of the corpus.

The shortest sensible sentence in the development corpus was 25 characters, so we first removed all the lines shorter than that from our open track corpus. The accuracy rose to 51.08%. Then we removed all lines that did not include one of the top 5 characters (in the DSL training data) for the language in question. Furthermore, we only kept the lines which included at least one of the top-5 words with at least 2 characters of the respective language. With these adjustments, the accuracy rose to 62.42%. Moreover, we created lists of characters starting and ending lines in the DSL training corpus.

---

[3] http://commoncrawl.org/

Domain ending	Country	Language	Size, raw (tokens)	Size, final (tokens)
.ba	Bosnia and Herzegovina	Bosnian	41,400,000	5,500,000
.hr	Croatia	Croatian	282,700,000	9,700,000
.rs	Serbia	Serbian	148,300,000	12,600,000
.my	Malaysia	Malay	239,700,000	8,100,000
.id	Indonesia	Indonesian	549,700,000	35,100,000
.br	Brazil	Portuguese	3,689,300,000	264,500,000
.pt	Portugal	Portuguese	307,000,000	13,400,000
.ar	Argentina	Spanish	909,900,000	27,500,000
.mx	Mexico	Spanish	1,092,400,000	51,000,000
.es	Spain	Spanish	2,865,900,000	46,200,000
.fr	France	French	4,878,600,000	240,800,000
.ca	Canada	French	7,414,500,000	13,600,000

Table 2: The languages and varieties of the sub-task 1 and the collected domains for the corpus used in the open tracks.

We chose almost all of the characters from both categories and kept only the lines starting and ending with those characters. We then sorted all the lines alphabetically and removed duplicates. Furthermore, we made a character set out of the whole DSL training corpus (all languages in one) and removed all lines that had characters which were not in the character set. After these changes we managed to get an accuracy of 68.34%. Moreover, we used the language identifier service that we had set up for the SUKI project web crawler, with almost 400 languages and dialects, and identified the language of each line. If Canadian or French lines were in French, they were accepted and so on also for the other languages and dialects. The accuracy rose to 69.19%. Subsequently, we instead used the language models created from the DSL training data and kept only the lines which were identified as the proper language or dialect. The accuracy rose to 74.66%. These accuracies were attained using language models with cut-off of 10,000 tokens. We did some optimizing and ended up with a cut-off of 75,000 tokens which gave us an accuracy of 80.93%. Additionally, we created a very simple sentence detection program and divided the corpora into sentences, keeping only complete sentences from each line with each sentence on its own line. Furthermore, we again removed all lines shorter than 25 characters after which we identified the lines using the project language identifier keeping only the lines identified with correct languages. Moreover, we identified the lines again using the DSL models and kept the lines identified with the corresponding dialect or language. The accuracy was now 83.15%. Subsequently, we again sorted the lines alphabetically and removed duplicates and after some optimizing of the parameters (using 100,000 tokens in the language models) the accuracy was 84.90%. The sizes of each language in the final corpus we created can be seen in the "Size, final (Gb)" column of the Table 2. In hindsight, there would be more straightforward ways to end up with the same corpus. By doing some of the before mentioned steps in another order, some other steps could be omitted completely, but we did not have time to redo the corpora creation process within the time constraints of the shared task.

Then we added the DSL training data to the corpora we created and the results on the development improved. We also tried to add the relevant parts of the 2nd edition of the shared task corpus, but including them did not improve the results on the development set. Instead, we finally added also the development material to the corpus to create the final language models for the open tracks of the test sets A, B1 and B2.

5   Results

In order to find the best possible parameters (n_{max}, c, and p), and language models for words (lowercased or not), we applied a simple form of the greedy algorithm separately for each development set. The use of capital letter words is not detailed in the description of the method. However, the language identifier begins with a language model for words which includes capital letters and if it is not applicable it backs off to using lowercased models for words and so on. The parameters for each run are included in Tables 3-8. We have also included the best results and the name of the winning team in each category.

5.1 Sub-task1

5.1.1 Test set A

For the test set A we only did one run for each of the closed and the open tracks. The results can be seen in the Table 3. On the closed track we used all of the training and the development data to create the language models.

Run	Accuracy	F1 (macro)	n_{max}	c	p	Cap. words	Low. words
SUKI closed	0.8879	0.8877	6	120,000	6.6	no	yes
tubasfs closed	0.8938	0.8938					
SUKI open	0.8837	0.8835	7	180,000	8.2	yes	yes
nrc open	0.8903	0.8889					

Table 3: Results for test set A (closed training).

5.1.2 Test set B1

For the test set B1 we did three runs on both the closed and the open tracks.

Closed training After the first two runs with the basic HeLI method, for the third run we used the unknown language detection thresholds we came up with in the 2015 edition of the shared task (Jauhiainen et al., 2015b). We first identified each tweet separately and removed all tweets that were supposedly in an unknown language. Then we identified the tweets that were left as one line. The results can be seen in Table 4.

Run	Accuracy	F1 (macro)	n_{max}	c	p	Cap. words	Low. words
SUKI run1	0.68	0.662	6	110,000	6.5	no	yes
SUKI run2	0.676	0.6558	0	110,000	6.5	no	yes
SUKI run3	0.688	0.6719	8	2,000,000	6.6	yes	yes
GWU_LT3	0.92	0.9194					

Table 4: Results for test set B1 (closed training).

Open training For the first run we did not do any preprocessing. Before the second run, we used the language identifier set up for our web crawler to remove those individual tweets that it detected to be of non-relevant language. For the third run we also removed all the http- and https-addresses from the tweets to be tested. The results can be seen in the Table 5.

Run	Accuracy	F1 (macro)	n_{max}	c	p	Cap. words	Low. words
SUKI run1	0.714	0.6999	6	180,000	8.1	yes	yes
SUKI run2	0.806	0.7963	8	2,000,000	6.6	yes	yes
SUKI run3	0.822	0.815	8	2,000,000	6.6	yes	yes
nrc	0.948	0.948					

Table 5: Results for test set B1 (open training).

5.1.3 Test set B2

For the test set B2 we did two runs on both the closed and the open tracks. On the second run of both tracks, our language identifier occasionally returned an unknown language as a result of our preprocessing that had emptied some of the lines completely. In order to comply with the way our results were handled by the shared task organizers, we used the 'pt-PT' which was the language identified for the majority of the lines with the unknown language in the first runs. The correct way to handle this problem would have been to put the exact answers from the first runs as the unknown language, but there was no time for this. The effects on the results should anyway be only fractions of a percent.

Closed training For the first run we did not do any preprocessing, but for the second run we used the unknown language detection in the same way as in the B1 closed track run 3. From the results in Table 6, it can be seen that this actually lowered the identification accuracy.

Run	Accuracy	F1 (macro)	n_{max}	c	p	Cap. words	Low. words
SUKI run1	0.642	0.6229	6	110,000	6.5	no	yes
SUKI run2	0.614	0.5991	6	110,000	6.5	no	yes
GWU_LT3	0.878	0.8773					

Table 6: Results for test set B2 (closed training).

Open training The results for the B2 open track can be seen in Table 7. For the first run we did not do any preprocessing. For the second run we used the language identifier set up for our web crawler to remove those individual tweets that it detected to be of non-relevant language. We also removed all the http- and https-addresses from the tweets to be tested.

Run	Accuracy	F1 (macro)	n_{max}	c	p	Cap. words	Low. words
SUKI run1	0.75	0.7476	6	180,000	8.1	yes	yes
SUKI run2	0.796	0.7905	8	2,000,000	6.6	yes	yes
nrc	0.9	0.9					

Table 7: Results for test set B2 (open training).

5.2 Sub-task2

For the sub-task 2 we made only one run on the closed track. The character n-grams in the language models created for the test set C also included capital letters due to the nature of the corpus, unlike in the regular HeLI method where the character n-grams are created from lowercased words. The results can be seen in Table 8.

Run	Accuracy	F1 (macro)	n_{max}	c	p	Cap. words	Low. words
SUKI run1	0.4883	0.4797	8	5,000	4.6	yes	no
MAZA	0.5117	0.5132					

Table 8: Results for test set C (closed training).

The best accuracy on the closed track was 51.17% and that of the open track 52.18%. Our system came 7th on the closed track with 48.83% accuracy.

6 Discussion

Seventeen teams provided results for the closed track of test set A, which is quite a large increase over the 9 teams of the previous year. We were surprised to achieve the second place in this track, considering that we did not really try to improve the system from the last year's shared task, where we were in the 4th place. Instead, we made it simpler than last year, leaving out the extra discriminating features as well as the first stage of language group identification. As of this writing, we do not have much information on the nature of the language identification methods the other teams used, so we can only compare our method with the methods used in the previous task. The winner of the 2015 shared task used Support Vector Machines (SVMs), which heavily rely on finding the discriminating features (Malmasi and Dras, 2015). SVMs were also used by the NRC (Goutte and Leger, 2015) and MMS (Zampieri et al., 2015a) teams, which shared the second place last year. The language identification method we propose is generative in nature. It does not rely on finding discriminating features between languages. The language models for each language can be built without any knowledge of the other languages to be included in the repertoire of the language identifiers. This makes adding more languages to the language identifier very easy, there is no need to change the already existing models or to compare the new language with the already existing ones. It is possible that the generative nature gives our method more robustness in the case that the development and test data are not from exactly the same source. We suspect that the reason that we did not fare so well with the test sets B1 and B2 is mostly our inability to handle the format of the tweets well enough. It would have been interesting to see how our method would have succeeded in an out-of-domain test without the preprocessing challenges.

References

Mohamed Al-Badrashiny, Heba Elfardy, and Mona Diab. 2015. Aida2: A hybrid approach for token and sentence level dialect identification in arabic. In *Proceedings of the 19th Conference on Computational Language Learning*, pages 42–51, Beijing, China.

Ahmed Ali, Najim Dehak, Patrick Cardinal, Sameer Khurana, Sree Harsha Yella, James Glass, Peter Bell, and Steve Renals. 2016. Automatic dialect detection in arabic broadcast speech. In *Interspeech 2016*, pages 2934–2938.

Kareem Darwish, Hassan Sajjad, and Hamdy Mubarak. 2014. Verifiably effective arabic dialect identification. In *Proceedings of the 2014 Conference on Empirical Methods in Natural Language Processing (EMNLP)*, pages 1465–1468, Doha, Qatar.

Heba Elfardy and Mona Diab. 2013. Sentence level dialect identification in arabic. In *Proceedings of the 51st Annual Meeting of the Association for Computational Linguistics*, pages 456–461, Sofia.

Heba Elfardy, Mohamed Al-Badrashiny, and Mona Diab. 2014. Aida: Identifying code switching in informal arabic text. In *Proceedings of The First Workshop on Computational Approaches to Code Switching*, pages 94–101, Doha, Qatar.

Archana Garg, Vishal Gupta, and Manish Jindal. 2014. A survey of language identification techniques and applications. *Journal of Emerging Technologies in Web Intelligence*, 6(4):388–400.

Cyril Goutte and Serge Leger. 2015. Experiments in discriminating similar languages. In *Proceedings of the Joint Workshop on Language Technology for Closely Related Languages, Varieties and Dialects (LT4VarDial)*, pages 78–84, Hissar, Bulgaria.

Cyril Goutte, Serge Léger, Shervin Malmasi, and Marcos Zampieri. 2016. Discriminating Similar Languages: Evaluations and Explorations. In *Proceedings of the 10th International Conference on Language Resources and Evaluation (LREC 2016)*.

Heidi Jauhiainen, Tommi Jauhiainen, and Krister Lindén. 2015a. The finno-ugric languages and the internet project. *Septentrio Conference Series*, 0(2):87–98.

Tommi Jauhiainen, Heidi Jauhiainen, and Krister Lindén. 2015b. Discriminating similar languages with token-based backoff. In *Proceedings of the Joint Workshop on Language Technology for Closely Related Languages, Varieties and Dialects (LT4VarDial)*, pages 44–51, Hissar, Bulgaria.

Tommi Jauhiainen, Krister Lindén, and Heidi Jauhiainen. 2015c. Language Set Identification in Noisy Synthetic Multilingual Documents. In *Proceedings of the Computational Linguistics and Intelligent Text Processing 16th International Conference, CICLing 2015*, pages 633–643, Cairo, Egypt.

Tommi Jauhiainen. 2010. Tekstin kielen automaattinen tunnistaminen. Master's thesis, University of Helsinki, Helsinki, Finland.

Nikola Ljubešic and Denis Kranjcic. 2014. Discriminating between very similar languages among twitter users. In *Proceedings of the Ninth Language Technologies Conference*, pages 90–94, Ljubljana, Slovenia.

Nikola Ljubešic and Denis Kranjcic. 2015. Discriminating between closely related languages on twitter. *Informatica*, 39.

Nikola Ljubešic, Nives Mikelic, and Damir Boras. 2007. Language indentification: How to distinguish similar languages? In *Information Technology Interfaces, 2007. ITI 2007. 29th International Conference on*, pages 541–546, Cavtat/Dubrovnik, Croatia.

Marco Lui. 2014. *Generalized language identification*. Ph.D. thesis, The University of Melbourne.

Wolfgang Maier and Carlos Gómez-Rodríguez. 2014. Language variety identification in spanish tweets. In *Proceedings of the EMNLP'2014 Workshop: Language Technology for Closely Related Languages and Language Variants (LT4CloseLang 2014)*, pages 25–35, Doha, Qatar.

Shervin Malmasi and Mark Dras. 2015. Language identification using classifier ensembles. In *Proceedings of the Joint Workshop on Language Technology for Closely Related Languages, Varieties and Dialects (LT4VarDial)*, pages 35–43, Hissar, Bulgaria.

Shervin Malmasi, Eshrag Refaee, and Mark Dras. 2015. Arabic Dialect Identification using a Parallel Multidialectal Corpus. In *Proceedings of the 14th Conference of the Pacific Association for Computational Linguistics (PACLING 2015)*, pages 209–217, Bali, Indonesia, May.

Shervin Malmasi, Marcos Zampieri, Nikola Ljubešić, Preslav Nakov, Ahmed Ali, and Jörg Tiedemann. 2016. Discriminating between similar languages and arabic dialect identification: A report on the third dsl shared task. In *Proceedings of the 3rd Workshop on Language Technology for Closely Related Languages, Varieties and Dialects (VarDial)*, Osaka, Japan.

Seppo Mustonen. 1965. Multiple discriminant analysis in linguistic problems. *Statistical Methods in Linguistics*, 4:37–44.

Bali Ranaivo-Malançon. 2006. Automatic identification of close languages–case study: Malay and indonesian. *ECTI Transaction on Computer and Information Technology*, 2(2):126–133.

Fatiha Sadat, Farnazeh Kazemi, and Atefeh Farzindar. 2014. Automatic identification of arabic language varieties and dialects in social media. In *Proceedings of the Second Workshop on Natural Language Processing for Social Media (SocialNLP)*, pages 22–27, Dublin, Ireland.

Wael Salloum, Heba Elfardy, Linda Alamir-Salloum, Nizar Habash, and Mona Diab. 2014. Sentence level dialect identification for machine translation system selection. In *Proceedings of the 52nd Annual Meeting of the Association for Computational Linguistics (Short Papers)*, pages 772–778, Baltimore, USA.

H. L. Shashirekha. 2014. Automatic language identification from written texts - an overview. *International Journal of Innovative Research in Computer and Communication Engineering*, 2(5):156–160.

Liling Tan, Marcos Zampieri, Nikola Ljubešic, and Jörg Tiedemann. 2014. Merging comparable data sources for the discrimination of similar languages: The dsl corpus collection. In *Proceedings of the 7th Workshop on Building and Using Comparable Corpora*, Reykjavik.

Jörg Tiedemann and Nikola Ljubešic. 2012. Efficient discrimination between closely related languages. In *Proceedings of COLING 2012*, pages 2619–2634, Mumbai.

Christoph Tillmann, Yaser Al-Onaizan, and Saab Mansour. 2014. Improved sentence-level arabic dialect classification. In *Proceedings of the First Workshop on Applying NLP Tools to Similar Languages, Varieties and Dialects*, pages 110–119, Dublin, Ireland.

Omar F. Zaidan and Chris Callison-Burch. 2014. Arabic dialect identification. *Computational Linguistics*, 40(1):171–202.

Marcos Zampieri and Binyam Gebrekidan Gebre. 2012. Automatic identification of language varieties: The case of portuguese. In *11th Conference on Natural Language Processing (KONVENS) - Empirical Methods in Natural Language Processing - Proceedings of the Conference on Natural Language Processing 2012*, pages 233–237, Vienna.

Marcos Zampieri, Binyam Gebrekidan Gebre, and Sascha Diwersy. 2012. Classifying pluricentric languages: Extending the monolingual model. In *Proceedings of the Fourth Swedish Language Technlogy Conference (SLTC2012)*, pages 79–80, Lund.

Marcos Zampieri, Binyam Gebrekidan Gebre, and Sascha Diwersy. 2013. N-gram language models and pos distribution for the identification of spanish varieties. In *Actes de TALN'2013 : 20e conférence sur le Traitement Automatique des Langues Naturelles*, pages 580–587, Sables d'Olonne.

Marcos Zampieri, Liling Tan, Nikola Ljubešić, and Jörg Tiedemann. 2014. A report on the dsl shared task 2014. In *Proceedings of the First Workshop on Applying NLP Tools to Similar Languages, Varieties and Dialects (VarDial)*, pages 58–67, Dublin, Ireland.

Marcos Zampieri, Binyam Gebrekidan Gebre, Hernani Costa, and Josef van Genabith. 2015a. Comparing approaches to the identification of similar languages. In *Proceedings of the Joint Workshop on Language Technology for Closely Related Languages, Varieties and Dialects (LT4VarDial)*, pages 66–72, Hissar, Bulgaria.

Marcos Zampieri, Liling Tan, Nikola Ljubešić, Jörg Tiedemann, and Preslav Nakov. 2015b. Overview of the dsl shared task 2015. In *Proceedings of the Joint Workshop on Language Technology for Closely Related Languages, Varieties and Dialects (LT4VarDial)*, pages 1–9, Hissar, Bulgaria.

Marcos Zampieri. 2013. Using bag-of-words to distinguish similar languages: How efficient are they? In *Computational Intelligence and Informatics (CINTI), 2013 IEEE 14th International Symposium on*, pages 37–41, Budapest.

ASIREM Participation at the Discriminating Similar Languages Shared Task 2016

Wafia Adouane[1], Nasredine Semmar[2], Richard Johansson[3]
Department of FLoV, University of Gothenburg, Sweden[1]
CEA Saclay – Nano-INNOV, Institut CARNOT CEA LIST, France[2]
Department of CSE, University of Gothenburg, Sweden[3]
`wafia.gu@gmail.com, nasredine.semmar@cea.fr`
`richard.johansson@gu.se`

Abstract

This paper presents the system built by ASIREM team for the Discriminating between Similar Languages (DSL) Shared task 2016. It describes the system which uses character-based and word-based n-grams separately. ASIREM participated in both sub-tasks (sub-task 1 and sub-task 2) and in both open and closed tracks. For the sub-task 1 which deals with Discriminating between similar languages and national language varieties, the system achieved an accuracy of 87.79% on the closed track, ending up ninth (the best results being 89.38%). In sub-task 2, which deals with Arabic dialect identification, the system achieved its best performance using character-based n-grams (49.67% accuracy), ranking fourth in the closed track (the best result being 51.16%), and an accuracy of 53.18%, ranking first in the open track.

1 Introduction

Automatic Language Identification (ALI) is the task of identifying the natural language of a given text or speech by a machine. It is a necessary task to build any language-dependent system. ALI is a well-established Natural Language Processing (NLP) task for many languages which are well represented on the Web. Nowadays, the challenge, however, is the identification of languages which are not well-represented on the Web, also called under-resourced languages, as well as the discrimination between similar languages (DSL) and language varieties (DLV).

The DSL Shared task 2016 consists of two sub-tasks; sub-task 1 and sub-task 2. Sub-task 1 (discriminating between similar languages and national language varieties) deals with twelve languages and language varieties grouped by similarity into 5 groups (Bosnian (bs), Croatian (hr), and Serbian (sr); Malay (my) and Indonesian (id); Portuguese: Brazil (pt-br) and Portugal (pt-pt); Spanish: Argentina (es-ar), Mexico (es-mx), and Spain (es-es); French: France (fr-fr) and Canada (fr-ca)). Sub-task 2 deals with Arabic dialect identification (Malmasi et al., 2016) including five Arabic varieties, namely Egyptian (EGY), Gulf (GLF), Levantine (LAV), North-African (NOR), and Modern Standard Arabic (MSA). We participated in both sub-tasks and we submitted four runs for both closed and open tracks (two for each). We trained a linear Support Vector Machines (SVM) classifier using both character-based and word-based n-grams as features.

The paper is organized as follows: in Section 2, we briefly describe some related work done for DSL and DLV tasks for both Arabic and other languages. In Section 3, we describe our system and the different runs we submitted. Then we present our results for each run in Section 4. We conclude by discussing the results and providing some suggestions to improve the current system.

2 Related Work

Discriminating between Similar Languages (DSL) and Discriminating between Language Varieties (DLV) are one of the serious bottlenecks, among others, of current automatic language identification tools. They are an even bigger challenge for under-resourced languages. DLV is a special case of DSL

Proceedings of the Third Workshop on NLP for Similar Languages, Varieties and Dialects,
pages 163–169, Osaka, Japan, December 12 2016.

where the languages to distinguish are very close. These tasks have recently attracted the intention of the research community, resulting in recurring competitions such as the DSL Shared Task (Goutte et al., 2016). DSL can be simply defined as a specification or a sub-task of Automatic Language Identification (ALI) (Tiedemann and Ljubešić, 2012). Many of the standard methods used for the ALI have been applied to the DSL and DLV tasks for some languages. Goutte et al. (2016) give a comprehensive bibliography of the recently published papers dealing with these tasks. Discriminating between Arabic varieties is also an active research area although limited work has been done, so far, to distinguish between written Arabic varieties. The main reason is the lack of annotated data (Benajiba and Diab, 2010). Zaidan (2012) in his PhD distinguished between four Arabic varieties (Modern Standard Arabic (MSA), Egyptian, Gulf and Levantine dialects) using character and word n-gram models. Elfardy and Diab (2013) identified MSA from Egyptian at a sentence level, Tillmann et al. (2014) proposed an approach to improve classifying Egyptian and MSA at a sentence level, and Saâdane (2015) in her PhD distinguished between Maghrebi Arabic (Algerian, Moroccan and Tunisian dialects) using morpho-syntactic information. Furthermore, Malmasi et al. (2015) used a parallel corpus to distinguish between six Arabic varieties, namely MSA, Egyptian, Tunisian, Syrian, Jordanian and Palestinian.

Distinguishing between spoken Arabic varieties is also an active research area as there are sufficient phone and TV program recordings which are easy to transcribed. "The problem is somewhat mitigated in the speech domain, since dialectal data exists in the form of phone conversations and television program recordings, but, in general, dialectal Arabic data sets are hard to come by" (Zaidan and Callison-Burch, 2014). Akbacak et al. (2009), Akbacak et al. (2011), Lei and Hansen (2011), Boril et al. (2012), and Zhang et al. (2013) are some examples of work done to distinguish between spoken Arabic varieties. Similarly to Goutte and Léger (2015), we experimented with both character-based and word-based n-grams as features. However, we used only one prediction step instead of two for both sub-tasks. Compared to the system proposed by Malmasi and Dras (2015), we used the same set of features with only one SVM classifier instead of an ensemble of SVM classifiers.

3   Methodology and Data

We used a supervised machine learning approach where we trained a linear SVM classifier (LinearSVC) as implemented in the Scikit-learn package[1]. In sub-task 1, we submitted two runs (run1 and run2). We experimented with different character-based and word-based n-grams and different combinations as features, and we reported only the best scoring features for each run. In run1: we used character-based 4-grams as features using TF-IDF weighting scheme. In run2: we used word-based unigrams. In both runs, we trained only on the released training dataset (Tan et al., 2014), and we used the development set for evaluating the system and selecting the best performing features. Word-based unigrams scored better than word based bigrams and trigrams and character-based 4-grams outperformed the rest of n-grams.

In sub-task 2 (Arabic dialects identification), we also submitted two runs for the closed track (run1 and run2) and two others for the open track (run3 and run4). In run1 and run3, we used a combination of character-based 5-grams and 6-grams as features using TF-IDF. In run2 and run4, we used word-based unigrams also weighted by TF-IDF. In all cases, we did not introduce any data pre-processing or Named Entity (NE) filtering. For sub-task 2, the released training data (Ali et al., 2016) consisted of ASR transcriptions of conversational speech in five Arabic varieties which are Egyptian (EGY), Gulf (GLF), Levantine (LAV), North-African (NOR), and Modern Standard Arabic (MSA). We noticed that the released training data contained many inconsistencies such as incomplete sentences, the use of different labels for the same sentence (chunk of text) and many speech segmentation errors. We did not have enough time to properly deal with these issues. All we did was clean the data by removing duplicate sentences having different labels. For training and evaluation, we trained our system on 80% of the released training dataset and we used the remaining data (20%) as a development set because the released data for this sub-task did not include a development set. Likewise, we evaluated the system and selected the best performing features, namely Word-based unigrams and the combination of character-based 5-grams and 6-grams.

---

[1] For more information see: http://scikit-learn.org/stable/.

In run3 and run4 (open track) we trained on a new dataset containing 18,000 documents (609,316 words in total) collected, manually by native speakers, from social media (real world data). The documents were originally written by users in Arabic script and we transliterated them using the Buckwalter Arabic transliteration scheme. This dataset contains 2,000 documents for each of the eight most popular high level[2] Arabic varieties (Algerian (ALG), Egyptian (EGY), Gulf (GLF), Levantine (LAV), Mesopotamian (KUI), Moroccan (MOR), Tunisian (TUN) dialects and MSA) plus Arabicized Berber[3]. The dataset was built as part of a Master's thesis project in Language Technology (Adouane, 2016), and is freely available for research from the first author.

4   Results

In sub-task 1, in both run1 and run2, we tested our system on test set A (closed track). Results are shown in Table 1.

Run	Baseline	Features	Accuracy	F1 (micro)	F1 (macro)	F1 (weighted)
run1	0.083	char 4-grams	**0.8779**	**0.8779**	**0.8778**	**0.8778**
run2	0.083	word unigrams	0.8717	0.8717	0.8714	0.8714

Table 1: Results for test set A (closed training).

The results show that Character-based 4-grams model (run1) scores slightly better than the word-based unigram model (run2), giving 0.8779 and 0.8717 accuracy respectively. Both models outperform the random baseline. Figure 1 shows the confusion matrix of the system as described in run1.

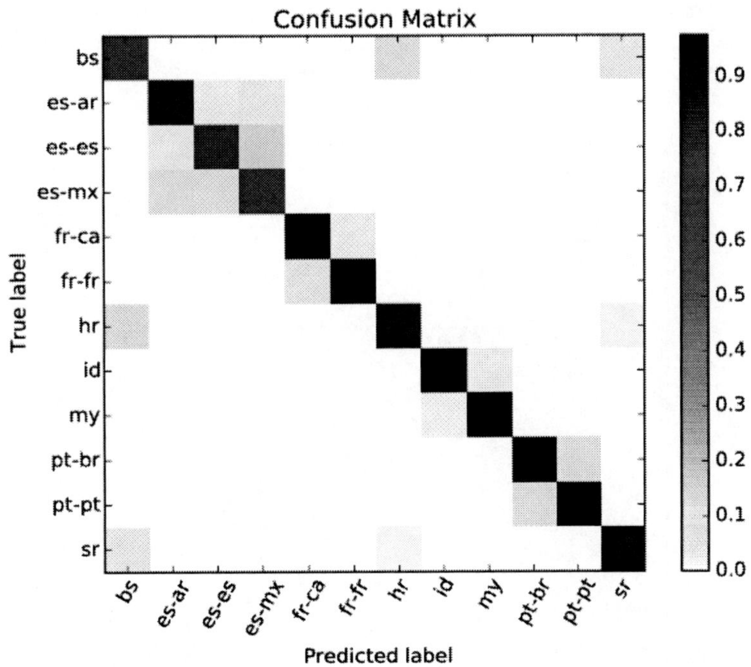

Figure 1: The confusion matrix of the system as in run1 (Table 1).

[2]We grouped local and regional varieties in one high level group.

[3]Berber or Tamazight is an Afro-Asiatic language widely spoken in North Africa and completely different from Arabic. It has 13 varieties and each has formal and informal forms. It has its unique script called Tifinagh but for convenience Latin and Arabic scripts are also used. Using Arabic script to transliterate Berber has existed since the beginning of the Islamic Era, see (Souag, 2004) for details.

The system is confused mostly between Spanish of Mexico and between Spanish of Argentina and Spanish of Spain. There is also confusion between Bosnian, Croatian and Serbian. Portuguese of Brazil is also confused with Portuguese of Portugal. Likewise, French of France is confused with French of Canada. Some confusions are also found between Indonesian and Malay. More or less, there is a confusion between all languages of the same group. The confusion is expected because those languages or language varieties are very similar.

As mentioned above, we participated in both closed and open track in sub-task 2 where we tested our system on the test set C and submitted two runs for each track. Table 2 and Table 3 show the evaluation results for the closed and open track respectively.

Run	Baseline	Features	Accuracy	F1 (micro)	F1 (macro)	F1 (weighted)
run1	0.2279	char 5+6-grams	**0.4968**	**0.4968**	**0.4914**	**0.4946**
run2	0.2279	word unigrams	0.4721	0.4721	0.4667	0.4711

Table 2: Results for test set C (closed training).

Run	Baseline	Features	Accuracy	F1 (micro)	F1 (macro)	F1 (weighted)
run3	0.2279	char 5+6-grams	**0.5318**	**0.5318**	**0.5255**	**0.5274**
run4	0.2279	word unigrams	0.4948	0.4948	0.4882	0.4912

Table 3: Results for test set C (open training).

The reported baseline in both tables is the majority class baseline because the samples in test set C were slightly unbalanced. It is clear that the combination of the character-based 5 and 6 grams scores better than the word-based unigram model in both closed and open tracks. The classification results outperformed the set baseline. The use of extra training dataset has improved the performance of the classifier compared to the use of the only provided training dataset.

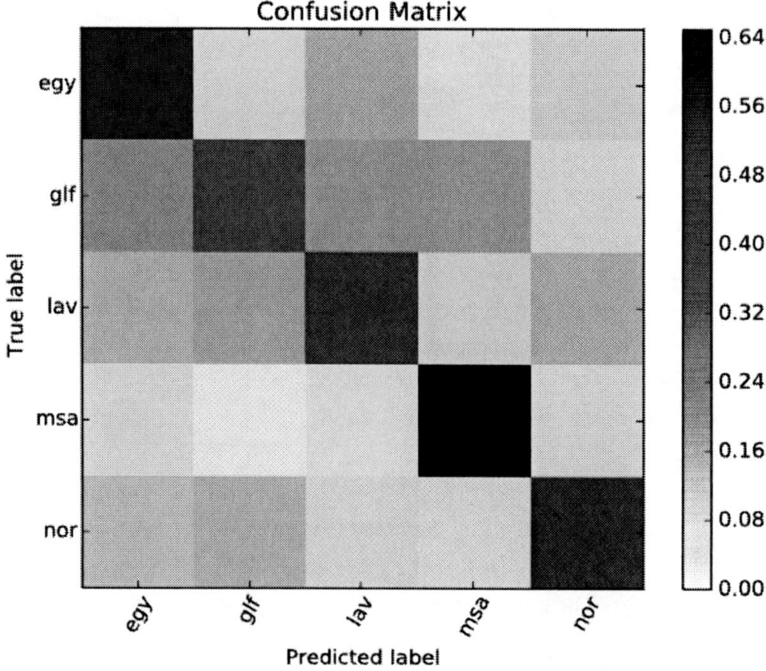

Figure 2: The confusion matrix of the system as in run1 (Table 2).

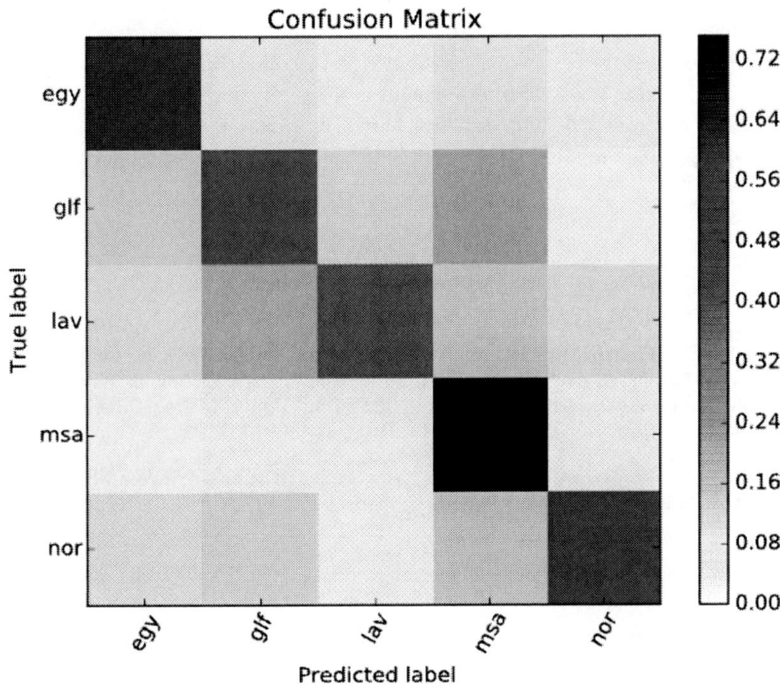

Figure 3: The confusion matrix of the system as in run3 (Table 3).

As shown in Figure 2 and Figure 3, the system misclassified all Arabic varieties with each other with different confusion degrees. Gulf Arabic is the most variety for which most mistakes are made, while MSA is the one that is most accurately recognized. Comparing between Figure 2 and Figure 3 shows that using extra training data has reduced the classification confusion in most cases, except for Levantine Arabic which is more confused with Gulf Arabic. This causes the number of correctly classified Levantine instances to decrease. It is also noticeable that there are more instances of all Arabic dialects confused with MSA. The results are expected as all these Arabic varieties use the same script with considerable vocabulary overlap and lots of false friends. Moreover, in the closed training, the used training dataset is very small.

5   Discussion

We have described our four submissions to the DSL Shared Task 2016 and presented the obtained results. We participated with the same system with no data preprocessing in both sub-task 1 and sub-task 2. Distinguishing between Arabic varieties (sub-task 2) is obviously more challenging than distinguishing between the languages included in sub-task 1. The main reason is of course related to the difference in linguistic properties between Arabic (all varieties included) and other languages. But most importantly, it is related to the quality of the data used in both training and evaluation. As mentioned above, the provided training data has many issues. Training the system on a larger manually collected dataset from social media domain (originally written texts in Arabic script) did not have a great effect on the performance of the system, especially that the test data (set C) consists of ASR transcripts which have many speech segmentation issues. It is worth mentioning also that we manually transliterated the new training dataset from Arabic script into Latin script (general replacement by mapping between letters using TextEdit) without any checking. There are some freely available scripts to do the transliteration automatically, but we preferred not to use them because of many encoding problems. The use of TF-IDF helped to get rid of most frequent (non-informative) words but only those seen in the training data which was very small in our case. Still we believe that the proposed system is very simple. There are many possible improvements which can be done, for instance combining character and word-based n-grams, the use of dialectal lexicons as extra resources, the filtering of Named Entities (NE) because they are dialect or region specific. Another possible improvement is the removal of all MSA stop-words because MSA vocabulary is used in all other Arabic varieties. However, before that, we need to improve the quality of the training/evaluation data to allow the system to learn better language models.

References

Wafia Adouane. 2016. Automatic detection of under-resourced languages: The case of Arabic short texts. Master's thesis, University of Gothenburg.

Murat Akbacak, Horacio Franco, Michael Frandsen, Saša Hasan, Huda Jameel, Andreas Kathol, Shahram Khadivi, Xin Lei, Arindam Mandal, Saab Mansour, Kristin Precoda, Colleen Richey, Dimitra Vergyri, Wen Wang, Mei Yang, and Jing Zheng. 2009. Recent advances in SRI's IraqComm TM Iraqi Arabic-English speech-to-speech translation system. In *Proceedings of IEEE ICASSP*, pages 4809–4813, Taipei.

Murat Akbacak, Dimitra Vergyri, Andreas Stolcke, Nicolas Scheffer, and Arindam Mandal. 2011. Effective Arabic dialect classification using diverse phonotactic models. In *INTERSPEECH'11*, pages 4809–4813, Florence, Italy.

Ahmed Ali, Najim Dehak, Patrick Cardinal, Sameer Khurana, Sree Harsha Yella, James Glass, Peter Bell, and Steve Renals. 2016. Automatic dialect detection in arabic broadcast speech. In *Interspeech 2016*, pages 2934–2938.

Yassine Benajiba and Mona Diab. 2010. A web application for dialectal Arabic text annotation. In *Proceedings of the LREC Workshop for Language Resources (LRs) and Human Language Technologies (HLT) for Semitic Languages: Status, Up-dates, and Prospects*.

Hynek Boril, Abhijeet Sangwan, and John H. L. Hansen. 2012. Arabic dialect identification – Is the secret in the silence? and other observations. In *INTERSPEECH 2012*, Portland, Oregon.

Heba Elfardy and Mona Diab. 2013. Sentence Level Dialect Identification in Arabic. In *Proceedings of the 51st Annual Meeting of the Association for Computational Linguistics (ACL-13)*, Sofia, Bulgaria.

Cyril Goutte and Serge Léger. 2015. Experiments in Discriminating Similar Languages. In *Proceedings of the Joint Workshop on Language Technology for Closely Related Languages, Varieties and Dialects (LT4VarDial)*, pages 78–84, Hissar, Bulgaria.

Cyril Goutte, Serge Léger, Shervin Malmasi, and Marcos Zampieri. 2016. Discriminating similar languages: Evaluations and explorations. In *Proceedings of the Tenth International Conference on Language Resources and Evaluation (LREC)*.

Yun Lei and John H. L. Hansen. 2011. Dialect classification via text-independent training and testing for Arabic, Spanish, and Chinese. In *IEEE Transactions on Audio, Speech, and Language Processing, 19(1)*, pages 85–96.

Shervin Malmasi and Mark Dras. 2015. Language Identification using Classifier Ensembles. In *Proceedings of the Joint Workshop on Language Technology for Closely Related Languages, Varieties and Dialects (LT4VarDial)*, pages 35–43, Hissar, Bulgaria.

Shervin Malmasi, Eshrag Refaee, and Mark Dras. 2015. Arabic Dialect Identification using a Parallel Multidialectal Corpus. In *Proceedings of the 14th Conference of the Pacific Association for Computational Linguistics (PACLING 2015)*, pages 209–217, Bali, Indonesia, May.

Shervin Malmasi, Marcos Zampieri, Nikola Ljubešić, Preslav Nakov, Ahmed Ali, and Jörg Tiedemann. 2016. Discriminating between Similar Languages and Arabic Dialect Identification: A Report on the Third DSL Shared Task. In *Proceedings of the 3rd Workshop on Language Technology for Closely Related Languages, Varieties and Dialects (VarDial)*, Osaka, Japan.

Houda Saâdane. 2015. Le traitement automatique de l'arabe dialectalisé: aspects méthodologiques et algorithmiques. In *PhD thesis*, Université Grenoble Alpes, France.

Lameen Souag. 2004. Writing Berber Languages: a quick summary. In *L. Souag. Archived from http://goo.gl/ooA4uZ, Retrieved on April 8th, 2016.*

Liling Tan, Marcos Zampieri, Nikola Ljubešic, and Jörg Tiedemann. 2014. Merging Comparable Data Sources for the Discrimination of Similar Languages: The DSL Corpus Collection. In *Proceedings of the 7th Workshop on Building and Using Comparable Corpora (BUCC)*, pages 11–15, Reykjavik, Iceland.

Jörg Tiedemann and Nikola Ljubešić. 2012. Efficient Discrimination Between Closely Related Languages. In *Proceedings of COLING*, pages 2619–2634.

Christoph Tillmann, Yaser Al-Onaizan, and Saab Mansour. 2014. Improved Sentence-Level Arabic Dialect Classification. In *Proceedings of the 1st Workshop on Applying NLP Tools to Similar Languages, Varieties and Dialects*, pages 110–119, Dublin, Ireland.

Omar F. Zaidan and Chris Callison-Burch. 2014. Arabic dialect identification. In *Computational Linguistics, 40(1)*, pages 171–202.

Omar F. Zaidan. 2012. *Crowdsourcing Annotation for Machine Learning in Natural Language Processing Tasks*. Ph.D. thesis, Johns Hopkins University.

Qinghai Zhang, Hynek. Boril, and John. H. L. Hansen. 2013. Supervector Pre-Processing for PRSVM-based Chinese and Arabic Dialect Identification. In *IEEE ICASSP'13*, pages 7363–7367, Vancouver, Canada.

Comparing two Basic Methods for Discriminating Between Similar Languages and Varieties*

Pablo Gamallo
Centro Singular de Investigación en
Tecnoloxías da Información (CiTIUS)
Univ. of Santiago de Compostela
Galiza

José Ramom Pichel
Imaxin—Software,
Galiza

Iñaki Alegria, Manex Agirrezabal
IXA Nlp group
Univ. of the Basque Country
UPV/EHU

`pablo.gamallo@usc.es`   `joseramompichel@imaxin.com`   `i.alegria@ehu.eus`

`manex.aguirrezabal@ehu.eus`

Abstract

This article describes the systems submitted by the Citius_Ixa_Imaxin team to the Discriminating Similar Languages Shared Task 2016. The systems are based on two different strategies: classification with ranked dictionaries and Naive Bayes classifiers. The results of the evaluation show that ranking dictionaries are more sound and stable across different domains while basic bayesian models perform reasonably well on in-domain datasets, but their performance drops when they are applied on out-of-domain texts.

1 Introduction

McNamee (2005) argued that language detection is a solved problem since the performance of most systems approaches 100% accuracy. However, this can be true only if we assume that the systems are tested on relatively long and well written texts. In recent experiments, the accuracy of the language detection starts to decrease much faster with respect to relatively longer texts having at least 400 characters (Tromp and Pechenizkiy, 2011). In consequence, language detection is not a solved problem if we consider noisy short texts such as those written in social networks. Apart from the size and the written quality of input texts, it is also necessary to take into account another important factor that can hurt the performance of language detectors, namely language proximity and variety detection. Closely related languages or language varieties are more difficult to identify and separate than languages belonging to different linguistic families.

DSL Shared Task 2016 (Malmasi et al., 2016; Goutte et al., 2016) is aimed to compare language identification systems on the specific task of discriminating between similar languages or varieties. This is the third edition of the shared taks, which is divided into two sub-tasks.

First, the sub-task 1 is focused on discriminating between similar languages and national language varieties, including five different groups of related languages or language varieties:

- Bosnian, Croatian, and Serbian

- Malay and Indonesian

- Portuguese varieties: Brazil and Portugal

- Spanish varieties: Argentina, Mexico, and Spain

- French varieties: France and Canada

The objective of sub-task 2 is the identification of Arabic varieties. As Arabic is mostly written using the modern standard, the sub-task is focused on conversational speech which is divided into many different diatopical varieties. For this purpose, the DSL organizers provided a dataset containing automatic speech recognition transcripts five Arabic varieties: Egyptian, Gulf, Levantine, North-African, and Modern Standard Arabic (Malmasi et al., 2015).

Proceedings of the Third Workshop on NLP for Similar Languages, Varieties and Dialects,
pages 170–177, Osaka, Japan, December 12 2016.

Our team, Citius_Ixa_Imaxin, participated in all DSL sub-tasks with the following objective: to compare two very basic methods for language detection and observe how they behave when they are applied on the difficult task of discriminating between similar languages or varieties. On the one hand, we describe and evaluate a ranking approach based on small dictionaries built according to the Zipf's law, i.e. the frequency of any word is inversely proportional to its rank in the frequency table. On the other hand, we also describe and evaluate a Naive Bayes system relying on word unigrams.

2   Related Work

Two types of models have been used for language detection in general: those made of n-grams of characters (Beesley, 1988; Dunning, 1994) and those based on word unigrams or dictionaries (Grefenstette, 1995; Rehurek and Kolkus, 2009). In the latter approaches, models are dictionaries built with words ranked by their frequency in a reference corpus, and their ranking is used to compute their "relevance" in the input text. In Cavnar and Trenkle (1994), they construct a language model by making use of the ranking of the most frequent character n-grams for each language during the training phase (n-gram profiles). So, even if this is an approach based on character n-grams, it also uses the ranking strategy which is characteristic of the dictionary-based approach.

According to Rehurek (2009), very simple dictionary-based methods are better suited to work on close varieties than other more complex methods for language identification. In order to verify such a hypothesis, in the DSL shared task we will compare a dictionary-based approach with a another standard strategy based on bayesian classification.

Two former editions of DSL shared task took place in the two previous years (Zampieri et al., 2015; Zampieri et al., 2014). One of the best systems in the two previous editions makes classification in two steps: it first makes a prediction about the language group and then it selects a specific language from that language group (Goutte et al., 2014; ?). In 2014 edition, it achieved the best performance in the closed submission task, while in 2015, it was the first system in the open task. At the last edition, the winner system in the closed submission track relies on an ensemble of SVM classifiers using features such as character n-grams from one to six n-grams (Malmasi and Dras, 2015). Notice that the two winner systems rely on complex strategies since the first one requires several steps to perform classification and the second one needs to work with several classifiers. By contrast, we propose very basic classifiers using just word unigrams (tokens) as features. One of our aims is to observe whether baseline strategies are able to be competitive in the DSL tasks.

Another related research direction has been on language identification on Twitter, giving rise to the Tweet-LID shared task (Zubiaga et al., 2014; Zubiaga et al., 2015). This competition aimed at recognizing the language of tweets written in English and in languages spoken on the Iberian peninsula such as Basque, Catalan, Spanish, Galician and Portuguese. Notice that some of these languages, namely Galician and Portuguese, are so close that they could be considered as two varieties of the same language.

3   Methodology and Data

In this section, we describe two basic strategies for language identification: a dictionary-based approach and a bayesian classifier, which also participated at TweetLID 2014 Shared Task (Gamallo et al., 2014).

3.1   Quelingua: A Dictionary-Based Approach

Quelingua[1] has been implemented using a dictionary-based method and a ranking algorithm. It is based on the observation that for each language, there is a set of words that make up a large portion of any text and their presence is to be expected as word distribution follows Zipf's law.

For each word w found in a corpus of a particular language, and for the N most frequent words in that corpus, we define its *inverse ranking* (IR) as follows:

$$IR(w) = N - (rank(w) - 1) \tag{1}$$

---

[1]Freely available at: `https://github.com/gamallo/QueLingua`

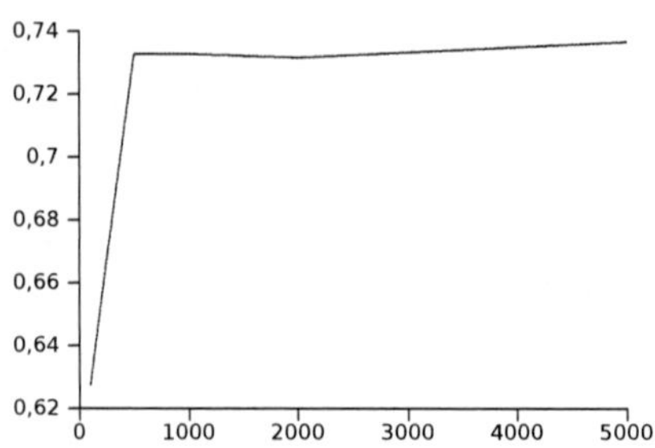

Figure 1: Growth curve of F1-Score (y axis) as a function of the dictionary size (x axis)

where $rank(w)$ is the rank of w in the dictionary of N most frequent words. For instance, if the dictionary contains 1000 words, the IR for the most frequent word (ranking 1) is 1000. Specifying the size N of the dictionary is a critical issue of the method. The final weight of a specific language $lang$ given a text is computed in equation 2, where K is the size of the input text:

$$weight(lang, text) = \sum_{i=1}^{K} IR(word_i) \qquad (2)$$

This is computed for all available languages, and that with the highest weight is selected as the detected language for the input text.

In order to give more coverage to the system, we added a suffix module containing the most frequent suffixes of the target languages. For instance, "-ção" is associated to Portuguese, "-ak" to Basque, "-ción" to Spanish and Galician, etc. This information can be automatically extracted or manually added to the module. The IR of any word that is not in the dictionary but has a suffix found in the suffix module is computed as the average IR, i.e.: $N/2$. However, for the DSL task, the suffix module has not been used because we did not find any relevant suffixes allowing to discriminate between similar varieties. This module is useful for distinguish between different languages within very short texts, but it is not suited to deal with similar varieties.

We performed some preliminary experiments focused on determining the best size of the dictionary (i.e. of the language model). Figure 1 depicts the growth curve of F1-Score as a function of the size of the dictionary for one of the varieties (es-ES). It shows that the peak is achieved with a size of 1000 words. We obtained similar results for all language varieties. So, for all tracks of the DSL shared task, Quelingua was trained with a dictionary of this size.

3.2 A Naive Bayes Classifier

To compare our dictionary-based system with a state-of-the-art approach, we implemented a Naive Bayes (NB) classifier based on the system we previously created for a sentiment analysis task, and described in Gamallo (2013). According to Winkelmolen and Mascardi (2011; Vatanen et al. (2010), language detection based on NB algorithms performs well on short texts. In Vatanen (2010), a NB classifier built with character n-gram models clearly outperformed the ranking method by Cavnar and Trenkle (1994) when the tests were performed on noisy short texts.

Our NB classifier was trained with two different models: a model based on character n-grams and another one based on word unigrams (bag of words). The smoothing technique used by our classifiers for unseen features (n-grams or words) is a version of Good-Turing estimation (Gale, 1995).

We made preliminary experiments on similar languages with both character n-grams and word unigrams. Concerning character-based models, the highest scores were reached using short n-grams. This was also predicted by Winkelmolen and Mascardi (2011; Vatanen et al. (2010), who claimed that NB classifiers for language detection perform better using short n-grams, with $n < 4$. However, in our preliminary experiments the best results were achieved using word unigrams, which outperformed the best character-based models. This is in accordance with Rehurek (2009), who tried to prove that word-based methods are more reliable than character-based models for language discrimination between similar languages/varieties. Therefore, for the tracks of DSL, we will only use word unigrams to train the bayesian classifiers.

4 Experiments

4.1 Training and Test Dataset

For the sub-task 1, the training corpus is a new version of the DSL corpus collection (DSLCC) (Tan et al., 2014). The corpus contains 20,000 instances per country, including excerpt extracted from journalistic texts. In total, the corpus contains 8.6M tokens. For the sub-task 2, the training corpus on Arabic varieties consists on over 7.5K automatic speech recognition transcripts for five varieties (**?**). In total, 331K tokens. These two corpora were used in the closed submission tracks, that is, in those tracks requiring systems to be trained with the corpus collection of the third edition. In order to participate in the open tracks, we also trained our two systems including the corpus released in the second edition of the DSL corpus collection (Zampieri et al., 2015). Given that this collection does not contain any data for Arabic dialects, we have not participated at the open submission track of sub-task 2.

4.2 Preprocessing

Before building the language models, we used a Named Entity Recognition system inspired by that described in Garcia and Gamallo (2015) in order to remove all proper names from the input texts. Even if proper names may help the system find the correct variety in many cases, we reckon that they are useful just because of extra-linguistic or cultural reasons. Proper names can prevent the classifier correctly identifying a specific national variety when the topic of the target text is a person or a location of a country with a different language variety. For this reason, we got rid of named entities before building the language models.

Test Set	Track	Method	Accuracy	F1 (micro)	F1 (macro)	F1 (weighted)
A	-	Random baseline	-	-	-	0.083
A	closed	Quelingua	0.7756	0.7756	0.771	0.771
A	closed	**NB**	0.8525	0.8525	0.8502	**0.8502**
A	open	Quelingua	0.7759	0.7759	0.7707	0.7707
A	open	**NB**	0.871	0.871	0.8694	**0.8694**
B1/B2	-	Random baseline	-	-	-	0.20
B1	closed	**Quelingua**	0.708	0.708	0.4454	**0.7127**
B1	closed	NB	0.082	0.082	0.049	0.1175
B1	open	Quelingua	0.664	0.664	0.3962	0.6339
B1	open	NB	0.094	0.094	0.054	0.1296
B2	closed	**Quelingua**	0.686	0.686	0.4988	**0.6983**
B2	closed	NB	0.282	0.282	0.1244	0.2987
B2	open	Quelingua	0.692	0.692	0.4345	0.6952
B2	open	NB	0.288	0.288	0.1318	0.3164
C	-	Majority class baseline	-	-	-	0.2279
C	closed	**Quelingua**	0.387	0.387	0.3795	**0.3817**
C	closed	NB	0.3032	0.3032	0.2667	0.2664

Table 1: Results for all runs of Quelingua and NB classifiers.

4.3 Results

Table 1 shows the results obtained by our two classifiers, *Quelingua* (dictionary-based) and *NB* (naive bayes). Four test sets were used for evaluation. Tests A, B1 and B2 belong to the sub-task 1 (5 language groups of similar varieties) while test C is used for sub-task 2 (Arabic varieties). In sub-task 1, test A

Run	Accuracy	F1 (micro)	F1 (macro)	F1 (weighted)
Quelingua	0.7756	0.7756	0.771	0.771
NB	0.8525	0.8525	0.8502	0.8502

Table 2: Results for test set A (closed training).

Run	Accuracy	F1 (micro)	F1 (macro)	F1 (weighted)
Quelingua	0.7759	0.7759	0.7707	0.7707
NB	0.871	0.871	0.8694	0.8694

Table 3: Results for test set A (open training).

Run	Accuracy	F1 (micro)	F1 (macro)	F1 (weighted)
Quelingua	0.708	0.708	0.4454	0.7127
NB	0.082	0.082	0.049	0.1175

Table 4: Results for test set B1 (closed training).

Run	Accuracy	F1 (micro)	F1 (macro)	F1 (weighted)
Quelingua	0.664	0.664	0.3962	0.6339
NB	0.094	0.094	0.054	0.1296

Table 5: Results for test set B1 (open training).

Run	Accuracy	F1 (micro)	F1 (macro)	F1 (weighted)
Quelingua	0.686	0.686	0.4988	0.6983
NB	0.282	0.282	0.1244	0.2987

Table 6: Results for test set B2 (closed training).

Run	Accuracy	F1 (micro)	F1 (macro)	F1 (weighted)
Quelingua	0.692	0.692	0.4345	0.6952
NB	0.288	0.288	0.1318	0.3164

Table 7: Results for test set B2 (open training).

Run	Accuracy	F1 (micro)	F1 (macro)	F1 (weighted)
Quelingua	0.387	0.387	0.3795	0.3817
NB	0.3032	0.3032	0.2667	0.2664

Table 8: Results for test set C (closed training).

contains newspaper texts. It is thus considered as an in-domain experiment as both training and test datasets belong to the same domain. By contrast tests B (B1 and B2) consist of social media data. As the training corpus is very different from the test dataset, it can be considered as an out-of-domain test. Test set C of sub-task 2 contains automatic speech recognition translations from Arabic varieties. Even if test C belongs to the same genre (spoken language) than the training dataset, it is likely that its content will belong to new and/or different domains than the training corpus.

Concerning the baselines depicted in the table (1), it is important to point out that test set A had 12 classes (i.e. different varieties) while test sets B1 and B2 had only 5 classes. The samples were evenly distributed across the classes and so a random baseline is used. The samples in test set C were slightly unbalanced, so a majority class baseline of 22.79% is used.

As it was stated above, closed submissions use only the training corpus provided by the DSL organizers, while open submissions also use the corpus provided by the previous version of the DSL shared task.

The results of Table 1 show that the best in-domain system is NB, while Quelingua is more stable and performs better accross different domains and genres. Considering the in-domain task (test A), NB scores are not very far from the best systems. For instance, it is less than 2 points far from the top system (0.869 *vs* 0.888) in the open submission. A similar system achieved the best score in the open submission of Tweet-LID shared task 2014 (Gamallo et al., 2014). Nevertheless, the performance of NB drops dramatically in out-of-domain tests (B1 and B2). The dictionary-based approach (Quelingua) achieve similar results in both in-domain and out-domain tests. It is the eighth best system (out of 14) in both B1 and B2 tests (closed submission). Such a result is acceptable if we consider that the system is very basic and simple: its models only make use of the 1k most frequent words per variety. It also outperforms NB in test C, even if the results are quite poor: position 16 out 18 systems and 13 points less than the best one: 0.381 *vs* 0.513. The poor results are likely due to the fact that we used the same preprocessing than that performed for the sub-task 1. However, the transcription of spoken language contains many metacharacters that could have been misinterpreted by our system.

To help readers to understand on which languages or groups of languages the two approaches performed better, we also include seven new tables with the confusion matrix for each test. Tables 2 and 3 for test A, tables 4, 5, 6, and 7 for tests B, and Table 8 for test C.

4.4 Efficiency

In terms of memory use, Quelingua loads a light dictionary of 136Kb (1000 words per language in sub-task 1), while the NB system requires loading much larger language models o(31Mb in sub-task 1, closed submission). Concerning speed, classification based on NB models is much slower than classification with the ranking method of Quelingua. More precisely, Quelingua is about 10 times faster than NB.

5 Discussion

We compared two very basic strategies for similar language/variety detection. We observed that Naive Bayes classifiers perform better on in-domain datasets than dictionary-based strategy, while the latter one is more stable across different domains and performs reasonably well on out-of-domain tests.

Besides the fact of performing reasonably well across different domains and genres, another benefit of the dictionary-based model is its small, transparent, and easy to handle ranked lexicon, which can be easily corrected and updated by human experts.

However, we must clarify that our Naive Bayes classifier is a class of model that can be quite sensitive to specific hyper-parameters (e.g. the kind of smoothing and the type of features - characters *vs* words). So, our work should be seen as just a comparison between a dictionary-based strategy and a particular parameterization of a Naive Bayes classifier.

In future work, we will measure the performance effects of using a manually corrected ranked vocabulary, since the dictionaries used in the described experiments were not corrected by humans. We will also analyze the growth curve of the F1-score obtained by the NB system over the corpus size. Besides, it will be interesting to compare these approaches with contextual-based strategies such as Markov Models, which were the best systems according to other evaluations (Padrò and Padrò, 2004). Finally, it will be very useful to perform a sound qualitative error analysis of the language varieties we know well: Portuguese, Spanish, and French. We have observed that many of the instances in the training dataset were annotated as belonging to a particular variety even if they did not contain any clear linguistic feature. In many cases, only cultural and extra-linguistic elements (e.g. a localized topic and named entities) could be used to discriminate between the related varieties. Further deeper analyses in this direction are required.

Acknowledgments

This work has been supported by TelePares project, MINECO, ref:FFI2014-51978-C2-1-R.

References

Kenneth R. Beesley. 1988. Language identifier: A computer program for automatic natural-language identication of on-line text. In *29th Annual Conference of the American Translators Association*, pages 47–54.

William B. Cavnar and John M. Trenkle. 1994. N-gram-based text categorization. In *Proceedings of the Third Symposium on Document Analysis and Information Retrieval*, Las Vegas, USA.

Ted Dunning. 1994. *Statistical Identification of Language*. Technical Report MCCS 94–273. New Mexico State University.

Willian Gale. 1995. Good-turing smoothing without tears. *Journal of Quantitative Linguistics*, 2:217–37.

Pablo Gamallo, Marcos Garcia, and Santiago Fernández-Lanza. 2013. Tass: A naive-bayes strategy for sentiment analysis on spanish tweets. In *Workshop on Sentiment Analysis at SEPLN (TASS2013)*, pages 126–132, Madrid, Spain.

Pablo Gamallo, Susana Sotelo, and José Ramom Pichel. 2014. Comparing ranking-based and naive bayes approaches to language detection on tweets. In *Workshop TweetLID: Twitter Language Identification Workshop at SEPLN 2014*, Girona, Spain.

Marcos Garcia and Pablo Gamallo. 2015. Exploring the effectiveness of linguistic knowledge for biographical relation extraction. *Natural Language Engineering*, 21(4):519–551.

Cyril Goutte, Serge Léger, and Marine Carpuat. 2014. The nrc system for discriminating similar languages. In *Proceedings of the First Workshop on Applying NLP Tools to Similar Languages, Varieties and Dialects (VarDial)*, pages 139–145, Dublin, Ireland.

Cyril Goutte, Serge Léger, Shervin Malmasi, and Marcos Zampieri. 2016. Discriminating Similar Languages: Evaluations and Explorations. In *Proceedings of the 10th International Conference on Language Resources and Evaluation (LREC 2016)*.

Gregory Grefenstette. 1995. Comparing two language identification schemes. In *Proceedings of the 3rd International Conference on the Statistical Analysis of Textual Data (JADT 1995)*.

Shervin Malmasi and Mark Dras. 2015. Language identification using classifier ensembles. In *Proceedings of the Joint Workshop on Language Technology for Closely Related Languages, Varieties and Dialects (LT4VarDial)*, pages 35–43, Hissar, Bulgaria.

Shervin Malmasi, Eshrag Refaee, and Mark Dras. 2015. Arabic Dialect Identification using a Parallel Multidialectal Corpus. In *Proceedings of the 14th Conference of the Pacific Association for Computational Linguistics (PACLING 2015)*, pages 209–217, Bali, Indonesia, May.

Shervin Malmasi, Marcos Zampieri, Nikola Ljubešić, Preslav Nakov, Ahmed Ali, and Jörg Tiedemann. 2016. Discriminating between similar languages and arabic dialect identification: A report on the third dsl shared task. In *Proceedings of the 3rd Workshop on Language Technology for Closely Related Languages, Varieties and Dialects (VarDial)*, Osaka, Japan.

Paul McNamee. 2005. Language identification: a solved problem suitable for undergraduate instruction. *Journal of Computing Sciences in Colleges*, 3:94–101.

Muntsa Padrò and Lluís Padrò. 2004. Comparing methods for language identification. *Procesamiento del Lenguage Natural*, 33:151–161.

Radim Rehurek and Milan Kolkus. 2009. Language identification on the web: Extending the dictionary method. *Lecture Notes in Computer Science*, pages 315–345.

Liling Tan, Marcos Zampieri, Nikola Ljubešic, and Jörg Tiedemann. 2014. Merging comparable data sources for the discrimination of similar languages: The dsl corpus collection. In *Proceedings of the 7th Workshop on Building and Using Comparable Corpora (BUCC)*, pages 11–15, Reykjavik, Iceland.

Erik Tromp and Mykola Pechenizkiy. 2011. Graph-based n-gram language identification on short texts. In *Proceedings of Benelearn 2011*, pages 27–35, The Hague, Netherlands.

Tommi Vatanen, Jaakko J. Väyrynen, and Sami Virpioja. 2010. Slanguage identification of short text segments with n-gram models. In *Proceedings of LREC-2010*.

Fela Winkelmolen and Viviana Mascardi. 2011. Statistical language identification of short texts. In *Proceedings of ICAAR*, pages 498–503.

Marcos Zampieri, Liling Tan, Nikola Ljubešić, and Jörg Tiedemann. 2014. A report on the dsl shared task 2014. In *Proceedings of the First Workshop on Applying NLP Tools to Similar Languages, Varieties and Dialects (VarDial)*, pages 58–67, Dublin, Ireland.

Marcos Zampieri, Liling Tan, Nikola Ljubešić, Jörg Tiedemann, and Preslav Nakov. 2015. Overview of the dsl shared task 2015. In *Proceedings of the Joint Workshop on Language Technology for Closely Related Languages, Varieties and Dialects (LT4VarDial)*, pages 1–9, Hissar, Bulgaria.

Arkaitz Zubiaga, Iñaki San Vicente, Pablo Gamallo, José Ramom Pichel, Iñaki Alegria, Nora Aranberri, Aitzol Ezeiza, and Víctor Fresno. 2014. Overview of tweetlid: Tweet language identification at sepln 2014. In *TweetLID - SEPLN 2014*, Girona, Spain.

Arkaitz Zubiaga, Iñaki San Vicente, Pablo Gamallo, José Ramom Pichel, Iñaki Alegria, Nora Aranberri, Aitzol Ezeiza, and Víctor Fresno. 2015. Tweetlid: a benchmark for tweet language identification. *Language Resources and Evaluation*, pages 1–38.

Advances in Ngram-based Discrimination of Similar Languages

Cyril Goutte
Multilingual Text Processing
National Research Council
Ottawa ON, Canada
Cyril.Goutte@gmail.com

Serge Léger
Human Computer Interaction
National Research Council
Moncton NB, Canada
Serge.Leger@nrc.ca

Abstract

We describe the systems entered by the National Research Council in the 2016 shared task on discriminating similar languages. Like previous years, we relied on character ngram features, and a combination of discriminative and generative statistical classifiers. We mostly investigated the influence of the amount of data on the performance, in the open task, and compared the two-stage approach (predicting language/group, then variant) to a flat approach. Results suggest that ngrams are still state-of-the-art for language and variant identification, that additional data has a small but decisive impact, and that the two-stage approach performs slightly better, everything else being kept equal, than the flat approach.

1 Introduction

We describe the systems submitted by the National Research Council Canada to the 2016 shared task on discriminating similar languages.

Discriminating similar languages and language variants is useful for several purposes. As the typical linguistic processing pipeline is tailored to a specific language and variant, it is important to have a reliable prediction of the language a text is written in, in order to use the appropriate linguistic tools. It may also be used for filtering data in order to build these specialized linguistic processing tools. In education, and language learning in particular, it may also be useful to identify precisely the variant familiar to a learner so that feedback can be tailored to the vocabulary or linguistic constructions they are familiar with. Finally, in security, it is highly relevant to identify the regional variant of the language used by a writer or poster.

Shared tasks on discriminating similar languages were organized in 2014 (Zampieri et al., 2014) and 2015 (Zampieri et al., 2015). This year's task continues in the same track, removing some of the easy languages (Czech and Slovak; Macedonian and Bulgarian), providing additional material for some of the harder variants (Serbo-Croat-Bosnian; Indonesian and Malay; Portuguese; Spanish), and adding new groups or variants (Mexican Spanish; French from Canada and France).

Like previous years, we relied on character ngram features, and a mixture of discriminative and generative statistical classifiers. Due to lack of time, we decided to eschew a full optimization of the feature sets and model combination, despite the fact that it provided excellent results in previous years (Goutte et al., 2014; Malmasi and Dras, 2015). Instead, we focused on two issues: the influence of the amount of data on the performance (open versus closed data), and the difference between a two-stage approach (predicting language/group, then variant) and a flat approach predicting the variant directly. To be clear, the "Advances" in the title of this paper do not relate to the performance and model we used this year, which are mostly similar to successful models of prior years. The intent is to advance our *understanding* of how these models works and what configurations are more effective.

An overview of the results of this shared task is presented in the shared task report (Malmasi et al., 2016). It provides a wider context for interpreting the results reported here, which we only compare to a few top systems. The shared task report also provides references to related work. The reader may also

Proceedings of the Third Workshop on NLP for Similar Languages, Varieties and Dialects,
pages 178–184, Osaka, Japan, December 12 2016.

lang	DSLCC v1.0	DSLCC v2.1	DSL 2016	crawl	Total (open)
bs	20,000	20,000	20,000	-	60,000
hr	20,000	20,000	20,000	-	60,000
sr	20,000	20,000	20,000	-	60,000
es-AR	20,000	20,000	20,000	-	60,000
es-ES	20,000	20,000	20,000	-	60,000
es-MX	-	20,000	20,000*	-	40,000*
fr-CA	-	-	20,000	40,000	60,000
fr-FR	-	-	20,000	-	20,000
id	20,000	20,000	20,000	-	60,000
my	20,000	20,000	20,000	-	60,000
pt-BR	20,000	20,000	20,000	-	60,000
pt-PT	20,000	20,000	20,000	-	60,000

Table 1: Statistics on the training data used for training our systems. (*: 2016 data was actually identical to DSLCC v2.1 data)

find a lot of references to related work (within and outside the shared tasks) in Section 2 of (Goutte et al., 2016).

In the following section, we describe the data we worked with, the features we extracted from the data, and the models we trained on these features. Section 3 summarizes our results on the shared task test set and compared them to a few key systems from other participants. Finally, we discuss those results and their significance in Section 4.

2 Data and Methods

We now describe the data we used for our two runs, the features we extracted from the data, and the models we trained on those features.

2.1 Data

In order to evaluate the impact of using additional data on the performance of the discriminative performance, we built "closed" systems on the 2016 training data only, and "open" systems using additional data.

The closed systems use the data provided for the 2016 evaluation only. This consisted of 20k sentences from the news domain for each of the twelve language variant, for a total of 240k sentences (column **DSL 2016** in Table 1). We joined the `train` and `dev` portions of the training data as we evaluate the performance using ten fold cross-validation rather than using a single development set.

The open systems used data from previous DSL shared tasks (DSLCC v1.0 and DSLCC v2.1, (Tan et al., 2014)), plus additional text crawled from the web site of the Québec journal *La Presse*. For each of the variants used in previous years, this results in 60k sentences per variant (20k per corpus). Mexican Spanish was not included in previous years, but the DSLCC v2.1 corpus released last year contained 20k sentences for that variant, for use in the "unshared" task that (unfortunately) received little attention. We did not realize before training our system that the 20k sentences provided for es-MX this year were actually identical to the material provided last year for that variant, which means that our material for the es-MX variant is actually the same 20k sentences duplicated. For fr-CA, we added 40k sentences from the web crawl of *La Presse*. We checked that the added material did not overlap with the material provided by the DSL organizers (for training or testing). For French, our training material was therefore unbalanced, with only 20k sentences for fr-FR versus 60k for fr-CA.

Due to lack of time, we did not take part in the Arabic dialect sub-task, despite its great interest.

2.2 Features

Character ngram counts have been popular and effective features since at least (Cavnar and Trenkle, 1994), and produced top results at previous evaluations (Goutte et al., 2014; Malmasi and Dras, 2015; Goutte and Leger, 2015). We therefore relied again on character ngrams. This year, however, we only used 6grams. The reasons for this choice are multiple:

- Optimizing the size and combination of ngram features produces small performance improvements. However this optimization also requires significant effort and time, which we did not have this year.

- In our experience from previous shared tasks, 6grams were almost always the best feature set. When they were not, they were very close.

- Our main focus this year was not on maximizing performance of a single system, but on investigating the influence of training data size and the difference between a flat and two-stage model.

Using character 6grams therefore ensures that we build systems with reasonable (if not top) performance, while removing the variability in the choice (or optimization) of the features. It allows us to evaluate the impact of the data size and model architecture, everything else being kept equal. In addition, as we had a limited number of hours to spend on the shared task, we avoided the effort associated with feature engineering and optimization.

2.3 Models

Having decided on the feature set and training data, we tried two competing approaches.

2.3.1 `run1`

In the 2014 and 2015 evaluations (Goutte et al., 2014; Goutte and Leger, 2015) , we used a two stage approach, where we

1. train a level-1 classifier to predict the language group, and

2. train a level-2 classifier to predict the variant within each group.

This approach is actually not too costly. On the one hand, the lower level classifiers are often binary classifiers trained on smaller amounts of data. On the other hand, the top level classifier focuses on a simpler task, with bigger differences between groups, so a simple multiclass probabilistic classifier can be trained efficiently with almost perfect performance.

Our `run1` implements this two-stage approach again. The top-level classifier is a probabilistic classifier (Gaussier et al., 2002) similar to Naïve Bayes, trained in a single pass over the data, making it suitable for large-scale training. Using ten fold cross-validation, we estimate that the error rate of that first stage on the open task is below 0.051% (335 errors out of 660k examples), i.e. roughly one mistake per 2000 examples.

The level-2 classifiers are Support Vector Machines (SVM) trained using SVM^{light} (Joachims, 1998). For the three groups with only two variants (French, Portuguese and Indonesian/Malay), we trained a single binary SVM classifier in each group, taking one variant as the positive class, and the other variant as the negative class. For the two groups with three variants (Spanish and Serbo-Croat-Bosnian), we trained three SVM classifiers in one-versus-all configuration: each variant is taken as the positive class, in turn, with the other two as the negative class. The outputs of the three classifiers are calibrated to make them comparable (Bennett, 2003). At prediction time, we pick the class with the highest calibrated classifier output. Although training SVM models can be slow for large datasets, we restrict ourselves to linear kernels, and we only use the examples within a group to estimate the model, which is a maximum of 180k examples. Once the SVM classifiers and calibration layers have been estimated, prediction is just a few dot-products away, and therefore extremely fast. In previous years, we also validated that this combination of discriminative approach and calibration provides slightly better performance than modeling the problem directly with a multiclass probabilistic classifier.

Run	A	B1	B2	Overall	(CV)
run1	**89.03**	**94.80**	**90.00**	**89.29**	92.50
run2	88.77	94.20	89.00	88.98	92.63
SUKI	88.37	82.20	79.60	87.79	
Citius	87.10	66.40	69.20	85.62	

Table 2: Predictive accuracy (in %) for the 2016 open track runs, for our two runs and two runner-ups, on the three official test sets and overall. Rightmost column gives cross-validation estimate, for comparison.

2.3.2 run2

In the 2015 evaluation (Zampieri et al., 2015), the best performing system in the closed task (Malmasi and Dras, 2015) used a "flat" approach, treating the entire problem as a single, multiclass classification, with excellent results, only slightly below the best overall performance on the open task for test set A and best overall for test set B.

We attempt to test this flat approach on our chosen feature set, as our run2. Note that the best approach in (Malmasi and Dras, 2015) uses an *ensemble* of classifiers trained on different feature spaces (words, word bigrams, character bigrams, 4grams and 6grams). As we focus on a single feature set, we did not reproduce the ensemble part of that approach. The key difference between run1 and run2 is really the two-stage vs. flat approach.

We use again Support Vector Machines trained using SVM^{light} in one-versus-all fashion. For each of the 12 variants, a binary classifier is trained using one variant as the positive class and the rest as negative examples. The output of each of the 12 classifiers is then calibrated into a proper probability (Bennett, 2003). At prediction time, a sentence is sent through each calibrated classifier, producing a proper probability. The prediction is the class with highest probability. Note that despite its conceptual simplicity, this approach is more costly than the two-stage approach, as it requires training 12 binary classifier on 660k examples each (for the *open* track; 240k for the *closed* track). In addition, class imbalance is more severe for this model.

3   Results

We made four submissions for each of the three test sets (A, B1 and B2): two models on the *open* and two models on the *closed* tracks. The performance of each model was also estimated on the full training set (train+dev partitions of the official data) using a stratified ten fold cross-validation.

When the test data was received, we simply processed test set A as it was provided, as it seemed to match the training data fairly well. For the twitter data (test sets B1 and B2), we did light preprocessing by removing markers for accounts and hashtags (@ and #), as well as URLs. For example the tweet:

```
RT @xxmarioo: savage #KimExposedTaylorParty https://t.co/7FpfbmqziQ
```

is turned, before being sent to the classifiers, into:

```
RT xxmarioo: savage KimExposedTaylorParty
```

Official results on the three test sets were obtained from the organizers. From these results, we compute an overall score which is the micro-averaged accuracy over classes and test sets. The two 'B' test sets contain only 500 exemples vs. 12,000 for test set 'A', so the overall score is a weighted average of the provided accuracies, with eights 12/13, 1/26 and 1/26 for A, B1 and B2, respectively. Note that, in a single-label multiclass evaluation like this one, micro-averaged accuracy, precision, recall and (as a consequence) F-scores are identical. They differ slightly from the *weighted* F_1 used as the official ranking metric, but differences are small, probably due to the fact that classes are balanced in the test data.

Table 2 shows the results for the *open* track, while Table 3 shows the results for the *closed* track. As a naïve baseline, we propose to use a "group-perfect random" baseline, i.e. a classifier that would correctly identify the language group (a very easy task) and would perform randomly on the variants

Run	A	B1	B2	Overall	(CV)
run1	88.59	91.40	**87.80**	88.67	89.26
run2	88.12	90.80	86.60	88.16	88.87
tubasfs	**89.38**	86.20	82.20	**88.98**	
GWU	88.70	**92.00**	**87.80**	88.79	

Table 3: Predictive accuracy (in %) for the 2016 closed track runs, on the three official test sets and overall. Rightmost column gives cross-validation estimate, for comparison.

	sr-hr-bs	español	français	id-my	portugês
sr-hr-bs	2994	3	1	1	1
español	1	2990	3	1	5
français	0	0	1996	0	4
id-my	1	0	2	1997	0
portugês	0	1	0	0	1999

Table 4: Language group confusion on test set A, run1: reference in rows, predicted in columns.

within a group. The accuracy of this baseline is $\frac{\#\text{groups}}{\#\text{variants}}$ which is 41.67% for test set A and 40% for test sets B1 and B2, resulting in an overall score of 41.54%.

According to the official ranking,[1] our run1 results yield the top performance in the *open* track, closely followed by our run2 results and the two runner-up systems (SUKI and Citius_Ixa_Imaxin). Another participant submitted only for the twitter data (B1 and B2) and is not included in Table 2.

On the closed track, our results are slightly below the top two systems overall (tubasfs and GWU), with slight variations across the three test sets. Our run1 yield top results on test set B2 and close on test set B1 (the difference amounts to 3 tweets out of 500), but was outperfomed on the larger test set A. Note that tubasfs, GWU and our run1 are within 0.3% of each other, which may not be highly significant, either practically or statistically. A more precise assessment of the significance of the differences ill require access to the individual predictions.

Table 4 shows the confusion table between language groups for run1 on test set A (other runs and conditions are similar). Overall, there are 16 to 24 language group mistakes on test set A, depending on the track, i.e. below 0.2% error rate. Although still very low, this is quite significantly above the cross-validation estimate of 0.05%. The reasons for this will require further investigation. Most mistakes are, as expected, between Spanish, Portuguese and/or French, but a few are surprising (e.g., two Indonesian sentences predicted as French). On test sets B, the only mistake observed on either run or condition is a Portuguese user predicted as Bosnian. Overall this suggests that the first stage group classifier has little impact on performance, as it costs us at most 0.2% in error rate.

Looking at the language variant confusion in Table 5 shows that errors are not uniformly distributed. There are more confusions between Serbian and Croatian in the news data, and about as many confusions between Bosnian and Serbian in the twitter data. The confusion between Croatian and Bosnian is consistently smaller than for the other two pairs. In Spanish, errors appear unbalanced, with many Mexican sentences incorrectly assigned to the other two variants. This is likely due to a combination of the smaller size of the Mexican data, and the fact that we duplicated the data by mistake, which underestimates the unbalance between the classes.

4 Discussion

In light of these results and considering the questions we were targetting, we can reach the following conclusions.

- Data size has a small but consistent impact on performance. Keeping the models equal, the difference in performance brought by training on the *open* data was 0.72% on average. As this involves

---

[1] Available from http://ttg.uni-saarland.de/vardial2016/dsl2016.html.

set:	A			B1+B2		
	sr	hr	bs	sr	hr	bs
sr	692	198	109	179	8	13
hr	112	880	6	13	195	2
bs	85	24	888	8	0	192

set:	A		
es-	-ar	-es	-mx
-ar	945	32	19
-es	81	878	35
-mx	175	152	673

set:	A	
fr-	-ca	-fr
-ca	937	63
-fr	77	919

set:	A	
	id	my
id	990	7
my	14	986

set:	A		B1+B2	
pt-	-br	-pt	-br	-pt
-br	956	44	189	11
-pt	59	940	21	179

Table 5: Language variant confusion for `run1`: reference in rows, predicted in columns.

training on three times more data, whether this is worth it in practice is debatable, but it clearly brought our `run1` above the best *closed* data result.

- The two-stage approach of predicting the group performs slightly but consistently better than the "flat" approach of predicting the variant directly. Keeping the data equal, the difference in performance between `run1` and `run2` was 0.41%, on average, in favour of the former. Again, this may not be a significant difference in practice, but given the advantage of the two stage approach in terms of training time, we think that this provides a convincing argument in favour of that approach. A side conclusion is that this suggests that the gain observed last year in the winning system (Malmasi and Dras, 2015) may be due to the ensemble combination, which could also be applied to the two stage approach.

- Our systems performed rather well on the twitter data, which seemed to be a challenge for several participants. Although that data was expected to be of lower quality than the journalistic material (language variety, frequent code switching and inventive character sequences), we also had a lot more material: segments in test set A had up to 88 words, whereas segments in test sets B1 and B2 had up to 6400. This was clearly helpful by providing better ngram statistics. It also helped that English was not among the candidate languages/variants as a lot of tweet material is clearly English. It would be interesting to check performance on single tweets.

- Previous work on twitter suggested that removing hashtags and account names altogether may yield a small performance gain (Lui and Baldwin, 2014). In this work, we decided to remove the # and @ characters alone, with the motivation that the hashtag or account *text* itself may point to the correct variant. A systematic evaluation of the different strategies is left to future work, although based on results from Lui and Baldwin (2014), we conjecture that it is unlikely to make a significant difference.

- The cross-validation estimates computed on the joint train+dev data yield optimistic estimates, especially on the open data. Although differences are expected, it is unusually large, and may suggest a domain mismatch between the test data and the training material. Another factor is that classes in the training data were imbalanced (fewer fr-FR and es-MX examples), whereas the test set is balanced. As a consequence, the fr-MX class is underpredicted compared to other Spanish variants. We did not observe the same effect on French, so this is still up for investigation.

- Our experience this year suggests that focusing on 6grams and removing the system combination (or ensemble) step makes it possible to set up competitive systems in very short time. The top performance this year was 89.3% accuracy, which is lower than last year, but still competitive (and on different test sets).

Acknowledgements

We wish to thank Marc Tessier at NRC for helping us acquire additional Canadian French data; the organizers for their hard work and for extending the submission deadline; the (anonymous) reviewers for many excellent suggestions.

References

Paul N. Bennett. 2003. Using asymmetric distributions to improve text classifier probability estimates. In *Proceedings of the 26th Annual International ACM SIGIR Conference on Research and Development in Informaion Retrieval*, SIGIR '03, pages 111–118, New York, NY, USA. ACM.

William Cavnar and John Trenkle. 1994. N-gram-based text categorization. *3rd Symposium on Document Analysis and Information Retrieval (SDAIR-94)*.

Éric Gaussier, Cyril Goutte, Kris Popat, and Francine Chen. 2002. A hierarchical model for clustering and categorising documents. In *Proceedings of the 24th BCS-IRSG European Colloquium on IR Research: Advances in Information Retrieval*, pages 229–247, London, UK, UK. Springer-Verlag.

Cyril Goutte and Serge Leger. 2015. Experiments in discriminating similar languages. In *Proceedings of the Joint Workshop on Language Technology for Closely Related Languages, Varieties and Dialects (LT4VarDial)*, pages 78–84, Hissar, Bulgaria.

Cyril Goutte, Serge Léger, and Marine Carpuat. 2014. The NRC system for discriminating similar languages. In *Proceedings of the First Workshop on Applying NLP Tools to Similar Languages, Varieties and Dialects (VarDial)*, pages 139–145, Dublin, Ireland.

Cyril Goutte, Serge Léger, Shervin Malmasi, and Marcos Zampieri. 2016. Discriminating Similar Languages: Evaluations and Explorations. In *Proceedings of the 10th International Conference on Language Resources and Evaluation (LREC 2016)*.

Thorsten Joachims. 1998. Text categorization with Suport Vector Machines: Learning with many relevant features. In Claire Nédellec and Céline Rouveirol, editors, *Proceedings of ECML-98, 10th European Conference on Machine Learning*, volume 1398 of *Lecture Notes in Computer Science*, pages 137–142. Springer.

Marco Lui and Timothy Baldwin. 2014. Accurate language identification of twitter messages. In *Proceedings of the 5th Workshop on Language Analysis for Social Media (LASM)*, pages 17–25, Gothenburg, Sweden, April. Association for Computational Linguistics.

Shervin Malmasi and Mark Dras. 2015. Language identification using classifier ensembles. In *Proceedings of the Joint Workshop on Language Technology for Closely Related Languages, Varieties and Dialects (LT4VarDial)*, pages 35–43, Hissar, Bulgaria.

Shervin Malmasi, Marcos Zampieri, Nikola Ljubešić, Preslav Nakov, Ahmed Ali, and Jörg Tiedemann. 2016. Discriminating between similar languages and arabic dialect identification: A report on the third DSL shared task. In *Proceedings of the 3rd Workshop on Language Technology for Closely Related Languages, Varieties and Dialects (VarDial)*, Osaka, Japan.

Liling Tan, Marcos Zampieri, Nikola Ljubešic, and Jörg Tiedemann. 2014. Merging comparable data sources for the discrimination of similar languages: The dsl corpus collection. In *Proceedings of the 7th Workshop on Building and Using Comparable Corpora (BUCC)*, pages 11–15, Reykjavik, Iceland.

Marcos Zampieri, Liling Tan, Nikola Ljubešić, and Jörg Tiedemann. 2014. A report on the dsl shared task 2014. In *Proceedings of the First Workshop on Applying NLP Tools to Similar Languages, Varieties and Dialects (VarDial)*, pages 58–67, Dublin, Ireland.

Marcos Zampieri, Liling Tan, Nikola Ljubešić, Jörg Tiedemann, and Preslav Nakov. 2015. Overview of the dsl shared task 2015. In *Proceedings of the Joint Workshop on Language Technology for Closely Related Languages, Varieties and Dialects (LT4VarDial)*, pages 1–9, Hissar, Bulgaria.

Discrimination between Similar Languages, Varieties and Dialects using CNN- and LSTM-based Deep Neural Networks

Chinnappa Guggilla
chinna.guggilla@gmail.com

Abstract

In this paper, we describe a system (CGLI) for discriminating similar languages, varieties and dialects using convolutional neural networks (CNNs) and long short-term memory (LSTM) neural networks. We have participated in the Arabic dialect identification sub-task of DSL 2016 shared task for distinguishing different Arabic language texts under closed submission track. Our proposed approach is language independent and works for discriminating any given set of languages, varieties and dialects. We have obtained 43.29% weighted-F1 accuracy in this sub-task using CNN approach using default network parameters.

1 Introduction

Discriminating between similar languages, language varieties is a well-known research problem in natural language processing (NLP). In this paper we describe about Arabic dialect identification. Arabic dialect classification is a challenging problem for Arabic language processing, and useful in several NLP applications such as machine translation, natural language generation and information retrieval and speaker identification (Zaidan and Callison-Burch, 2011).

Modern Standard Arabic (MSA) language is the standardized and literary variety of Arabic that is standardized, regulated, and taught in schools, used in written communication and formal speeches. The regional dialects, used primarily for day-to-day activities present mostly in spoken communication when compared to the MSA. The Arabic has more dialectal varieties, in which Egyptian, Gulf, Iraqi, Levantine, and Maghrebi are spoken in different regions of the Arabic population (Zaidan and Callison-Burch, 2011). Most of the linguistic resources developed and widely used in Arabic NLP are based on MSA.

Though the language identification task is relatively considered to be solved problem in official texts, there will be further level of problems with the noisy text which can be introduced when compiling languages texts from the heterogeneous sources. The identification of varieties from the same language differs from the language identification task in terms of difficulty due to the lexical, syntactic and semantic variations of the words in the language. In addition, since all Arabic varieties use the same character set, and much of the vocabulary is shared among different varieties, it is not straightforward to discriminate dialects from each other (Zaidan and Callison-Burch, 2011). Several other researchers attempted the language varsities and dialects identification problems. Zampieri and Gebre (2012) investigated varieties of Portuguese using different word and character n-gram features. Zaidan and Callison-Burch (2011) proposed multi-dialect Arabic classification using various word and character level features.

In order to improve the language, variety and dialect identification further, Zampieri et al. (2014), Zampieri et al. (2015b) and Zampieri et al. (2015a) have been organizing the Discriminating between Similar Languages (DSL) shared task. The aim of the task is to encourage researchers to propose and submit systems using state of the art approaches to discriminate several groups of similar languages and varieties. Goutte et al. (2014) achieved 95.7% accuracy which is best among all the submissions in 2014 shared task. In their system, authors employed two-step classification approach to predict first

Proceedings of the Third Workshop on NLP for Similar Languages, Varieties and Dialects,
pages 185–194, Osaka, Japan, December 12 2016.

the language group of the text and subsequently the language using SVM classifier with word and character level n-gram features. Goutte and Leger (2015) and Malmasi and Dras (2015) achieved 95.65% and 95.54% state of the art accuracies under open and closed tracks respectively in 2015 DSL shared task. Goutte et al. (2016) presents a comprehensive evaluation of state of-the-art language identification systems trained to recognize similar languages and language varieties using the results of the first two DSL shared tasks. Their experimental results suggest that humans also find it difficult discriminating between similar languages and language varieties. This year, DSL 2016 shared task proposed two sub-tasks: first sub-task is about discriminating between similar languages and national language varieties. Second sub-task is about Arabic dialect identification which is introduced first time in DSL 2016 shared task. We have participated in the sub-task2 of dialect identification on Egyptian, Gulf, Levantine, and North-African, and Modern Standard Arabic (MSA) Arabic dialects. We describe about dataset used for dialect classification in section 4.

In classifying Arabic dialects, Elfardy and Diab (2013), Malmasi and Dras (2014), Zaidan and Callison-Burch (2014), Darwish et al. (2014) and Malmasi et al. (2015) employed supervised and sem-supervised learning methods with and without ensembles and meta classifiers with various levels of word, character and morphological features. Most of these approaches are sensitive to the topic bias in the language and use expensive set of features and limited to short texts. Moreover, generating these features can be a tedious and complex process. In this paper, we propose deep learning based supervised techniques for Arabic dialect identification without the need for expensive feature engineering. Inspired by the advances in sentence classification (Kim, 2014) and sequence classification (Hochreiter and Schmidhuber, 1997) using distributional word representations, we use convolutional neural networks (CNN) and long short-term memory (LSTM)-based deep neural network approaches for Arabic dialect identification.

The rest of the paper is organized as follows: in section 2, we describe related work on Arabic dialect classification. In section 3, we introduce two deep learning based supervised classification techniques and describe about the proposed methodology. We give a brief overview about the dataset used in the shared task in section 4, and also we present experimental results on dialect classification. In section 5, we discuss about results and analyse various types of errors in dialect classification and conclude the paper. Additional analysis and comparison with the other submitted systems are available in the 2016 shared task overview (Malmasi et al., 2016)

2 Related Work

In recent years, a very few researchers have attempted the task of automatic Arabic dialect identification. Zaidan and Callison-Burch (2011) developed an informal monolingual Arabic Online Commentary (AOC) annotated dataset with high dialectal content. Authors in this work applied language modelling approach and performed dialect classification tasks on 4 dialects (MSA and three dialects) and two dialects (Egyptian Arabic and MSA) and reported 69.4% and 80.9% accuracies respectively. Several other researchers (Elfardy and Diab, 2013; Malmasi and Dras, 2014; Zaidan and Callison-Burch, 2014; Darwish et al., 2014) also used the same AOC and Egyptian-MSA datasets and employed different categories of supervised classifiers such as Naive Bayes, SVM, and ensembles with various rich lexical features such as word and character level n-grams, morphological features and reported the improved results.

Malmasi et al. (2015) presented a number of Arabic dialect classification experiments namely multi-dialect classification, pairwise binary dialect classification and meta multi-dialect classification using the Multidialectal Parallel Corpus of Arabic (MPCA) dataset. Authors achieved 74% accuracy on a 6-dialect classification and 94% accuracy using pairwise binary dialect classification within the corpus but reported poorer results (76%) between Palestinian and Jordanian closely related dialects. Authors also reported that a meta-classifier can yield better accuracies for multi-class dialect identification and shown that models trained with the MPCA corpus generalize well to other corpus such as AOC dataset. They demonstrated that character n-gram features uniquely contributed for significant improvement in accuracy in intra-corpus and cross-corpus settings. In contrast, Zaidan and Callison-Burch (2011; Elfardy and Diab (2013; Zaidan and Callison-Burch (2014) shown that word unigram features are the best features for Arabic dialect classification. Our proposed approach do not leverage rich lexical, syntactic features, instead learns abstract representation of features through deep neural networks and distributional representations of words from the training data. Proposed approach handles n-gram features with varying context window-sizes sliding over input words at sentence level.

Habash et al. (2008) composed annotation guidelines for identifying Arabic dialect content in the Arabic text content, by focusing on code switching. Authors also reported annotation results on a small data set (1,600 Arabic sentences) with sentence and word-level dialect annotations.

Biadsy et al. (2009; Lei and Hansen (2011) performed Arabic dialect identification task in the speech domain at the speaker level and not at the sentence level. Biadsy et al. (2009) applied phone recognition and language modeling approach on larger (170 hours of speech) data and performed four-way classification task and reported 78.5% accuracy rate. Lei and Hansen (2011) performed three-way dialect classification using Gaussian mixture models and achieved an accuracy rate of 71.7% using about 10 hours of speech data for training. In our proposed approach, we use ASR textual transcripts and employ deep-neural networks based supervised sentence and sequence classification approaches for performing multi-dialect identification task.

In a more recent work, Franco-Salvador et al. (2015) employed word embeddings based continuous Skip-gram model approach (Mikolov et al., 2013a; Mikolov et al., 2013b) to generate distributed representations of words and sentences on HispaBlogs[1] dataset, a new collection of Spanish blogs from five different countries: Argentina, Chile, Mexico, Peru and Spain. For classifying intra-group languages, authors used averaged word embedding sentence vector representations and reported classification accuracies of 92.7% on original text and 90.8% accuracy after masking named entities in the text. In this approach, authors utilizes sentence vectors generated from averaged word embeddings and uses logistic regression or Support Vector Machines (SVMs) for detecting dialects where as in our proposed approach, we build the task of dialect identification using end to end deep neural representation by learning abstract features and feature combinations through multiple layers. Our results are not directly comparable with this work as we use different Arabic dialect dataset.

3 Methodology

Deep neural networks, with or without word embeddings, have recently shown significant improvements over traditional machine learning–based approaches when applied to various sentence- and document-level classification tasks.

Kim (2014) have shown that CNNs outperform traditional machine learning–based approaches on several tasks, such as sentiment classification, question type classification, and subjectivity classification, using simple static word embeddings and tuning of hyper-parameters. Zhang et al. (2015) proposed character level CNN for text classification. Lai et al. (2015; Visin et al. (2015) proposed recurrent CNN while Johnson and Zhang (2015) proposed semi-supervised CNN for solving text classification task. Palangi et al. (2016) proposed sentence embedding using LSTM network for information retrieval task. Zhou et al. (2016) proposed attention-based bidirectional lstm Networks for relation classification task. RNNs model text sequences effectively by capturing long-range dependencies among the words. LSTM-based approaches based on RNNs effectively capture the sequences in the sentences when compared to the CNN and SVM-based approaches. In subsequent sub sections, we describe our proposed CNN and LSTM based approaches for multi-class dialect classification.

3.1 CNN-based Dialect Classification

Collobert et al. (2011) adapted the original CNN proposed by LeCun and Bengio (1995) for modelling natural language sentences. Following Kim (2014), we present a variant of the CNN architecture with four layer types: an input layer, a convolution layer, a max pooling layer, and a fully connected softmax layer. Each dialect in the input layer is represented as a sentence (dialect) comprised of distributional word embeddings. Let $v_i \in \mathbb{R}^k$ be the k-dimensional word vector corresponding to the ith word in the

---

[1]https://github.com/autoritas/RD-Lab/ tree/master/data/HispaBlogs

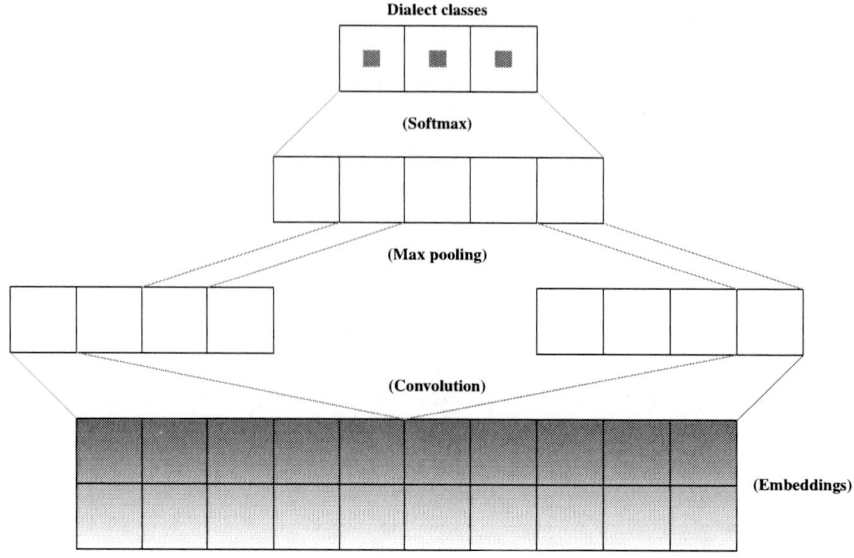

Figure 1: Illustration of convolutional neural networks with an example dialect

sentence. Then a dialect S of length ℓ is represented as the concatenation of its word vectors:

$$S = v_1 \oplus v_2 \oplus \cdots \oplus v_\ell. \tag{1}$$

In the convolution layer, for a given word sequence within a dialect, a convolutional word filter P is defined. Then, the filter P is applied to each word in the dialect to produce a new set of features. We use a non-linear activation function such as rectified linear unit (ReLU) for the convolution process and max-over-time pooling (Collobert et al., 2011; Kim, 2014) at pooling layer to deal with the variable dialect size. After a series of convolutions with different filters with different heights, the most important features are generated. Then, this feature representation, Z, is passed to a fully connected penultimate layer and outputs a distribution over different labels:

$$y = \mathrm{softmax}(W \cdot Z + b), \tag{2}$$

where y denotes a distribution over different dialect labels, W is the weight vector learned from the input word embeddings from the training corpus, and b is the bias term.

3.2 LSTM-based Dialect Classification

In case of CNN, concatenating words with various window sizes, works as n-gram models but do not capture long-distance word dependencies with shorter window sizes. A larger window size can be used, but this may lead to data sparsity problem. In order to encode long-distance word dependencies, we use long short-term memory networks, which are a special kind of RNN capable of learning long-distance dependencies. LSTMs were introduced by Hochreiter and Schmidhuber (1997) in order to mitigate the vanishing gradient problem (Gers et al., 2000; Gers, 2001; Graves, 2013; Pascanu et al., 2013).

The model illustrated in Figure 2 is composed of a single LSTM layer followed by an average pooling and a softmax regression layer. Each dialect is represented as a sentence (S) in the input layer. Thus, from an input sequence, $S_{i,j}$, the memory cells in the LSTM layer produce a representation sequence $h_i, h_{i+1}, \ldots, h_j$. Finally, this representation is fed to a softmax layer to predict the dialect classes for unseen input dialects.

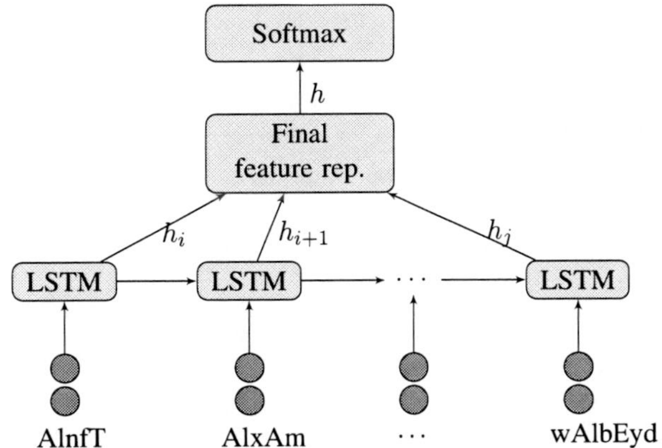

Figure 2: Illustration of LSTM networks with an example dialect

3.3 Experimental Setup

We modeled dialect classification as a sentence classification task. We tokenized the corpus with white space tokenizer. We performed multi-class 5-way classification on the given arabic data set containing 5 language dialects. We used Kim's (2014) Theano implementation of CNN [2] for training the CNN model and a variant of the standard Theano implementation[3] for training the LSTM network. We initialized and used the randomly generated embeddings in both the CNN and LSTM models in the range $[-0.25, 0.25]$. We used 80% of the training set for training and 20% of the data for validation set and performed 5-fold cross validation in CNN. In LSTM, we used 80% of the given training set for building the model and rest 20% of the data is used as development set. We updated input embedding vectors during the training. In the CNN approach, we used a stochastic gradient descent–based optimization method for minimizing the cross entropy loss during the training with the Rectified Linear Unit (ReLU) non-linear activation function. We used default window filter sizes set at $[3, 4, 5]$. In the case of LSTM, model was trained using an adaptive learning rate optimizer-adadelta (Zeiler, 2012) over shuffled mini-batches with the sigmoid activation function at input, output and forget gates and tanh non-linear activation function at cell state. Post competition we performed experiments without and with average pooling using LSTM networks and reported the results as shown in tables 5 and 6.

Hyper Parameters. We used hyper-parameters such as drop-out for avoiding over-fitting), and batch size and learning rates on 20% of the cross-validation/development set. We varied batch sizes, drop-out rate, embedding sizes, and learning rate on development set. We obtained the best CNN performance with learning rate decay 0.95, batch size 50, drop-out 0.5, and embedding size 300 and ran 20 epochs on cross validated dataset. For LSTM, we got the best results on development set with learning rate 0.001, drop-out 0.5, and embedding size 300, batch-size of 32 and at 12 epochs. We used same settings similar to the development set but varied drop-out rate over [0.5,0.6,0.7] and obtained best results on test set using drop-out 0.7. We obtained best results on test set with drop-out 0.5 using average pooling.

Pre-compiled Embeddings. We used the gensim (ehek and Sojka, 2010) word2vec program to compile embeddings from the given training corpus. We compiled 300-dimensional embedding vectors for the words that appear at least 3 times in the Arabic dialect corpus, and for rest of the vocabulary, embedding vectors are assigned uniform distribution in the range of $[-0.25, 0.25]$. We used these pre-compiled embeddings in LSTM and reported run2 results in the test set.

4 Datasets and Results

In this section we describe about DSL 2016 shared task data sets and the experimental results.

---

[2] https://github.com/yoonkim/CNN_sentence
[3] http://deeplearning.net/tutorial/lstm.html

	egy	glf	lav	msa	nor	Total
Train	1578	1671	1758	999	1612	7618
Test	315	256	344	274	351	1540
Total	1893	1927	2102	1273	1963	9158

Table 1: The distribution of training and test data sets

4.1 Datasets

In 2016, for the first time the DSL shared task included a sub-task on Arabic dialects for 5 dialects: Egyptian, Gulf, Levantine, North-African, and Modern Standard Arabic (MSA) As dialects are mostly used in conversational speech, DSL 2016 shared task supplied training and test datasets (Malmasi et al., 2016) containing ASR transcripts. Test set contains uniform distribution of dialects related to ASR texts. The distribution of training and test splits are shown in table 1. The samples in test set are slightly unbalanced.

4.2 Results

We evaluated the given test set using both LSTM and CNN and presented the results as shown in table 2. DSL shared task results are evaluated using weighted-F1 measure for ranking of various participating systems. Due to the imbalance of classes in the test set, majority baseline is used in this Arabic dialect classification task. We have obtained run1 results (0.1779 F1-weighted) with LSTM-based dialect classification model using random embedding weights at the input layer. Run2 results (0.1944 F1) are obtained using LSTM-model with pre-compiled word embeddings. Though run2 results are better than run1 but LSTM-model poorly performed when compared to the base line results (0.2279 weighted-F1) on the test set. We have obtained fairly comparable results on experimental held-out development set without pre-compiled embeddings as shown in table 3. We identified that the poor results on test set are due to the bug in the code of LSTM-results compilation. Post competition, we fixed the bug and re-evaluated results on test set as shown in tables 5 and 6. We observe that LSTM without using pooling before the softmax layer, performed slightly better (0.4231 F1-weighted) than using average pooling (0.4172 F1-weighted). LSTM without pooling classified 'egy', 'msa' and 'nor' dialects more accurately than the LSTM with average pooling. LSTM with average pooling performed better than the LSTM without pooling in classifying 'glf' and 'lav' dialect classes. Run 3 results are obtained using CNN classification model without using pre-compiled embeddings. We observe that the CNN performance (0.4329 F1-weighted) is better than the LSTM performance (0.4231 F1-weighted). The performance of different dialect classes accuracy using CNN is visualized in the confusion matrix as shown in figure 3. We also present the 5-fold cross validation results as shown in the table 4. CNN in cross validation setting outperformed LSTM-results on development set in four dialect classes (egy,lav,msa,nor) where as LSTM performed better in case of 'glf' dialect classification. It took 24 hours to perform 5-fold cross validation using CNN on a single CPU, 8-GB RAM, Intel, i7-processor machine. We have also tried building model using CNN and LSTM on sub-task1 but took 10 days of time to train on entire training set and unable to test it on the test set and produce results in-time. The limitation of CNN and LSTM is that they need more time to train on on CPU machines and this can be avoided by using GPU machines.

Test Set	Track	Run	**Accuracy**	**F1 (micro)**	**F1 (macro)**	**F1 (weighted)**
run1	C	closed	0.1961	0.1961	0.1715	0.1779
run2	C	closed	0.2162	0.2162	0.1876	0.1944
run3	C	closed	0.4377	0.4377	0.4364	**0.4329**
baseline	-	-	-	-	-	0.2279

Table 2: Results for test set C for all runs (closed training).

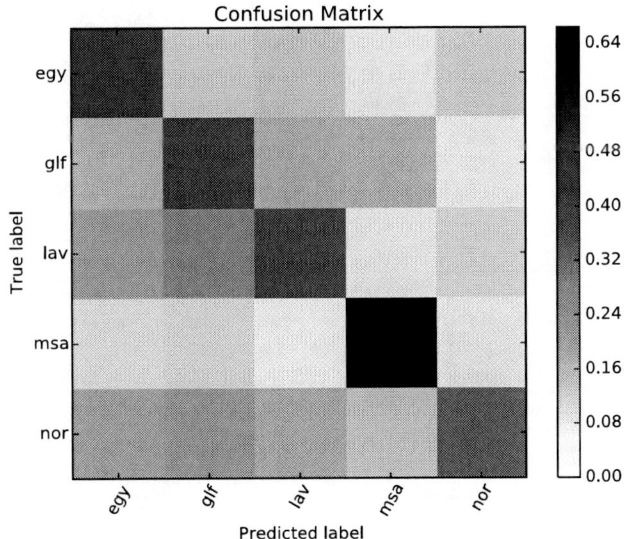

Figure 3: Run3 confusion matrix using CNN multi-class classification

	Precision	Recall	f1-score
egy	0.5694	0.5484	0.5587
glf	0.4444	0.5562	0.4940
lav	0.4704	0.4389	0.4541
msa	0.5922	0.6731	**0.6301**
nor	0.5444	0.4171	0.4723

Table 3: LSTM experimental results (run1) on development set without embeddings after 12 epochs of training.

5   Discussion and Conclusion

We can assess the degree of confusion between various dialect classes from the confusion matrix of CNN classification model as shown in figure 3. MSA and Egypt are the dialects that are more accurately identified when compared to the other dialects. North-african and Laventine have the highest degree of confusion, mostly with Egypt and gulf Arabic dialects. This might be due to the geographically in close contact with these languages. We also observe significant amount of confusion between gulf and the Egyptian and leventine dialects. In our experiments, we observed that CNN performed better than the LSTM for Arabic dialect classification. There are number of potential directions to improve the dialect classification accuracy. One possible future work might be to compile the common vocabulary among most confusing dialect classes and for these vocabulary compile the word embeddings from large, unlabeled dialect corpora using neural networks, and encode both syntactic and semantic properties of words. Studies have found the learned word vectors to capture linguistic regularities and to collapse similar words into groups (Mikolov et al., 2013b).

As our proposed CNN model is built using default network parameters, tuning of hyper-parameters can significantly improve the dialect classification accuracy and this will be considered as our future work. Learning word embeddings from the larger dialect corpus and using them in the input layer of CNN and LSTM networks can also improve the dialect classification accuracy. Since Arabic language dialects are morphologically rich and pose various syntactic and semantic challenges at word level, experimenting with character level CNNs and bi-directional LSTMs can be more useful for accurate classification of

	Precision	Recall	f1-score
egy	0.5582	0.6363	0.5947
glf	0.4716	0.4629	0.4672
lav	0.6153	0.4861	0.5432
msa	0.6597	0.7356	**0.6956**
nor	0.5750	0.6174	0.5954

Table 4: CNN Average 5-fold cross-validation results (run3) without embeddings after 20 epochs

	Precision	Recall	f1-score
egy	0.4444	0.4190	0.4314
glf	0.3172	0.2305	0.2670
lav	0.4179	0.4215	0.4197
msa	0.4605	0.6606	**0.5427**
nor	0.4637	0.4188	0.4401
F1 (macro)	-	-	**0.4202**
F1 (weighted)	-	-	**0.4232**

Table 5: LSTM experimental results on test set **without pooling**

	Precision	Recall	f1-score
egy	0.4353	0.3523	0.3895
glf	0.2678	0.3516	0.3040
lav	0.4059	0.4389	0.4218
msa	0.5301	0.5146	**0.5222**
nor	0.4662	0.4131	0.4381
F1 (macro)	-	-	**0.4151**
F1 (weighted)	-	-	**0.4172**

Table 6: LSTM experimental results on test set **with average pooling**

various Arbaic dialects. As our proposed approach do not rely much on language specific analysis on the corpus, it can be easily adapted to more similar languages, varieties and classification tasks.

References

Fadi Biadsy, Julia Hirschberg, and Nizar Habash. 2009. Spoken arabic dialect identification using phonotactic modeling. In *Proceedings of the eacl 2009 workshop on computational approaches to semitic languages*, pages 53–61. Association for Computational Linguistics.

Ronan Collobert, Jason Weston, Léon Bottou, Michael Karlen, Koray Kavukcuoglu, and Pavel Kuksa. 2011. Natural language processing (almost) from scratch. *The Journal of Machine Learning Research*, 12:2493–2537.

Kareem Darwish, Hassan Sajjad, and Hamdy Mubarak. 2014. Verifiably effective arabic dialect identification. In *EMNLP*, pages 1465–1468.

Heba Elfardy and Mona T Diab. 2013. Sentence level dialect identification in arabic. In *ACL (2)*, pages 456–461.

Marc Franco-Salvador, Paolo Rosso, and Francisco Rangel. 2015. Distributed representations of words and documents for discriminating similar languages. In *Proceedings of the Joint Workshop on Language Technology for Closely Related Languages, Varieties and Dialects (LT4VarDial)*, pages 11–16, Hissar, Bulgaria.

Felix A. Gers, Jürgen Schmidhuber, and Fred Cummins. 2000. Learning to forget: Continual prediction with LSTM. *Neural Computation*, 12(10):2451–2471.

Felix Gers. 2001. *Long Short-term Memory in Recurrent Neural Networks*. Ph.D. thesis, Universität Hannover.

Cyril Goutte and Serge Leger. 2015. Experiments in discriminating similar languages. In *Proceedings of the Joint Workshop on Language Technology for Closely Related Languages, Varieties and Dialects (LT4VarDial)*, pages 78–84, Hissar, Bulgaria.

Cyril Goutte, Serge Léger, and Marine Carpuat. 2014. The nrc system for discriminating similar languages. In *Proceedings of the First Workshop on Applying NLP Tools to Similar Languages, Varieties and Dialects (VarDial)*, pages 139–145, Dublin, Ireland.

Cyril Goutte, Serge Léger, Shervin Malmasi, and Marcos Zampieri. 2016. Discriminating Similar Languages: Evaluations and Explorations.

Alex Graves. 2013. Generating sequences with recurrent neural networks. *CoRR*, abs/1308.0850.

Nizar Habash, Owen Rambow, Mona Diab, and Reem Kanjawi-Faraj. 2008. Guidelines for annotation of arabic dialectness. In *Proceedings of the LREC Workshop on HLT & NLP within the Arabic world*, pages 49–53.

Sepp Hochreiter and Jürgen Schmidhuber. 1997. Long short-term memory. *Neural Computation*, 9(8):1735–1780.

Rie Johnson and Tong Zhang. 2015. Semi-supervised convolutional neural networks for text categorization via region embedding. In *Advances in neural information processing systems*, pages 919–927.

Yoon Kim. 2014. Convolutional neural networks for sentence classification. In *Proceedings of the 2014 Conference on Empirical Methods in Natural Language Processing*, pages 1746–1751.

Siwei Lai, Liheng Xu, Kang Liu, and Jun Zhao. 2015. Recurrent convolutional neural networks for text classification. In *AAAI*, pages 2267–2273.

Yann LeCun and Yoshua Bengio. 1995. Convolutional networks for images, speech, and time series. In Michael A. Arbib, editor, *The Handbook of Brain Theory and Neural Networks*, pages 255–258. MIT Press, Cambridge, MA.

Yun Lei and John HL Hansen. 2011. Dialect classification via text-independent training and testing for arabic, spanish, and chinese. *IEEE Transactions on Audio, Speech, and Language Processing*, 19(1):85–96.

Shervin Malmasi and Mark Dras. 2014. Arabic native language identification. In *Proceedings of the Arabic Natural Language Processing Workshop (EMNLP 2014)*, pages 180–186. Citeseer.

Shervin Malmasi and Mark Dras. 2015. Language identification using classifier ensembles. In *Proceedings of the Joint Workshop on Language Technology for Closely Related Languages, Varieties and Dialects (LT4VarDial)*, pages 35–43, Hissar, Bulgaria.

Shervin Malmasi, Eshrag Refaee, and Mark Dras. 2015. Arabic Dialect Identification using a Parallel Multidialectal Corpus. In *Proceedings of the 14th Conference of the Pacific Association for Computational Linguistics (PACLING 2015)*, pages 209–217, Bali, Indonesia, May.

Shervin Malmasi, Marcos Zampieri, Nikola Ljubešić, Preslav Nakov, Ahmed Ali, and Jörg Tiedemann. 2016. Discriminating between similar languages and arabic dialect identification: A report on the third dsl shared task. In *Proceedings of the 3rd Workshop on Language Technology for Closely Related Languages, Varieties and Dialects (VarDial)*, Osaka, Japan.

Tomas Mikolov, Ilya Sutskever, Kai Chen, Greg S Corrado, and Jeff Dean. 2013a. Distributed representations of words and phrases and their compositionality. In *Advances in Neural Information Processing Systems 26*, pages 3111–3119.

Tomas Mikolov, Wen-tau Yih, and Geoffrey Zweig. 2013b. Linguistic regularities in continuous space word representations. In *Proceedings of the 2013 Conference of the North American Chapter of the Association for Computational Linguistics: Human Language Technologies*, pages 746–751.

Hamid Palangi, Li Deng, Yelong Shen, Jianfeng Gao, Xiaodong He, Jianshu Chen, Xinying Song, and Rabab Ward. 2016. Deep sentence embedding using long short-term memory networks: Analysis and application to information retrieval. *IEEE/ACM Transactions on Audio, Speech, and Language Processing*, 24(4):694–707.

Razvan Pascanu, Tomas Mikolov, and Yoshua Bengio. 2013. On the difficulty of training recurrent neural networks. In *Proceedings of the 30th International Conference on Machine Learning*, volume 3, pages 1310–1318.

Radim ehek and Petr Sojka. 2010. Software framework for topic modelling with large corpora. In *Proceedings of the LREC 2010 Workshop on New Challenges for NLP Frameworks*.

Francesco Visin, Kyle Kastner, Kyunghyun Cho, Matteo Matteucci, Aaron Courville, and Yoshua Bengio. 2015. Renet: A recurrent neural network based alternative to convolutional networks. *arXiv preprint arXiv:1505.00393*.

Omar F Zaidan and Chris Callison-Burch. 2011. The arabic online commentary dataset: an annotated dataset of informal arabic with high dialectal content. In *Proceedings of the 49th Annual Meeting of the Association for Computational Linguistics: Human Language Technologies: short papers-Volume 2*, pages 37–41. Association for Computational Linguistics.

Omar F Zaidan and Chris Callison-Burch. 2014. Arabic dialect identification. *Computational Linguistics*, 40(1):171–202.

Marcos Zampieri and Binyam Gebrekidan Gebre. 2012. Automatic identification of language varieties: The case of portuguese. In *KONVENS2012-The 11th Conference on Natural Language Processing*, pages 233–237. Österreichischen Gesellschaft für Artificial Intelligende (ÖGAI).

Marcos Zampieri, Liling Tan, Nikola Ljubešić, and Jörg Tiedemann. 2014. A report on the dsl shared task 2014. In *Proceedings of the First Workshop on Applying NLP Tools to Similar Languages, Varieties and Dialects (VarDial)*, pages 58–67, Dublin, Ireland.

Marcos Zampieri, Binyam Gebrekidan Gebre, Hernani Costa, and Josef van Genabith. 2015a. Comparing approaches to the identification of similar languages. In *Proceedings of the Joint Workshop on Language Technology for Closely Related Languages, Varieties and Dialects (LT4VarDial)*, pages 66–72, Hissar, Bulgaria.

Marcos Zampieri, Liling Tan, Nikola Ljubešić, Jörg Tiedemann, and Preslav Nakov. 2015b. Overview of the dsl shared task 2015. In *Proceedings of the Joint Workshop on Language Technology for Closely Related Languages, Varieties and Dialects (LT4VarDial)*, pages 1–9, Hissar, Bulgaria.

Matthew D. Zeiler. 2012. ADADELTA: An adaptive learning rate method. *CoRR*, abs/1212.5701.

Xiang Zhang, Junbo Zhao, and Yann LeCun. 2015. Character-level convolutional networks for text classification. In *Advances in Neural Information Processing Systems*, pages 649–657.

Peng Zhou, Wei Shi, Jun Tian, Zhenyu Qi, Bingchen Li, Hongwei Hao, and Bo Xu. 2016. Attention-based bidirectional long short-term memory networks for relation classification. In *The 54th Annual Meeting of the Association for Computational Linguistics*, page 207.

Language and Dialect Discrimination Using Compression-Inspired Language Models

Paul McNamee
Johns Hopkins University
Human Language Technology Center of Excellence
mcnamee@jhu.edu

Abstract

The DSL 2016 shared task continued previous evaluations from 2014 and 2015 that facilitated the study of automated language and dialect identification. This paper describes results for this year's shared task and from several related experiments conducted at the Johns Hopkins University Human Language Technology Center of Excellence (JHU HLTCOE). Previously the HLTCOE has explored the use of compression-inspired language modeling for language and dialect identification, using news, Wikipedia, blog, and Twitter corpora. The technique we have relied upon is based on prediction by partial matching (PPM), a state of the art text compression technique. Due to the close relationship between adaptive compression and language modeling, such compression techniques can also be applied to multi-way text classification problems, and previous studies have examined tasks such as authorship attribution, email spam detection, and topical classification. We applied our approach to the multi-class decision that considered each dialect or language as a possibility for the given shared task input line. Results for testset A were in accord with our expectations, however results for testsets B and C were notably worse.

1 Introduction

Automated language identification (LID) can be defined as the task of predicting the dominant language being used by the author of a text. Often the decision task is formulated as selecting one language from a fixed inventory of languages, although it is not uncommon to extend the problem to indicating "none of the above" when it is believed that the text is not written in one of the listed languages. For comparatively large input texts (*i.e.,* texts longer than a sentence or two), choosing between only a few languages, or when it is diverse languages that are being considered, high levels of accuracy can be achieved (*i.e.,* over 99%).

The *Discriminating between Similar Languages* (DSL) shared task was started in 2014 and it is now in its third year. The DSL'16 task (Malmasi et al., 2016) is focused on distinguishing between highly related languages, which is a more challenging problem than the general case. Examples include distinguishing between mutually-intelligible variants of a regional language (*e.g.,* Bosnian, Croatian, and Serbian variants of Serbo-Croatian) or among dialects of imperial languages (*e.g.,* between African, European, and South American Portuguese).

A variety of approaches have been used for language identification since the increased availability of multilingual corpora in the early 1990s. These include vector comparisons (*e.g.,* cosine similarity) (Damashek, 1995), language modeling (Dunning, 1994; Grefenstette, 1995), and supervised machine learning (Baldwin and Lui, 2010; Zampieri, 2013).

In recent years, there has been increased interest in LID due to the the growth of international (*i.e.,* multilingual) social media platforms. Such user-generated texts tend to be short, less grammatical, and contain highly variable spellings and the frequent use of abbreviations, shorthands, emoticons, and other confounding phenomena which can complicate language identification.

Proceedings of the Third Workshop on NLP for Similar Languages, Varieties and Dialects,
pages 195–203, Osaka, Japan, December 12 2016.

In this paper we discuss the use of compression-inspired language models for predicting the language of texts. In Section 2 we describe classification using the prediction by partial matching algorithm. In Section 3 we report experiments on language identification. In Section 4 we discuss our participation in the DSL'16 challenge and briefly summarize results. Section 5 briefly mentions a few related studies.

2   Prediction by Partial Matching

Prediction by Partial Matching (PPM) is a data compression algorithm developed in the early 1980s when RAM, external storage, and network bandwidth were considerably less abundant than is the case today.

2.1   Overview

Cleary and Witten described the algorithm (1984) and presented two methods for smoothing probability estimates (termed Methods *A* and *B*). A few years later Moffat investigated engineering improvements to the algorithm and introduced a set of parameter estimation enhancements collectively known as Method *C* (or PPM-C).

PPM is based on a variable-order Markov language model that contains a parameter N which is the maximal order. When used to compress data files, observations from previously seen data are used to estimate the likelihood of observing a symbol[1] in a given context. Generally longer contexts are used when available, starting with the maximal order N. However, the method backs off to use shorter contexts when a symbol has not been observed in a longer context. Crucially, a context-dependent *penalty*[2] is applied when backing off is required.

As an example, seeing a 'z', 't', or 'c' is not uncommon following a left-context of "[space] q u i" in English. But an 'h' would be very unlikely. To represent 'h' after "q u i" it will be necessary to back-off using the estimates from shorter contexts such as "u i". If an 'h' has never been observed after "u i" then the process continues, with an additional penalty, and further recursive backoff for 'h' after a context of a single symbol ('i').

The A/B/C/D variants of PPM differ in how they model backoff, or "escape" probabilities. The later variants of PPM (*e.g.,* PPM-C or PPM-D) are considered to achieve more compact codes than the earlier versions.

2.2   Compression-inspired Classification

Adaptive compression is concerned with representing symbols in a minimal number of bits, based on a model trained from a given history (or dataset). This approach can be turned on its head in the following way. Given several models $M_1, M_2, ..., M_n$, each trained from different datasets, and a input text fragment T, choose the model that will encode T in the fewest number of bits. This type of analysis is commonly used with traditional Markov language models (*e.g.,* Dunning (1994)).

PPM and related compression techniques have been applied to a variety of classification tasks. Frank *et al.* (2000) used PPM for topical text classification tasks using the Reuters 21578 dataset; their results were not at the level of the state of the art.

The earliest use of entropy-based compression techniques for language identification can probably be attributed to Teahan (2000). He examined several large texts in six Western European languages; his illustration of the method was simplistic, but clear. In the same study he conducts additional experiments in authorship attribution and topic identification.

Between 2005 and 2007, the NIST Text REtrieval Conference (TREC) ran an evaluation of email spam detection. Methods based on compression-inspired language models such as PPM and Dynamic Markov Compression (DMC) were among the top performing approaches (Bratko et al., 2006; Cormack, 2008).

One explanation for why compression-based methods succeed for authorship attribution, language identification, and spam detection, is that decisions can be informed based on short contexts (*e.g.,* character n-grams of lengths 3 to 7). Tasks like topic classification would appear to be a less good fit.

---

[1]This could be a byte, an UTF-8 character, or a even a word if the stream was at the word level.

[2]This penalty is sometimes called the escape probability.

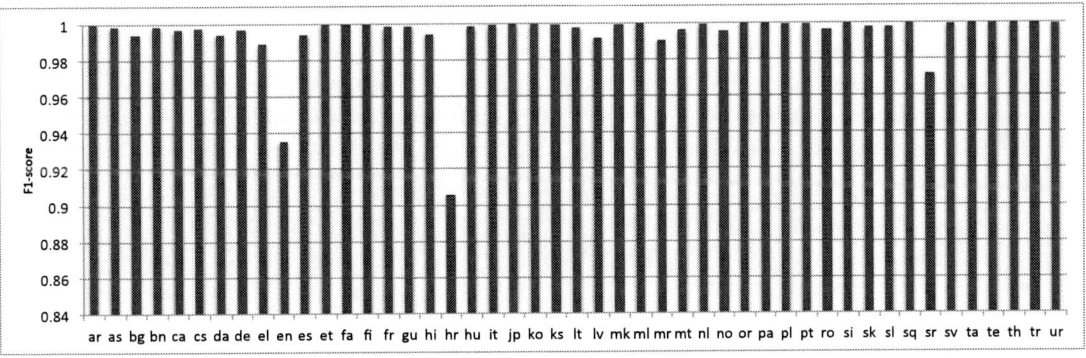

Figure 1: F_1 score by language for 47-way LID classification. Data are single sentences. Both training and test exemplars were drawn from "high quality" corpora (e.g., Europarl, EMILLE, Leipzig, and other national corpora).

3   LID Experiments

In these experiments we use PPM-A, a decision that was undertaken based on the fact our existing software (Bergsma et al., 2012) relies on hash-tables to store frequency counts. Refactoring the source code to use suffix trees would make it easier to adopt the parameter estimate techniques in PPM-C, but we did not have time before this year's evaluation to consider such a change.

3.1   Initial Testing

For some very preliminary experiments, we begain by assembling a 47-language collection from extant corpora, including well-known sources such as Europarl (v5), the Leipzig corpus, the EMILLE corpus, and other available national corpora. Using 90k sentences for training, and 10k sentences for testing, we attempted the 47-way classification task using PPM-A with order $n = 4$, attaining a macro-averaged F_1 score of 99.4%. This seemed promising. Furthermore, the majority of the mistakes were in Bosnian, Croatian, and English data, and much of the error was due to mis-labelled data. The per-language F_1 scores are shown in Figure 1.

The use of Wikipedia text was considered for training and experimentation in a greater number of languages. However, there are a great many instances of code switching or "English pollution", where articles in a given language's Wikipedia contain much text written in other languages, especially English. For these and other pragmatic reasons, we encourage caution when using Wikipedia corpora for language identification training or testing.

3.2   DSL '15

To prepare for the DSL'16 shared task, we experimented with the shared task data from 2015 (DSLCC version 2.0, test set A). We sought to investigate the effects of the PPM maximal order, the use of case normalization, the directionality of scoring text, additional text normalizations, and the use of outside data.

In the sections below we report our findings using the accuracy scores reported by the *evaluate.py* script released with the 2015 data. Because the compression-based classifier does not require tuning hyper-parameters, both the *task1-train* and *task1-dev* files were used to build a model and scoring was done against the *task1-test* file.

As we were not concerned with confusions between dissimilar languages (*e.g.*, we were not worried about confusing Argentine Spanish for Indonesian or Serbian), we did not rely on hierarchical decision making (*e.g.*, predicting language family first, and then a specific language or dialect).

3.2.1 Maximal order

Maximal orders of $n = 4$ or $n = 5$ often seem to work well. To consider a wider range of possibilities, we looked at values of n from 3 to 6. In this first trial, no normalization of case, punctuation, etc... was performed. Each input line was scored in two ways, either from left-to-right (LTR) or from right-to-left (RTL). Results are shown in Table 1.

Order	LTR	RTL
3	90.96	90.99
4	92.87	92.78
5	93.11	93.03
6	92.93	92.79

Table 1: Comparison of PPM order and direction of processing.

Using a maximal order of $n = 5$ achieved the overall best result, and $n = 3$ was notably worse.

3.2.2 Case normalization

Next transformation of the input texts to lower-case was examined. Results are shown in Table 2. Somewhat surprisingly, a slight decline in performance occurs when case information is removed. An order of $n = 5$ is still the best choice.

Order	LTR	RTL
3	89.75	89.96
4	92.85	92.85
5	92.96	92.89
6	92.80	92.67

Table 2: Comparison of PPM order and case-folding. Performance drops without case information.

3.2.3 Digit conflation and bidirectionality

Arguably Roman digits should not be very indicative of language. Therefore we explored mapping the digits $[1 - 9]$ to the digit 1 (chosen as a representative). Also, rather than score the input text in only one direction, we also considered bidirectional scoring. To produce a bidirectional score the forward (*i.e.,* LTR) and backward (*i.e.,* RTL) probabilities were combined. The bidirectional probability was computed as follows:

$$p_{bi} = \sqrt{p_{ltr} \times p_{rtl}} \tag{1}$$

Table 3 shows a very slight adjustment from conflating digits compared to the results in Table 1 when scoring in only one direction. However, combining evidence from both directions seems to help materially.

A score of 93.34 would have been ranked 7th if it were an official submission in 2015 according to Table 5 in Zampieri *et al.* (2015).

Order	LTR	RTL	Both
3	91.01	91.01	**91.06**
4	92.92	92.82	**93.04**
5	93.13	93.16	**93.34**
6	92.99	92.79	**93.15**

Table 3: Use of case preservation, digit conflation, and combination of directionality. Our best results for the DSL'15 dataset.

3.2.4 External Data

Generally with supervised learning using greater amounts of data to build models leads to higher levels of performance. Therefore we tried one additional experiment where 20k sentences were added to the training set. We used 20k sentences from Wikipedia text for Bosian, Croatian, Serbian, Indonesian, and Malaysian. We used newspaper sources for Iberian Spanish (EFE), Brazilian Portuguese (Folha), and European Portuguese (Publico). No data were added for Czech, Slovakian, Bulgarian, Macedonian, Argentine Spanish, or the unknown category "xx".

The results in Table 4 were disappointing; an average of about 1.3 points in accuracy were lost. One possible conjecture could be that the test data are drawn from a similar distribution as the training data. Were that to be the case, then adding external data that is not *i.i.d.* to the training and test data could be expected to be more harmful than helpful.

Order	LTR	RTL	Both
3	88.54	88.41	88.55
4	91.25	90.91	91.15
5	92.07	01.67	92.06
6	91.70	91.54	92.00

Table 4: Augmenting training data using external corpora – compare results to Table 3. The use of additional data degrades performance.

4 Participation in DSL'16

As a result of the trials reported in Section 3 we anticipated that our best results would be obtained using an order of $n = 5$, preserving case, conflating digits, and scoring text bidirectionally. As use of external corpora had not improved in our earlier results, we did not submit any "open" results, restricting models to using the provided training data.

We spent approximately one day working with the DSL'15 data in preparation for the current evaluation. About 3 hours was spent working on the DSL'16 task and preparing submissions.

4.1 Submitted Runs

Table 5 describes the characteristics of the submitted runs. The B1 and B2 partitions were treated identically to each other.

Task	Run	Conditions
A	1 - closed	PPMA (5), bidirectional, case preserved, digit-folding
A	2 - closed	PPMA (5), bidirectional, lower-cased, all non-letter, non-whitespace characters deleted
B	1 - closed	PPMA (5), bidirectional, case preserved, digit-folding
B	2 - closed	PPMA (5), bidirectional, lower-cased, all non-letter, non-whitespace characters deleted
C	1 - closed	PPMA (4), bidirectional, no text normalization
C	2 - closed	PPMA (5), bidirectional, no text normalization
C	3 - closed	PPMA (6), bidirectional, no text normalization

Table 5: Characteristics of submitted runs.

Results for each run are given in Table 6 below.

4.2 Discussion

4.2.1 Test Set A

The Task 1 (Test Set A) data (Tan et al., 2014) was fairly similar to the DSL'15 task, and our submission was ranked around what we would expect. The accuracy of our hltcoe-closed-A-run1 (A1) submission was 0.8772 and ranked 10th out of 17 teams. The maximum reported accuracy was 0.8938, and the

Test Set	Track	Run	Accuracy	F1 (micro)	F1 (macro)
A	closed	run1	0.8772	0.8772	0.8769
A	closed	run2	0.8727	0.8727	0.8729
B1	closed	run1	0.5300	0.5300	0.5101
B1	closed	run2	0.5460	0.5460	0.4934
B2	closed	run1	0.5100	0.5100	0.4965
B2	closed	run2	0.5540	0.5540	0.5132
C	closed	run1	0.4123	0.4123	0.4111
C	closed	run2	0.3870	0.3870	0.3803
C	closed	run3	0.3909	0.3909	0.3858

Table 6: Results for all hltcoe runs.

lowest score was 0.8253. With twelve classes, a purely random baseline would have an accuracy of only 0.083; however, most languages or dialects only have one or two other confusable classes, so it is natural to expect performance above 0.33 or 0.50.

From Table 6 we can compare the effectiveness of our two Task-1 submissions. Run 1 (case preserved, minimal normalization) was marginally more effective than Run 2 which employed more aggressive text normalization. The confusion matrix[3] for Run 1 is given below in Table 7 and graphially in Figure 2. Bosnian and Mexican Spanish proved to be the most challenging classes.

	bs	es-ar	es-es	es-mx	fr-ca	fr-fr	hr	id	my	pt-br	pt-pt	sr
bs	749	0	0	0	0	0	132	0	0	0	0	119
es-ar	0	869	58	71	0	0	1	0	0	1	0	0
es-es	0	56	813	126	0	3	0	0	0	0	2	0
es-mx	0	111	178	711	0	0	0	0	0	0	0	0
fr-ca	0	0	0	0	875	125	0	0	0	0	0	0
fr-fr	0	0	0	0	17	981	0	0	1	1	0	0
hr	137	1	0	0	0	0	852	0	0	0	0	10
id	0	0	0	0	0	0	0	984	15	0	0	1
my	0	0	0	0	0	0	0	40	960	0	0	0
pt-br	0	0	0	0	0	0	0	0	0	947	53	0
pt-pt	0	0	0	0	0	0	0	0	0	84	916	0
sr	116	0	0	0	0	1	13	0	0	0	0	870

Table 7: Confusion maxtrix for hltcoe run 1 (test set A – closed training).

4.2.2 Social Media data

As the DSL'15 data had been single sentences from journalistic texts, we had expected the DSL'16 social media data to be single tweets with one message per line. We were preparing submissions just hours before the deadline, and it came as quite a surprise upon unpacking the test-set zip file to find that the data contained multiple tweets per line, and that a given user's tweets could be in multiple languages. Due to time limitations it wasn't feasible for us to do anything other than treat the input like the data in Test Set A and simply ignore this phenomena. Thus, the input line was treated as one, possibly long message.

Additionally, we did not remove any hashtags, URLs, or other potentially English-looking twitter phenomena. Together these two factors contributed to our very low ranking on this test set (*i.e.,* last of 14 systems).

---

[3] Note the ISO 639-1 digraph for Malaysian is ms, however, the released data was mistakenly labeled as my, the code for Burmese. The my label was retained for consistency with other papers.

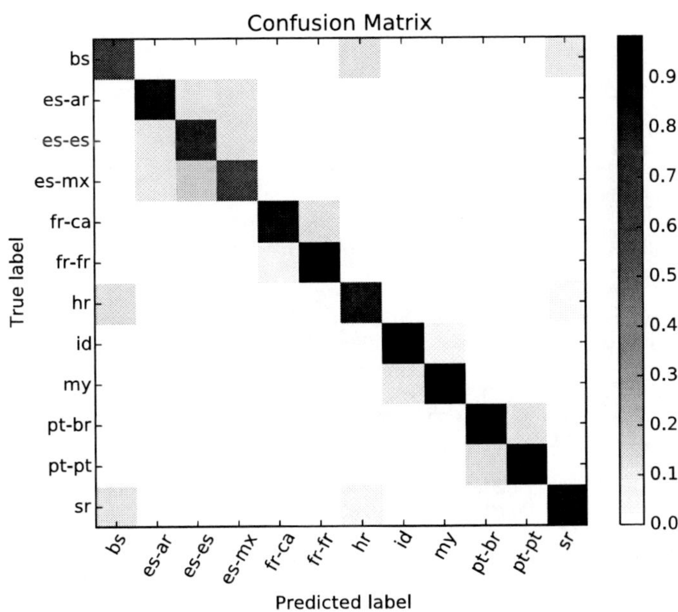

Figure 2: Graphical depiction of the confusion matrix for hltcoe run 1 (test set A – closed training).

4.2.3　Task 2 / Test Set C dataset

It also came as a last-minute surprise to find that the dialectal Arabic dataset was phonetically encoded and not expressed in native orthography. We had previously worked with written dialect identification using the test sets produced by Zaidan and Callison-Burch (2011; 2014). Working with automatically produced phonetic representations is undoubtably a more challenging task, but not one that we were prepared for. In hindsight, it would have been worthwhile to examine the training data beforehand. Our runs were ranked 15th of 18 systems.

5　Related Work

Use of character-level n-grams for LID is not new. Cavnar and Trenkle (1994) developed the TextCat system, which has served as a publicly available LID baseline for over two decades.

Information-theoretic and compression-based techniques have been used for LID for some time. Besides Teahan's early work (2000), such approaches were "rediscovered" by Benedetto *et al.* (2002), generating some controversy in the computational linguistics community (Goodman, 2002).

Bobicev submitted results to the DSL'15 shared task using the PPM-C variant (2015). Our results appear similar to her published results on the 2015 task; we suspect that her use of PPM-C vs. our use of PPM-A is probably responsible for her higher score (94.14 vs. 93.34) on that dataset.

Other recent work in language detection includes: (Baldwin and Lui, 2010; Gottron and Lipka, 2010; Lui and Baldwin, 2011; Tromp and Pechenizkiy, 2011; Bergsma et al., 2012; Carter et al., 2013; Brown, 2014).

6　Conclusions

We think compression-inspired classification is a reasonable technique for tasks such as language and dialect identification which are highly informed from short character n-grams. Use of PPM-A with a maximal order of $n = 5$ was most effective and notably better than a value of $n = 3$. Scoring texts bidirectionally consistently improved performance. Our middle of the pack ranking in the Task-1 evaluation was on par with our expectations given our post-hoc testing with the DSL'15 dataset. In future work we would like to determine whether different methods for estimating escape probabilities, such as PPM-C, can yield superior results.

References

Timothy Baldwin and Marco Lui. 2010. Language identification: The long and the short of the matter. In *Proc. HLT-NAACL*, pages 229–237.

Dario Benedetto, Emanuele Caglioti, and Vittorio Loreto. 2002. Language trees and zipping. *Physical Review Letters*, 88(4):2–5.

Shane Bergsma, Paul McNamee, Mossaab Bagdouri, Clayton Fink, and Theresa Wilson. 2012. Language identification for creating language-specific twitter collections. In *Proceedings of the second workshop on language in social media*, pages 65–74. Association for Computational Linguistics.

Victoria Bobicev. 2015. Discriminating between similar languages using ppm. In *Joint Workshop on Language Technology for Closely Related Languages, Varieties and Dialects*, page 59.

Andrej Bratko, Gordon V. Cormack, Bogdan Filipic, Thomas R. Lynam, and Blaz Zupan. 2006. Spam filtering using statistical data compression models. *JMLR*, 6:2673–2698.

Ralf D Brown. 2014. Non-linear mapping for improved identification of 1300+ languages. In *Empirical Methods in Natural Language Processing*.

Simon Carter, Wouter Weerkamp, and Manos Tsagkias. 2013. Microblog language identification: Overcoming the limitations of short, unedited and idiomatic text. *Language Resources and Evaluation*, 47(1):195–215.

William B. Cavnar and John M. Trenkle. 1994. N-gram-based text categorization. In *Proc. Symposium on Document Analysis and Information Retrieval*, pages 161–175.

John G. Cleary, Ian, and Ian H. Witten. 1984. Data compression using adaptive coding and partial string matching. *IEEE Transactions on Communications*, 32:396–402.

Gordon V. Cormack. 2008. Email spam filtering: A systematic review. *Found. Trends Inf. Retr.*, 1(4):335–455, April.

Marc Damashek. 1995. Gauging similarity with n-grams: Language-independent categorization of text. *Science*, 267(5199):843.

Ted Dunning. 1994. Statistical identification of language. Technical Report 94-273, Computing Research Laboratory, New Mexico State University.

Eibe Frank, Chang Chui, and Ian H. Witten. 2000. Text categorization using compression models. In *Proc. DCC-00, IEEE Data Compression Conference, Snowbird, US*, pages 200–209. IEEE Computer Society Press.

J. Goodman. 2002. Extended Comment on Language Trees and Zipping. *eprint arXiv:cond-mat/0202383*, February.

Thomas Gottron and Nedim Lipka. 2010. A comparison of language identification approaches on short, query-style texts. In *Proc. ECIR*, pages 611–614.

Gregory Grefenstette. 1995. Comparing two language identication schemes. In *Proc. Third International Conference on Statistical Analysis of Text*.

Marco Lui and Timothy Baldwin. 2011. Cross-domain feature selection for language identification. In *Proc. IJCNLP*, pages 553–561.

Shervin Malmasi, Marcos Zampieri, Nikola Ljubešić, Preslav Nakov, Ahmed Ali, and Jörg Tiedemann. 2016. Discriminating between Similar Languages and Arabic Dialect Identification: A Report on the Third DSL Shared Task. In *Proceedings of the 3rd Workshop on Language Technology for Closely Related Languages, Varieties and Dialects (VarDial)*, Osaka, Japan.

Liling Tan, Marcos Zampieri, Nikola Ljubešic, and Jörg Tiedemann. 2014. Merging comparable data sources for the discrimination of similar languages: The dsl corpus collection. In *Proceedings of the 7th Workshop on Building and Using Comparable Corpora (BUCC)*, pages 11–15, Reykjavik, Iceland.

William John Teahan. 2000. Text classification and segmentation using minimum cross-entropy. In *Proc. RIAO*, pages 943–961.

Erik Tromp and Mykola Pechenizkiy. 2011. Graph-based n-gram language identication on short texts. In *Proc. 20th Machine Learning conference of Belgium and The Netherlands*, pages 27–34.

Omar F. Zaidan and Chris Callison-Burch. 2011. The arabic online commentary dataset: an annotated dataset of informal arabic with high dialectal content. In *Proc. ACL*, pages 37–41.

Omar F Zaidan and Chris Callison-Burch. 2014. Arabic dialect identification. *Computational Linguistics*, 40(1):171–202.

Marcos Zampieri, Liling Tan, Nikola Ljubešic, Jörg Tiedemann, and Preslav Nakov. 2015. Overview of the DSL shared task 2015. In *Joint Workshop on Language Technology for Closely Related Languages, Varieties and Dialects*, page 1.

Marcos Zampieri. 2013. Using bag-of-words to distinguish similar languages: How efficient are they? In *Computational Intelligence and Informatics (CINTI), 2013 IEEE 14th International Symposium on*, pages 37–41. IEEE.

Arabic Language WEKA-Based Dialect Classifier for Arabic Automatic Speech Recognition Transcripts

Areej Alshutayri , Eric Atwell , AbdulRahman AlOsaimy
James Dickins, Michael Ingleby and Janet Watson
University of Leeds, LS2 9JT, UK
ml14aooa@leeds.ac.uk, E.S.Atwell@leeds.ac.uk,
scama@leeds.ac.uk, J.Dickins@leeds.ac.uk,
inglebymeltham@binternet.com, J.C.E.Watson@leeds.ac.uk

Abstract

This paper describes an Arabic dialect identification system which we developed for the Discriminating Similar Languages (DSL) 2016 shared task. We classified Arabic dialects by using Waikato Environment for Knowledge Analysis (WEKA) data analytic tool which contains many alternative filters and classifiers for machine learning. We experimented with several classifiers and the best accuracy was achieved using the Sequential Minimal Optimization (SMO) algorithm for training and testing process set to three different feature-sets for each testing process. Our approach achieved an accuracy equal to 42.85% which is considerably worse in comparison to the evaluation scores on the training set of 80-90% and with training set 60:40 percentage split which achieved accuracy around 50%. We observed that Buckwalter transcripts from the Saarland Automatic Speech Recognition (ASR) system are given without short vowels, though the Buckwalter system has notation for these. We elaborate such observations, describe our methods and analyse the training dataset.

1 Introduction

Language Identification or Dialect Identification is the task of identifying the language or dialect of a written text. The task of Arabic dialect identification may require both computer scientists and Arabic linguistics experts. The Arabic language is one of the worlds major languages, and there is a common standard written form used worldwide, Modern Standard Arabic (MSA). MSA is based on the text of the Quran, the holy book of Islam; and MSA is taught in Arab schools, and promoted by Arab civil as well as religious authorities and governments. There are many dialects spoken around the Arab World; Arabic dialectologists have studied hundreds of local variations, but generally agree these cluster into five main regional dialects: Iraqi Dialect (IRQ), Levantine Dialect (LAV), Egyptian Dialect (EGY), North Africa Dialect (NOR), and Gulf Dialect (GLF) which is a subclass of Peninsular Arabic. Studies in Arabic dialectology focus on phonetic variation (Alorifi, 2008; Biadsy et al., 2009; Horesh and Cotter, 2016; Sadat et al., 2014). Horesh and Cotter (Horesh and Cotter, 2016) confirmed that past and current research is focussed on phonetic and phonological variation between Arabic dialects: all examples that they presented are of phoneme variation, and they did not mention any work on text, or corpus-based research, or of lexical or morpho-syntactic or grammar variation. However, Arabic spoken dialect does include local words, phrases, and even local variant morphology and grammar. With the spread of informal writing, for example on social networks and in local-dialect blogs, news and other online sources, Arabs are starting to write in their dialects. Because of the dominance of the MSA standard, there are no official writing standards for Arabic dialects, so spelling, morphology, lexis and grammar can be subject to individual transcription choice: it is up to a dialect speaker to decide how to write down their text. Dialect speakers have been taught from school to write down everything in MSA, so they may well normalise or translate into MSA rather than phonetically transcribe words and utterances. Pronunciation of vowels in words constitute one of the key differences between Arabic dialects; but in written MSA, most vowels are omitted, leaving few clues to distinguish the source dialect.

Proceedings of the Third Workshop on NLP for Similar Languages, Varieties and Dialects,
pages 204–211, Osaka, Japan, December 12 2016.

All this makes it challenging to collect an Arabic dialects texts corpus. Previous DSL shared tasks (Zampieri et al., 2015) were based on officially recognised and differentiated languages (Bosnian v Croatian v Serbian, Malay v Indonesian etc.) with readily-available published sources: Each example is a short text excerpt of 20100 tokens, sampled from journalistic texts . Local and national Arabic news sources and other journalistic text may include some local words but are still permeated and dominated by MSA, so a DSL Arabic dialects journalisic text data-set would be contaminated with MSA/dialect code-switching, and blocks of MSA. The DSL organisers tried instead to gather dialect data more directly from dialect speakers, and tried to avoid the problem of translation into MSA by using Automatic Speech Recognition rather than human scribes. However, these texts were often much shorter than 20-100 words, sometimes only 1 or 2 word utterances; and these short utterances could be common to two or more dialects, with no further indicators for differentiation. Arabic linguistics experts in our team found clear evidence of MSA in numerous dialect texts, possibly introduced by the ASR transcription method; and numerous short utterance instances which had no linguistic evidence of a specific Arabic dialect.

The DSL shared task (Malmasi et al., 2016) was to identify Arabic dialects in texts in five classes: EGY, GLF, LAV, NOR, and MSA; in utterance/phrase level identification which is more challenging than document dialect identification, since short texts have fewer identifying features. Arabic dialects classification is becoming important due to the increasing use of Arabic dialect in social media, and the importance of identification of the dialect before machine translation takes place, or search and retrieval of data (Lu and Mohamed, 2011). Furthermore, identifying the dialect may improve the Part-Of-Speech tagging: for example, the MADAMIRA toolkit identifies the dialect (MSA or EGY) prior to the POS tagging (Pasha et al., 2014). The task of Sentiment Analysis of texts, classifying the text as positive or negative sentiment, is also dialect-specific, as some diagnostic words (especially negation) differ from one dialect to another.

In this paper we describe our method for defining features and choosing the best combination of classifier and feature-set for this task. We show the results of different variants of SMO with different feature-tokenizers. Finally, we conclude the paper by discuss the limitations that affected our results.

2   Related Work

There have been many studies about Arabic dialect Identification. One of these studies presented by Zaidan and Callison-Burch (Zaidan and Callison-Burch, 2014). The authors focused on three Arabic dialects: Levantine, Gulf, and Egyptian and they created a large data set called the Arabic Online Commentary Dataset (AOCD) contained words in all dialects from readers' comments on the three online Arabic newspapers. They obtained 1.24M words from Al-Ghad newspaper (from Jordan to cover Levantine dialect), 18.8M form Al-Riyadh newspaper (from Saudi Arabia to cover Gulf dialect), and 32.1M form Al-Youm Al-Sabe newspaper (from Egypt to cover Egyptian dialect). They classify dialect using Nave Bayes and used wordGram and charcterNGram as features and trained the classifier using unigram, bigram, and trigram models for word, and unigram, trigram, and 5-gram for character model. Based on the dataset they used in training process they found that a unigram word model achieved best accuracy when examine the classifier using 10-fold cross validation (Zaidan and Callison-Burch, 2014). Another study built a system called LAHGA proposed to classify EGY dialect, LEV dialect, and MAG dialect (Lu and Mohamed, 2011). The authors used Tweets as a dataset for training and testing processes. Then begin manually identifying features by reading thousands of tweets and extracting features. They used three different classifiers, which are Nave Bayes classifier, Logistic Regression classifier, and Support Vector Machine classifier. The testing phase was divided into manual testing and cross-validation. During the manual testing process, they removed all noise and chosen 90 tweets, 30 from each dialect, whereas in a 10-flod cross-validation there is not any human intervention. The LAHGA performance shows 90% on a manual test and 75% on cross-validation.

Another research study to classify Arabic dialects used a sentence-level approach to classify whether the sentence was MSA or Egyptian dialect (Elfardy and Diab, 2013). They based the study on a supervised approach using Nave Bayes classifier which was trained on labelled sentences with two types of features: Core Features to indicate if the given sentence is dialectal or non-dialectal. Meta Features to estimate whether the sentence is informal or not. The system accuracy was about 85.5%.

3   Data

The data for the shared task provided from the DSL Corpus Collection (Ali et al., 2016) is a dataset containing ASR transcripts of utterances by Arabic dialect speakers; there was no guarantee that each utterance was unique to a dialect. The task is performed at the utterance-level and they provided us with two sets. The first set is for training and contains 7,619 utterances labelled and divided unevenly between 5 classes that cover four Arabic dialects (EGY, GLF, LAV, NOR), and MSA (it is not clear how MSA speakers were procured as MSA is not a spoken dialect). Table 1 shows the number of utterances for each class. The second set is for testing, consisting of 1,540 unlabelled utterances. The utterance length ranged from one word to 3305 words with an average of 40 words/utterance and standard deviation = 60. The number of utterances with word count less than 10 words is 1761 = 23.1%. Figure 1 shows the utterances distribution over utterance length.

Classes	Number of utterances
EGY	1578
GLF	1672
LAV	1758
NOR	1612
MSA	999

Table 1: The number of utterances for each class.

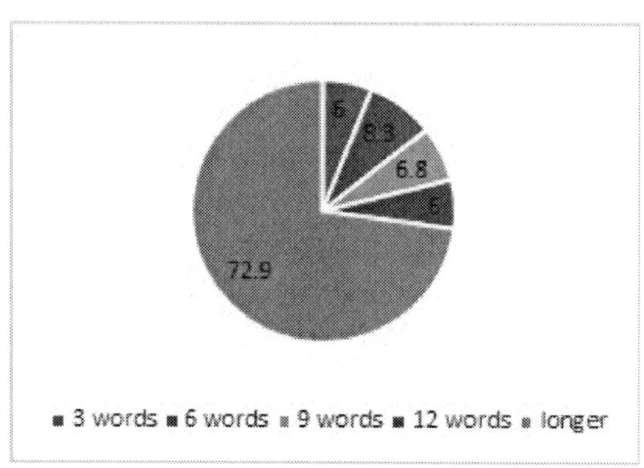

Figure 1: The sentences distribution over sentence length.

4   Method

At the beginning we tried to choose the best classifier for the Arabic Dialects Identification (ADI) task from a set of classifiers provided by WEKA (Hall et al., 2009) by measuring the performance of several classifiers on testing with the training dataset, 10-fold cross-validation, and by percentage split which divides the training set into 60% for training and 40% for testing. Table 2 reports results for a range of classifiers that we tried, using the WEKA StringToWordVector filter with WordTokenizer to extract words as features from utterance-strings. SMO was the best performing classifier. Table 3 shows the results of SMO using CharacterNGram Tokenizer with Max=3 and Min=1. Word Tokenizer method, also known as bag of words, is a filter that converts the utterances into a set of attributes that represents the occurrence of words (delimited by space, comma, etc) from the training set. It is designed to keep the n (which we set to 1000) top words per class. NGramWord Tokenizer is similar to Word Tokenizer with the exception that ability to also include word-sequences with the max and min number of words; while CharacterNGram Tokenizer counts 1-2- and/or 3-character n-grams in the utterance-string.

The second column in table 2 shows the results on the same (dialect-labelled) data as those used to train classifier. Third column represents the results on 10-fold cross-validation. The fourth column shows the results on a randomly selected 40% of original training data for test of classifiers trained on the other 60%. After running the experiments in Table 2, we realised that 10-fold cross-validation is very time-consuming (at least 10 times the duration of evaluation on training set or 60:40 percentage split) but produces the same classifier ranking, so we did not repeat the 10-fold cross-validation for table 3.

Classifier	Evaluate on training set	10-fold cross-validation	60% train, 40% test
NaiveBayes	47.09	45.01	43.93
SMO	**89.29**	**52.82**	**50.13**
J48	72.28	43.26	41.5
ZeroR	23.07	23.07	22.41
JRip	35.67	32.76	32.51

Table 2: The accuracy of different classifiers (WordTokenizer).

Classifier	Evaluate on training set	60% train, 40% test
SMO	**94.46**	**53.08**
J48	88.36	37.53
REPTree	53.71	35.56
JRip	41.62	36.35

Table 3: The accuracy of different classifiers (CharacterNGramTokenizer).

Looking at table 2, we noticed that by using SMO we got 6803 utterances correctly classified and 816 utterances misclassified. To improve the identification results we output the misclassified utterances and converted the text from Buckwalter to normal readable Arabic script because looking at the Buckwalter texts is difficult even if you know the Buckwalter transliteration system (Buckwalter, 2002). Then, we asked our Arabic linguistic experts to examine some of the texts which were misclassified, and try to find features which might correctly predict the dialect. Figure 2 shows example of misclassified utterances. The example shows the instance 4 is actually labelled class 2:GLF but the classifier made an error and predicted class 3:NOR.

```
inst#    actual  predicted        error prediction
4            2:GLF                  3:NOR
"$Ahd AlgrAfyk tfAqmh  Q    GLF"
شاهد الغرافيك تفاقمه"                Q    GLF"

15           2:GLF                  4:LAV
"$Ark wEqb Eqdyn llywm Em byEtrDwA mEkm lkn  Q    GLF"
شارك وعقب عقدين لليوم عم بيعترضوا معكم لكن"        Q        GLF"
```

Figure 2: Example of misclassified sentences.

The Arabic linguistics experts analysed the shortcomings in the misclassified utterances from the training data. They found that numerous texts are too short to say anything about their dialect origins, for example: $Ark is a short one-word text which appears unchanged labelled as different dialects. Some of the utterance seem to be entirely MSA despite having dialect labels, possibly due to the Automatic Speech Recognition method used; and a lot of the utterance have at least some MSA in them. Some utterances that have recognisable dialect words often have words -which are shared between two or more dialects. They even found some utterances labelled as one dialect but evidently containing words not from that dialect; for example in utterance (254) labelled as LAV in the training set contains a non-LAV lexical item, see figure 3.

```
inst#        actual  predicted        error prediction
254              4:LAV                    2:GLF
"<ElAmy h*A Hqh ly$   Q   LAV"
"إعلامي هذا حقه ليش     Q   LAV"  This is not LAV, Hqh ly$
is not LAV
```

Figure 3: Example of mislabelled sentences.

This analysis led us to conclude that it is impossible in principle for WEKA to classify all instances correctly. There is a proportion of texts that cannot be classified, and this sets a ceiling on accuracy that it is possible to achieve approximate to 90-91%.

4.1 Sequential Minimal Optimization (SMO)

SMO is the WEKA implementation of the Support Vector Machines classifier (SVM) which have been developed for numeric prediction and classifying data by constructing N-dimensional hyper plane to separate data optimally into two categories (Ayodele, 2010). SMV works to find a hypothesis h that reduces the limit between the true error in h will make it on unseen test data and the error on the training data (Joachims, 1998). SMV achieved best performance in text classification task due to the ability of SVM to remove the need for feature selection which means SVM eliminate a high-dimensional feature spaces resulting from the frequent of occurrence of word wi in text. In addition, SVM automatically find good parameter settings (ibid).

4.2 Term Frequency (TF)

Term Frequency represent the frequency of particular word in text (Gebre et al., 2013). Based in our task we found some words usually frequent in one dialect more than other dialects. So we used the weight of TF to indicate the importance of a word in text.

4.3 Inverse Document Frequency (IDF)

Invers Document Frequency tried to scale the weight of frequent words if it appear in different texts (more than one dialects) that is mean a word which appear in many dialect we cannot used as feature (Gebre et al., 2013).

4.4 Features

The first experiments to choose the best classifier to identify Arabic dialects showed that SMO is the best machine learning classifier algorithm, but we may increase accuracy by adjusting parameters and features taken into account.

The WordTokenizer setting assumes features are words or character-strings between spaces while the CharacterNGramTokenizer assumes features are 1/2/3-character sequences. We used the WEKA StringToWordVector filter with WordTokeniser which splits the text into words between delimiters: (full-stop, comma, semi-colon, colon, parenthesis, question, quotation and exclamation mark). After that, we decided to use SMO, but we suggested trying character n-Grams as units, instead of words as units. We used CharacterNGramTokenizer to splits a string into an n-gram with min and max gram. We tried to set Max and Min both to 1 gives a model based on single characters; max and min both to 2 is a char-bigram model; max and min both to 3 gives us a trigram model; max and min to 4 gives a 4-gram model, table 4 shows the results of different gram values when evaluating with the training set and a 60:40 percentage split of the training set. Table 4 suggests that 4-gram model may be inappropriate as the training data is not sufficiently large.

Features	Evaluate on training set	60% train, 40% test
Character UniGram	43.23	41.11
Character BiGram	78.08	52.4
Character TriGram	**94.62**	49.87
Character FourGram	85.01	50.39

Table 4: The accuracy of SMO classifier with CharcterNGram.

In addition, to improve performance we tried to replace the dimensions of the feature vector with their IDF and TF weight which is a standard method from Information Retrieval (Robertson, 2004). We supposed the models were very similar: (3-1) has all the trigrams of (3-3) and also some bigrams and unigrams but these probably are common to all or most dialects and so do not help in discrimination. However, the Task rules stated that we were restricted to trying our three best classifiers, so at this stage we had to choose three "Best" results. Sometimes the training set score is high, but the 60:40 percentage split score is low; and sometimes the 60:40 percentage split score is high but the Training set score is poor. So, we decided to use 60:40 percentage split as our guide to choose the best combination, because using the training set for training as well as evaluation may over-fit to the training set. Figure 4 below shows the chart that summarises the above four tables for different combinations of TF/IDF and WC values with SMO classifier.

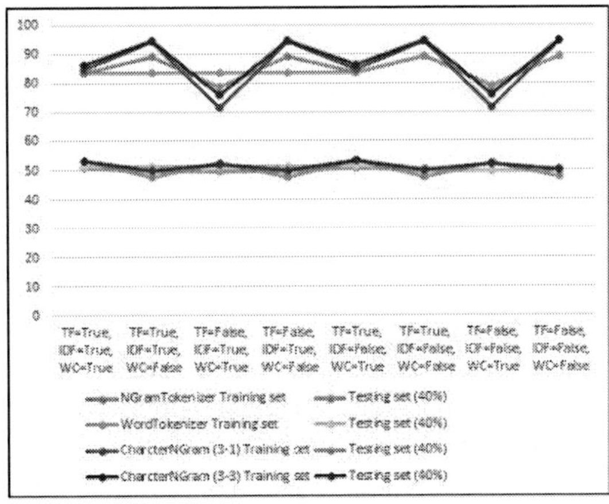

Figure 4: Summary of different combinations of TF/IDF and WC values with SMO classifier.

5 Results

We finally evaluated our system using the supplied separate test data set and submitted three different results using SMO classifier with three different features-sets:

Run1: is obtained by using CharacterNGram, Max=3, Min=3, IDF=True, TF=True, WC=True. We got accuracy around 42%.

Run2: is obtained by using WordTokenizer, IDF=True, TF=True, WC=True, we removed ' delimiter because it is used as a letter in Buckwalter transcription. The performance of this model equals to 37%.

Run3: is obtained by using NGramTokenizer, Max=3, Min=1, IDF=True, TF=True, WC=True, also we removed ' delimiter as in Run2. We got accuracy equals to 38%. Table 5 shows the results of the three runs.

Run	Accuracy	F1 (weighted)
1	42.86	43.49
2	37.92	38.41
3	38.25	38.71

Table 5: The results of the three classifiers.

6   Conclusion

We built systems that classify Arabic dialects in shared task by using WEKA data analytic tool and SMO machine learning algorithm after testing variants of SMO with different tokenizers, IDF, TF, WC values, and comparing results tested on training set (around 80-90% correct) as against using 60% to train and separate 40% for test (around 50% correct). By testing our system on the testing data set we got an average accuracy of 42.85%. We think that we got a low accuracy due to ASR transcription because the most of the misclassified instances are not readily classifiable even by three human Arabic Linguistic experts, which provides strong evidence that a Machine Learning classifier can do no better. Clearly if the training data contains inappropriately-transcribed text and mislabelled instances, this will reduce the ceiling of accuracy that any classifier can achieve. We think that we might combine WordTokenizer and CharacterNGram in the future to improve the results.

References

Ahmed Ali, Najim Dehak, Patrick Cardinal, Sameer Khurana, Sree Harsha Yella, James Glass, Peter Bell and, and Steve Renals. 2016. Automatic dialect detection in arabic broadcast speech. *Interspeech2016*, pages 2934–2938.

Fawzi S Alorifi. 2008. *Automatic Identification of Arabic Dialects Using Hidden Markov Models*. Thesis.

Taiwo Oladipupo Ayodele. 2010. Types of machine learning algorithms.

Fadi Biadsy, Julia Hirschberg, and Nizar Habash. 2009. Spoken arabic dialect identification using phonotactic modeling, 31 March.

Tim Buckwalter. 2002. Arabic transliteration. *URL http://www. qamus. org/transliteration. htm.*

Heba Elfardy and Mona Diab. 2013. Sentence level dialect identification in arabic. In *Proceedings of the 51st Annual Meeting of the Association for Computational Linguistics*, page 456461.

Binyam Gebrekidan Gebre, Marcos Zampieri, Peter Wittenburg, and Tom Heskes. 2013. Improving native language identification with tf-idfweighting. In *Proceedings of the Eighth Workshop on Innovative Use of NLP for Building Educational Applications*, pages 216–223. Association for Computational Linguistics.

Mark Hall, Eibe Frank, Geoffrey Holmes, Bernhard Pfahringer, Peter Reutemann, and Ian H. Witten. 2009. The weka data mining software: An update. *SIGKDD Explorations*, 11(1):10–18.

Uri Horesh and William M. Cotter. 2016. Current research on linguistic variation in the arabic-speaking world. *Language and Linguistics Compass*, 10(8):370–381.

Thorsten Joachims. 1998. Text categorization with support vector machines: Learning with many relevant features.

Man Lu and Moustafa Mohamed. 2011. Lahga: Arabic dialect classifier. Report, December 13, 2011.

Shervin Malmasi, Marcos Zampieri, Nikola Ljubei, Preslav Nakov, Ahmed Ali, Jrg Tiedemann, and Liling Tan. 2016. Discriminating between similar languages and arabic dialect identification: A report on the third dsl shared task. In *Proceedings of the 3rd Workshop on Language Technology for Closely Related Languages, Varieties and Dialects (VarDial)*.

Arfath Pasha, Mohamed Al-Badrashiny, Mona Diab, Ahmed El Kholy, Ramy Eskander, Nizar Habash, Manoj Pooleery, Owen Rambow, and Ryan M. Roth. 2014. Madamira: A fast, comprehensive tool for morphological analysis and disambiguation of arabic.

Stephen Robertson. 2004. Understanding inverse document frequency: On theoretical arguments for idf. *Journal of Documentation*, 60(5):503–520.

Fatiha Sadat, Farnazeh Kazemi, and Atefeh Farzindar. 2014. Automatic identification of arabic language varieties and dialects in social media. In *Proceedings of the Second Workshop on Natural Language Processing for Social Media (SocialNLP)*, pages 22–27.

Omar F. Zaidan and Chris Callison-Burch. 2014. Arabic dialect identification. *Computational Linguistics*, 40(1):171–202.

Marcos Zampieri, Binyam Gebrekidan Gebre, Hernani Costa, and Josef van Genabith. 2015. Comparing approaches to the identification of similar languages. In *Proceedings of the Joint Workshop on Language Technology for Closely Related Languages, Varieties and Dialects*, pages 66–72. Association for Computational Linguistics.

An Unsupervised Morphological Criterion for Discriminating Similar Languages

Adrien Barbaresi

Austrian Academy of Sciences (ÖAW-AC)

Berlin-Brandenburg Academy of Sciences and Humanities (BBAW)

`adrien.barbaresi@oeaw.ac.at`

Abstract

In this study conducted on the occasion of the Discriminating between Similar Languages shared task, I introduce an additional decision factor focusing on the token and subtoken level. The motivation behind this submission is to test whether a morphologically-informed criterion can add linguistically relevant information to global categorization and thus improve performance. The contributions of this paper are (1) a description of the unsupervised, low-resource method; (2) an evaluation and analysis of its raw performance; and (3) an assessment of its impact within a model comprising common indicators used in language identification. I present and discuss the systems used in the task A, a 12-way language identification task comprising varieties of five main language groups. Additionally I introduce a new off-the-shelf Naive Bayes classifier using a contrastive word and subword n-gram model ("Bayesline") which outperforms the best submissions.

1 Introduction

Language identification is the task of predicting the language(s) that a given document is written in. It can be seen as a text categorization task in which documents are assigned to pre-existing categories. This research field has found renewed interest in the 1990s due to advances in statistical approaches and it has been active ever since, particularly since the methods developed have also been deemed relevant for text categorization, native language identification, authorship attribution, text-based geolocation, and dialectal studies (Lui and Cook, 2013).

As of 2014 and the first Discriminating between Similar Languages (DSL) shared task (Zampieri et al., 2014), a unified dataset (Tan et al., 2014) comprising news texts of closely-related language varieties has been used to test and benchmark systems. A second shared task took place in 2015 (Zampieri et al., 2015), an analysis of recent developments can be found in Goutte el al. (2016). The documents to be classified are quite short and may even be difficult to distinguish for humans, thus adding to the difficulty and the interest of the task.

The present study was conducted on the occasion of the third DSL shared task (Malmasi et al., 2016). It focuses on submissions to task A, a 12-way language identification task comprising varieties of five main language groups: Bosnian (bs), Croatian (hr), and Serbian (sr); Argentine (es-AR), Mexican (es-MX), and Peninsular Spanish (es-ES); Québec French (fr-CA) and Metropolitan French (fr-FR); Malay (*Bahasa Melayu*, my) and Indonesian (*Bahasa Indonesia*, id); Brazilian Portuguese (pt-BR) and European Portuguese (pt-PT). Not all varieties are to be considered equally since differences may stem from extra-linguistic factors. It is for instance assumed that Malay and Indonesian derive from a millenium-old *lingua franca*, so that shorter texts have been considered to be a problem for language identification (Bali, 2006). Besides, the Bosnian/Serbian language pair seems to be difficult to tell apart whereas Croatian distinguishes itself from the two other varieties mostly because of political motives (Ljubešić et al., 2007; Tiedemann and Ljubešić, 2012).

Proceedings of the Third Workshop on NLP for Similar Languages, Varieties and Dialects,
pages 212–220, Osaka, Japan, December 12 2016.

The contributions of this paper are (1) a description of an unsupervised, low-resource method comprising morphological features; (2) an evaluation and analysis of its raw performance; and (3) an assessment of its impact in a model comprising common indicators used in language identification. In addition, I will demonstrate that an off-the-shelf method working on the subtoken level can outperform the best submissions in the shared task. The remainder of this paper is organized as follows: in section 2 the method is presented, a evaluation follows in section 3, the systems used for the shared task is described and a new baseline for task A is proposed in section 4.

2 Method

2.1 General principles

Statistical indicators such as character- and token-based language models have proven to be efficient on short text samples, especially character n-gram frequency profiles from length 1 to 5 (Cavnar and Trenkle, 1994). In the context of the shared task, a simple approach using n-gram features and discriminative classification achieved competitive results (Purver, 2014). Although features relying on the output of instruments may yield useful information such as POS-features used for Spanish (Zampieri et al., 2013), the diversity of the languages to classify as well as the prevalence of statistical methods call for low-resource methods that can be trained and applied easily.

Morphological features are not prominent in the literature, although the indirect word stemming performed by character n-grams is highlighted (Cavnar and Trenkle, 1994), and morphological ending frequency mentioned as future work topic (Bali, 2006). The motivation behind this submission was to test whether a morphologically-informed criterion can add linguistically relevant information to the global decision and thus improve performance. This article protocols an attempt at developing an unsupervised morphological model for each language present in the shared task. In order for this to be used in competition, it has to be learned from the training data ("closed" submission track).

The method is based on segmentation and affix analysis. The original idea behind this simple yet efficient principle seems to go back to Harris' letter successor variety which grounds on transitional probabilities to detect morpheme boundaries (Harris, 1955). The principle has proven valuable to construct stem dictionaries for document classification (Hafer and Weiss, 1974), it has been used in the past by spell-checkers (Peterson, 1980; Jones and Silverman, 1985), as it is linguistically relevant and computationally efficient. Relevant information is stored in a trie (Fredkin, 1960), a data structure allowing for prefix search and its reverse opposite in order to look for sublexicons, which greatly extends lexical coverage. Forward (prefix) and backward (suffix) tries are used in a similar fashion, albeit with different constraints. This approach does not necessarily perform evenly across languages; it has for example led to considerable progress in morphologically-rich languages such as Arabic (Ben Hamadou, 1986) or Basque (Agirre et al., 1992).

Similar approaches have been used successfully to segment words into morphemes in an unsupervised way and for several languages. A more recent implementation has been the RePortS algorithm which gained attention in the context of the PASCAL challenge (Keshava and Pitler, 2006; Dasgupta and Ng, 2007; Demberg, 2007) by outperforming most of the other systems. The present approach makes similar assumptions as the work cited and adapts the base algorithm to the task at hand, that is the identification of in- and out-of-vocabulary words and ultimately language identification. I have used this method in previous work to overcome data sparsity in the case of retro-digitized East German corpora, an under-resourced variety of written German, as I showed that it could trump full-fledged morphological analysis to predict whether a given token is to be considered as part of the language or as an error (Barbaresi, 2016a). The present experiment consists of testing if an unsupervised morphological analysis of surface forms can be useful in the context of similar language discrimination.

2.2 Current implementation

In order to build the corresponding models, a dictionary is built by observing unigrams in the training data for each language, then prefix and suffix trees are constructed using this dictionary. An affix candidate list is constituted by decomposing the tokens in the training data and the residues are added to the list if they are under a fixed length. The 5% most frequent affixes are stored and used in the identification phase, as relative corpus frequency is an efficient model construction principle (Dasgupta and Ng, 2007). Parameter tuning, that is the determination of the best result for the shared task settings, is performed empirically, in a one-against-all way with the concurrent languages. Token and affix length as well as frequency-based thresholds and blacklists have been tested. In the end, only token and affix length constraints have been used, as blacklisting in the higher or lower frequency range did not lead to noticeable improvements.

The identification algorithm aims at the decomposition into possibly known parts. It consists of two main phases: first a prefix/suffix search over respective trees in order to look for the longest possible known subwords, and secondly sanity checks to see if the rest could itself be an affix or a word out of the dictionary. If $\alpha\beta$ is a concatenation absent of the dictionary and if α and β are both identified as longest affix and in-vocabulary words, then $\alpha\beta$ is considered to be part of the target language. If one of the components is a word and if the other one is in the affix dictionary, then the token is also considered valid. The segmentation can be repeated twice if necessary, it can thus identify up to 4 components. It is performed both forward and backward since tests showed small improvements in cross-language efficiency.

For example, the token *cantalapiedra* in the Spanish corpus is not necessarily in the dictionary, but it can be decomposed into *canta+lapiedra* and ultimately into *canta+la+piedra*. The method can be robust: *especialemente* for instance can be considered to be a spelling error, but it can still be decomposed into *especial+e+mente* and qualifies as a word if the remaining *e* is in the affix list of the corresponding variety; in this particular context this is not the case, and the token is not considered to be a valid word. In the Malay/Indonesian corpus, the token *abdul_rahman* is probably a Twitter username, and its parts *abdul* and *rahman* are both in the dictionary. If punctuation signs are added to the affix list, then this token is correctly analyzed as part of the target language. On the opposite side, the token *mempertanyakan* (to put into question, to doubt) is only present in the Indonesian corpus, and the affix *memper-* is more frequent in this corpus. The model for Malay decomposes the word as *mempe+r+tanyakan*, because the word *mempe* is seen once in the training data (which stems from a spelling error: *mempe ngerusikan* should be spelled *mempengerusikan* and analyzed as *mem+pengerusi+kan*). Since *r* is in the affix list it concludes that *mempertanyakan* is a valid word. The right decomposition would have been *memper+tanyakan* or even *memper+tanya+kan*. This composite could easily be a valid Malay word but it is more frequent in Indonesian. Since *memper-* does not occur as a token, it is not decomposed correctly. Additionally, the model does not presently yield information about such frequency effects.

The models are indeed restricted to concatenative morphology, and the fact that a stem has to be in the dictionary is a strong limitation impeding performance (Demberg, 2007), in particular recall. However, it has been kept here as it prevents the models from overgenerating because of differences in the languages examined.

3   Evaluation

After empirical testing, the smallest possible token length for learning and searching is fixed to 5 characters, there is no upper bound on token length, and the maximum affix length is set to 2 to provide a safer setting overall, although affix lengths of 3 or 4 occasionally lead to better results. Despite the possibility of populating a blacklist out of common tokens present in the lower and higher frequency ranges, experiments have not been conclusive, so that no blacklisting has been used for the task.

3.1   Raw performance

Table 1 describes the results of morphological training. The coverage displayed is the total percentage of words considered to be in-dictionary by the model, for the target language and for the concurrent language(s) respectively. For Southeastern-European languages, I find a lower lexical overlap than Tiedemann and Ljubešić (2012). The Spanish varieties have the smallest coverage spread. The assumption that Malay and Indonesian feature more than 90% lexical similarity (Bali, 2006) is only partially confirmed: it seems that Indonesian has more to do with Malay than vice versa and the news samples used

Trad. assumed	Languages		Coverage		Benchmark (precision)		
lang. type	Target	Concurrent	Target	Other	Baseline	Method	Bayesline
	bs	hr,sr	0.88	0.84	0.70	0.71	0.81
Fusional	hr	bs,sr	0.90	0.79	0.87	0.87	0.83
	sr	bs,hr	0.90	0.76	0.92	0.92	0.86
	es-AR	es-ES,es-MX	0.96	0.89	0.85	0.86	0.79
Fusional	es-ES	es-AR,es-MX	0.95	0.92	0.69	0.69	0.58
	es-MX	es-AR,es-ES	0.93	0.92	0.66	0.65	0.78
Fusional	fr-CA	fr-FR	0.97	0.87	0.92	0.92	0.95
	fr-FR	fr-CA	0.94	0.92	0.84	0.85	0.85
Agglutinative	id	my	0.95	0.85	0.98	0.97	0.98
	my	id	0.96	0.78	0.99	0.98	0.99
Fusional	pt-BR	pt-PT	0.95	0.89	0.89	0.91	0.93
	pt-PT	pt-BR	0.95	0.89	0.92	0.93	0.93

Table 1: Results of morphological induction on training set in terms of coverage and precision of classification on the development set. The unigram baseline and unigram Bayesline (Tan et al. 2014) are given for comparison.

for the tests seem to be relatively easy to tell apart, since they feature the largest coverage spread. This distinction within the Bahasa complex and the rest is reflected as being traditionally assumed in language typology. However, finer differences do exist between fusional/inflectional languages (Dryer and Haspelmath, 2013)[1], and the results of the morphological induction phase constitute further evidence of subtle differences, among other things on the morpholexical level.

Concerning the benchmark, the method is compared to a unigram baseline in terms of raw precision: for each instance, potential candidates (alphabetic tokens of 5 characters and more) are analyzed and classified as in- or out-of-vocabulary. The number of in-vocabulary tokens is divided by the number of candidates, and the instance is classified according to the model which yields the highest proportion of recognized tokens. This proportion has to be strictly superior to all others, which means that this indicator (as all unigram models) can be undecided due to coverage problems, especially in short instances. Thus, I used precision as a benchmark in order to judge cases where the indicator actually predicts something, in other words the positive predictive value.

The precision displayed has been calculated accordingly on the development set, by using the highest score per instance and taking language families in isolation, i.e. by reducing the 12-way classification to a 2- or 3-way one. The method mostly achives equal or better results than the unigram baseline, which proves that the concept is working, and that it might lead to better predictions for unseen samples. A "Bayesline" is used as implemented for the previous DSL editions (Tan et al., 2014), it grounds on unigrams for the sake of comparison and integrates a Naive Bayes classifier[2], whereas the baseline and my method yield "raw" results at this point. In line with expectations, the Bayesline generally achieves better results. There are interesting discrepancies though: Argentine Spanish and Serbian seem to stand out in a morpholexical perspective, meaning that the method could add relevant information to a global system.

3.2 Impact in a composite system

The morphological criterion is not meant to be used by itself, but rather as a part of a combination of features which are learned and weighted by statistical learning techniques as usually done in the literature (Goutte et al., 2016). Since the criterion does not systematically lead to an unequivocal result, it will be treated as a sparse feature by the models. The question is now to determine both the impact and the

---

[1] http://wals.info/chapter/26

[2] `CountVectorizer(analyzer='word', ngram_range=(1,1))`, followed by a multinomial Naive Bayes classifier

Language	Morphology		Char 4-grams		Word bigrams	
	LM	RF	LM	RF	LM	RF
bs	***	**	.	*	***	*
hr	.	*		*	***	*
sr	***	*	***	*	*	.
es-AR	***	*	.	.	**	.
es-ES		**	.	**	***	*
es-MX	***	**	*	*	***	.
fr-CA	*	**	***	**	***	.
fr-FR	***	***		*	***	.
id	***	***	*	**	***	.
my	***	**	***	*	**	.
pt-BR	***	**	***	*	***	.
pt-PT	***	**	***	**	***	.

Table 2: Results of relevance tests on development set
Linear model (LM) significance levels: 0 "***" 0.001 "**" 0.01 "*" 0.05 "." 0.1 " " 1
Random Forest (RF) relative feature importances: $> 80\%$ "***" $> 60\%$ "**" $> 40\%$ "*" $> 20\%$ "."

potential for generalization of the morphological criterion presented in this article, all the more since the closed training sets are restricted in size.

To test for variable significance, two distinct classification models are applied. The first one consists of a regression analysis using a linear model, from a family of models commonly used to classify data and select variables (Friedman et al., 2009), and previously used for classification of web documents in web corpus construction (Barbaresi, 2015). The second one resides in random forests (Breiman, 2001). It has been shown that in spite of their variability they can be used for interpretation, with respect to variable importance, and also for feature selection in terms of model efficiency (Genuer et al., 2010). Previous editions of the shared task have highlighted that higher-order character n-grams and lower-order word n-grams allow for an efficient combination of accuracy and efficiency (Goutte et al., 2014; Malmasi and Dras, 2015). Following from these results, character 4-grams and word bigrams are taken as a reference for relevance tests.

Table 2 shows that word bigrams are the most relevant indicator according to the linear model, the morphological criterion is used the most by the random forests. Overall, the most relevant feature is the morphological criterion, although it is not equally important across all languages (especially for 3-way concurrencies) and although the overall model is well-balanced. In fact, nearly all if not all the features tend to be used even after feature selection by both methods, which means that the criterion introduced here qualifies as relevant input from a statistical point of view and may be used as a sparse feature to discriminate similar languages.

4   Shared task systems

The systems described in this section have been submitted as team XAC (Cross-Academies). An additional Bayesline is introduced, used as a system component. It only became apparent after the release of the gold dataset that it actually performs better on it than all other features and, most importantly, better than the other competing systems.

After significance tests conducted as described above, a combination of features has been used to set up a classification system for the DSL shared task. The instances in the data are tokenized using the *SoMaJo* tokenizer (Proisl and Uhrig, 2016), which achieves state-of-the-art accuracies on both web and CMC data for German. As it is rule-based, it is deemed efficient enough for the languages of the shared task. The features used comprise instance statistics such as length or number of capital letters and most importantly the following series of continuous variables yielded by models trained for each language variety: the normalized morphological criterion (feature scaling by standardization); character and word n-grams language models perplexities on lowercase tokenized text, respectively character 5-grams with Kneser-Ney smoothing (Kneser and Ney, 1995) as computed by *OpenGrm* (Roark et al., 2012); and word 2-, 3-, and 4-grams with modified Kneser-Ney smoothing as computed by *KenLM* (Heafield, 2011; Heafield et al., 2013); the online learning toolkit *Vowpal Wabbit* (Langford et al., 2007; Langford et al., 2009), which achieved the best performance when used separately on the development set; and probabilities given by the Bayesline proposed below (as a Naive Bayes classifier yields probabilities for each category). It was not clear in the development data that this new Bayesline would perform better when applied alone on the gold set, the combination appeared to lead to the best overall performance.

Classification is performed using existing implementations by the *scikit-learn* toolkit (Pedregosa et al., 2011). Random forests (Breiman, 2001) were used in the two first runs because of encouraging results on the development set, but they were outperformed by a gradient boosting classifier (Friedman, 2001) on the test set as shown in Table 3 (run 3), probably because of the robustness of this method, which is known to perform well with heterogeneous features. The baseline is calculated according to the DSL Bayesline (Tan et al., 2014) as described above, with an adapted setting to focus on character 4-grams.[3]

The best run was ranked 8th out of 17 teams on the task A in closed training, i.e. without using external resources or past DSL data, with an accuracy of 0.879; the baseline of the first edition was 0.859 and the best ranked submission reached an accuracy of 0.893. The confusion matrix on Figure 1 hints at a lower classification accuracy concerning the three-way concurrencies, Spanish in particular. I hypothesize that statistical models reach their limits here, especially concerning the Mexican Spanish, which is both heavily influenced by other varieties and not homogeneous enough, so that frequency information cannot be used reliably. Finally, the results on the gold set are not in line with the development set, where cross-validated accuracies around 0.92 have been observed. The systems used may have been too complex or not well-weighted.

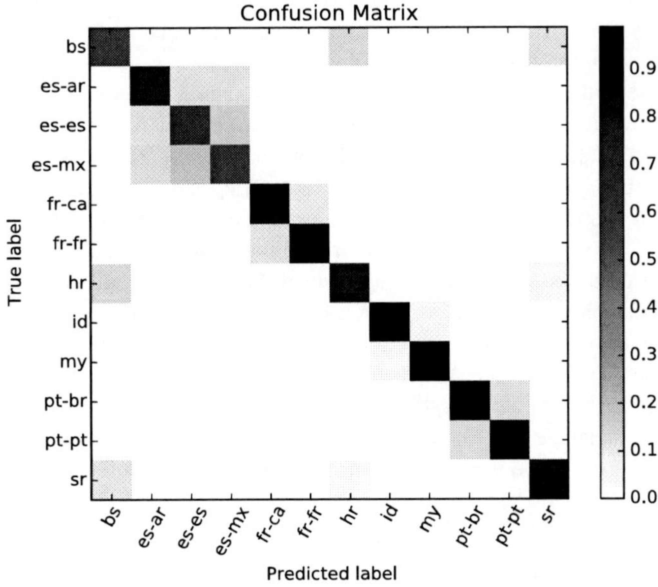

Figure 1: Confusion matrix for test set A (closed training)

In view of this I would like to introduce a refined version of the Bayesline (Tan et al., 2014) in the form of a similar off-the-shelf Naive Bayes classifier using a contrastive subword n-gram model[4], which

---

[3] `CountVectorizer(analyzer='char', ngram_range=(4,4))`

[4] `TfidfVectorizer(analyzer='char', ngram_range=(2,7), strip_accents=None, lowercase=True)` followed by `MultinomialNB(alpha=0.005)`, adapted from https://web.archive.org/web/2016-

outperforms the best teams for task A (with an accuracy of 0.902), even without taking the development data into consideration (accuracy of 0.898). This shows that meaningful word and subword features can give a boost to existing systems, even if they are based on simple extraction methods and/or used alone.

Run	Accuracy	F1 (micro)	F1 (macro)	F1 (weighted)
Reference Bayesline	0.859	0.859	0.858	0.858
run 1	0.861	0.861	0.860	0.860
run 2	0.870	0.870	0.869	0.869
run 3	0.879	0.879	0.879	0.879
Proposed Bayesline	0.902	0.902	0.902	0.902

Table 3: Results for test set A (closed training). Bayeslines inspired by Tan et al. (2014)

Finally, I wish to bring to the reader's attention that I tried to gather web texts for an open submission using existing techniques (Barbaresi, 2013; Barbaresi, 2016b) and focusing on top-level domains. Although the quality of corpora did not seem to be a problem apart from the Bosnian domain (.ba), the variation contained in web texts was not a good match for the news texts of the shared task. As observed in previous editions, performance decreased as further texts were included, so that no open submission was made.

5 Conclusion

I have presented a method to build an unsupervised morphological model for all the languages of the shared task. The resulting segmentation analysis is not the most efficient feature in itself, but I have shown that this criterion qualifies as relevant input from a statistical point of view and may be used as a sparse feature to discriminate similar languages. A reasonable hypothesis is that it adds new linguistically motivated information, dealing with the morpho-lexical logic of the languages to be classified, also yielding insights on linguistic typology. Unevenly distributed characteristics across the languages account for noise which is filtered accordingly by the models.

Meaningful subword features could well give a boost to existing systems, even if they are based on simple extraction methods. In fact, an off-the-shelf Naive Bayes classifier using a contrastive word and subword n-gram model outperforms the best submission for classification across 12 languages, which casts the best possible light on this topic. In this respect, future work includes a refinement of feature extraction processes on this level, especially concerning frequency, whose role in linguistically relevant units is more difficult to assess, probably because more training data is needed than for character n-grams.

The efficiency of the proposed Bayesline as well as the difficulty to reach higher scores in open training could be explained by artificial regularities in the test data. The results for the Malay/Indonesian pair are striking, this clear distinction does not reflect the known commonalities between these varieties. This seems to be an artifact of the data which feature standard language of a different nature than the continuum "on the field", that is between both countries and within Indonesia. The conflict between in-vitro and real-world language identification has already been emphasized in the past (Baldwin and Lui, 2010), it calls for the inclusion of web texts into the existing task reference.

Acknowledgements

Thanks to three anonymous reviewers for their comments, to Antonio Ruiz Tinoco (Sophia University) for his input on variation in Spanish, and to Artem Sharandin (Russian Academy of Sciences) for his help with Bahasa Melayu.

References

Eneko Agirre, Inaki Alegria, Xabier Arregi, Xabier Artola, A Díaz de Ilarraza, Montse Maritxalar, Kepa Sarasola, and Miriam Urkia. 1992. XUXEN: A spelling checker/corrector for Basque based on two-level morphology.

0403184050/http://scikit-learn.org/stable/auto_examples/text/document_classification_20newsgroups.html

In *Proceedings of the 3rd conference on Applied Natural Language Processing*, pages 119–125. Association for Computational Linguistics.

Timothy Baldwin and Marco Lui. 2010. Language Identification: The Long and the Short of the Matter. In *Human Language Technologies: The 2010 Annual Conference of the North American Chapter of the Association for Computational Linguistics*, pages 229–237. Association for Computational Linguistics.

Ranaivo-Malançon Bali. 2006. Automatic Identification of Close Languages–Case Study: Malay and Indonesian. *ECTI Transaction on Computer and Information Technology*, 2(2):126–133.

Adrien Barbaresi. 2013. Challenges in web corpus construction for low-resource languages in a post-BootCaT world. In *6th Language & Technology Conference, Less Resourced Languages special track*, pages 69–73.

Adrien Barbaresi. 2015. *Ad hoc and general-purpose corpus construction from web sources*. Ph.D. thesis, École Normale Supérieure de Lyon.

Adrien Barbaresi. 2016a. Bootstrapped OCR error detection for a less-resourced language variant. In Stefanie Dipper, Friedrich Neubarth, and Heike Zinsmeister, editors, *Proceedings of the 13th Conference on Natural Language Processing (KONVENS 2016)*, pages 21–26. University of Bochum.

Adrien Barbaresi. 2016b. Efficient construction of metadata-enhanced web corpora. In *Proceedings of the 10th Web as Corpus Workshop*, pages 7–16. Association for Computational Linguistics.

Abdelmajid Ben Hamadou. 1986. A compression technique for Arabic dictionaries: the affix analysis. In *Proceedings of the 11th Conference on Computational Linguistics*, pages 286–288. Association for Computational Linguistics.

Leo Breiman. 2001. Random Forests. *Machine Learning*, 45(1):5–32.

William B. Cavnar and John M. Trenkle. 1994. N-Gram-Based Text Categorization. In *Proceedings of the 3rd Annual Symposium on Document Analysis and Information Retrieval*, pages 161–175.

Sajib Dasgupta and Vincent Ng. 2007. High-performance, language-independent morphological segmentation. In *HLT-NAACL*, pages 155–163.

Vera Demberg. 2007. A language-independent Unsupervised Model for Morphological Segmentation. In *Annual Meeting of the Association for Computational Linguistics*, volume 45, pages 920–927.

Matthew S. Dryer and Martin Haspelmath, editors. 2013. *WALS Online*. Max Planck Institute for Evolutionary Anthropology, Leipzig.

Edward Fredkin. 1960. Trie Memory. *Communications of the ACM*, 3(9):490–499.

Jerome Friedman, Trevor Hastie, and Robert Tibshirani. 2009. *The Elements of Statistical Learning*, volume 1. Springer, 2nd edition.

Jerome H. Friedman. 2001. Greedy Function Approximation: A Gradient Boosting Machine. *The Annals of Statistics*, 29(5):1189–1232.

Robin Genuer, Jean-Michel Poggi, and Christine Tuleau-Malot. 2010. Variable selection using Random Forests. *Pattern Recognition Letters*, 31(14):2225–2236.

Cyril Goutte, Serge Léger, and Marine Carpuat. 2014. The NRC system for discriminating similar languages. In *Proceedings of the 1st Workshop on Applying NLP Tools to Similar Languages, Varieties and Dialects*, pages 139–145.

Cyril Goutte, Serge Léger, Shervin Malmasi, and Marcos Zampieri. 2016. Discriminating Similar Languages: Evaluations and Explorations. In *Proceedings of the 10th International Conference on Language Resources and Evaluation (LREC 2016)*, pages 1800–1807. European Language Resources Association (ELRA).

Margaret A. Hafer and Stephen F. Weiss. 1974. Word Segmentation by Letter Successor Varieties. *Information Storage and Retrieval*, 10:371–385.

Zellig S. Harris. 1955. From Phoneme to Morphemes. *Language*, 31(2):190–222.

Kenneth Heafield, Ivan Pouzyrevsky, Jonathan H. Clark, and Philipp Koehn. 2013. Scalable modified Kneser-Ney language model estimation. In *Proceedings of the 51st Annual Meeting of the Association for Computational Linguistics*, pages 690–696.

Kenneth Heafield. 2011. KenLM: Faster and smaller language model queries. In *Proceedings of the Sixth Workshop on Statistical Machine Translation*, pages 187–197. Association for Computational Linguistics.

Mark A. Jones and Alex Silverman. 1985. A spelling checker based on affix classes. In Jagdish C. Agrawal and Pranas Zunde, editors, *Empirical Foundations of Information and Software Science*, pages 373–379. Springer US, Boston, MA.

Samarth Keshava and Emily Pitler. 2006. A simpler, intuitive approach to morpheme induction. In *Proceedings of 2nd Pascal Challenges Workshop*, pages 31–35.

Reinhard Kneser and Hermann Ney. 1995. Improved backing-off for m-gram language modeling. In *Proceedings of the IEEE International Conference on Acoustics, Speech, and Signal Processing (ICASSP)*, pages 181–184.

John Langford, Lihong Li, and Alexander L. Strehl. 2007. Vowpal wabbit (fast online learning). Technical report. http://hunch.net/∼vw/.

John Langford, Lihong Li, and Tong Zhang. 2009. Sparse Online Learning via Truncated Gradient. *Journal of Machine Learning Research*, 10(Mar):777–801.

Nikola Ljubešić, Nives Mikelić, and Damir Boras. 2007. Language identification: how to distinguish similar languages? In *29th International Conference on Information Technology Interfaces*, pages 541–546. IEEE.

Marco Lui and Paul Cook. 2013. Classifying English Documents by National Dialect. In *Proceedings of the Australasian Language Technology Association Workshop*, pages 5–15.

Shervin Malmasi and Mark Dras. 2015. Language Identification using Classifier Ensembles. In *Proceedings of the Joint Workshop on Language Technology for Closely Related Languages, Varieties and Dialects*, pages 35–43.

Shervin Malmasi, Marcos Zampieri, Nikola Ljubešić, Preslav Nakov, Ahmed Ali, and Jörg Tiedemann. 2016. Discriminating between Similar Languages and Arabic Dialect Identification: A Report on the Third DSL Shared Task. In *Proceedings of the 3rd Workshop on Language Technology for Closely Related Languages, Varieties and Dialects (VarDial)*.

F. Pedregosa, G. Varoquaux, A. Gramfort, V. Michel, B. Thirion, O. Grisel, M. Blondel, P. Prettenhofer, R. Weiss, V. Dubourg, J. Vanderplas, A. Passos, D. Cournapeau, M. Brucher, M. Perrot, and E. Duchesnay. 2011. Scikit-learn: Machine learning in Python. *Journal of Machine Learning Research*, 12:2825–2830.

James L. Peterson. 1980. Computer programs for detecting and correcting spelling errors. *Communications of the ACM*, 23(12):676–687.

Thomas Proisl and Peter Uhrig. 2016. SoMaJo: State-of-the-art tokenization for German web and social media texts. In *Proceedings of the 10th Web as Corpus Workshop*, pages 57–62. Association for Computational Linguistics.

Matthew Purver. 2014. A Simple Baseline for Discriminating Similar Languages. In *Proceedings of the First Workshop on Applying NLP Tools to Similar Languages, Varieties and Dialects*, pages 155–160.

Brian Roark, Richard Sproat, Cyril Allauzen, Michael Riley, Jeffrey Sorensen, and Terry Tai. 2012. The OpenGrm open-source finite-state grammar software libraries. In *Proceedings of the ACL 2012 System Demonstrations*, pages 61–66. Association for Computational Linguistics.

Liling Tan, Marcos Zampieri, Nikola Ljubešić, and Jörg Tiedemann. 2014. Merging Comparable Data Sources for the Discrimination of Similar Languages: The DSL Corpus Collection. In *Proceedings of the 7th Workshop on Building and Using Comparable Corpora*, pages 11–15.

Jörg Tiedemann and Nikola Ljubešić. 2012. Efficient discrimination between closely related languages. In *Proceedings of COLING*, pages 2619–2633.

Marcos Zampieri, Binyam Gebrekidan Gebre, and Sascha Diwersy. 2013. N-gram language models and POS distribution for the identification of Spanish varieties. In *Proceedings of TALN 2013*, pages 580–587.

Marcos Zampieri, Liling Tan, Nikola Ljubešić, and Jörg Tiedemann. 2014. A Report on the DSL Shared Task 2014. In *Proceedings of the First Workshop on Applying NLP Tools to Similar Languages, Varieties and Dialects*, pages 58–67.

Marcos Zampieri, Liling Tan, Nikola Ljubešić, Jörg Tiedemann, and Preslav Nakov. 2015. Overview of the DSL Shared Task 2015. In *Proceedings of the Joint Workshop on Language Technology for Closely Related Languages, Varieties and Dialects*, pages 1–9.

QCRI @ DSL 2016: Spoken Arabic Dialect Identification Using Textual Features

Mohamed Eldesouki, Fahim Dalvi, Hassan Sajjad, *and* **Kareem Darwish**

Qatar Computing Research Institute

Hamad bin Khalifa University

Doha, Qatar

{*mohamohamed, faimaduddin, hsajjad, kdarwish*}`@qf.org.qa`

Abstract

The paper describes the QCRI submissions to the shared task of automatic Arabic dialect classification into 5 Arabic variants, namely Egyptian, Gulf, Levantine, North-African (Maghrebi), and Modern Standard Arabic (MSA). The relatively small training set is automatically generated from an ASR system. To avoid over-fitting on such small data, we selected and designed features that capture the morphological essence of the different dialects. We submitted four runs to the Arabic sub-task. For all runs, we used a combined feature vector of character bigrams, trigrams, 4-grams, and 5-grams. We tried several machine-learning algorithms, namely Logistic Regression, Naive Bayes, Neural Networks, and Support Vector Machines (SVM) with linear and string kernels. Our submitted runs used SVM with a linear kernel. In the closed submission, we got the best accuracy of 0.5136 and the third best weighted F1 score, with a difference of less than 0.002 from the best system.

1 Introduction

The Arabic language has various dialects and variants that exist in a continuous spectrum. They are a result of an interweave between the Arabic language that spread throughout the Middle East and North Africa and the indigenous languages in different countries. With the passage of time and the juxtaposition of cultures, dialects and variants of Arabic evolved and mutated. Among the varieties of Arabic, so-called Modern Standard Arabic (MSA) is the lingua franca of the Arab world, and it typically used in written and formal communications. On the other hand, Arabic dialects, such as Egyptian and Levantine, are usually spoken and used in informal communications, especially on social networks such as Twitter and Facebook.

Automatically identifying the dialect of a piece of text or of a spoken utterance can be beneficial for a variety of practical applications. For instance, it can aid Machine Translation (MT) systems in choosing the most appropriate model for translation.

In this paper we describe our dialect identification system that we used for Arabic dialect identification (sub-task 2) in the 2016 DSL shared task (Malmasi et al., 2016). We submitted a total of 4 runs to the shared task; 2 closed runs and 2 open runs. For closed runs, participants are only allowed to use the provided training set. For open runs, external resources are allowed. We tried several combinations of features such as bag-of-words features based-on words or character n-grams where terms are weighed by term frequency (tf) or term frequency and inverse document frequency (tf-idf). We also experimented with several machine learning classifiers including logistic regression, naive Bayes, neural networks, and Support Vector Machines (SVM) with different kernels. Our best run used an SVM classifier with a linear kernel trained on character n-gram features. Our best run achieved an accuracy of 0.5136 and an F-measure 0.5112. Compared to the systems that participated in the shared task, our system obtained the best accuracy and the third highest weighted F1 score, with a difference of less than 0.002 from the best system.

Proceedings of the Third Workshop on NLP for Similar Languages, Varieties and Dialects,
pages 221–226, Osaka, Japan, December 12 2016.

2   Related Work

Arabic dialect identification work could be divided into two main streams, namely: (1) the creation of dialectal Arabic resources , and (2) the development of approaches and techniques for dialect identification. Here we present the most pertinent related work.

One of the early attempts to build Dialectal Arabic annotated resources was done by the COLABA project (Diab et al., 2010). The project harvested blogs about social issues, religion, and politics in four Arabic dialects, namely Egyptian, Iraqi, Levantine (Syrian, Lebanese, Palestinian, and Jordanian) and to a lesser extent Maghrebi. The blogs data was collected via a set of identified URLs as well as 40 dialectal queries from 25 annotators. The project attempted to tackle the non-standard orthography issues of Arabic dialects by defining a phonological scheme which they referred to as CCO. They used lexical features to select the most dialectal content based on the percentage of non-MSA words in the document being identified. They didn't mention any statistics about the data they collected. They used Information Retrieval (IR) for extrinsic evaluation.

The AOC dataset (Zaidan and Callison-Burch, 2011; Zaidan and Callison-Burch, 2014) was created from the content and comments of three newspapers namely Al-Ghad, Al-Riyadh and Al-Youm Al-Sabe', which originate from Jordan, Saudi Arabia, and Egypt respectively. The authors assumed that readers commenting on the different newspapers would use MSA or the dialect of the country of the newspaper. Thus, they considered all the dialectal comments extracted from Al-Ghad as Levantine, from Al-Riyadh as Gulf, and from Al-Youm Al-Sabe' as Egyptian. Out of 3.1 million sentences in AOC, they manually annotated about 108K sentences using crowdsourcing. They considered dialect classification as a language identification task. They built language models for MSA and each of the three dialects and used them to score text segments. The segment would be assigned a label corresponding to the language model with the lowest perplexity. They achieved an accuracy of 69.4%.

Mubarak and Darwish (2014) used user geographical information to build a multi-dialectal corpus from Twitter. Out of 175M tweets collected using Twitter API, they managed to annotate about 6.5M tweets with their dialects. Also, they conducted some analysis on the vocabulary distribution of different Arabic variants. Using the AOC dataset (Zaidan and Callison-Burch, 2011) and MSA corpus composed of 10 years worth of Aljazeera articles (about 114M tokens), they extracted about 45,000 n-grams (uni-, bi-, and tri-) and then manually label them as either MSA, Egyptian, Levantine, Gulf, Iraqi, or Maghrebi. They found that MSA words compose more than 50% of the words in the dialectal text and about 2500 n-gram are truly dialectal.

By showing that many of the most frequent discriminating words for Egyptian Arabic are in fact MSA words, Darwish et al. (2014) argued that Arabic dialect identification system built on the AOC dataset is biased towards the topics in the newspapers from which the corpus was built. Therefore, they discussed the need to identify lexical and linguistic features such as morphological patterns, word concatenations, and verb negation constructs to distinguish between dialectal Arabic and MSA. For evaluation, they used the Egyptian part of the LDC2012T09 corpus. They achieved an accuracy of 94.6% using lexical lists of dialectal words and verbs.

A new Multidialectal Parallel Corpus of Arabic (MPCA) released by Bouamor et al. (2014) was used by Malmasi et al. (2015) to train an SVM classifier to distinguish between MSA, Egyptian, Syrian, Jordanian, Palestinian and Tunisian. The classifier was a meta-classifier that was trained over the probabilities of an ensemble of classifiers that have been trained over different sets of word-level and character-level n-grams. They achieved an accuracy of 74%.

3   Dataset and Methodology

This section analyzes the dataset provided by the shared task and discusses the methodologies and approaches for both preparing the data and for developing our Arabic dialect identification system.

3.1   Dialectal Arabic Dataset

The DSL organizers provided a training dataset that is composed of Automatic Speech Recognition (ASR) transcripts (Ali et al., 2016), where utterances (or sentences) are labeled as Egyptian (EGY), Gulf

(GLF), Levantine (LAV), North-African (NOR), or Modern Standard Arabic (MSA). Each sentence is provided in a separate line in the following tab-delimited format:

```
sentence <tab> target-dialect-label
```

The Arabic sentences are transliterated into the Buckwalter encoding scheme. The training set has 7,619 sentences with a total of 315,829 words, of which 55,992 are unique. The average sentence length is 41 words. Table 1 shows the distribution of sentences, words, and unique words for the different variants. The numbers show that Egyptian has the longest sentences with an average of 53.8 words per sentence.

count	LAV	GLF	NOR	EGY	MSA	Total
sentences	**1,758**	1,672	1,612	1,578	999	7,619
words	66,219	64,081	51,593	**84,949**	48,987	315,829
unique words	19,198	17,842	20,271	**20,836**	13,607	55,992

Table 1: The distribution of sentences, words, and unique words for the different Arabic variants.

As expected, the frequent words are mostly stopwords with the words *fy* (in), *mn* (from), and *mA* (what) being the most frequent words across dialects. We retained stopwords as they are important for identifying dialects.

The data used in this shared task is different from data mentioned in the literature in that it is composed of ASR transcripts, and dialects are more common in conversational speech. Since the data was not manually revised (as part of the challenge), we found the following drawbacks in the data:

- The sentences are often quite incoherent and many sentences make no sense.

- Some lines have identical sentences, but with different dialect labels. Consider the following example (line 16 through line 19 in the dataset file):

```
16        $Ark Q EGY
17        $Ark Q GLF
18        $Ark Q LAV
19        $Ark Q NOR
```

Such problems complicate the dialect identification task. Furthermore, the nature and the distribution of the words and phrases in such data is different than the one extracted from sources such as blogs, forums, and tweets. Therefore, using such data to train a classifier (without taking into consideration the aforementioned issues) may yield a classifier that does not capture real patterns for a generalized dialect identifier.

Data Preparation: To perform offline experiments before submitting the official shared task runs, we split the provided training data into an 80/20 train/dev partitions, which would allow us to measure the effectiveness of different classification schemes. However, we used the entire set for training when submitting the final runs.

For some runs, we excluded sentences that are shorter than a certain threshold of words. We tried several threshold between 1 and 5. Furthermore, we also considered removing words with document frequency less than and/or greater than certain thresholds.

3.2   Methodology

We experimented with several supervised learning algorithms to perform a five-way classification among the five dialect classes. Apart from Multinomial Naive Bayes, we also trained a one-vs-rest logistic regression model and multi-class SVM with linear or string kernels. For SVM optimization, we used Stochastic Gradient Descent (SGD) over multiple passes on the dataset. We also trained a two layer neural network model over the dataset and evaluated its performance. With each of these learning algorithms, we tried several features including word level features and character level features. The shared task allowed for closed runs, in which we were allowed to use the provided training set exclusively, and open runs, in which we were allowed to use external resources. For the open runs, we augmented the shared task training data with the AOC data. Following is the description of the features that we used to train these models.

3.2.1 Word level features

Given that words are small units of semantic meaning, experimenting with word level features was the natural choice. We used words as follows:

Unigrams: As a baseline, we used word unigrams as features. We experimented with using raw word counts in a given sentence, term frequencies (tf), and term frequency and inverse document frequency (tf-idf) vectors.

N-grams: To capture contextual information, we experimented with bigrams and trigrams from the dataset. We collected all bigrams and trigrams and treated each one of them as a term. Our feature vector was then the tf-idf vector over these bigrams or trigrams. This may help capture word ordering differences among different dialects. Moreover, several n-grams only occur in certain dialects, which helps us create a more discriminating feature vector over the sentences in the dataset.

N-gram combinations: Finally, after noticing that all three of the previously computed features, unigrams, bigrams and trigrams provides its own advantage over the dataset, we decided to experiment with different combinations of these features, such as unigrams with bigrams, bigrams with trigrams, all three n-grams, etc. This resulted in a very high-dimensional feature vector.

3.2.2 Character level features

These features are more fine-grained than word level features, which would enable our models to learn morphological and utterance based features. Working with more fine-grained features was also shown to be useful in other natural language processing tasks such as machine translation (Sennrich et al., 2016). Character-based models have also been used in literature to convert Egyptian dialect to MSA in order to aid machine translation of Egyptian dialect (Sajjad et al., 2013; Durrani et al., 2014). Hence, this motivates the use of character level features for this task.

Character N-grams: Similar to word level features, we experimented with character-level bigrams, trigrams, 4-grams and 5-grams. The motivation behind this was drawn from word examples from different dialects that only differ in a few characters. The average word length in the dataset for the closed task is around 4.5 characters. Thus, we decided not to try values of n that are higher than 5.

Character N-gram combinations: Again, similar to word level features, we noticed that each of the n-gram features provided additional discriminating information for our classifiers, and hence we experimented with several combinations.

4 Results

As mentioned in section 3.1, we split the provided training set into training and dev splits. We report here our results on the dev split and on the official shared task runs. Tables 2 and 3 report on the accuracy of different experimental conditions with various learning algorithms and features on the dev set. The last column of Table 3 shows the performance of our best system. Our best system was trained on character bigrams, trigrams, 4-grams and 5-grams together. For this system, we also ignored all sentences of 3 words or less during training, as this has been shown to improve performance. As explained in section 3.1, shorter sentences in the corpus are not very discriminatory in this particular dataset. Hence, keeping them in the training corpus leads to sub-optimal performance. The linear SVM gave us the best results.

Table 4 shows the performance of our best model in the shared task. The baseline is based on the majority class, and our model performs significantly better than the baseline in the closed track. Figure 4 also shows the confusion matrix of our best model on the dev and official test sets. The best performance was achieved on the MSA class, while the worst was on the Gulf dialect. For the open track, our results were considerably poorer than those for the closed class even though we employed more training data. This could be explained by the significant difference in genre and lexical distribution between the task's training data and the AOC data.

More sophisticated models such as the SVM with a string kernel and a 2 Layer neural network did not perform as well as the linear SVM. This is potentially due to the limited size of the training set that does not allow the parameters to be adequately learned from the existing data to generalize as well.

	Raw Counts	Term Frequencies	Unigrams TF-IDF	Bigrams TF-IDF	trigrams TF-IDF	1,2,3-grams TF-IDF
Naive Bayes	0.5450	0.4339	0.4832	0.4504	0.3544	0.4734
Logistic Regression	0.5556	0.5227	0.5694	0.4523	0.3432	0.5082
SVM (linear)	0.5503	0.5457	**0.5976**	0.4931	0.3958	0.5700
2 Layer NN	0.5030	0.5312	0.5477	0.4536	0.3787	0.4845

Table 2: Accuracy on dev set with various word-level features

	Bigrams TF-IDF	Trigrams TF-IDF	4-grams TF-IDF	5-grams TF-IDF	2,3,4,5-grams TF-IDF	Best system
Naive Bayes	0.5030	0.5273	0.4668	0.4655	0.3702	0.3468
Logistic Regression	0.5654	0.6213	0.6318	0.6108	0.6377	0.6619
SVM (linear)	0.5378	0.6154	0.6410	0.6404	0.6588	**0.7007**
2 Layer NN	0.5352	0.6062	0.5845	0.5819	0.6009	0.6237

Table 3: Accuracy on dev set with various character-level features

Test Set	Track	Run	Accuracy	F1 (micro)	F1 (macro)	F1 (weighted)
C	-	baseline	0.2279	-	-	-
C	closed	run1	**0.5136**	**0.5136**	**0.5091**	**0.5112**
C	closed	run2	0.5117	0.5117	0.5023	0.5065
C	open	run1	0.3792	0.3792	0.3462	0.352
C	open	run2	0.3747	0.3747	0.3371	0.3413

Table 4: Results for all runs on the hidden test set.

5 Conclusion

In this paper, we described our Arabic dialect detection system that we used to submit four runs to sub-task 2 of the 2016 DSL shared task, which involves the automatic identification of 5 Arabic variants, namely Egyptian, Gulf, Levantine, North-African, and MSA. The training data for the sub-task at hand differs from data used in the literature in two ways, namely:

- The training data is relatively small,

- the training data is composed of ASR output, which makes the data difficult to work with.

For classification, we tried several machine-learning models. Our best performing model used an SVM classifier with a linear kernel that is trained on combined character n-gram where n = 1, 2, 3, 4, and 5 with tf-idf weighting. In the closed submission, we got the best accuracy of 0.5136 and the third best weighted F1 score, with a difference of less than 0.002 from the best system.

For future work, we plan to apply more powerful techniques, such as recurrent neural networks over both words and characters to capture the differences between the dialects better. We will be using larger datasets, since these models usually require large amounts of data to perform well.

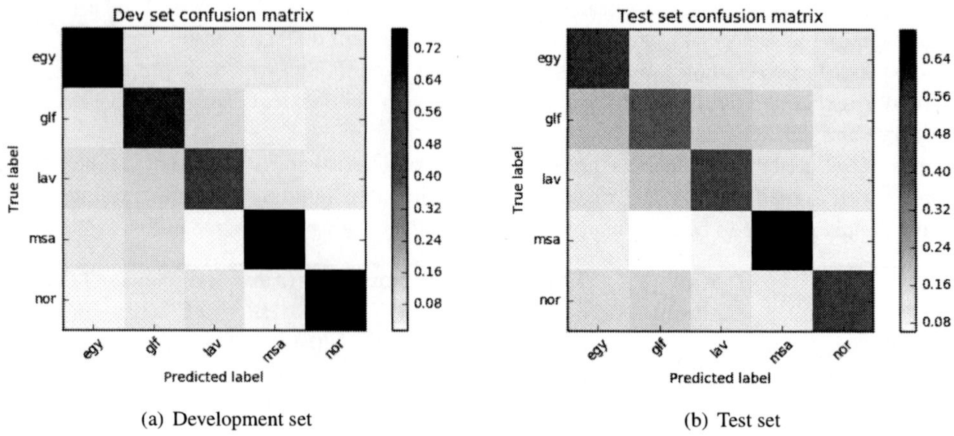

(a) Development set   (b) Test set

Figure 1: Confusion matrix for our best model

References

Ahmed Ali, Najim Dehak, Patrick Cardinal, Sameer Khurana, Sree Harsha Yella, James Glass, Peter Bell, and Steve Renals. 2016. Automatic dialect detection in arabic broadcast speech. In *Interspeech 2016*, pages 2934–2938.

Houda Bouamor, Nizar Habash, and Kemal Oflazer. 2014. A multidialectal parallel corpus of arabic. In *LREC*, pages 1240–1245.

Kareem Darwish, Hassan Sajjad, and Hamdy Mubarak. 2014. Verifiably effective arabic dialect identification. In *EMNLP*, pages 1465–1468.

Mona Diab, Nizar Habash, Owen Rambow, Mohamed Altantawy, and Yassine Benajiba. 2010. Colaba: Arabic dialect annotation and processing. In *Lrec workshop on semitic language processing*, pages 66–74.

Nadir Durrani, Yaser Al-Onaizan, and Abraham Ittycheriah. 2014. Improving egyptian-to-english smt by mapping egyptian into msa. In *International Conference on Intelligent Text Processing and Computational Linguistics*, pages 271–282. Springer.

Shervin Malmasi, Eshrag Refaee, and Mark Dras. 2015. Arabic Dialect Identification using a Parallel Multidialectal Corpus. In *Proceedings of the 14th Conference of the Pacific Association for Computational Linguistics (PACLING 2015)*, pages 209–217, Bali, Indonesia, May.

Shervin Malmasi, Marcos Zampieri, Nikola Ljubešić, Preslav Nakov, Ahmed Ali, and Jörg Tiedemann. 2016. Discriminating between similar languages and arabic dialect identification: A report on the third dsl shared task. In *Proceedings of the 3rd Workshop on Language Technology for Closely Related Languages, Varieties and Dialects (VarDial)*, Osaka, Japan.

Hamdy Mubarak and Kareem Darwish. 2014. Using twitter to collect a multi-dialectal corpus of arabic. *ANLP 2014*, page 1.

Hassan Sajjad, Kareem Darwish, and Yonatan Belinkov. 2013. Translating dialectal Arabic to English. In *Proceedings of the 51st Annual Meeting of the Association for Computational Linguistics (Volume 2: Short Papers)*, ACL '13, pages 1–6, Sofia, Bulgaria.

Rico Sennrich, Barry Haddow, and Alexandra Birch. 2016. Neural machine translation of rare words with subword units. In *Proceedings of the 54th Annual Meeting of the Association for Computational Linguistics (Volume 1: Long Papers)*, pages 1715–1725, Berlin, Germany, August. Association for Computational Linguistics.

Omar F Zaidan and Chris Callison-Burch. 2011. The arabic online commentary dataset: an annotated dataset of informal arabic with high dialectal content. In *Proceedings of the 49th Annual Meeting of the Association for Computational Linguistics: Human Language Technologies: short papers-Volume 2*, pages 37–41. Association for Computational Linguistics.

Omar F Zaidan and Chris Callison-Burch. 2014. Arabic dialect identification. *Computational Linguistics*, 40(1):171–202.

Tuning Bayes Baseline for dialect detection

Hector-Hugo Franco-Penya
Dublin Institute of Technology
francoph@tcd.ie

Liliana Mamani Sanchez
University College Dublin
mamanisl@tcd.ie

Abstract

This paper describes an analysis of our submissions to the Dialect Detection Shared Task 2016. We proposed three different systems that involved simplistic features, to name: a Naive-bayes system, a Support Vector Machines-based system and a Tree Kernel-based system. These systems underperform when compared to other submissions in this shared task, since the best one achieved an accuracy of ∼0.834.

1 Introduction

The problem of discriminating similar languages has been tackled in previous years in the context of shared tasks (Zampieri et al., 2014; Zampieri et al., 2015b). Here, there are promising results for dialect detection, being the best results around 95.54% and for an open challenge, the best results yield around 95.65%.

Despite these positive results, some research issues remain to be solved such as: domain adaptation, inclusion of new languages and classifier performance in terms of processing time.

The DSL 2014 Shared Task aimed to discriminate dialects within each of these 6 groups: Group A (Bosnian, Croatian, Serbian), Group B (Indonesian, Malay), Group C (Czech, Slovak), Group D (Brazilian Portuguese, European Portuguese), Group E (Castilian Spanish, Argentine Spanish), and Group F (American English, British English). The 2015 version of this Shared task considered the first 5 groups plus an additional group comprising Bulgarian and Macedonian. The 2016 version (Malmasi et al., 2016) where our systems were competing differs to previous tasks in the addition of a new variety of Spanish language: Mexican Spanish. Additionally, a second task aims to test dialect identification systems in Arabic language datasets.

Our submissions mainly addressed the sub-task 1 for automatically discriminating between similar languages and language varieties. We took into account two principles: a) to design lightweight systems given that such a system should work in an online environment, and b) to design systems that would involve using grammatical information without the recurring to sophisticated parsers.

This paper is structured as follows: Section 2 provides a brief context for our work in the state of the art of language detection. Section 3 describes the core of our experiments. Section 4 outlines our results and an analysis of the relevance of the proposed methods. Finally, we conclude with Section 6.

2 Related Work

Zampieri et al. (2012) and Zampieri et al. (2013) developed a computationally efficient method for detecting Spanish and French dialects, which produces highly accurate results based on a naive Bayes method. They address dialection detection in text extracted from newspaper articles. Since one of our systems is mainy based in this method we provide a more detailed explanation in Section 3.3.

The previous DSL shared task was hold in 2015, in for which nine systems where submitted to the close challenge. The best system was developed by (Malmasi and Dras, 2015). It consists of an ensemble of SVM classifiers trained with character ngrams and word unigrams and bigrams.

Other approaches were based on two stage classification, the first stage was designed to classify the group of languages and the second stage to differentiate between dialects (Goutte and Serge, 2015; Fabra-

Proceedings of the Third Workshop on NLP for Similar Languages, Varieties and Dialects,
pages 227–234, Osaka, Japan, December 12 2016.

Boluda et al., 2015; Acs et al., 2015). Zampieri et al. (2015a) created a system based on Support Vector Machines that has features in form of TF-IDF and also token base back-off (Jauhiainen et al., 2015), an interesting method that split unknown tokens (unknown in the training data sets) into character n-grams until it is found some examples on the training data set that can be use to derived probabilities.

3 Methods

This section briefly describes the resources and methods used to develop our systems.

3.1 Datasets

The training datasets provided by the shared task organizers were created based on text from newspapers articles. One in-domain test set and also two out of domain twitter base data sets were made available for testing purposes; these two twitter data sets were collected in a different manner to the news dataset.

3.2 Pre-processing

Punctuation marks, brackets, parenthesis, hyphens, and multiple blank spaces were removed. Also, sentences were standardized to be all in upper-case. This pre-processing simplifies the text and that could be beneficial on classification tasks with scarce amount of training data, but could also lose relevant information for the classification, for instance (Tan et al., 2012) claim that in Malaysian numbers are written with decimal point while in Indonesian are written using colons.

3.3 Naive Bayes, bi-gram language model

Our best system is a re-creation of the lightweight naive bayes bi-gram-word classification model described in (Zampieri et al., 2015a; Zampieri et al., 2013; Zampieri et al., 2012; Zampieri and Gebre, 2012; Tiedemann and Ljubešić, 2012; Baldwin and Lui, 2010) for detecting Spanish dialects, Portuguese dialects (from Brazil or Portugal), between Bosnian, Croatian and Serbian, and other languages. This model has been extensively tested in different scenarios in the aforementioned works and we deemed it was a good starting point for our experiment and it seemed less demanding in terms of processing times. Its implementation was also described in language identification studies (Tiedemann and Ljubešić, 2012).

The formula used to calculate the likelihood of a given text belonging to a language or dialect L is:

$$P(L|text) = argmax_L \sum_{i=1}^{N} log(P_l(n_i|L)) + log(P(L)))$$

(1)

where N is the number of n-grams, $P_l(n_i|L)$ is the Laplace probability of the n_i n-gram appearing on the language model L and $P(L)$ is the ratio of the number of n-grams used to build the language model L divided by the total amount of n-grams used to build all language models.

$$P_l(ng|L) = \frac{C(ng|L) + \alpha}{N + B}$$

(2)

where $\alpha = 1$. $C(ng|L)$ is the number of times the n-gram ng appears on the text used to build the language model L. N is the total number of n-grams extracted from the text used to build L, and B is the total number of unique n-grams found at the text used to build the language model L.

The best results on the discerning western languages development data set where reach using bi-grams, therefore bi-grams models where used to for both tasks.

3.4 SVM

Support Vector Machines are among the most used algorithms for classification problems. Baldwin and Lui (2010) successfully used SVMs in language identification. It was also used in previous shared tasks in different setups (Purver, 2014; Zampieri et al., 2015a; Malmasi and Dras, 2015).

Each unique word on the train data set was assigned a unique index. Using these indexes, a sparse vector was created for each sentence of the training and testing data set. Words which did not appear on the training data set were ignored. The appearance of a word was flagged as a single occurrence on the projected vector independently of how many times that word appeared on the sentence. For this experiment the multi-class setup of lib-SMV was used.

4 Analysis of Results

This shared task is about classifying sentences, and context plays a crucial role. Nonetheless, the authors think it is worth to discuss the importance of dialect detection when the dialect of a short piece of language cannot be detected by neither humans or machines.

Two scenarios appear likely: a) such piece of language is standard amongst language variations and understood by the great majority of native speakers of the corresponding language, or b) It is too specific in a dialect and in a register within that dialect that there is there is no body of comparison that allows detection.

For the second case, let us consider the domain register of the dataset used during the training phase of the experiments.

4.1 Training times

The naive Bayes model is quickly trained because it just requires to calculate n-grams probabilities and has a linear computational cost (see Table 1). SVM is has a quadratic computational time, and the training time is measured in hours or minutes, except for the Arabic data set, which is measured in seconds due to its small size.

All experiments were done in a laptop with an Intel Core i7-5600U processor at 2.60GHz with 2 Cores and 16GB of RAM.

Method	Sub-task	Set	unigrams	bigrams
SVM	1	train	5.5 hours	5 hours
SVM	2	train	30 seconds	12 seconds
SVM	1	dev	20 minutes	14 minutes
Bayes	1	train	11 seconds	17 seconds
Bayes	2	train	<1 second	<1 second
Bayes	1	dev	<1 second	<1 second

Table 1: Training times for both training datasets: Sub-task 1(for Roman Alphabet Languages) and Sub-task 2 (for the Arabic language)

5 Overview

The official results for our submissions are shown in Table 2. They correspond to two of the systems described in Section 3. This table shows the accuracy, micro and macro and weighted F1 for each of the submitted classifications. Test set A is the in-domain composed by text from newspaper articles. Test datasets B1 and B2 are composed by text extracted from twitter microposts, in two different ways. Test set C is composed by Arabic text extracted by Automatic Speech Recognition.

Test Set	Run	Accuracy	F1 (micro)	F1 (macro)	F1 (weighted)
A	run1(Bayes)	0.8377	0.8377	0.8317	0.8317
A	run2(SVM)	0.5848	0.5848	0.5802	0.5802
B1	run1(Bayes)	0.806	0.806	0.5667	0.7934
B1	run2(SVM)	0.594	0.594	0.3949	0.4739
B2	run1(Bayes)	0.74	0.74	0.4543	0.7268
B2	run2(SVM)	0.588	0.588	0.3394	0.543
C	run1(Bayes)	0.3584	0.3584	0.3492	0.3455

Table 2: Results for all runs (for the closed track)

Table 3 shows the confusion matrix for the in-domain test set A per language. When a word cannot be identified as belonging to any language model the system classifies as "bs" by default, that is why the

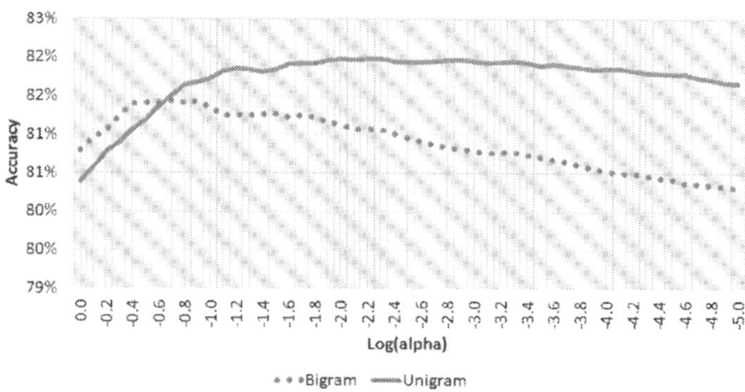

Figure 1: Accuracy graph for Lidstone smoothing factor (development data set)

first column (predicted bs) shows more false positives than other languages. This confusion table shows that the system classifies the language of a sentence with an accuracy of about 99.5%.

	bs+hr+sr	es	fr	id-my	pt
bs+hr+sr	2994	3	1	1	1
es	3	2994	1	1	1
fr	9	1	1989	0	1
id-my	7	2	2	1988	1
pt	3	1	1	0	1995

Table 3: Language confusion matrix

Table 4 shows the confusion matrix for all dialects. Table 5 shows Precision, Recall and F1 of each dialect, in domain test set. Here the Indonesian and Malasian (Group B) show the highest F1-scores, and Bosnian, Croatian and Serbian (group A) show the lowest F1-scores.

Table 6 shows the confusion matrix for the twitter testing data sets B1 and B2, the tables are simplified because there are only testing samples for group D:Portuguese and group A: Bosnian, Croatian and Serbian, rows corresponding to other dialects where removed as only contain zeros, but those dialects may appear in the column section to identify false positives, which in this case are es-es, fr-fr and id.

B1	bs	es-ar	es-es	es-mx	fr-ca	fr-fr	hr	id	my	pt-br	pt-pt	sr
bs	500		2				247					251
es-ar		861	126	12			1					
es-es	2	70	909	16		1		1			1	
es-mx		191	350	459								
fr-ca					863	137						
fr-fr	6		1		46	943	3				1	
hr	78		1				871					50
id	5	1	1			2		976	14		1	
my	2							40	958			
pt-br	1									945	54	
pt-pt	2		1			1				95	901	
sr	79					1	52	1		1		866

Table 4: Confusion matrix results

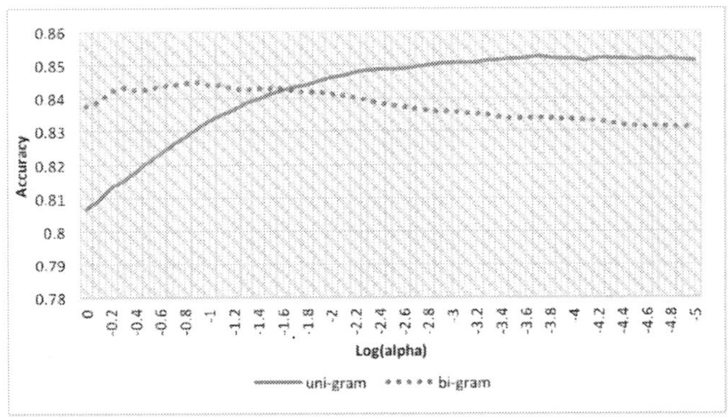

Figure 2: Accuracy graph for Lidstone smoothing factor for A (in-domain test).

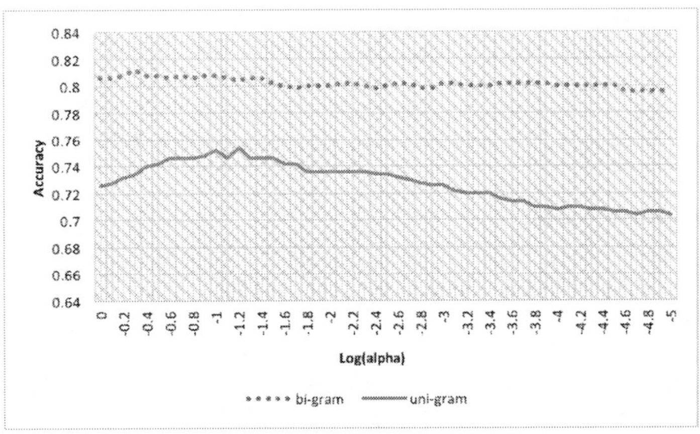

Figure 3: Accuracy graph for Lidstone smoothing factor for B1 (first out-of-domain twitter data set)

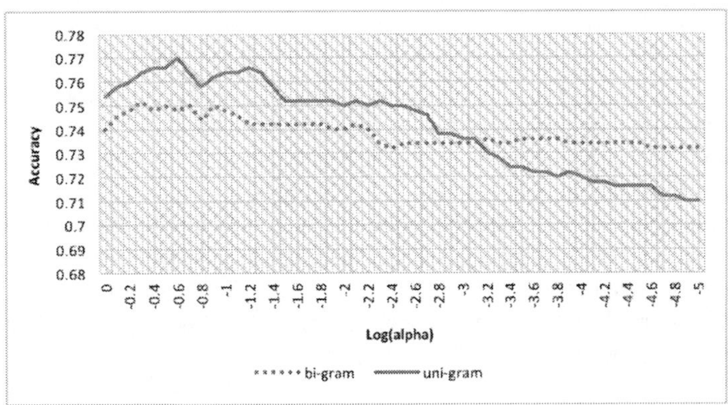

Figure 4: Accuracy graph for Lidstone smoothing factor for B2 (second out-of-domain twitter data set)

	bs	es-ar	es-es	es-mx	fr-ca	fr-fr	hr	id	my	pt-br	pt-pt	sr
Precision	50	86	91	46	86	94	87	98	96	95	90	87
Recall	43	43	40	49	49	46	43	49	50	48	48	43
F1	46	58	55	47	62	62	57	65	65	63	63	57

Table 5: Precision, Recall and F1 of each dialect, in domain test set (in percentages)

	Predicted							
	bs-hr-sr dialects			Portuguese		Others		
B1	bs	hr	sr	pt-br	pt-pt	es-es	fr-fr	id
bs	36	6	56	.	.	1	.	1
hr	2	90	8	.	.	.	.	.
sr	1	.	99	.	.	.	.	.
pt-br	.	.	.	99	1	.	.	.
pt-pt	.	.	.	21	79	.	.	.
B2	bs	hr	sr	pt-br	pt-pt	es-es	fr-fr	id
bs	34	7	57	.	.	1	.	1
hr	4	87	9	.	.	.	.	.
sr	1	.	99	.	.	.	.	.
pt-br	3	.	.	88	9	.	.	.
pt-pt	2	.	.	34	62	1	1	.

Table 6: Simplified confusion matrix for the twitter test datasets B1 and B2.

5.1 Lidstone smoothing factor

With Lidstone smoothing factor α set to one, the probability formula results in the Laplace probability, however with $\alpha < 1$ the probability results in Lidstone smoothing (Tan et al., 2012).

Extensive experimentation using Laplace probability has been carried out ($\alpha = 1$) (Baldwin and Lui, 2010; Tan et al., 2012; Zampieri and Gebre, 2012; Zampieri et al., 2013; Zaidan and Callison-Burch, 2014), but non as far as the authors of this article know using an optimization of Lidstone smoothing.

An investigation carried out after the submission deadline for the experiment using the development set, shows that an accuracy of 80.4% for uni-grams using Laplace probabilities could be improved to 82.0% (increment of 1.6%) with Lidstone smoothing using an alpha value of $\alpha = 0.01$.

The tuning of the parameter α seems to improve the uni-grams language model more than the bi-grams language model to the extent that the uni-gram model outperforms the bi-gram one. This is an important observation because it was believed that the bi-gram model outperforms the uni-gram model, and that is what happens with $\alpha = 1$, this is why the results of the bi-gram model where submitted to the shared task evaluation.

Figure 1 shows how the accuracy changes along with the parameter α. The smallest the α value the higher weight of infrequent words on the results of the experiment.

It is a plausible hypothesis that uni-gram models are less likely to capture name entities that consist on multiple words and therefore not only outperforms the bi-gram model but also adapts better to new domains. This expectation is not observed on the results show on other data sets, for instance Figure 2 shows a similar trend by the crossing point from which uni-grams outperform bi-grams $10^{-1.6}$ is much lower than the one suggested by the development set $10^{-0.6}$. Also the out of domains data sets, B1 shows a graph for which bi-grams always outperform uni-grams (See Figure 3), and B2, shows opposite trends as the in-domain testing set (see Figure 3).

6 Concluding Remarks

Observations on the tuning of the smoothing factor (Section 3.3) are important contributions of this work. This results indicates that with proper selection of the α parameter the word base uni-gram model tends to outperforms the word base bi-gram model. This is important because previous published research used the default parameter $\alpha = 1$ and it looks like bi-gram word base models outperform uni-gram models, where the results shown on this article point otherwise. Uni-gram word base models can have smaller dictionaries which probably are less attached to the training set domain and that could lead to better domain adaptation, this hypothesis needs further investigation.

The optimal value for the alpha parameter seems to be substantially lower than the default set on Laplace probabilities, about $\alpha = 0.01$ for words uni-grams and $\alpha = 0.2$ for words bi-grams, where the crossing point from which the uni-grams model outperform the bi-grams model is $\alpha = 0.25$ $(10^{-0.6})$ this values are derivative from the development set.

This article re-produces a successfully naive Bayes language classifier approach for the automatic classification. The system was trained with for two different groups of languages, the first task contains twelve different languages or dialects group in five different clusters according to their similarity. The groups are: Group A (Bosnian, Croatian, and Serbian), Group B (Malay and Indonesian), Group C (Portuguese: Brazil and Portugal), Group D (Spanish: Argentina, Mexico, and Spain), Group E (French: France and Canada).

Classifying sentences among this groups of languages is not a novel task if analysed on individual groups but what is novel is to discriminate with all twelve groups together, except on previous shared tasks.

As an interesting observation using naive Bayes about 4.2% of the in-domain test set of Argentinian-Spanish is classified as Castilian-Spanish, where almost no Argentinian-Spanish samples are classified as Mexican-Spanish (0.4%). However with the SVM model, this trend is reversed, with SVM still 3% of Argentinian-Spanish samples are misclassified as Spanish, and 13% are misclassified as Mexican-Spanish.

Regarding the second task, classifying Arabic languages/dialects, the results obtained using naive Bayes differ in great manner from the naive Bayes system described in (Zaidan and Callison-Burch, 2014) where the accuracy for each dialect ranges between 69.1% to 86.5%. The data sets are not the same, but the difference could be due to a problem on encoding Arabic characters.

References

Judit Acs, László Grad-Gyenge, Thiago Bruno, Rodrigues de Rezende Oliveira, and Vale do Sao Francisco. 2015. A two-level classifier for discriminating similar languages. In *Proceedings of the Joint Workshop on Language Technology for Closely Related Languages, Varieties and Dialects, LT4VarDial*, volume 15, pages 73–77.

Timothy Baldwin and Marco Lui. 2010. Language Identification: The Long and the Short of the Matter. *Proceedings of the 2010 Conference of the North American Chapter of the Association for Computational Linguistics: Human Language Technologies (NAACL HLT '12)*, (June):229–237.

Raül Fabra-Boluda, Francisco Rangel, and Paolo Rosso. 2015. NLEL UPV Autoritas participation at Discrimination between Similar Languages (DSL) 2015 Shared Task. In *Joint Workshop on Language Technology for Closely Related Languages, Varieties and Dialects*, page 52.

Cyril Goutte and Leger Serge. 2015. Experiments in Discriminating Similar Languages. In *Proceedings of the Joint Workshop on Language Technology for Closely Related Languages, Varieties and Dialects 2015*, pages 78–84, Bulgaria.

Tommi Jauhiainen, Heidi Jauhiainen, Krister Lindén, and Others. 2015. Discriminating similar languages with token-based backoff. In *Proceedings of the Joint Workshop on Language Technology for Closely Related Languages, Varieties and Dialects*.

Shervin Malmasi and Mark Dras. 2015. Language Identification using Classifier Ensembles. In *Joint Workshop on Language Technology for Closely Related Languages, Varieties and Dialects*, pages 35–43.

Shervin Malmasi, Marcos Zampieri, Nikola Ljubešić, Preslav Nakov, Ahmed Ali, and Jörg Tiedemann. 2016. Discriminating between similar languages and arabic dialect identification: A report on the third dsl shared task. In *Proceedings of the 3rd Workshop on Language Technology for Closely Related Languages, Varieties and Dialects (VarDial)*, Osaka, Japan.

Matthew Purver. 2014. A Simple Baseline for Discriminating Similar Languages. *Proceedings of the First Workshop on Applying NLP Tools to Similar Languages, Varieties and Dialects*, pages 155–160.

Liling Tan, Marcos Zampieri, and Nikola Ljubeši. 2012. Merging Comparable Data Sources for the Discrimination of Similar Languages : The DSL Corpus Collection. In *Proceedings of the 7th Workshop on Building and Using Comparable Corpora: Building Resources for Machine Translation Research*, Reykjavik, Iceland.

Jörg Tiedemann and Nikola Ljubešić. 2012. Efficient Discrimination Between Closely Related Languages. *Coling 2012*, (December 2012):2619–2634.

Omar F. Zaidan and Chris Callison-Burch. 2014. Arabic dialect identification. *Computational Linguistics*, 40(1):171–202, March.

Marcos Zampieri and Binyam Gebrekidan Gebre. 2012. Automatic Identification of Language Varieties: The Case of Portuguese. In *Proceedings of KONVENS 2012*, pages 233–237.

Marcos Zampieri, Binyam Gebrekidan Gebre, and Sascha Diwersy. 2012. Classifying Pluricentric Languages: Extending the Monolingual Model on. *Proceedings of the Fourth Swedish Language Technlogy Conference (SLTC2012)*, pages 79–80.

Marcos Zampieri, Binyam Gebrekidan Gebre, and Sascha Diwersy. 2013. N-gram Language Models and POS Distribution for the Identification of Spanish Varieties. In *Proceedings of TALN 2013 (Volume 2: Short Papers)*, pages 580–587, Les Sables d'Olonne, France, June. ATALA.

Marcos Zampieri, Liling Tan, Nikola Ljubešić, Jörg Tiedemann, and Nikola Ljube. 2014. A Report on the DSL Shared Task 2014. *Proceedings of the First Workshop on Applying NLP Tools to Similar Languages, Varieties and Dialects*, (2013):58–67.

Marcos Zampieri, Binyam Gebrekidan Gebre, Hernani Costa, and Josef Van Genabith. 2015a. Comparing Approaches to the Identification of Similar Languages. *Joint Workshop on Language Technology for Closely Related Languages, Varieties and Dialects (LT4VarDial'15). 2nd Discriminating between Similar Languages Shared Task (DSL'15)*, page 7.

Marcos Zampieri, Liling Tan, Nikola Ljubešić, Jörg Tiedemann, and Preslav Nakov. 2015b. Overview of the DSL Shared Task 2015. *Proceedings of the Joint Workshop on Language Technology for Closely Related Languages, Varieties and Dialects*, (2014):1–9.

Vanilla Classifiers for Distinguishing between Similar Languages

Alina Maria Ciobanu, Sergiu Nisioi, Liviu P. Dinu
Solomon Marcus Center for Computational Linguistics,
Faculty of Mathematics and Computer Science,
University of Bucharest
alina.ciobanu@my.fmi.unibuc.ro,
sergiu.nisioi@gmail.com,
ldinu@fmi.unibuc.ro

Abstract

In this paper we describe the submission of the UniBuc-NLP team for the Discriminating between Similar Languages Shared Task, DSL 2016. We present and analyze the results we obtained in the closed track of sub-task 1 (Similar languages and language varieties) and sub-task 2 (Arabic dialects). For sub-task 1 we used a logistic regression classifier with tf-idf feature weighting and for sub-task 2 a character-based string kernel with an SVM classifier. Our results show that good accuracy scores can be obtained with limited feature and model engineering. While certain limitations are to be acknowledged, our approach worked surprisingly well for out-of-domain, social media data, with 0.898 accuracy (3rd place) for dataset B1 and 0.838 accuracy (4th place) for dataset B2.

1 Introduction

Automatic language identification is the task of determining the language in which a piece of text is written using computational methods. In today's context of multilingualism, and given the rapid development of the online repositories of cross-language information, language identification is an essential task for many downstream applications (such as cross-language information retrieval or question answering), to route the documents to the appropriate NLP systems, based on their language.

Although language identification has been intensively studied in the recent period, there are still questions to be answered. Language identification is still a challenging research problem for very similar languages and language varieties, for very short pieces of text, such as tweets, or for documents involving code-switching (the practice of mixing more languages within a single communication).

The DSL 2016 shared task (Malmasi et al., 2016) tackles two interesting aspects of language identification: similar language and language varieties (with in-domain and out-of-domain – social media data – test sets) and Arabic dialects. In this paper we present the submission of the UniBuc-NLP team for the closed track (using only the training data provided by the organizers) of both sub-tasks.

2 Related Work

Most approaches to language identification are based on character n-grams. Dunning (1994) was one of the very first who used them. He proposed a statistical method for language identification based on Markov models to compute the likelihood of the character n-grams. Ever since, character n-grams have been employed to discriminate between a wide variety of closely related languages and dialects. Maier and Gómez-Rodríguez (2014) performed language classification on tweets for Spanish varieties, with character n-grams as features and using the country of the speaker to identify the variety. Trieschnigg et al. (2012) discriminated between Dutch dialects (and several other languages) using a large collection of folktales. They compared several approaches to language identification and reported good results when using the method of Cavnar and Trenkle (1994), based on character n-grams. Sadat et al. (2014) performed language identification on Arabic dialects using social media texts. They obtained better results with Naive Bayes and n-gram features (2-grams) than with a character n-gram Markov model for

Proceedings of the Third Workshop on NLP for Similar Languages, Varieties and Dialects,
pages 235–242, Osaka, Japan, December 12 2016.

most of the Arabic dialects. Gottron and Lipka (2010) conducted a comparative experiment of classification methods for language identification in short texts, discriminating between languages from various language families and using n-gram features. Their results show that Naive Bayes classifier performs best and that errors occur for languages from the same family, reinforcing the hypothesis that language identification is more difficult for very similar languages.

Word n-grams have also proven effective for discriminating between languages and language varieties. Malmasi and Dras (2015) achieved the best performance in the closed track of the DSL 2015 shared task, experimenting with classifier ensembles trained on character and word n-gram features. Goutte and Leger (2015) obtained a very good performance in the same competition using statistical classifiers and employing a combination of character and word n-grams as features. Zampieri and Gebre (2012) made use of a character n-gram model and a word n-gram language model to discriminate between two varieties of Portuguese. They reported the highest accuracy when using character 4-grams and reached the conclusion that orthographic and lexical differences between the two varieties have more discriminative power than lexico-syntactic differences.

Other features, such as exclusive words, the format of the numbers (Ranaivo-Malancon, 2006), blacklists (Tiedemann and Ljubesic, 2012), syllable n-grams (Maier and Gómez-Rodríguez, 2014) or skipgrams have been employed and shown useful for this task.

3   Data

The organizers released two training datasets for the 2016 DSL shared task: a dataset of similar languages and language varieties (for sub-task 1) and a dataset of Arabic dialects (for sub-task 2).

The dataset for sub-task 1 is a new version of the DSL Corpus Collection (Tan et al., 2014). It contains instances written in the following languages and language varieties (organized by groups of similarity):

Language	Lang. code	Group code	Avg. sent. lenth	Avg. word length
Bosnian	bs		31.38	5.21
Croatian	hr	bs-hr-sr	37.30	5.30
Serbian	sr		34.28	5.09
Indonesian	id	id-my	34.34	5.84
Malay	my		26.01	5.91
Portuguese (Brazil)	pt-BR	pt	39.94	4.90
Portuguese (Portugal)	pt-PT		36.70	4.92
Spanish (Argentina)	es-AR		41.70	4.98
Spanish (Mexico)	es-MX	es	30.96	4.78
Spanish (Spain)	es-ES		45.06	4.84
French (France)	fr-FR	fr	37.13	4.69
French (Canada)	fr-CA		30.20	4.69

Table 1: Statistics for the dataset of similar languages and language varieties (sub-task 1).

The dataset consists of 20,000 instances (18,000 for training and 2,000 for development) in each language or language variety, extracted from journalistic texts. In Table 1 we report several statistics for this dataset. The average sentence length varies from 26.01 (for Malay) to 45.06 (for the Spanish variety used in Spain). We observe a high variance for the average sentence length within some of the language groups (the difference between the average sentence length of Indonesian and Malay is ∼8, and between the average sentence length of the Spanish variety spoken in Spain and the one spoken in Mexico is ∼14). The average word length varies from 4.69 (for both versions of French) to 5.91 (for Malay), with a low variance within groups.

Comparing these statistics with those extracted from the sub-task 1 test sets, we notice that while the average sentence length values for test set A are similar to those of the training set, for test sets B1 and B2 – social media data – sentences are significantly shorter, as expected, ranging from an average of 11.33 for Portuguese (Brazil) to an average of 13.39 for Serbian. The average word length values for B1 and B2 are also smaller than those for test set A and the training set, but the differences are not as significant as the differences regarding the length of the sentences.

The dataset for sub-task 2 contains automatic speech recognition transcripts (Ali et al., 2016) written in the following Arabic dialects: Egyptian, Gulf, Levantine, North-African, and Modern Standard Arabic. In Table 2 we report several statistics for this dataset. The average sentence length ranges from 35.41 (for North-African) to 60.57 (for Egyptian). All the Arabic dialects have the average word length lower than 4.

Dialect	Dialect code	# instances	Avg. sent. lenth	Avg. word length
Egyptian	EGY	1,578	60.57	3.65
Gulf	GLF	1,672	43.21	3.64
Levantine	LAV	1,758	42.01	3.63
North-African	NOR	1,612	35.41	3.74
Modern Standard Arabic	MSA	999	56.94	3.80

Table 2: Statistics for the dataset of Arabic dialects (sub-task 2).

4 Our Approach

In this section we describe and analyze the methods we used for discriminating between similar languages, language varieties and dialects. We used standard linear classifiers with basic n-grams features.[1]

4.1 Classifiers

Logistic Regression

For sub-task 1 we used a logistic regression classifier with word unigrams and bigrams as features. The features are tf-idf (Salton and Buckley, 1988) weighted and we keep only the features that occur at least 3 times in the training set. We use the L_2 distance for term vectors and the default regularization constant $C = 1$ without performing any grid search for best parameters. We use the wrapper of the scikit learn Python library (Pedregosa et al., 2011) over the Liblinear logistic regression implementation (Fan et al., 2008). The main advantages of this model are its simplicity and training speed.

SVM + String Kernel

On the Arabic dataset we decided to use string a kernel based on character n-grams, since the text is obtained through ASR systems and most certainly the transcript contains errors. Character n-grams are able to cover sub-parts of words and can theoretically increase the overall classification accuracy, especially in a language recognition task. We used a string kernel in combination with a support vector machine classifier. A kernel function can be used either to embed the data in a higher dimensional space to achieve linear separability, or to replace the dot product between vectors with values that are more appropriate for the data used. Previous studies on text classification revealed that character n-gram-based string kernels can be effective tools for authorship attribution, native language identification or plagiarism detection (Grozea and Popescu, 2010).

The kernel we propose is computed by summing the number of common character n-grams between two examples, where n varies between 2 and 7. Formally, given an alphabet A, we define the mapping function $\Phi_n : \mathcal{D} \rightarrow \{0, 1\}^{Q_n}$ for an example $e \in \mathcal{C}$ in the corpus to be the vector of all the binary values of existence of the n-gram g in the document:

$$\Phi_n(e) = [\phi_g(e)]_{g \in A^n}$$

---

[1]The source code to reproduce our results is available at `https://gitlab.com/nlp-unibuc/dsl2016-code`.

The function $\phi_g(e) = 1$ if the n-gram g is in the example e and equal to zero otherwise. Computationally, Q_n depends on all the possible character n-grams between two examples at certain instance.

The corresponding Gram matrix K of size $|\mathcal{C}| \times |\mathcal{C}|$ has the following elements:

$$K_{ij} = \sum_{n=2}^{n \leq 7} < \Phi_n(e_i) \Phi_n(e_j) >$$

The Gram matrix is then normalized to the $[0, 1]$ interval:

$$K_{ij} = \frac{K_{ij}}{\sqrt{K_{ii}K_{jj}}} \tag{1}$$

The kernel function, in our case, is computed between every pair of training and testing examples. This type of approach is less scalable for large amounts of data, which is the main reason for not applying this technique on sub-task 1. However, additional optimizations can be taken into consideration, such as using just the upper half of the symmetric Gram matrix, aggregating multiple kernels trained on sub-samples of the data or hashing techniques for faster computation. In our vanilla approach we did not make use of any of these techniques.

In practice, kernel methods over strings for text classification work remarkably well covering fine-grained similarities such as content, punctuation marks, affixes etc., however one important downside of this method is usually the lack of linguistic features available within the classifier, making almost impossible to analyze from the Gram matrix the actual features that lead to good or bad results.

4.2 Experiments

Using the experimental setup previously described, we developed several systems for discriminating between similar languages and language varieties (sub-task 1) and between Arabic dialects (sub-task 2).

The organizers provided three test datasets, two for sub-task 1 and one for sub-task 2. In Table 3 we provide a brief characterization of the datasets:

Dataset	Description	Task	# instances
A	In-domain: newspaper texts	Sub-task 1	12,000
B1	Out of domain: social media data	Sub-task 1	500
B2	Out of domain: social media data	Sub-task 1	500
C	ASR texts from Arabic dialects	Sub-task 2	1,540

Table 3: Test datasets for DSL 2016.

Sub-task 1

Our two runs for sub-task 1 are as follows:

- **Run 1:** a one-level system. The first system consists of a single logistic regression classifier that predicts the language or language variety.

- **Run 2:** a two-level system. The second system consists of multiple logistic regression classifiers: we train a classifier to predict the language group ("inter-group classifier"), and one classifier for each language group ("intra-group classifier"), to predict the language or language variety within the group.

For the one-level system we obtained 0.8441 accuracy when evaluating on the development dataset. For the two-level system we obtained 0.9972 accuracy for the inter-group classifier, and the following values for the intra-group classifiers: 0.7510 for es, 0.8940 for fr, 0.9207 for pt, 0.7848 for bs-hr-sr, 0.9820 for id-my.

Test Set	Run	Accuracy	F1 (micro)	F1 (macro)	F1 (weighted)
A	Run 1	0.8624	0.8624	0.8620	0.8620
A	**Run 2**	**0.8648**	**0.8648**	**0.8643**	**0.8643**
B1	**Run 1**	**0.8980**	**0.8980**	**0.7474**	**0.8969**
B1	Run2	0.8940	0.8940	0.7429	0.8915
B2	Run1	0.8360	0.8360	0.5970	0.8358
B2	**Run2**	**0.8380**	**0.8380**	**0.5236**	**0.8378**

Table 4: The results of the UniBuc-NLP team for sub-task 1.

Test Set	Run	Accuracy	F1 (micro)	F1 (macro)	F1 (weighted)
C	run1	0.3948	0.3948	0.3891	0.3938
C	run2	0.4747	0.4747	0.4729	0.4732
C	**run3**	**0.4753**	**0.4753**	**0.4732**	**0.4742**

Table 5: The results of the UniBuc-NLP team for sub-task 2.

In Table 4 we report the results that we obtained for the test datasets. Our best results for each dataset are as follows: 0.8648 accuracy (11th place) for dataset A, 0.8980 accuracy (3rd place) for dataset B1 and 0.8380 accuracy (4th place) for dataset B2. For two of the three datasets (A, B2), the two-level system obtained better results than the one-level system. However, our highest accuracy (0.8990) was obtained by the one-level system for dataset B1.

Lang. code	Top 10 informative features
bs	povrije ,fbih, rs, poslije, km, prenosi, je, sarajevo, bh, bih
hr	tko, hdz, je, hrvatska, milijuna, u, te, kuna, tijekom, s
sr	evra, deo, srbije, predsednik, dve, vreme, gde, da, pre, posle
id	tim, tak, indonesia, mengatakan, di, bahwa, saat, dari, karena, bisa
my	ialah, encik, turut, apabila, selepas, boleh, berkata, daripada, beliau, kerana
pt-BR	para, ela, voce, do, em, brasil, r, e, o, ele
pt-PT	acores, o seu, a sua, numa, equipa, num, e, euros, a, portugal
es-AR	productores, empresas, ar, de rosario, el, santa fe, de, y, argentina, rosario
es-MX	mexicano, gadafi, mil, el, mexico, dijo, en, la, que, de
es-ES	alicante, murcia, del, ayer, han, la, y, euros, el, ha
fr-FR	d, paris, euros, est, et, les, le, l, france, vous
fr-CA	des, dit, de, de montreal, mme, quebecois, m, canada, montreal, quebec

Table 6: The most informative features for the one-level system for sub-task 1.

In Tables 6 and 7 we report the most informative features for each class. With few exceptions, most of the informative features are unigrams. While for the language classifiers many of these features are named entities (such as references to geographical regions or names of persons), as expected, for the language group classifier (Table 7a) the situation is different: mostly very short words prove to have high discriminative power. Among others, we identified definite and indefinite articles – "los" (es), "le" (fr) – and functional words – "nao" (pt), "dalam" (id-my) – ranked among the most informative features.

Despite the fact that quite many of the top features are named entities, which could a suggest a topic bias in classification, our systems obtain a good performance on out-of-domain data, ranking 3rd and 4th on the social media datasets.

Both our systems outperform significantly a random baseline that obtains 0.0883 F1 score for dataset A and 0.20 for datasets B1 and B2.

Group code	Top 10 informative features
bs-hr-sr	da, ce, iz, su, od, na, za, u, i, je
id-my	dari, pada, dalam, ini, untuk, dengan, itu, di, yang, dan
pt	nao, a, com, um, as, os, em, do, o, e
es	una, las, con, de, la, del, en, los, el, y
fr	au, une, pour, d, du, l, des, les, et, le

(a) Level 1: language groups.

Lang. code	Top 10 informative features
bs	sarajeva,sarajevu, fbih, rs, poslije, prenosi, km, sarajevo, bh, bih
hr	hrvatska, tisuca, hdz, tko, milijuna, te, no, kuna, tijekom, s
sr	evra, deo, srbije, predsednik, dve, gde, vreme, da, pre, posle
id	harus, tak, indonesia, tim, mengatakan, bahwa, dari, saat, bisa, karena
my	encik, turut, bahawa, apabila, selepas, boleh, berkata, daripada, beliau, kerana
pt-BR	eles, equipe, voce, sao paulo, federal, ela, em um, brasil, r, ele
pt-PT	numa, lisboa, acores, num, o seu, a sua, este, equipa, euros, portugal
es-AR	provincial, produccion, productores, empresas, mercado, empresa, santa fe, de rosario, argentina, rosario
es-MX	pri, de mexico, japon, pues, gadafi, mexicano, libia, mil, dijo, mexico
es-ES	ayuntamiento, espana, y a, murcia, alicante, han, cantabria, ayer, euros, ha
fr-FR	est, l, sarkozy, 2, francais, paris, 1, euros, vous, france
fr-CA	canadiens, ottawa, harper, m, du quebec, de montreal, quebecois, canada, montreal, quebec

(b) Level 2: languages.

Table 7: The most informative features for the two-level system for sub-task 2.

Sub-task 2

Our three runs for sub-task 2 are as follows:

- **Run 1**: SVM + string kernel with n-gram size $n \in \{ 2,...,5 \}$.

- **Run 2**: SVM + string kernel with n-gram size $n \in \{ 2,...,6 \}$.

- **Run 3**: SVM + string kernel with n-gram size $n \in \{ 2,...,7 \}$.

In Table 5 we report the results that we obtained for the test dataset. As expected, the accuracy of the system increases as the range of n-grams becomes wider. Our best result for sub-task 2 is 0.4753 accuracy (8th place). In Figures 1, 2 and 3 we render the confusion matrices for the classification of the Arabic dialects. We observe a different behavior for the five classes, along the three runs: for EGY and LAV, the number of correctly classified instances is very similar over the three runs. For GLF there is a slight increase in correctly classified instances at run 2. For MSA the increase is significant (from 92 in run 1 to 190 – more than double – in run 2), and for NOR there is a certain decrease (from 180 in run 1 to 145 in run 2).

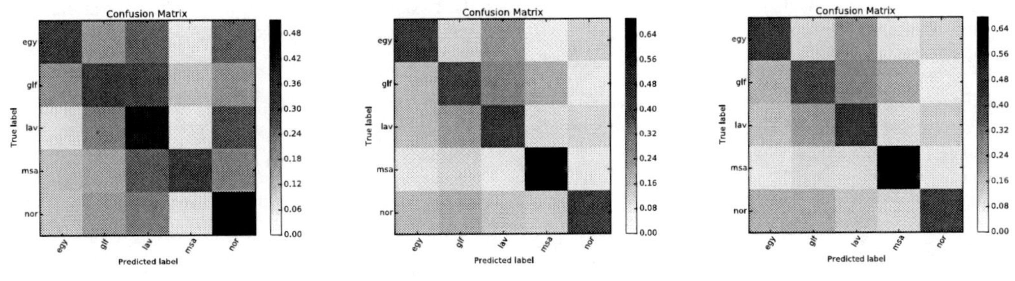

<table>
<tr><td>Figure 1: Run 1</td><td>Figure 2: Run 2</td><td>Figure 3: Run 3</td></tr>
</table>

5 Conclusions

In this paper we described the submission of the UniBuc-NLP team for the DSL 2016 shared task. We participated in the closed track of both sub-tasks (sub-task 1: similar languages and language varieties, sub-task 2: Arabic dialects), submitting a total of 5 runs (2 for sub-task 1 and 3 for sub-task 2). We used linear classification methods based on word and character n-gram features. For sub-task 1 we used a logistic regressions classifier with tf-idf feature weighting and for sub-task 2 an SVM classifier with a string kernel. Our best system obtains 89.80% accuracy for sub-task 1, dataset B1 (3rd place). Our results suggest that relatively good results may be obtained with plain vanilla linear classifiers, with no hyper-parameter optimization or special feature selection. When compared to other competitors in the shared task, our logistic regression results were at most 0.03% lower compared to the top score on sub-task 1, dataset A and among the top scoring for the datasets B1 and B2. On the Arabic dataset, the kernel method stands 0.04% from the first position and while additional parameters can improve the model, we believe the dataset created using ASR had a great impact on the results. To conclude, plain vanilla methods can be *good enough* to distinguish between similar languages, however we are still a long way from claiming this task *solved* and clearly more research is needed in this direction to create robust models that capture linguistic variation.

6 Acknowledgments

This work was supported by a grant of the Romanian National Authority for Scientific Research and Innovation, CNCS/CCCDI UEFISCDI, project number PN-III-P2-2.1-53BG/2016, within PNCDI III.

References

Ahmed Ali, Najim Dehak, Patrick Cardinal, Sameer Khurana, Sree Harsha Yella, James Glass, Peter Bell, and Steve Renals. 2016. Automatic dialect detection in arabic broadcast speech. In *Interspeech 2016*, pages 2934–2938.

William B. Cavnar and John M. Trenkle. 1994. N-Gram-Based Text Categorization. In *Proceedings of the 3rd Annual Symposium on Document Analysis and Information Retrieval, SDAIR 1994*, pages 161–175.

Ted Dunning. 1994. Statistical Identification of Language. Technical report, Computing Research Laboratory, New Mexico State University.

Rong-En Fan, Kai-Wei Chang, Cho-Jui Hsieh, Xiang-Rui Wang, and Chih-Jen Lin. 2008. LIBLINEAR: A Library for Large Linear Classification. *Journal of Machine Learning Research*, 9:1871–1874.

Thomas Gottron and Nedim Lipka. 2010. A Comparison of Language Identification Approaches on Short, Query-Style Texts. In *Proceedings of the 32nd European Conference on Advances in Information Retrieval, ECIR 2010*, pages 611–614.

Cyril Goutte and Serge Leger. 2015. Experiments in Discriminating Similar Languages. In *Proceedings of the Joint Workshop on Language Technology for Closely Related Languages, Varieties and Dialects*, pages 78–84.

Cristian Grozea and Marius Popescu. 2010. Encoplot - performance in the second international plagiarism detection challenge - lab report for PAN at CLEF 2010. In *CLEF (Notebook Papers/LABs/Workshops)*, volume 1176 of *CEUR Workshop Proceedings*. CEUR-WS.org.

Wolfgang Maier and Carlos Gómez-Rodríguez. 2014. Language Variety Identification in Spanish Tweets. In *Proceedings of the Workshop on Language Technology for Closely Related Languages and Language Variants, LT4CloseLang 2014*, pages 25–35.

Shervin Malmasi and Mark Dras. 2015. Language Identification using Classifier Ensembles. In *Proceedings of the Joint Workshop on Language Technology for Closely Related Languages, Varieties and Dialects*, pages 35–43.

Shervin Malmasi, Marcos Zampieri, Nikola Ljubešić, Preslav Nakov, Ahmed Ali, and Jörg Tiedemann. 2016. Discriminating between similar languages and arabic dialect identification: A report on the third dsl shared task. In *Proceedings of the 3rd Workshop on Language Technology for Closely Related Languages, Varieties and Dialects (VarDial)*, Osaka, Japan.

F. Pedregosa, G. Varoquaux, A. Gramfort, V. Michel, B. Thirion, O. Grisel, M. Blondel, P. Prettenhofer, R. Weiss, V. Dubourg, J. Vanderplas, A. Passos, D. Cournapeau, M. Brucher, M. Perrot, and E. Duchesnay. 2011. Scikit-learn: Machine Learning in Python. *Journal of Machine Learning Research*, 12:2825–2830.

Bali Ranaivo-Malancon. 2006. Automatic Identification of Close Languages – Case study: Malay and Indonesian. *ECTI Transactions on Computer and Information Technology*, 2(2):126–134.

Fatiha Sadat, Farnazeh Kazemi, and Atefeh Farzindar. 2014. Automatic identification of arabic dialects in social media. In *Proceedings of the First International Workshop on Social Media Retrieval and Analysis, SoMeRA 2014*, pages 35–40.

Gerard Salton and Christopher Buckley. 1988. Term-weighting approaches in automatic text retrieval. *Information Processing Management*, 24(5):513 – 523.

Liling Tan, Marcos Zampieri, Nikola Ljubešic, and Jörg Tiedemann. 2014. Merging comparable data sources for the discrimination of similar languages: The dsl corpus collection. In *Proceedings of the 7th Workshop on Building and Using Comparable Corpora (BUCC)*, pages 11–15, Reykjavik, Iceland.

Jörg Tiedemann and Nikola Ljubesic. 2012. Efficient discrimination between closely related languages. In *COLING 2012, 24th International Conference on Computational Linguistics, Proceedings of the Conference: Technical Papers, 8-15 December 2012, Mumbai, India*, pages 2619–2634.

Dolf Trieschnigg, Djoerd Hiemstra, Mariët Theune, Franciska de Jong, and Theo Meder. 2012. An exploration of language identification techniques for the Dutch folktale database. In *Workshop on Adaptation of Language Resources and Tools for Processing Cultural Heritage, LREC 2012*, pages 47–51.

Marcos Zampieri and Binyam Gebrekidan Gebre. 2012. Automatic Identification of Language Varieties: The Case of Portuguese. In *Proceedings of the 11th Conference on Natural Language Processing, KONVENS 2012*, pages 233–237.

N-gram and Neural Language Models
for Discriminating Similar Languages

Andre Cianflone and **Leila Kosseim**
Dept. of Computer Science & Software Engineering
Concordia University
{a_cianfl|kosseim}@encs.concordia.ca

Abstract

This paper describes our submission (named `clac`) to the 2016 Discriminating Similar Languages (DSL) shared task. We participated in the closed Sub-task 1 (Set A) with two separate machine learning techniques. The first approach is a character based Convolution Neural Network with a bidirectional long short term memory (BiLSTM) layer (CLSTM), which achieved an accuracy of 78.45% with minimal tuning. The second approach is a character-based n-gram model. This last approach achieved an accuracy of 88.45% which is close to the accuracy of 89.38% achieved by the best submission, and allowed us to rank #7 overall.

1 Introduction

Discriminating between languages is often the first task to many natural language applications (NLP), such as machine translation or information retrieval. Current approaches to address this problem achieve impressive results in ideal conditions: a small number of unrelated or dissimilar languages, enough training data and long enough sentences. For example, Simões et al. achieved an accuracy of 97% on the discrimination of 25 languages in TED talks (Simões et al., 2014). However, in the case of discriminating between similar languages or dialects, such as French Canadian and European French, or Spanish varieties, the task is more challenging (Goutte and Leger, 2015). This problem is addressed specifically in the DSL shared task at VarDial 2016 (DSL 2016). In comparison to results from Simões et al. who achieved a 97% accuracy, the best performing system at DSL 2016 achieved only an 89.38% accuracy.

This paper describes our system and submission at the DSL 2016 shared task. The shared task is split into two main sub-tasks. Sub-task 1 aims at discriminating between similar languages and national language varieties; whereas Sub-task 2 focuses on Arabic dialect identification. We will only describe the specifics of Sub-task 1, for which we submitted results. For Sub-task 1, participants could chose between the closed submission, where only the use of the DSL Corpus Collection, provided by the organisers (see Section 3), was allowed; or the open task which permitted the use of any external data for training. Participants could also submit runs for two different data sets: Set A, composed of newspaper articles, and Set B, composed of social media data. We only participated in the closed Sub-task 1 using Set A. Hence, our task was to discriminate between 12 similar languages and national language varieties using only the newspaper articles provided in the DSL corpus as training set. For a full description of all sub-tasks, see the overview paper (Malmasi et al., 2016), which also discusses data and results for all participants.

It was our first participation to the DSL task, and registered late to the shared task. Hence our system is the result of a 3 person-week effort. We started with very little existing code. We had experimented previously with neural language models (NLM) and wanted to evaluate their applicability to this task. In addition, we believed that a convolutional plus long-short term memory network (CLSTM) would be appropriate for the task given their success in several other NLP tasks (see Section 2 for details). In the

Proceedings of the Third Workshop on NLP for Similar Languages, Varieties and Dialects,
pages 243–250, Osaka, Japan, December 12 2016.

end, we managed to submit 3 runs: run1 and run2 consist of standard character-based n-gram models; while run3 is the CLSTM. Our best performance was achieved by run1, with an accuracy of 88.45% ranking it 7th among the 17 participants, and arriving very close to the top run which had an accuracy of 89.38%. Alas, our run3, the CLSTM, attained an accuracy of 78.45% but benefited from very minimal tuning.

2   Related Work

Through the years, statistical language identification has received much attention in Natural Language Processing. The standard technique of character n-gram modeling has traditionally been very success-ful for this application (Cavnar and Trenkle, 1994), but other statistical approaches such as Markov models over n-grams (Dunning, 1994), dot products of word frequency vectors (Dafmashek, 1995), and string kernels in support vector machines (Kruengkrai et al., 2005) have also provided impressive results. However, as noted by (Baldwin and Lui, 2010), more difficult situations where languages are similar, less training data is available or the text to identify is short can significantly degrade performance. This is why, more recently, much effort has addressed more difficult questions such as the language identifi-cation of related languages in social media texts (e.g. (Zubiaga et al., 2014)) and the discrimination of similar languages (e.g. (Zampieri et al., 2015; Malmasi et al., 2016)).

The second Discriminating Similar Languages shared task (DSL 2015) aimed to discriminate between 15 similar languages and varieties, with an added "other" category. At this shared task, the best accuracy was 95.54% and was achieved by (Malmasi and Dras, 2015). The authors used two classes of features: character n-grams (with n=1 to 6) and word n-grams (with n=1 to 2). Three systems were submitted for evaluation. The first was a single Support Vector Machine (SVM) trained on the features above; while the other two systems were ensemble classifiers, combining the results of various classifiers with a mean probability combiner. A second team at DSL 2015 relied on a two-stage process, first predicting the language group and then the specific language variant (Goutte and Leger, 2015). This team achieved an accuracy of 95.24%. As (Goutte et al., 2016) note, many other techniques were also used for the task, such as TF-IDF and SVM, token-based backoff, prediction by partial matching with accuracies achieving between 64.04% and 95.54%. An interesting experiment at DSL-2015 consisted in having two versions of the corpora, where one corpus was the original newspaper articles; while the other substituted named entities with placeholders. The aim was to evaluate how strong a clue named entities are in the identification of language varieties. By relying heavily on geographic names, for example, which are highly correlated to specific nations, it was thought that accuracy would increase significantly. However, surprisingly, accuracy on the modified data set was only 1 to 2 percentage points lower than the original data set for all systems (Goutte et al., 2016).

Given the recent success of Recurrent Neural Networks in many NLP tasks, such as machine trans-lation (Bahdanau et al., 2015) and image captioning (Karpathy and Fei-Fei, 2015), we believed that an interesting approach for the DSL task would be to use solely characters as inputs, and add the ability to find long-distance relations within texts. Neural models are quite efficient at abstracting word meaning into a dense vector representation. Mikolov et al. for example, developed an efficient method to repre-sent syntactic and semantic word relationships through a neural network (Mikolov et al., 2013) and the resulting vectors can be used in a variety of NLP tasks. For certain NLP tasks however, Convolutional Neural Networks (ConvNets), extensively studied in computer vision, have been shown to be effective for text classification. For example, (Zhang et al., 2015) experimented with ConvNets on commonly used language data sets, such as topic classification and polarity detection. A key conclusion of their study is that traditional methods, such as n-grams, work best for small data sets, whereas character ConvNets work best for data sets with millions of instances. Since the DSL data set contained a few thousand instances (see Section 3), we decided to give it a try. Further, it has been shown recently that augmenting ConvNets with Reccurrent Neural Networks (RNNs) is an effective way to model word sequences (Kim et al., 2016), (Choi et al., 2016). For this reason, we developed a neural model based on the latter method.

3 Data Set

Because we participated in the closed task, we only used the DSL Corpus Collection (Set A) (Tan et al., 2014) provided by the organisers. The data set contained 12 languages organised into 5 groups: two groups of similar languages and three of national language varieties.

Group 1:   Similar languages: Bosnian, Croatian, and Serbian
Group 2:   Similar languages: Malay and Indonesian
Group 3:   National varieties of Portuguese: Brazil and Portugal
Group 4:   National varieties of Spanish: Argentina, Mexico, and Spain
Group 5:   National varieties of French: France and Canada

Table 1 illustrates statistics of the shared task data set. As shown in the table, the data set is equally divided into 12 similar languages and national language varieties with 18,000 training instances for each language. On average, each instance is 35 tokens long and contain 219 characters.

Group		Language	Code	Train.	Dev.	Test	Av. # char.	Av. # token
1	1	Bosnian	bs	18,000	2,000	1,000	198	31
	2	Croatian	hr	18,000	2,000	1,000	240	37
	3	Serbian	sr	18,000	2,000	1,000	213	34
2	4	Malaysian	my	18,000	2,000	1,000	182	26
	5	Indonesian	id	18,000	2,000	1,000	240	34
3	6	Spanish (Argentina)	es-AR	18,000	2,000	1,000	254	41
	7	Spanish (Spain)	es-ES	18,000	2,000	1,000	268	45
	8	Spanish (Mexico)	es-MX	18,000	2,000	1,000	182	31
4	9	Portuguese (Brazil)	pt-BR	18,000	2,000	1,000	241	40
	10	Portuguese (Portugal)	pt-PT	18,000	2,000	1,000	222	36
5	11	French (Canada)	fr-CA	18,000	2,000	1,000	175	28
	12	French (France)	fr-FR	18,000	2,000	1,000	216	35
Total				216,000	24,000	12,000	219	35

Table 1: Statistics of DSL 2016 Data set A. We list the number of instances across languages for the Training, Development and Test sets. The last two columns represent the average number of characters and average number of tokens of the training set.

Since the results of our CLSTM model (See Section 4.2) were lower than expected during the development phase, we attempted to increase the size of the training set. Using the data set from DSL-2015, we could find additional training data for most languages, with the exception of French. We therefore attempted to use publicly vailable corpora for French. For Canadian French, we used the Canadian Hansard[1]; whereas for France French, we used the French monolingual news crawl data set (2013 version) from the ACL 2014 Ninth Workshop on Statistical Machine Translation[2]. However, upon closer investigation, this last corpus clearly contained non-French news content, heavily referencing locations and other international entities. Additionally, the majority of the Canadian French Hansard is translated from English, possibly not being representative of actual Canadian French. We experimented with these two additional data sets, but the accuracy of our models was far from our closed task equivalent. Given our short development time, we decided to drop the open task, and train our models on only the given DSL 2016 Data Set A.

4 Methodology

As indicated in Section 1, we experimented with two main approaches: a standard n-gram model to use as baseline, and a convolution neural network (ConvNet) with bidirectional long-short term memory recurrent neural network (BiLSTM), which we refer to as CLSTM.

---

[1]http://www.isi.edu/natural-language/download/hansard/
[2]http://www.statmt.org/wmt14/translation-task.html

4.1 N-gram Model

Our baseline is a standard text-book character-based n-gram model (Jurafsky and Martin, 2014). Because we used a simple baseline, the same unmodified character set (including no case-folding) is used for both of our approaches, for easier later comparison. During training, the system calculates the frequency of each n-gram for each language. Then, at test time, the model computes a probability distribution over all possible languages and selects the most probable language as the output. Unseen n-grams were smoothed with additive smoothing with $\alpha = 0.1$. As discussed in Section 5, surprisingly, this standard approach was much more accurate than our complex neural network. We experimented with different values for n with the development set given (see Section 3). As table 2 shows, the accuracy peaks at sizes $n = 7$ and $n = 8$; while larger n-grams degrade in performance and explode in memory use. The curse of dimensionality seriously limits this type of approach.

N-gram size	Accuracy
1	0.5208
2	0.6733
3	0.7602
4	0.7523
5	0.8035
6	0.8303
7	**0.8424**
8	**0.8474**

Table 2: Accuracy across n-grams of sizes 1 to 8 with the development Set A.

4.2 Convolution Neural Network with Long Short Term Memory (CLSTM)

Our second approach is a Convolution Neural Network with a Bidirectional Long Short Term Memory layer (CLSTM). The goal of this approach was to build a single neural model without any feature engineering, solely taking the raw characters as input. Using characters as inputs has the added advantage of detecting language patterns even with little data available. For example, a character based neural model can predict the word *running* as being more likely to be in English than *courir* if it has seen the word *run* in English training texts. In a word based model that has not seen the word in this form, *running* would be represented as a random vector. Given the heavy computational requirements of training neural models and the limited time we had, we could not develop an ensemble neural model system, which could combine the strength of diverse models.

The input to the model is the raw text where each character in an instance has been mapped to its one-hot representation. Each character is therefore encoded as a vector of dimension d, where d is a function of the maximum number of unique characters in the corpus. Luckily, the languages share heavily in alphabets and symbols, limiting d to 217. A fixed number of characters l is chosen from each instance. Since our texts are relatively short, as observed by the character average column in Table 1, we set l to 256. Shorter texts are zero padded, while longer instances are cut after the first 256 characters. Our input matrix A is thus a $d \times l$ matrix where elements $A_{ij} \in \{0, 1\}$. The input feeds into three sequences of convolutions and max-pooling. We used temporal max-pooling, the 1D version equivalent in computer vision. Our ConvNet parameters are heavily based on (Zhang et al., 2015)'s empirical research who observed that the temporal max-pooling technique is key to deep convolutional networks with text. We further improved results on our development set by stacking the ConvNet with a Bidirectional LSTM (BiLSTM). The BiLSTM effectively takes the output of the ConvNet as its input. As shown in Table 3, the two LSTM layers are merged by concatenation and followed by a fully connected layer with 1024 units. ReLU is used as activation function and loss is measured on cross-entropy and optimized with the Adam algorithm (Kingma and Ba, 2015). The system is built as a single neural network with no pre-training. We could not test much wider networks due to lack of computing capability. However, as experienced by (Zhang et al., 2015), it seems that much wider networks than our own would result in little, if any, performance improvement. The model is built in Keras[3] and TensorFlow[4].

Layer	Type	Features	Kernel	Max-pooling
1	Convolutional	256	7	3
2	Convolutional	256	7	3
3	Convolutional	256	3	3
4	LSTM (left)	128	-	-
5	LSTM (right)	128	-	-
6	Dense	1024	-	-

Table 3: Layers used in our neural network. The Features column represents the number of filters for the convolutional layers and hidden units for LSTM and Dense layers. Layers 4 and 5 are merged by concatenation to form the BiLSTM layer. Dropout was added between layer 6 and the output layer (not listed in the table).

With the development set provided, the accuracy of the CLSTM approach reached 82% on average which was below but comparable to the n-gram model. Additionally, our tests on the development set showed that adding the BiLSTM on top of our ConvNet does indeed increase performance. We were able to improve accuracy by 2 to 3% on average, with little additional computing time.

5 Results and Discussion

We submitted 3 runs for the closed test Set A: `run1` – the N-gram of size 7, `run2` – the N-gram of size 8, and `run3` – the CLSTM model. Table 4 shows the overall results of all 3 runs on the official test set. As the table shows, the standard n-gram model significantly outperformed the CLSTM model. It is interesting to note that the difference between the two n-grams is negligible. This was also observed during training (see Section 4.1). Recall from Table 2 that the accuracy peaked at sizes $n = 7$ and $n = 8$ on the development set reaching 84.74%. The 3.71% increase with the test set was a welcome surprise. On the other hand, the CLSTM performed about 3.55% lower during the test than it did at training time, decreasing from an average of 82% to 78.46%. Overall, as Table 5 shows, our `run1` (labeled `clac`) ranked #7 with respect to the best runs of all 17 participating teams.

Run	Description	Accuracy	F1 (micro)	F1 (macro)	F1 (weighted)
Run 1	N-gram 7	0.8845	0.8845	0.8813	0.8813
Run 2	N-gram 8	0.8829	0.8829	0.8812	0.8812
Run 3	CLSTM	0.7845	0.7845	0.7814	0.7814

Table 4: Results of our 3 submissions on test set A (closed training).

Table 6 shows the confusion matrix for our best run, the N-gram of size 7. For comparative purposes, we have added the confusion matrix in Table 7 for our third and lesser performing model, the CLSTM. As shown in Tables 6 and 7, for all language groups the N-gram performed significantly better than the CLSTM. However, with both models, misclassifications outside of a language group are sparse and statistically insignificant. This may indicate that a two-stage hierarchical process, as proposed by (Goutte and Leger, 2015), is not necessary for the models we propose.

As shown in Tables 6 and 7, the major difficulty for our models was the classification of the Spanish varieties in Group 3. It seems that the addition of Mexican Spanish is a significant challenge to discriminating national varieties of Spanish. At DSL 2015, (Goutte and Leger, 2015) were able to classify European Spanish and Argentine Spanish with an 89.4% accuracy, lower than for other languages. Given the low variability among the best performing systems (see Table 5), and the lower performance with respect to previous iterations of the DSL shared task, this was likely a challenge for all systems at DSL 2016.

---

[3] https://keras.io/
[4] https://www.tensorflow.org/

Rank	Team	Run	Accuracy	F1 (weighted)
1	tubasfs	run1	0.8938	0.8937
2	SUKI	run1	0.8879	0.8877
3	GWU_LT3	run3	0.8870	0.8870
4	nrc	run1	0.8859	0.8859
5	UPV_UA	run1	0.8833	0.8838
6	PITEOG	run3	0.8826	0.8829
7	**clac**	**run1**	**0.8845**	**0.8813**
8	XAC	run3	0.8790	0.8786
9	ASIREM	run1	0.8779	0.8778
10	hltcoe	run1	0.8772	0.8769
11	UniBucNLP	run2	0.8647	0.8643
12	HDSL	run1	0.8525	0.8516
13	Citius_Ixa_Imaxin	run2	0.8525	0.8501
14	ResIdent	run3	0.8487	0.8466
15	eire	run1	0.8376	0.8316
16	mitsls	run3	0.8306	0.8299
17	Uppsala	run2	0.8252	0.8239

Table 5: Results for all systems, data set A, closed track. Our system "clac" ranked 7th.

| | | Group | | | | | | | | | | | | |
| | | 1 | | | 2 | | 3 | | | 4 | | 5 | | |
Group	Code	bs	hr	sr	my	id	es-ar	es-es	es-mx	pt-br	pt-pt	fr-ca	fr-fr	F1
1	bs	674	182	142			1		1					0.75
	hr	76	911	11					1		1			0.86
	sr	54	15	928		1					1		1	0.89
2	my				992	8								0.99
	id				13	985	1					1		0.99
3	es-ar						927	58	15					0.83
	es-es						92	875	29		2		2	0.81
	es-mx						219	218	563					0.70
4	pt-br									956	44			0.95
	pt-pt									54	946			0.95
5	fr-ca											972	28	0.93
	fr-fr				2					1	3	109	885	0.92

Table 6: Confusion matrix for the n-gram of size 7, test Set A. We also add the F1 score in the last column.

6 Conclusion

Although, it still achieved an accuracy of 78.46% with very little tuning and training set, we are disappointed in the performance of the CSLTM. Based on the empirical study of (Zhang et al., 2015), character based ConvNets performed in line with traditional methods with data sets in the hundreds of thousands, and better with data sets in the millions. Since the shared task data set size was in between, it was not clear which approach would perform best. We believe that a deep neural network can outperform the traditional n-gram model for this task, but only once the data set size is dramatically increased and given more time to experiment on the network parameters and structure. Since only raw texts are necessary, i.e. containing no linguistic annotations, increasing the data set does not constitute a problem.

As future work, we would like to explore once again the open task. With the addition of Mexican Spanish, France French and Canadian French, discriminating similar languages continues to be a challenge. In Table 5 we see how the top 7 teams are within a 1% spread, but all below 90% accuracy. We believe that with a very large data set, a neural model could automatically learn key linguistic patterns to differentiate similar languages and possibly perform better than the current iteration of our CLSTM.

		Group												
		1			2		3			4		5		
Group	Code	bs	hr	sr	my	id	es-ar	es-es	es-mx	pt-br	pt-pt	fr-ca	fr-fr	F1
1	bs	697	172	129		1	1							0.67
	hr	249	726	23		1	1							0.75
	sr	130	43	826						1				0.83
2	my				909	91								0.94
	id				23	975		1		1				0.94
3	es-ar					2	816	87	93	2				0.71
	es-es			1			173	633	190	1	1		1	0.62
	es-mx						304	309	385	1			1	0.46
4	pt-br			1			1			847	150	1		0.83
	pt-pt		1				4			183	811		1	0.83
5	fr-ca											972	28	0.90
	fr-fr	1						1		1	1	178	818	0.88

Table 7: Confusion matrix for the CLSTM, test Set A. We also add the F1 score in the last column.

Acknowledgement

The authors would like to thank the anonymous reviewers for their feedback on the paper. This work was financially supported by a grant from the Natural Sciences and Engineering Research Council of Canada (NSERC).

References

Dzmitry Bahdanau, Kyunghyun Cho, and Yoshua Bengio. 2015. Neural machine translation by jointly learning to align and translate. In *Advances in Neural Information Processing Systems (NIPS 2015)*, pages 649–657, Montreal, Canada, December.

Timothy Baldwin and Marco Lui. 2010. Language identification: The long and the short of the matter. In *Human Language Technologies: The 2010 Annual Conference of the North American Chapter of the Association for Computational Linguistics*, HLT 2010, pages 229–237, May.

William B. Cavnar and John M. Trenkle. 1994. N-gram-based text categorization. In *Proceedings of the 3rd Annual Symposium on Document Analysis and Information Retrieval (SDAIR 1994)*, pages 161–175, Las Vegas, Nevada, April.

Keunwoo Choi, George Fazekas, Mark Sandler, and Kyunghyun Cho. 2016. Convolutional Recurrent Neural Networks for Music Classification. arXiv preprint arXiv:1609.04243 – Submitted to the 42nd IEEE International Conference on Acoustics, Speech and Signal Processing (ICASSP 2017).

Marc Dafmashek. 1995. Gauging similarity with n-grams: Language-independent categorization of text. *Science*, 267(5199):843–848.

Ted Dunning. 1994. Statistical identification of language. Technical report, MCCS 940-273, Computing Research Laboratory, New Mexico State University.

Cyril Goutte and Serge Leger. 2015. Experiments in discriminating similar languages. In *Proceedings of the Joint Workshop on Language Technology for Closely Related Languages, Varieties and Dialects (LT4VarDial)*, pages 78–84, Hissar, Bulgaria, September.

Cyril Goutte, Serge Léger, Shervin Malmasi, and Marcos Zampieri. 2016. Discriminating similar languages: Evaluations and explorations. In *Proceedings of the Tenth International Conference on Language Resources and Evaluation (LREC 2016)*, Portoroz, Slovenia, May.

Dan Jurafsky and James H. Martin. 2014. *Speech and Language Processing*. Pearson custom library. Prentice Hall, Pearson Education International.

Andrej Karpathy and Li Fei-Fei. 2015. Deep visual-semantic alignments for generating image descriptions. In *Proceedings of the IEEE Conference on Computer Vision and Pattern Recognition*, pages 3128–3137, Boston, MA, USA, June.

Yoon Kim, Yacine Jernite, David Sontag, and Alexander M Rush. 2016. Character-aware neural language models. In *Proceedings of the Thirtieth AAAI Conference on Artificial Intelligence (AAAI 2016)*, pages 2741–2749, Phoenix, Arizona, USA, February.

Diederik Kingma and Jimmy Ba. 2015. Adam: A method for stochastic optimization. In *Proceeding of the 2015 International Conference on Learning Representation (ICLR 2015)*, San Diego, California.

Canasai Kruengkrai, Prapass Srichaivattana, Virach Sornlertlamvanich, and Hitoshi Isahara. 2005. Language identification based on string kernels. In *Proceedings of the 5th International Symposium on Communications and Information Technologies (ISCIT 2005)*, pages 896–899.

Shervin Malmasi and Mark Dras. 2015. Language identification using classifier ensembles. In *Proceedings of the Joint Workshop on Language Technology for Closely Related Languages, Varieties and Dialects (LT4VarDial)*, pages 35–43, Hissar, Bulgaria, September.

Shervin Malmasi, Marcos Zampieri, Nikola Ljubešić, Preslav Nakov, Ahmed Ali, and Jörg Tiedemann. 2016. Discriminating between Similar Languages and Arabic Dialect Identification: A Report on the Third DSL Shared Task. In *Proceedings of the 3rd Workshop on Language Technology for Closely Related Languages, Varieties and Dialects (VarDial)*, Osaka, Japan, December.

Tomas Mikolov, Ilya Sutskever, Kai Chen, Greg S Corrado, and Jeff Dean. 2013. Distributed representations of words and phrases and their compositionality. In *Advances in neural information processing systems (NIPS 2013)*, pages 3111–3119, Lake Tahoe, USA, December.

Alberto Simões, José João Almeida, and Simon D Byers. 2014. Language identification: a neural network approach. In *3rd Symposium on Languages, Applications and Technologies (SLATE 2014)*, pages 251–265. Schloss Dagstuhl-Leibniz-Zentrum für Informatik GmbH.

Liling Tan, Marcos Zampieri, Nikola Ljubešic, and Jörg Tiedemann. 2014. Merging Comparable Data Sources for the Discrimination of Similar Languages: The DSL Corpus Collection. In *Proceedings of the 7th Workshop on Building and Using Comparable Corpora (BUCC)*, pages 11–15, Reykjavik, Iceland.

Marcos Zampieri, Liling Tan, Nikola Ljubešic, Jörg Tiedemann, and Preslav Nakov. 2015. Overview of the DSL shared task 2015. In *Proceedings of the Joint Workshop on Language Technology for Closely Related Languages, Varieties and Dialects (LT4VarDial)*, pages 1–9.

Xiang Zhang, Junbo Zhao, and Yann LeCun. 2015. Character-level convolutional networks for text classification. In *Proceedings of the 29th Annual Conference on Neural Information Processing Systems (NIPS 2015)*, pages 649–657, Montreal, Canada, December.

Arkaitz Zubiaga, Iñaki San Vicente, Pablo Gamallo, José Ramón Pichel, Iñaki Alegria, Nora Aranberri, Aitzol Ezeiza, and Víctor Fresno. 2014. Overview of TweetLID: Tweet Language Identification at SEPLN 2014. In *Twitter Language Identification Workshop at SEPLN 2014*, pages 1–11, Girona, Spain, September.

Author Index

Association for Computational Linguistics
209 N. Eighth Street
Stroudsburg, Pennsylvania 18360

ISBN 978-1-5108-3328-9